'DAILY SPIRITUAL DIET'

1st Quarter
January-April

ELIZABETH DAS

English

Copyright © 2023 *ELIZABETH DAS.*

All rights reserved for audio, eBook (digital), and paper book. No part of this book may be used or reproduced by any means, graphic, electronic, or mechanical, including photocopying, recording, taping, or by any information storage retrieval system without the written permission of the author except in the case of brief quotations embodied in critical articles and reviews. Because of the dynamic nature of the internet, any web address links contained in this book may have changed since publication and may no longer be valid. Any people depicted in stock imagery provided by Thinkstock are models, and such images are beings used for illustrative purposes only. Certain Stock imagery © Thinkstock. Excerpt From: Elizabeth Das: "DAILY SPIRITUAL DIET'

DAILY SPIRITUAL DIET:

PAPERBACK :978-1-961625-00-6

Ebook-EPUB:978-1-961625-01-3

Digital Online:978-1-961625-02-0

Library of Congress Control Number: 2023944250

PREFACE

On January 1, 2018. I was at home alone, resting on the sofa. I heard my Lord's voice commanding me to write. In my spirit, He meant for me to do it every day. I clarified my process and topics and verbalized my intention to write daily. Divine communication gave me the inspiration for writing. As per the divine plan, I harked to the message for the day shared by the LORD. I wrote the content. I recorded it and uploaded it on YouTube. For 365 days, I took notes from the Lord. I have a message for all who will accept it. Under the instructions of the Holy Spirit, I learned Satan organizes religion, organizations, denominations, and non-denominations. These systems do not have the power to help you follow Jesus; instead, they will lead you to another building with a brand name, where you will learn about Jesus, but not about His power and His might. I once read an article by a satanic prophetess who claimed that to establish Satan's kingdom, we must convert people to the majority religion, which is Christianity. How can the Kingdom of Jesus be destroyed? Use the same proven tactics. Focus on what is prohibited. If Jesus overturned a table, constructed a den, and confined thieves there. The chief advantage of calling a structure a church is that people will not understand that their physical body embodies the church of Jehovah God. In addition, individuals who are impoverished, malnourished, addicted, alcoholic, spiritually controlled, or oppressed will not attain salvation.

Rather than relying on individuals trained and taught by the Holy Spirit, establish a theological school that covers all of our divided and contradictory teachings and trains men for teaching and preaching.

This is an excellent plan! This plan not only sounds good but can also be successful. Continue focusing on women since they can serve as our spokespeople. She still enjoys window shopping, finding good deals, and living a glamorous lifestyle.

They display godliness but reject true power. These types of doctrines may gratify the desires of the greedy, the lustful, and those driven by pride. I have realized that living within the confines of formal religious communities can hinder individuals from seeking and finding God through personal inquiry and prayer. The religious leadership may be a promoter of certain literature that may be the work of false teachers or prophets. It may also impede the home meetings from reaching out to our family, neighbors, and friends. This is defining total control. In addition, religious organizations are preachers of the WORD, but they are not always practitioners of the WORD. Their instructions distract believers from doing what Jesus commanded, directing them to obey group leaders. The teachings are effective only if you follow them without deviation. We are following everything but the teachings of Jesus. I recommended you study the teachings of Jesus, as he instructed his followers to do so. Jesus declared he is the Way, the Truth, and the Life. Following Jesus is the way to attain eternal life. I needed many years of searching to break free from Satan's deceptive hold and discover the Truth. The Lord has provided us with clear guidance on how to recognize His loyal disciples and how not to be led astray by Satan's deceptive schemes.

The text says that the apostle will work wonders, healings, and miracles in the city. Instead of religious restrictions, shouldn't we focus on these fruits out there? The New Testament says that the Lord will come and live in us when we repent and are immersed in Jesus 'name to wash away our sins. Therefore, we become Holy Spirit residents, or as some may say, the house of the Lord Jesus. It is now that our body serves as the church. While it is necessary to establish fellowship with our brothers and sisters in Christ from home to home and city to city, building establishments are unnecessary. One is called to work.

We must preach the good news of the gospel, which includes performing supernatural acts such as healing the sick, restoring the brokenhearted, casting out demons, and restoring sight to the blind. Supernatural power comes from the Holy Spirit. The Spirit does all healing, miracles, and deliverance living within us. We need to go out and work as Jesus did. Learning the Lord's ways requires surrendering and yielding to His Spirit. If we do not do this, then we will not acknowledge God's deliverance from various ailments, such as oppression, possession, sickness, brokenness, physical disabilities, and depression. The Lord will take care of everything, and you will go back home feeling joyous. This is a testament to the brilliance of the plan of God! There are many rewards for being a disciple of God. Access to provisions, protection, peace, and working privileges are bonuses. As a follower, you will inherit a beautiful mansion in heaven. Life's journey will soon end. This book may help you understand God's plan with clarity. I have been studying the Bible through practice, and you, too, can be a student by abiding by its teachings. May the Lord send you faithful prophetic, evangelistic, pastoral, teaching, and apostolic ministers to equip you for service in the armies of God. Follow Jesus. Amen.

Author Elizabeth Das

Contents

JANUARY

JANUARY 1	2
THE WORD OF GOD!	2
JANUARY 2	5
THE CHOICES ARE YOURS!	5
JANUARY 3	8
CALL ON GOD!	8
JANUARY 4	11
HEART!	11
JANUARY 5	14
WALK IN THE SPIRIT!	14
JANUARY 6	17
WHAT IS FAITH?	17
JANUARY 7	20
POWER OF THE WORD GAME!	20
JANUARY 8	23
GOD IS MAKING A NEW THING FOR YOU!	23
JANUARY 9	26
FAITH IN GOD IS TARGETED!	26
JANUARY 10	29
SPIRITUAL POLLUTION!	29
JANUARY 11	31
REALITY TEST!	31
JANUARY 12	34
DREAM!	34
JANUARY 13	36
SIMPLE WAYS OF GOD!	36
JANUARY 14	39
WAGES OF SINS ARE DEATH!	39
JANUARY 15	42
YOU ARE UNLIMITED!	42
JANUARY 16	45
GOD'S WAY OF COMMUNICATION!	45

JANUARY 17	48
YOUR MIND!	48
JANUARY 18	51
A BLESSING HUNTER!	51
JANUARY 19	54
ACCOUNTING IN THE KINGDOM!	54
JANUARY 20	58
WHAT MAKES DIFFERENCE?	58
JANUARY 21	61
LET US STAND FOR JESUS!	61
JANUARY 22	64
YOUR SIN WILL HAUNT YOU!	64
JANUARY 23	67
JESUS GIVES THE KINGDOM KEY, WHICH HAS A REVELATION OF HIM.	67
JANUARY 24	71
WAY TO ESCAPE!	71
JANUARY 25	74
DO YOU HAVE ROOM FOR ME?	74
JANUARY 26	77
YOUR ASSIGNMENT IN THE KINGDOM!	77
JANUARY 27	80
"POWER OF THANKFULNESS!	80
JANUARY 28	83
I ATTACH THE REWARD TO YOUR ACTIONS!	83
JANUARY 29	86
DIRT!	86
JANUARY 30	89
DO NOT FAIL GOD!	89
JANUARY 31	92
BIBLE IS A MIRROR OF YOUR SPIRIT!	92

FEBRUARY

FEBRUARY 1	96
LORD, SET THE CAPTIVE FREE!	96
FEBRUARY 2	99
EXAMPLE!	99

FEBRUARY 3	102
TREASURE IN EARTHEN VESSELS!	102
FEBRUARY 4	105
THEY KNEW HIM NOT!	105
FEBRUARY 5	108
ARE YOU CHARGED UP?	108
FEBRUARY 6	111
GOD IS IRREPLACEABLE!	111
FEBRUARY 7	114
THE BODY IS THE CARRIER OF THE SPIRIT!	114
FEBRUARY 8	117
DO YOU WONDER WHAT HAPPENED TO PEOPLE?	117
FEBRUARY 9	121
CONSISTENCY IS OMNIPOTENT!	121
FEBRUARY 10	124
CONTINUE THE LORD'S MISSION!	124
FEBRUARY 11	127
SATAN'S MISSION IN THE CHURCH	127
FEBRUARY 12	130
SPEAKS BLESSINGS OVER YOURSELF	130
FEBRUARY 13	133
WE NEED HUMBLE LEADERS	133
FEBRUARY 14	136
WE ARE PILGRIM AND STRANGER	136
FEBRUARY 15	139
DO NOT BE DECEIVED	139
FEBRUARY 16	142
ARE YOU SEEKING GOD?	142
FEBRUARY 17	145
GIVE BIRTH TO THE GODLY NATION	145
FEBRUARY 18	148
LEARNING FROM THE HOLY SPIRIT	148
FEBRUARY 19	152
YOUR WORDS ARE THAT POWERFUL!	152

FEBRUARY 20	155
THE KINGDOM OF GOD IS HIDDEN	155
FEBRUARY 21	158
GOD DOES SURGERY	158
FEBRUARY 22	161
MY PEOPLE HAVE FORGOTTEN ME DAILY	161
FEBRUARY 23	164
JESUS IS THE HOPE OF SALVATION.	164
FEBRUARY 24	167
LIFE-GIVING POWER IN THE BLOOD.	167
FEBRUARY 25	170
GUN HAS REPLACED THE BIBLE.	170
FEBRUARY 26	173
GOD, INCREASE MY CAPACITY.	173
FEBRUARY 27	176
SET YOUR PRIORITY IN ORDER.	176
FEBRUARY 28	179
ACTION HAS AN ATTACHMENT.	179
FEBRUARY 29	182
FEW ARE CHOSEN!	182

MARCH

MARCH 1	186
ARE YOU PUZZLED?	186
MARCH 2	189
TOILING OR WITH EASE?	189
MARCH 3	192
GIVE ME THE TRUTH!	192
MARCH 4	195
POWER OF PRAISE!	195
MARCH 5	198
LEARN TO SEEK GOD!	198
MARCH 6	201
GOD BEAUTIFIES MEEK WITH SALVATION!	201
MARCH 7	204
JESUS LOVES ME!	204

MARCH 8	207
I PRAY YOUR FAITH FAILS NOT!	207
MARCH 9	210
A LITTLE HELP CAN REVIVE AND RESTORE!	210
MARCH 10	213
LEARN TO CRY OUT!	213
MARCH 11	216
TAKE COUNSEL FROM GOD!	216
MARCH 12	219
THE DOCTRINE OF GOD VS THE DOCTRINE OF MAN!	219
MARCH 13	222
LET LOST FIND THE WAY OUT!	222
MARCH 14	225
WAITING IS THE KEY TO RECEIVING PROMISES!	225
MARCH 15	228
FIVE FOOL, FIVE WISE!	228
MARCH 16	231
THE RIGHTEOUS SHALL NOT BE MOVED!	231
MARCH 17	234
DO YOU KNOW WHAT'S AVAILABLE?	234
MARCH 18	237
RECONNECT WITH GOD!	237
MARCH 19	240
GOOD SEED VS TARE!	240
MARCH 20	243
WE WORK IN ADVERSITY!	243
MARCH 21	246
GET VIOLENT. TAKE IT BY FORCE!	246
MARCH 22	249
DO NOT RUIN MY REPUTATION!	249
MARCH 23	252
YOU CAN DO NOTHING WITHOUT ANOINTING!	252
MARCH 24	255
YOU CAN MAKE GOD MOVE!	255

MARCH 25	258
LET GOD DO HIS WORK!	258
MARCH 26	261
AUTHORITY APPOINTED BY JESUS CHRIST!	261
MARCH 27	265
HUNT FOR THE HIGHEST BLESSINGS!	265
MARCH 28	268
GIFTS OF THE SPIRIT ARE AVAILABLE!	268
MARCH 29	271
DO NOT LIVE UNDER THE PRIVILEGES!	271
MARCH 30	274
ONE ACCORD AND ONE MIND!	274
MARCH 31	277
TAKE IT BACK FROM SATAN!	277
APRIL	
APRIL 1	281
YOU CAN RESURRECT!	281
APRIL 2	284
ACTIVATE YOUR FAITH!	284
APRIL 3	287
AN ACTIVE CHRISTIAN FULFILLS	287
GOD'S PLAN!	287
APRIL 4	290
UNDERSTAND THE SPIRIT OPERATION!	290
APRIL 5	293
VISION WITH REVELATION!	293
APRIL 6	296
HOW TO MAKE ONE FALL!	296
APRIL 7	299
HOW DOES THE KINGDOM WORK?	299
APRIL 8	302
SEND THE WORD!	302
APRIL 9	305
INCLINE TO GOD!	305

APRIL 10	308
REBUKE THE STOPPER AND BLOCKER!	308
APRIL 11	311
BLESSING OF GOD ADDS NO SORROW TO IT!	311
APRIL 12	314
GOD PICKS THE LOWLY!	314
APRIL 13	317
REPENTANCE IS A FOUNDATION!	317
APRIL 14	320
SATAN's VERSION BIBLE!	320
APRIL 15	324
CHANGE YOUR LIFE STORY!	324
APRIL 16	327
SYSTEM OF THE KINGDOM!	327
APRIL 17	330
TRUTH VERSUS FALSE!	330
APRIL 18	333
TAKE THE LAMP AND LIGHT!	333
APRIL 19	336
RELIGION IS CONFUSING!	336
APRIL 20	339
THE WINDOW OF HEAVEN!	339
APRIL 21	342
SIN NO MORE!	342
APRIL 22	345
MINISTRY IS OUT THERE!	345
APRIL 23	348
SOUL TRAFFICKING!	348
APRIL 24	351
NOT EXTERNAL, BUT THE INTERNAL ATTACK WILL DESTROY!	351
APRIL 25	354
SEEK FOR THE GREATER!	354
APRIL 26	357
HOW CAN YOU GET DECEIVED AGAIN?	357

APRIL 27	360
WHAT IS MY JOB?	360
APRIL 28	363
GOD'S WORKS AND PLANS ARE IN ORDER!	363
APRIL 29	366
WE MUST KNOW WHAT IS AVAILABLE.	366
APRIL 30	369
CHANGE TO ENTER THE PROMISED LAND!	369

JANUARY

JANUARY 1

THE WORD OF GOD!

Happy New Year! Starting this year, let's dedicate ourselves to the study of God's Word. Let us experience how powerful the WORDS of God are. What impact does it have on us, as the creation of God?

The Bible is the manual that the Creator has provided for His creation. I encourage you to begin the year by reading and applying The WORD to your life. Begin by reading both the Old and New Testaments. Take the time to study, meditate, and live according to God's Word.

Success is the goal in today's culture, but what is the real strategy for reaching it? Biblical evidence with historical records tells us that a successful man has a connection to a supernatural power called God.

David had his success by keeping God's Word. By studying the Scripture, we gain hope for success.

Romans 15:4, tells us, "For whatsoever things were written aforetime were written for our learning, that we through patience and comfort of the scriptures might have hope."

How can you achieve success? By reading and obeying the Word of God, one can attain success. God's Word is eternal.

Isaiah, 40:8, tells us, *"The grass withereth, the flower fadeth: but the word of our God shall stand forever."*

Those who practice what the Word teaches are considered wise.

Matthew, 7:24 says, "Therefore whosoever heareth these sayings of mine and doeth them, I will liken him unto a wise man, which built his house upon a rock..."

What is the Word of God?

Hebrew 4:12 tells us, "For the word of God is quick, and powerful, and sharper than any two-edged sword, piercing even to the dividing asunder of soul and spirit, and of the joints and marrow, and is a discerner of the thoughts and intents of the heart."

Success can be found by following the Word of God. The Word of God first comes into the mind, then it goes into man's heart (spirit), and then it comes out from your innermost being when a need arises by speaking the Word to your situation. Try it and see what happens.

JANUARY 1

Being perfect at birth is impossible, but living by the Word leads to perfection. Rely on the guidance provided by God's Word.

Proverb 30:5 tells us, "Every word of God is pure: he is a shield unto them that put their trust in him."

The Word of God is a lamp and a light. Through the Word of God, we gain insight into the required change, as the Word is Light. Also, people will see the light shining through you. If you obey the Word, you will be on the path with Light.

Psalm 119:105 says, "Thy word is a lamp unto my feet and a light unto my path."

The Words of God have been tried seven times. It is the unadulterated pure Word.

Psalm 12:6 tells us, "The words of the LORD are pure words: as silver tried in a furnace of earth, purified seven times."

Are you seeking prosperity and success?

Read what Joshua 1:8 tells us: "This book of the law shall not depart out of thy mouth; but thou shalt meditate therein day and night, that thou mayest observe to do according to all that is written therein: for then thou shalt make thy way prosperous, and then thou shalt have good success."

Read the Bible to observe it. The Word of God is above all names of God. That is why Jesus used the Word of God when Satan came to tempt.

Psalms 138:2b, says, "... for thou hast magnified thy word above all thy name."

In this world, we are fighting against an unseen enemy named Satan, along with his cohorts of unclean angels and demons. The Word of God is the sole weapon against these invisible adversaries. Don't bring a gun when facing your unseen enemy; instead, arm yourself with the sword of the Spirit, which is the Word of God.

No one is above the Word of God. The followers of Jesus followed the instructions in the Word. A humble man's strength lies in his obedience to the Word of God, relying on God's power. When you stand on the Word, your life becomes unshakable, firmly grounded on solid ground. Life is filled with unpredictable twists and turns, but with guidance from the Word of God, you can triumph and be unstoppable. God Himself will be the source of your unstoppable elevation.

Follow the Word of God, as it is the most important book to read. By obeying the teachings of God, you can become a disciple of Jesus Christ. By obeying the Word, Jesus learned, and you can do the same.

Ephesians 6:17 tells us, "And take the helmet of salvation, and the sword of the Spirit, which is the word of God:"

It's important to remember that the Bible is God's Word, meant to be studied and followed. Starting this year with a deep study of the Word of God is essential. When praying for any situation, claim the Word of God. Let the Word of God be the foundation of your daily life. May the Lord Bless you and give you a divine understanding of His Word! May the Holy Spirit teach you and guide you through the Word!

Those who were successful in the past were those who followed the Word of God during their lifetime. We share a common word to represent this particular time in our lives. Seek refuge in the Scriptures for shield and buckler protection. Although God's commandments are still important, the blood of Jesus has replaced the animal sacrifices of the Old Testament.

Make sure not to use the Word of God as a tool for debating or arguing when you read and study it. Keep in mind that it is the Word of God, not yours. Do not interpret this from a personal perspective. You don't have to join any church, particularly one that alters the Word of God to suit their beliefs or lifestyle.

The Word of God has the power to free you from various chains, yokes, bondages, confusion, and the world.

Give studying and applying the Bible to your life a try. The Word brings an end to hardships, confusion, and toiling. It drives away depression, discouragement, and poverty, replacing them with prosperity. Your family is protected by angels. Your possessions will be safeguarded by the impenetrable hedge of protection. Amen! God Bless you!

LET US PRAY

Lord, how blessed we are that you have given us the Word of God in our languages. We recognize that only your Word has accurate information for each situation, problem, and trouble. Our hearts overflow with gratitude for the perfect help it offers. May we be blessed with genuine teachers who grasp, adhere to, and preserve the Word. We have learned that many do not have the Word of God, but we seek You knowing that You are the alpha and omega of the Bible. You are the Word of the Bible. Nothing can harm us if we keep it. Our long life and our seeking of success are in this book called the Bible. It is a light, a lamp, and a truth to freedom. It is a Sword to chop off the head of Satan and much more. The Lord instructed us to share it with others, and the most effective approach is to live according to God's Word. Jesus, guide us as we seek to do this in your name! God bless you! Amen!

JANUARY 2

THE CHOICES ARE YOURS!

The amazing aspect is that God didn't make us like robots but as unique individuals. We can exercise our free will when making choices. The Bible teaches us that our choices have consequences, according to God's word. God created us to live on earth and gave us the Bible as our life instruction. The earth is under the ownership of the Lord, but He has allowed us certain privileges that come with conditions. If we listen to and follow Jehovah God, our life can be the absolute best.

It is possible to point fingers at Eve, Adam, or someone else for the issues we confront on Earth. Self-examination requires us to start by looking in the mirror. We cannot be excused; we are fully responsible for our actions and choices in life.

Jehovah God provided instructions in the Holy Bible for us to live securely and receive blessings. Obeying His word leads to excellent results while disobeying brings terrible consequences. When it comes to wise counsel, is there anyone better than God? Take heed of Jehovah, the only wise God, and follow His instructions.

If you decide against aiding the underprivileged, including the poor, widows, orphans, and laborers, you will miss out on blessings. During this time of grace, there are individuals appointed by God to serve as apostles, evangelists, prophets, teachers, and pastors. The blessings of God are not confined to a church building. Failing to offer water to prophets or God's workers results in the loss of promised blessings.

If we follow God's voice instead of false prophets and teachers, our lives will be blessed. Taking titles doesn't make us pastors, evangelists, prophets, etc. God has given the title to whom He seems capable of the position.

During times of famine, Prophet Elijah survived by staying faithful to God. By following the prophet's instructions, the widow of Zarephath and her son were able to survive the famine.

You may ask yourself, "Why don't I experience the Lord this way in my life?"

Examine yourself and ask, "Do I go to God before I decide?" Do I choose the narrow road called the way of God? Am I deciding to follow Jesus and bear my cross? Follow God's instructions, put them to use, and watch the outcomes.

The priest Eli chose his wicked sons instead of God. God has called and appointed him to serve as a priest. God punished Eli for his bad choices by removing him from the priesthood and cursing his future generations. Just like others, we should learn from failure and avoid repeating disobedient choices.

ELIZABETH DAS

Remember what Jesus said in

John 5:14 "Afterward Jesus findeth him in the temple, and said unto him, Behold, thou art made whole: sin no more, lest a worse thing come unto thee."

The message of Jesus remains unchanged.

He said in John 8:11, "And Jesus said unto her, neither do I condemn you: go, and sin no more."

Hello parents and grandparents, choose to live by God's commandments. Make sure your children understand how crucial it is to make good decisions in their lives. Your soul will find rest if you choose to do this. There will come a day when you won't have to wait in a prison line to see them. You can have peace of mind about their location and activities as you trust their decisions. Making the right decisions allows children to bring peace to their parents' nights.

I pray that your children will be blessed with parents who will instruct them in the ways of the Lord. Life becomes purposeful when you choose to obey God.

May the Lord acknowledge you as a wise parent for imparting godly wisdom to your children. Choosing wisdom is a way to gain favor from the Lord, regardless of being a woman or a man. Blessings await those who prioritize obedience to the Lord above the fear of death.(for example, stoning, death by lions, death by fire, or any persecution).

It's up to you to make the choice. The fear of someone can lead people to become their followers. There's no need to be afraid. In your moments of need, God will come to your aid. He cannot be stopped, as He is unstoppable and will fulfill His promises as stated in His Word. Accept this truth or risk being led astray by the temptations of the flesh, materialism, and arrogance.

Raise the Bible to your eyes and affirm, "This is my guide, and I will pass it on to my children." Stay sincere and dedicated to receive blessings. Satan lures the flesh, but by making the correct choice, you can make him vanish!

Read the Word of God for knowledge. Examine the successes of those who stayed true to the Bible and the failures of those who deviated. Look at the examples of individuals who failed to fulfill their callings, like King Saul, Eve, Adam, Eli the Priest, Jehu the King, and more. Moreover, the study looks at the role of Biblical figures like Daniel, King David, King Asa, Moses, and Joshua. Today, we witness these men as prominent examples for us. Their relationship with God is revealed through obedience. They brought blessings to themselves, as well as to others and future generations. Your destiny is shaped by the choices you make in God's plan.

Read today's Deuteronomy Chapter 11. *Deuteronomy 11:12 reads, "A land which the Lord thy God careth for: the eyes of the Lord thy God are always upon it, from the beginning of the year even unto the end of the year. 13 And it shall come to pass, if ye shall hearken diligently unto my commandments which I command you this day, to love the Lord your God, and to serve him with all your heart and with all your soul, 14 That I will give you the rain of your land in his due season, the first rain and the latter rain, that thou mayest gather in thy corn, and thy wine, and thine oil. 15 And I will send grass in thy fields for thy cattle, that thou mayest eat and be full.16 Take heed to yourselves, that your heart be not deceived, and ye turn aside, and serve other gods, and worship them; 17 And then the Lord's wrath be kindled against you, and he shut up the heaven, that there be no rain, and that the land yield, not her fruit; and lest ye perish quickly from off the good land which the Lord giveth you. 26 Behold, I set before you this day a blessing and a curse; 27 A blessing, if ye obey the commandments of the LORD your God, which I command you this day: 28 And a curse if ye will not obey the commandments of the LORD your God, but turn aside out of the way which I command you this day, to go after other gods, which ye have not known."*

I urge all of you, my friends, to read and obey the Holy Bible, the Book of Life. To live according to God's teachings, dedicate time to studying and understanding the Bible. By doing this, you will receive blessings from God. Don't dismiss it, but rather read it diligently and keep the word in your heart.

"Thy word have I hid in my heart, that I might not sin against thee." (Psalm 119:11)

Remember, the decision is yours and no one's. Make sure to select the right choices. Make sure that you aren't misled by religious authorities or your family members when it comes to making the right decisions. Reading the Bible will lead you to the truth and a fulfilling life.

Deuteronomy 30:19 tells us, "I call heaven and earth to record this day against you, that I have set before you life and death, blessing and cursing: therefore choose life, that both thou and thy seed may live:..."

Remember, Daniel chose the lion's den. Shadrach, Meshach, and Abednego chose to enter the fiery furnace and praise God. Paul the Apostle and John Baptist were beheaded, as they knew their fate would fulfill God's plan.

Don't try to justify yourself by blaming your church, organization, family, or the liberal country you live in. Your choices will be your responsibility. When the Book of Life is opened on the Day of judgment, only you will be accountable for your actions. Will they be able to find out your name? You'll be labeled as a goat or a sheep based on the choices you make. Make a decision today: left or right. Amen! God Bless!

LET US PRAY

May the LORD give you a wise heart. His Holy Spirit guides and instructs you as you fulfill your purpose on this earth. O Lord, our Father in Heaven, we come to you knowing that you are the one and only God who loves and takes care of us. May our righteous path guide us to a place of sunshine, hope, eternal blessings, and divine protection! Lord, we appreciate being chosen to serve you and seek assistance to perform at our best. In Jesus 'Name! Amen! God Bless You!

JANUARY 3

CALL ON GOD!

"Call unto me, and I will answer thee, and show thee great and mighty things, which thou knowest not." (Jeremiah 33:3)

In the evening, I got a call from a woman whose son was in legal trouble. She was worried about her son; if he was found guilty, then he would be deported. The morning of the court case arrived, and she had no idea what her son would be up against. Charges were filed by a prostitute against her son. She devised a trap, making it seem like she required his help. When he attempted to assist her, she began screaming and contacted the police. She used her gender as an advantage to exploit this innocent boy. She took legal action against the young man who was simply trying to assist her.

Despite his innocence, the young man still felt anxious about the court's decision. We need to be aware of the trap the enemy has set for us.

Our God has the power to rescue us from the net's trap, thank goodness.

"For without cause have they hid for me their net in a pit, which without cause they have dug for my soul. Let destruction come upon him at unawares, and let his net that he hath hid catch himself: into that very destruction let him fall." (Psalm 35:7-8).

"He brought me up out of a horrible pit, out of the miry clay, and set my feet upon a rock, and established my goings." (Psalm 40:2.).

During the previous night, his mother was working at the hospital. She felt overwhelmed by the thought of the son being separated from his family the next day. As soon as she called me in tears, I started praying in tongues as the Holy Spirit moved through me. The depression cloud disappeared right away. She was relieved of the falsehoods spread by the enemy.

God is a good God! Call on Him! Go to someone who can pray over your situation. Reach out to someone who has a direct line to God. Our God has performed countless miracles and will always listen to the prayers of His followers.

"Likewise the Spirit also helpeth our infirmities: for we know not what we should pray for as we ought: but the Spirit itself maketh intercession for us with groanings which cannot be uttered." (Romans 8:26)

She wanted to know if she could reach out to me on the morning of the court day. I said, "Yes." She called the next morning since it was the court for her son. We offered our prayers, and I informed her that you were about to receive an amazing surprise. The situation will be resolved powerfully. The connection between the Almighty God and someone is evident when the Holy Spirit speaks through their mouth. After an hour, she called me and exclaimed, you won't believe what just happened.

I said I would too. Expect God to go above and beyond, granting you more than you can even fathom. Crying out to Him is the only way for this to take place. If you're too proud to tell God about your troubles and don't cry out to Him, don't expect any assistance from Him.

According to the young man's mother, the court found no evidence against her son in the computer. She mentioned that even their lawyer provided evidence in the form of written documents filed against him. God decided to dismiss the case.

When we reached out to the Lord, His command summoned angels to step in, eradicating all court computer data.

She was joyful and kept telling me I cannot believe this. What a mighty God!

Difficulties are a part of everyone's life.

Always remember to seek guidance from the Lord. Experience the amazing and awe-inspiring miracles by calling upon Jesus. Present your situation before the altar of God. Either cry in a closet or seek solace on a mountain to connect with God. Seek out a place to connect with God and lay your petitions at His feet. Reach out to Him.

There was a lot of suffering within the Jewish community in Babylon. The devil intended to eradicate the bloodline of the Messiah. By proclaiming fasting and prayer, Queen Esther successfully overturned the judgment. The case against the enemy can be turned around and they can be destroyed by utilizing the weapons of confession of sins, fasting, and prayer.

Psalm 50:15, tells us, "And call upon me in the day of trouble: I will deliver thee, and thou shalt glorify me."

Moses defended the rights of his enslaved people. The existence of Daniel, magicians, soothsayers, and astrologers was in danger. Daniel went to offer his prayers. God is patiently waiting for you to witness His mighty power. Seek God for any situation you're facing, whether it's poverty, addiction, or health issues. By calling upon Jesus, you will witness extraordinary things beyond your imagination. Witness doors opening, poverty transforming into prosperity, sickness healing, deliverance occurring, war leading to victory, and bondage giving way to freedom. However, the greatest thing is saving your soul. Pray to Jesus, the One true God, and unlock the ability to enter the unseen supernatural domain and accomplish extraordinary tasks beyond human capabilities. Don't forget, you possess the Key. Reach out to Him!

Psalm 40:3 says, "And he hath put a new song in my mouth, even praise unto our God: many shall see it, and fear, and shall trust in the Lord. 4 Blessed is that man that maketh the Lord his trust, and respecteth not the proud, nor such as turn aside to lies."

LET US PRAY

Lord, we come before Your altar, the Lord of Isaac who provided the lamb and rescued him. Lord of Jacob, who delivered him from many trials and troubles. The God of David, who delivered him from his mortal enemy. The Lord of Israel, Abraham, and Isaac hear you when you cry out to HIM! May the Lord help in the time of your distress! Your Lord, answer every prayer you pray for your children and grandchildren! The Lord be your guide till the end of this world? The Lord be your guide. You call upon Him and He will answer in the time of your need. Our God has ears to hear and eyes to see. He has the power to save you, deliver you, and set you free. Our God is merciful. Call on Him and see how good He is. Anyone who seeks diligently will find Him. God is not a respecter of any. God has His children in mind. He looks into their heart to find whose heart is leaning on Him. Since not everyone is calling on Him, he cannot help everyone. Call on Him and see what He does for you. Amen! In Jesus 'Name! God Bless You!

JANUARY 4

HEART!

The heart's essential facts are found in the Bible. Every detail within our body has been created by God. He is aware of the important functions carried out by each organ.

God says in Jeremiah 17:9, The heart is deceitful above all things, and desperately wicked: who can know it? 10 I, the Lord, search the heart, I try the reins, even to give every man according to his ways, and according to the fruit of his doings.

By exploring the Bible's perspective on the heart, you'll analyze your own heart. The nature of a man's heart remains deceitful and wicked, no matter our perspective. It's important to be cautious of how you perceive yourself. Your true identity is reflected in your actions, not your beliefs.

Proverbs 4:23 tells us to "Keep thy heart with all diligence; for out of it are the issues of life."

The source of life is hidden within your heart.

In the Bible, God communicates the truth of the heart. Jeremiah cautions that one should not make claims about knowing others or oneself, as God describes the human heart as deceitful and wicked.

King David, deceived by his own heart, committed adultery and murdered Bathsheba's husband. God observed and confronted him for his actions. David repented and wrote this beautiful prayer when he acknowledged the state of his heart.

Psalms 51:10 Create in me a clean heart, O God; and renew a right spirit within me. 11 Cast me not away from thy presence; and take not thy holy spirit from me. 12 Restore unto me the joy of thy salvation; and uphold me with thy free spirit.

In Matthew 15:18, But those things which proceed out of the mouth come forth from the heart; and they defile the man. 19 For out of the heart proceed evil thoughts, murders, adulteries, fornications, thefts, false witness, blasphemies:

Our hearts must be guided by God's laws and commandments.

Proverbs 23:19 gave a guiding principle to us: "Hear thou, my son, and be wise, and guide thine heart in the way."

ELIZABETH DAS

We must guard our hearts with diligence.

2 Chronicles 16:9 tells us, "For the eyes of the LORD run to and fro throughout the whole earth, to shew himself strong in the behalf of them whose heart is perfect toward him."

Proverbs 3: provides us with the necessities needed to keep our hearts clean: 1 My son, forget not my law; but let thine heart keep my commandments: 2 For the length of days, and long life, and peace, shall they add to thee.

Joshua 22: tells us to 5 But take diligent heed to do the commandment and the law, which Moses the servant of the Lord charged you, to love the Lord your God, and to walk in all his ways, and to keep his commandments, and to cleave unto him, and to serve him with all your heart and with all your soul.

Your heart is what matters to God, not your outward appearance. To keep the heart purified and clean, we need to give it extra attention.

Proverb 3: reminds us to 3 Let not mercy and truth forsake thee: bind them about thy neck; write them upon the table of thine heart: 4 So shalt thou find favour and good understanding in the sight of God and man. 5 Trust in the Lord with all thine heart; and lean not unto thine own understanding. 6 In all thy ways acknowledge him, and he shall direct thy paths.

Understanding that God has the power to transform our hearts is crucial.

In I Samuel 10:1, during the anointing of King Saul, "Samuel took a vial of oil, and poured it upon his head, and kissed him, and said, Is it not because the LORD hath anointed thee to be captain over his inheritance? 9 And it was so, that when he had turned his back to go from Samuel, God gave him another heart: and all those signs came to pass that day."

God is fully capable of renewing our hearts that He created. Seek it out, request it - The Lord will supply.

Ezekiel 36: says that 26 A new heart also will I give you, and a new spirit will I put within you: and I will take away the stony heart out of your flesh, and I will give you a heart of flesh. 27 And I will put my spirit within you, and cause you to walk in my statutes, and ye shall keep my judgments, and do them.

I bear witness that God can transform people's hearts when they turn to Him. He cares for them and eliminates any remnants of the evil that once haunted their hearts. The quality of our life is determined by the state of our heart—it shapes all aspects of our lives. If you let God take care of your heart, its problems will go away. The problem lies in our inability to identify the condition of our hearts. We enjoy receiving praise rather than being confronted with facts. Nonetheless, when the opportunity arises to validate, our heart expresses an entirely different narrative. We tend to neglect the fact that we are unaware of the true essence of our hearts. It is important to read and hold the Word of God in our hearts. It holds the key to a compassionate heart.

Psalm 119:11 says, "Thy word have I hid in mine heart, that I might not sin against thee."

The Word of God will protect you from making the wrong choices if you let it fill your heart. Amen! God Bless!

LET US PRAY

Heavenly Father, creator of our heart, where our life starts. It is in your hands to control our hearts entirely. You hold the master switch of the heart. Our prayers are directed to the Lord, who grants us a renewed heart and spirit. May love, joy, and peace fill our hearts to the brim. Our countenance reflects our heart. Lord, keep our hearts! Guide our hearts in Your ways and commandments. May our speech be as powerful as a sword, carrying the Word with conviction. Mend our inner beings. The Word of God strengthens our hearts to do right. We thank you for your power to create a clean heart within. Create in us a pure heart, O Lord, in Jesus's Name. Amen! God bless you!

JANUARY 5

WALK IN THE SPIRIT!

Exercise the spirit by walking in the spirit. The significance placed on our physical bodies outweighs the attention given to our spirits in today's world. Without nourishing our spirit with spiritual food, it becomes weak and unhealthy. We have become apathetic and unaware of our spiritual being. We do not recognize the condition of our spiritual health; it is dying.

Profitable exercise for our spirit can be found in the Bible, leading to salvation for you and those who hear your message.

Paul writes in *I Timothy 4:8 For bodily exercise profiteth little: but godliness is profitable unto all things, having promise of the life that now is, and of that which is to come.9 This is a faithful saying and worthy of all acceptation.10 For, therefore, we both labor and suffer reproach because we trust in the living God, who is the Saviour of all men, especially those who believe.11 These things command and teach.*

The exercises mentioned in the following verses are meant for our spirit.

I Timothy 4:12 Let no man despise thy youth; but be thou an example of the believers, in word, in conversation, in charity, in spirit, in faith, in purity.13 Till I come, give attendance to reading, to exhortation, to doctrine.14 Neglect not the gift that is in thee, which was given thee by prophecy, with the laying on of the hands of the presbytery.15 Meditate upon these things; give thyself wholly to them; that thy profiting may appear to all.16 Take heed unto thyself, and unto the doctrine; continue in them: for in doing this thou shalt both save thyself, and them that hear thee.

According to the Bible, we are encouraged to walk in the spirit. The world is talking about physical health, exercise, fitness, and body shape. Many techniques and devices have been introduced to ensure excellent physical fitness.

Despite achieving physical perfection, we continue to battle various emotional, mental, and physical ailments. Why? We don't use spiritual exercise to strengthen our spiritual self. The state of our spiritual health is mentioned in the Bible. Even with a perfect physical appearance, one's inner self can still be filled with evil that harms their mind and body.

My neighbor married a man who had a couple of sons. In addition, she had boys from a previous marriage. Every time I saw her, she was sick. She underwent multiple surgeries, one after another. There is a discrepancy in how she treats her sons compared to her husband's sons. Even though he couldn't reach the pedal, her husband's little son still managed to deliver newspapers in the early morning. In the cold and rainy early morning, he was accompanied by his fellow brothers. I questioned myself, what sort of individuals are these? The absence of smiles on her face created an environment of fear for her husband's children, who would always hide and refrain from playing or speaking whenever she was present. They ended up divorcing at a later time. However, I constantly witnessed her being ill. Although her sickness was not physical, it affected her spiritually. Beautiful looks are less important compared to love. Although she was stunning, she struggled with several spiritual illnesses. The way children acted in her presence made me realize that this lady needed to show kindness and love to little ones. Physical sickness is many times caused by the sickness of one's spirit.

Galatians 5: tells us,17 For the flesh lusteth against the spirit, and the spirit against the flesh: and these are contrary the one to the other: so that ye cannot do the things that ye would.18 But if ye be led of the Spirit, ye are not under the law.

Start your spiritual exercise by reading and following the following verses from

Galatians 5:22 But the fruit of the spirit is love, joy, peace, long-suffering, gentleness, goodness, faith, 23 Meekness, temperance: against such there is no law. 24 And they that are Christ's have crucified the flesh with the affections and lusts. 25 If we live in the spirit, let us also walk in the spirit.

Walking is a great way to improve your physical health. Your spirit will be healthier by walking in the spirit.

By engaging in spiritual exercises such as love, joy, and patience, you can achieve both inner and outer beauty and health.

Give more importance to your inner being (Spirit) rather than just your external appearance. Make prayer and fasting a priority in your schedule;Your spiritual being will become more powerful, while your physical body will become less strong.

Galatians 5:19 tells us, "Now the works of the flesh are manifest, which are these; Adultery, fornication, uncleanness, lasciviousness, 20 Idolatry, witchcraft, hatred, variance, emulations, wrath, strife, seditions, heresies, 21 Envyings, murders, drunkenness, reveling, and such like: of the which I tell you before, as I have also told you in time past, that they which do such things shall not inherit the kingdom of God."

Outwardly, someone might seem attractive, but they are unwell both internally and externally. You can't address the inner issues by focusing solely on adorning and painting the outer self. The only person you will deceive is yourself.

We neglected the well-being of our inner selves. Begin working out to improve your spiritual well-being. Seek guidance from God, our spiritual Father, and engage in spiritual exercises.

To start, open the Bible and familiarize yourself with the Scripture for your spiritual workout. Witness the transformation in your beauty and health through this spiritual exercise. Achieve your best spirit health by embracing spiritual walks;the act of walking is a pleasant and beneficial exercise.

May the Holy Spirit serve as a powerful guide in your spiritual journey! In Jesus's name, I pray that you are blessed with a spirit that is healthy and strong. Amen!

LET US PRAY

Lord, our heavenly Father, we are grateful for teaching us the need for our spiritual health. Teach us the way of God, and let us walk in the divine instruction of the Holy Spirit. Holy Spirit, we ask you to guide and teach us the way of the spirit. We mortify our flesh and its desires. Lord, give us His goodness, truth, and righteousness. Thank you for giving us a powerful Holy Spirit to take over any situation. He is the best teacher to keep us from falling away from the truth. We desire to walk in the Word of God. It gives perfect soundness to our souls. How wonderful is it to have your gifts of the spirit? Heavenly Father, please give us the word for each life situation. In Jesus 'name! Amen! God bless you!

JANUARY 6

WHAT IS FAITH?

In the realm of heaven, faith is a valuable currency. To purchase an item online, we require a credit card. The Bible teaches that faith serves as your charge card to place orders with God. Connect with God directly through the royal line, and your charges will be based on your faith balance.

Hebrews 11:1 tells us, "Now faith is the substance of things hoped for, the evidence of things not seen."

Whether wealthy or poor, having Faith makes you rich. Even with millions of dollars, one can still feel miserable and impoverished without Faith.

Where do you choose to place your Faith? Failure is inevitable if you continue to have Faith in perishable things such as your bank account, education, degree, job, or health. Trusting in God and His Word guarantees that you'll receive all the promised blessings.

A soldier in Matthew 8:8 said to Jesus, *"The centurion answered and said, Lord, I am not worthy that thou shouldest come under my roof: but speak the word only, and my servant shall be healed."*

This centurion's trust was in the Lord. When someone has faith and believes, the Lord can fulfill His desires.

Having faith is valuable, but where you put your faith is equally crucial. Use your faith currency to obtain healing, victory, and numerous other rewards when confronted with sickness, war, trouble, or unfavorable circumstances. Only if it is in the Lord will you receive it.

The Word of God is a book that bears witness to Jesus, the One in whom you should place your Faith. The data endures after being processed seven times in the fire. God's Word is everlasting and cannot be destroyed.

Occasionally, individuals express frustration, saying "I have faith, yet I do not see the outcomes." It is in you, not in the promises of God. The key to obtaining the right result lies in having more faith. Doubt, worry, fear, and other factors hinder progress and limit opportunities for growth. To achieve positive results, have Faith and disregard obstacles. It's definitely going to happen! The super source of mega power is none other than God. The Book known as the Bible holds the source of superpower. Practice continuous reading, belief, obedience, and application of the Bible.

Roman 10:17 tells us, "So then faith cometh by hearing, and hearing by the word of God."

The Bible contains accounts of non-believers who eventually became believers. Is there anything you sacrifice by believing? Doubt, fear, and worry are Satan's weapons against Faith. Your faith will undergo trials.

Jesus said in Luke 1:37, "For nothing will be impossible with God."

Believe in the Word and bring your circumstances to God to experience His limitless capabilities.

I place complete trust in God in every aspect of my life. He will not lie, cheat, or fail me. I've placed all my belief and confidence in the Lord Jesus. My job, which I had held for 21 years, was taken away by God, who advised me to accept a modest retirement check instead of a disability check. Though it felt impossible to make it through, God assured me that He would take care of me. There was no alternative source to rely on. Following the Lord's instruction, I had a peaceful sleep. There's no greater way to learn than by obeying and trusting the Lord's guidance. I was relieved when I experienced both back trouble and cancer. I listened to the various promises of God tailored to each situation. During my time in a wheelchair, God reassured me.

Proverbs 4:12. "When thou goest, thy steps shall not be straitened; and when thou runnest, thou shalt not stumble."

Don't waste time trying to figure out or resolve your situation. Allow Him to handle the calculations and overcome any tests or challenges. Obey His voice as He guides you on this exciting new adventure.

My God is both a provider and a faithful fulfiller of promises. Today, I am walking and free from cancer, no longer needing the wheelchair. Praise the Lord!

It's really that straightforward. Regardless of your unfamiliarity with the situation, he will diagnose and heal you without any cost. Faith is the only currency you require.

Hebrew 11:2 "For by it (faith) the elders obtained a good report."

Friends, you have been fully rescued from the devil's clutches by His precious blood. Why are you subjecting yourself to the burdens of illness, debt, addiction, poverty, and various hardships? Dive into the Bible, explore the Word, and acquire everything you desire. It is accessible; just bring heavenly currency called faith. According to the Word of God, having strong faith will lead to wealth.

Matthew 9:29,30a "Then touched he their eyes, saying, according to your Faith be it unto you. And their eyes were opened."

Do you see? God and His redeeming Book, the Bible, are all you need on this earth. With the Word residing in your heart and mind, you are abundant because your Heavenly Father is the ultimate owner of everything.

Psalm 50:10 "For every beast of the forest is mine and the cattle upon a thousand hills." Amen!

LET US PRAY

Lord, we humbly come to your altar, an altar of mercy. Give us faith as you give us generously. We would like to have faith in operation for all situations. Knowing You in Your might and power is essential for us to keep our faith in You. Help us, O Lord, to study your Word and to apply. Knowing the result will be beyond us. It will be supernatural. Our God keeps His Word if we stand on it and claim it. Lord, remove all doubt, fear, and worry. You are more than enough for us. You are all that we need. Let our eyes turn to You, knowing our help cometh from the Lord, the Maker of heaven and earth. Creator Sustainer of the living and breathing soul! No one but You have the power to raise the dead, give life to all, and keep us from harm and danger. Help us believe and trust that you are the only Jehovah's Savior, Jesus Christ, God in the flesh in Jesus's Name! Amen! God bless you!

JANUARY 7

POWER OF THE WORD GAME!

Proverb 18:21 tells us that "Death and life are in the power of the tongue: and they that love it shall eat the fruit thereof."

The act of speaking in both positive and negative ways yields opposite results. By speaking positively, you have the power to create, but by speaking negatively, you have the power to destroy. By responding positively, you surrender your problem to the Lord, who believes in the possibility of all things. You'll be caught in the devil's trap, which aims to kill, steal, and destroy if your response is negative. Master the art of speaking God's Word in every situation you encounter. Avoid empowering the devil by speaking negatively about the situation.

Just a couple of days ago, I got to be in charge of hosting a cooking show. The producers gave me a salad cutter machine as a thank-you for hosting. Despite their promise, they did not give a salad cutter as expected. Instead of getting upset, I stayed positive and said, "God will give me something better.

Within just a few days, God blessed me with something even better than a salad master machine. The Veggie Bullet is an electric device that can quickly chop up any ingredient, while the SaladMaster Machine is a manual tool that requires laborious effort.

On a different occasion, I needed a robe, so I requested a specific one from God. I placed my trust in Him to give me a robe. Someone gifted me a lovely robe during Christmas a few years ago. It was both wonderfully soft and lovely. At a later point, I found myself in need of another one. Following my morning prayer, I was contacted by a friend who requested me to go to Sam's Club. She said, "I have something to return?" I said, "Sure."

After returning her items, she wished to browse for a little while.

During our walk, she spotted the robe and instantly stopped. She initiated the act of feeling and touching the robe. "Take a look at how incredibly soft and nice this robe is," she exclaimed. I expressed that Christmas had not yet arrived, but she was insistent on buying it for me. I was happy. In the morning, I made a request to God for a robe. Do you understand how important your words are? Express the words, and your heavenly Father will be attentive. I said, "Please give me." I simply said, "Give me," knowing Jesus is my provider. Jesus proclaimed that if you ask, you will be given.

Genesis 22:7 tells us, "And Isaac spake unto Abraham his Father, and said, My Father: and he said, Here am I, my son. And he said, Behold the fire and the wood: but where is the lamb for a burnt offering? 8 And

Abraham said, My son, God will provide himself a lamb for a burnt offering: so they went both of them together."

And that's when everything changed.

Verse 13 says, "And Abraham lifted up his eyes, and looked, and behold behind him a ram caught in a thicket by his horns: and Abraham went and took the ram and offered him up for a burnt offering in the stead of his son."

If you are sick, say: "Jesus is my health; through His stripes, I am healed. Take authority and say, I rebuke this sickness; leave my body. Say, I Command the sickness to leave in Jesus 'name."

Matthew 12:37 says, "For by thy words thou shalt be justified, and by thy words, thou shalt be condemned."

Through the use of words, God brought about creation.

Psalm 33:6 tells us, "By the word of the LORD were the heavens made; and all the host of them by the breath of his mouth."

Proverb 21:23 says, "Whoso keepeth his mouth and his tongue keepeth his soul from troubles."

Speak positive words like: "My children will be mighty men and women of God. My health is excellent and will remain so. In the name of Jesus, I will receive what I desire. God will direct me to tranquil waters. He will bring back what I lost. He will provide me with knowledge, wisdom, riches, understanding, health, wealth, and everything I require.

Revelation 5:12 says, "Worthy is the Lamb that was slain to receive power, and riches, and wisdom, and strength, and honor, and glory, and blessing."

If we assert our ownership, everything mentioned in the previous verses can be ours to inherit. Our knowledge of the Savior is essential. Let's assume we have the knowledge and understanding of what needs to be done. Nobody will experience poverty, hunger, homelessness, thirst, illness, or heartbreak. The only way to receive everything from our God is by knowing and claiming it.

Keep your faith in God, for He alone has the power to accomplish everything. She said, I would touch His garment and be made whole, not healed, but made authentic; that is, mind, soul, body, and spirit will be sound and healing.

Ask Him to send His Word. Everything I wish for will be taken care of by him.

Psalms 52:8-9 says, "But I am like a green olive tree in the house of God: trust in the mercy of God forever and ever. I will praise thee forever because thou hast done it: and I will wait on thy name; for it is good before thy saints."

Don't forget, life is essentially a game of words. Say to yourself, "I am above, I am first, I am highly favored, I am the head. No weapons formed against me can prosper. I have the strength of an eagle. I will mount up like an eagle. I will run and not faint." Speak with faith by believing in your heart and enjoy all you receive from our generous God.

Find all positive words and speak them over yourself and others. See what it does for you and others. The same is true if you speak negative words. It will be a nightmare. No one will want to be around you if you speak negative words. You inevitably create an atmosphere where the devil thrives when you speak negative words.

Continue to read the Bible, which is the Word of the living God. Experience the creation of the unseen realm. Amen! God Bless you!

LET US PRAY

Heavenly Father, it is good to know that you have given us the power to be called your children. Thank you for the Word of God and thank you for directing our lives. Through you, we declare that we have life and abundance in abundance. We ask for your divine protection to cover us. We thank you for showing the power of speaking words into existence. Only the Lord has the power to create. The Lord is the only source of power and blessings for His children. May the Lord teach us through His Spirit to claim all that pertains to us. The God we know is mighty, all-powerful, all-knowing, and ever-present, and provides help in times of trouble. In the name above all names, Jesus, we are blessed. Thank you, Lord, for your living Word; we bless your Holy name in Jesus 'name! God bless you. Amen!

JANUARY 8

GOD IS MAKING A NEW THING FOR YOU!

There is a major transformation happening this year, on a global and personal level. In the Bible, there are references to innovative approaches, unfamiliar destinations, and groundbreaking ideas. We need to understand God's interpretation of new things.

Isaiah 43:18 tells us, "Remember ye not the former things, neither consider the things of old."

This year, get ready for both big and small changes, my friends. Maybe you're making changes in your church, job, and location. Don't forget, God is creating new things for you. Take a moment to relax, breathe deeply, and come along on our journey with Lord Jesus. Look forward to the new journey ahead and forget the past.

Explore new things. Experience a one-of-a-kind ride through life and make the most of what awaits you. You might be asking yourself what's going on. God is responsible for the transformation happening in you and your life. I pray that God expands your imagination and grants you spiritual insight to view things from a different angle.

Revelation 21:5 says, "And he that sat upon the throne said, Behold, I make all things new. And he said unto me, Write: for these words are true and faithful."

Is lying within God's nature? No, take it as a rain check and cash it today. He is giving you all the details about your new possessions.

I pray, "Lord, make my day new and better when I wake up. I want to know all of your thoughts and plans for me. Pray for divine wisdom and fresh insights to reach your full potential.

2 Corinthians 5:17 tells us, "Therefore if any man be in Christ, he is a new creature: old things are passed away; behold, all things are become new."

I can still vividly remember the day I surfaced from the water following my baptism in the name of Jesus. The first time I had that experience, it completely changed my life. That was an experience I had never had previously. When they immersed me in the Name of Jesus, I emerged from the water as a completely new individual.

ELIZABETH DAS

I experienced a tremendous transformation that I can't fully describe. The experience of forgiveness of sins is incredibly powerful. I had a sensation of being as light as a feather as if I could effortlessly glide on water. On that day, I transformed into a completely different being! A person who is born again.

Romans 6:3 tells us, "Know ye not that so many of us as were baptized into Jesus Christ were baptized into his death? 4 Therefore we are buried with him by baptism into death: that like as Christ was raised from the dead by the glory of the Father, even so, we also should walk in newness of life."

Following the Word of God by faith, as stated in the Bible, is the ultimate way to bring about renewal. Unless you follow the Word of God, you won't truly understand its power.

God says in Isaiah 43:19, "Behold; I will do a new thing; now it shall spring forth; shall ye not know it? I will even make a way in the wilderness and rivers in the desert."

In Israel, God is turning empty spaces into water-filled places and creating rivers out of previously dry land. Take a closer look at the developments occurring in desert countries within the Arab nations. Explore the UAE, Qatar, and other countries, and compare their transformation from 20 or 30 years ago.

Ephesians 2:15 says, "Having abolished in his flesh the enmity, even the law of commandments contained in ordinances; for to make in himself of twain one new man, so making peace;"

By shedding His Blood on the Cross, Jesus liberated us from laws that couldn't remove our sins. Keep in mind that the Cross and blood are responsible for your present life. There's an experience awaiting you in this dispensation that will change you. You will experience a wonderful renewal from the Lord, both within and around you.

Ephesians 4:24 tells us, "And that ye put on the new man, which after God is created in righteousness and true holiness."

Follow the guidance of the Bible by embracing God's righteousness and holiness. You have a job this year; then you will be what He created in the Garden of Eden, a man in His image. Open yourself to a new life in Christ and let God's glory shine brightly within you. Embrace a new highway of faith and claim your well-deserved triumph.

Hebrews 8:13 says, "In that he saith, A new covenant, he hath made the first old. Now that which decayeth and waxeth old are ready to vanish away."

God is making even a new covenant, not just jobs, roads, locations, and surroundings. Enter this year in the new covenant, which is called the New Testament. Read and experience by obeying where you need to establish your relationship and be a partaker of this New Covenant.

Isaiah 65:17 says, "For, behold, I create new heavens and a new earth: and the former shall not be remembered, nor come into mind."

Find joy in your new surroundings and seek the new heaven and earth. God is in creating business. Continue going on a new road until you meet Jesus. May you enjoy an everlasting existence with the Creator, who constantly renews all things.

JANUARY 8

Wishing you a safe trip on the Heavenly Highway. May you find happiness in your new heavenly abode, where golden roads replace cement.

Embrace the transformative power of daily experiences. There is a great deal of information you must study regarding how to please the Lord and what actions to refrain from. Expect numerous trials, but also anticipate glorious victories. Hear the Lord and obey; it is the life worth living on earth. Your experiences will serve as an inspiration for others to enjoy. Your story will serve as a beacon of hope and salvation for others.

You are now focusing on something different.

Philippians 4:6-9 tells us, "Be careful for nothing; but in everything by prayer and supplication with thanksgiving let your requests be made known unto God. 7 And the peace of God, which passeth all understanding, shall keep your hearts and minds through Christ Jesus. 8 Finally, brethren, whatsoever things are true, whatsoever things are honest, whatsoever things are just, whatsoever things are pure, whatsoever things are lovely, whatsoever things are of good report; if there be any virtue, and if there be any praise, think on these things. 9 Those things, which ye have both learned, and received, and heard, and seen in me, do: and the God of peace shall be with you."

LET US PRAY

Lord, we thank you that the day we repent and are baptized in your precious name, a new experience starts. We consider it a privilege to help others discover the transformative power of forgiveness for sins. May our souls be filled with boldness, strength, courage, and love. Lord anoints us with mighty anointing. We are grateful for the beautiful impact you have on our lives. Our Lord's promises are amazing. Thank you for ensuring our safety and brightening our day with the sunshine. Thank you for the food and all the daily provisions. Our heart is grateful to you. We are deeply appreciative that we can distribute all the resources you have generously given us. When we travel, the earth is full of surprises, riches, and amazement. When we finally witness heaven, it will be the most extraordinary story. We cannot comprehend the unimaginable heaven, but we express gratitude for everything you have done and will do. All is new and gorgeous, so thank you, Lord, in Jesus 'name! Amen! God Bless You!

JANUARY 9

FAITH IN GOD IS TARGETED!

Ephesians 6:16 Above all, taking the shield of faith, wherewith ye shall be able to quench all the fiery darts of the wicked.

Remember, the devil prowls and knows the thoughts and desires of your mind. He knows what you stand for. His mission is to find a way to shake your faith and test your loyalty to our Lord Jesus Christ.

Job:1:8 And the Lord said unto Satan, Hast thou considered my servant Job, that there is none like him in the earth, a perfect and an upright man, one that feareth God, and escheweth evil?

The Lord knows every single thing about us. I knew Job was perfect and upright. The Lord blessed him with abundance, wealth, and a near-perfect God-fearing life.

Keeping God's commandments most often results in material blessings as well.

The devil then attacked Job's health and attempted to destroy his will. Job's faith in the Lord was his shield, and faith is inherently power, so the devil was defeated.

If you are going through any type of trial, whether it be regarding your wealth, children, health, or financial issues, then what you need to find is a scripture that will shield your faith. The only thing you need is faith. Your faith should be in the Word of God. Your faith should not be in anything else.

What is faith?

Hebrews 11:1 says, "faith is the substance of things hoped for, the evidence of things not seen."

After Job lost everything, he says in

Job 1:21, "Naked came I out of my mother's womb, and naked shall I return thither: the Lord gave, and the Lord hath taken away; blessed be the name of the Lord."

Wow! Did you perceive the understanding of Job?

Job learned all material things God provided him were not of prime importance. His faith led his path and made the Lord his Shepard and the basis of his will.

2 Corinthians 4:18 While we look not at the things which are seen, but at the things which are not seen: for the things which are seen are temporal; but the things which are not seen are eternal.

Was Job tested for wealth or health? No, Job's faith was tried. His uprightness, fear of God, and perfect walk with God was tested. The devil hunts your walk with God.

Is your belief conditional? Are you serving God because you have a good time, or do you not lose what you already have? No, your relationship with God has nothing to do with the temporal things you own. God allowed all trials in Job's life and can give double what was lost. You must believe and trust in God and have no other selfish reason for serving and believing in God.

Your love for God must be unconditional, without worry or fear of loss or gain. God gives things on earth.

Look at the devil's argument with God:

Job 1:9 Then Satan answered the Lord, and said, Doth Job fear God for naught? 10 Hast not thou made a hedge about him, and about his house, and about all that he hath on every side? Thou hast blessed the work of his hands, and his substance is increased in the land.

Being Christian, we know we have a hedge of protection around our wealth, home, children, and health. In short, God protects us if we are God-fearing, righteous, and holy living people. We must love the Lord with all our heart, mind, soul, and strength.

Job 42:12 says, "So the LORD blessed the latter end of Job more than his beginning: for he had fourteen thousand sheep, and six thousand camels, and a thousand yoke of oxen, and a thousand she asses."

Job had a close relationship with understanding God.

Job 42:1 Then Job answered the LORD, and said, 2 I know that thou canst do everything and that no thought can be withholden from thee. 3 Who is he that hideth counsel without knowledge? Therefore have I uttered that I understood not; things too wonderful for me, which I knew not. 4 Hear, I beseech thee, and I will speak: I will demand of thee, and declare thou unto me. 5 I have heard of thee by the hearing of the ear: but now mine eye seeth thee. 6 Wherefore I abhor myself, and repent in dust and ashes.

Wow, what we see here is pure repentance.

Also, Job forgave his friends who spoke evil and judged him wrong.

Job 42:10 And the LORD turned the captivity of Job, when he prayed *for his friends: also the LORD gave Job twice as much as he had before. 11 Then came there unto him all his brethren, and all his sisters, and all they that had been of his acquaintance before and did eat bread with him in his house: and they bemoaned him, and comforted him over all the evil that the LORD had brought upon him: every man also gave him a piece of money, and every one an earring of gold. 12 So the LORD blessed the latter end of Job more than his beginning: for he had fourteen thousand sheep, and six thousand camels, and a thousand yoke of oxen, and a thousand she asses. 13 He had also seven sons and three daughters.*

Many of the trials of your faith will bring double blessings.

I pray the Lord gives you faith to shield your life with the Holy Spirit and blood of Jesus so that you may see double blessings one day. Let the devil's plans be destroyed. May God strengthen you to stand and not move. Keep your faith in the Lord!

LET US PRAY

We are grateful to you, Lord, for giving us a measure of faith with provision to increase by hearing your word. Lord, we need faith in the word of God to increase faith every day by hearing and obeying the scripture. Helping us to keep faith in the Lord is a blessing. We know that the crown of righteousness will be given to them. It is an actual crown that will not be taken away. We know our faith will be tried; please grant faith with the gift of strength and faithfulness. Do not let our faith fail. Our faith in the Lord will not bring shame. God rewards those who diligently seek after Him. By faith, we achieve what was promised to us. It is by faith we receive healing and deliverance. We thank you for the Armor of God given us with the sword of your word. It is faith that takes us higher. Lord, give faith to your people, the strength to pass all our trials by keeping faith in you in Jesus's name! Amen! God bless you!

JANUARY 10

SPIRITUAL POLLUTION!

We are living in toxic spiritual pollution. Why? The real world we need to pay attention to is the Spiritual World, but we pay no attention.

The Lord instructed Moses on how to live to serve a holy God. God gave divine laws, commandments, and instructions to walk with divine guidance. He mapped out all to walk in a clean, heavenly, pollution-free environment. How nice!

The divine direction, called Torah, was for the chosen descendants of Abraham. After Jesus sheds His blood, we all can partake of this divine calling. We need to pay attention to what thus saith the Lord! We must look for the true prophets and teachers of the Lord to hear from Him.

It is my and your responsibility to look for the true prophet appointed by the Lord, not the churches, organizations, and denominations. Our God has the government to keep us safe all the way. But do we care to keep our path in His divine direction, or are we like Mother Eve? We deviate from godly instruction influenced by the lust of eyes, flesh, and pride of life. The people who were interested in it polluted the world.

Matthew 24:37 But as the days of Noah were, so shall the coming of the Son of man be. 38 For as in the days that were before the flood they were eating and drinking, marrying and giving in marriage, until the day that Noe entered into the ark, 39 And knew not until the flood came, and took them all away; so shall also the coming of the Son of man be.

Our ungodly acts can easily contaminate our world. People become the contaminated generation to bear when they don't follow the righteous ways of the Lord. Our generation has reached that contamination today.

2 Peter 2:5 And spared not the old world, but saved Noah the eighth person, a preacher of righteousness, bringing in the flood upon the world of the ungodly;

God created the earth for His creation to flourish. There would be no spiritual pollution on earth if His creation took heed to God's divine ways, commandments, and laws. The righteous God can still save us since His idea of creating the earth is to multiply.

Hebrews 11:7 By faith Noah, being warned of God of things not seen as yet, moved with fear, prepared an ark to save his house; by the which he condemned the world, and became heir of the righteousness which is by faith.

Spiritual pollution is devastating, making it harder to find the right way. Why is that? Since our spiritual world became religious. The building has cross without God. God has the same direction, agenda, and guidance for us. A religious denomination and organization have kicked out the true prophet, and teachers like King Ahab did.

2 Chronicle 11:13 And the priests and the Levites that were in all Israel resorted to him out of all their coasts. 14 For the Levites left their suburbs and their possession, and came to Judah and Jerusalem: for Jeroboam, and his sons had cast them off from executing the priest's office unto the LORD:

The northern kingdom of Israel became idol worshipers as soon as this evil king came. These corrupt misguiding leaders polluted the country.

The country went into captivity, finally no more in the year 722. END OF THE NORTHERN KINGDOM - Israel. They were taken to Assyrian by Shalmaneser.

Why does history repeat? It is the nature of humans to walk away and be led by the flesh. It is carelessness on our part, like Esau, King Solomon, King Saul, Eve, and Adam. We do not see our life as happy and fruitful by keeping God's ways. We do not see the devil who is real, ready for every opportunity you give to destroy you. It is we; our flesh and our pride misguide us.

We cause self-harm and trouble. Our major problem is ignoring the instruction given by the Lord. Please pay attention to the instructions which are good for you.

LET US PRAY

Heavenly Father, we come to your altar asking for the ear to hear and eyes to see. We know that if we do right, all things will be fine. If we do wrong, then it is our wrong choice. We need the Spirit of perception and discernment to do right. Put hunger and thirst for Word and love for you. Lord, not paying attention, we have brought judgment, curses, and chaos. Today we turn to you; forgive us. Wash in the blood and make us new in Jesus's name. Amen! God bless you!

JANUARY 11

REALITY TEST!

How to check reality? God has mighty wisdom. His wisdom allows us to discern between right and wrong, lies and truth. Not everything that glitters is gold.

Having faith in various deities does not mean they are all equivalent to God. Divine wisdom from God is necessary to uncover the truth.

King Solomon asked God to give him the wisdom t's people. What he asked for was granted by God. At one point, he encountered a difficult case. Two harlots living in the same house, and both delivered babies. The baby was accidentally smothered by the mother while they were sleeping. She was conceited and changed her dead baby for life. How can this case be proven in those days? The real mother is discovered through a practical test set by a wise king. The King asks for a sword to cut the baby. Observe the responses from genuine and false mothers.

1 King 3:26 Then spake the woman whose the living child was unto the King, for her bowels yearned upon her son, and she said, O my Lord, give her the living child, and in no wise slay it. But the other said, Let it be neither mine nor thine, but divide it. 27 Then the King answered and said, Give her the living child, and in no wise slay it: she is the mother thereof.

Biological parents will feel pain when you are in pain. True parents will ensure your protection from any harm. They will ensure that your needs are met and that you have a place to stay. Deception is part of the Devil's plan. Seek wisdom from God and discover the true one. It is necessary to test and distinguish between the true God and the false. Not all spirits should be trusted, as there is a single God responsible for creating humanity. Not everyone who asserts themselves as a god or goddess truly is one. Being God is not determined by simply claiming to be God.

The real God will shower you with blessings, not curses.

In 1998, it was estimated by UNICEF that there were 11 million children who lived on the streets of India. We, as Christians, are similar to our true Father, Jesus. We understand their feelings completely. The conversion of the heart is done by God, not by man. Once they discover their true Father God, who provides for them. God wouldn't want His creation to suffer from hunger, poverty, pain, or destruction. The biological mother wouldn't want any harm to come to her son. Those who serve Jesus, the true God, stand out, whether they are individuals, nations, or countries. The country's idol worship, poverty, bread begging, sickness, impoverishment, and confusion about languages, customs, and caste systems are prevalent. As I learned of

11 million children in India who are on the streets, I knew why poverty is unthinkable in a country that worships idols.

Bible speaks to us: Matthew 25:34 Then shall the King say unto them on his right hand, Come, ye blessed of my Father, inherit the kingdom prepared for you from the foundation of the world: 35 For I was an hungred, and ye gave me meat: I was thirsty, and ye gave me drink: I was a stranger, and ye took me in: 36 Naked, and ye clothed me: I was sick, and ye visited me: I was in prison, and ye came unto me. 37 Then shall the righteous answer him, saying, Lord, when saw we thee an hungered, and fed thee? Or thirsty, and gave thee drink? 38 When saw we thee a stranger, and took thee in? or naked, and clothed thee? 39 Or when saw we thee sick, or in prison, and came unto thee? 40 And the King shall answer and say unto them, Verily I say unto you, In as much as ye have done it unto one of the least of these my brethren, ye have done it unto me.

Reflect on the example of a real shepherd, and our role as the sheep in his pastures. His thoughts and actions on our behalf.

John 10:11 I am the good shepherd: the good shepherd giveth his life for the sheep. 12 But he that is a hireling, and not the shepherd, whose own the sheep are not, seeth the wolf coming, and leaveth the sheep, and fleeth: and the wolf catcheth them, and scattereth the sheep. 13 The hireling fleeth because he is a hireling and careth not for the sheep. 14 I am the good shepherd, and know my sheep, and am known of mine. 15 As the Father knoweth me, even so, know I the Father: I lay down my life for the sheep.

Finding the true creator, your Father God, is your responsibility. He will provide care for you as you become part of His pasture as a Sheep.

God has given His word; let us see what He says in

Exodus 20:4 Thou shalt not make unto thee any graven image or any likeness of anything that is in heaven above, or that is in the earth beneath, or that is in the water under the earth. 5 Thou shalt not bow down thyself to them, nor serve them: for I the Lord thy God am a jealous God, visiting the iniquity of the fathers upon the children unto the third and fourth generation of them that hate me; 6 And shewing mercy unto thousands of them that love me, and keep my commandments.

Finding and serving a real God is a blessing; His name is Jesus. Jesus is our creator. Jesus means Jehovah's Savior. The term savior originated from the Greek word Sozo, which encompasses the meanings of healer, deliverer, and savior. He will rescue you from the deception of false teachers, prophets, and fake deities who cannot bring healing, deliverance, salvation, or change to your circumstances.

We should witness how many individuals bear witness to the existence of the one true God, Jesus. I was in a wheelchair; he made me walk. He delivered me from cancer, and healed my tonsils. Throughout my life, I've never taken any form of medicine. Jesus claimed that he has paid for your sicknesses by enduring 39 lashes and shedding life-giving blood. Jesus sacrificed his life for us, and that life flows through our veins. I've also authored the book "I Did It His Way" by Elizabeth Das. The book states the facts of following the instruction of God; we receive all of what the Lord has promised.

Christians are just like Jesus, their Father. We have a love for humanity. In contrast to certain religions, we don't believe in using physical harm or violence as a means of conversion. Instead: Our goal is to feed the hungry without exploiting their strength and life to get rich. Love is what we genuinely cherish, as our God is characterized by love. Our mission is to aid, not torment. The true Father God does not promote violence or harm towards others. Pray that your eyes are opened by the Lord. Could you imagine doing that to your kids? Will you? Real God would not harm. Don't wait any longer, start seeking truth, find Jesus, and experience Him. We don't show reverence to everything crafted by humans. Seeing, hearing, walking, and talking are not possible for them. I worship the one who has created my ear, eyes, legs, hand, spirit, and body. Seek to know God's true identity today. Would you like to uncover the identity of the true God, creator, and Father? Watch what transpires!

LET US PRAY

Lord Jesus, your creations are in a state of darkness, poverty, bondage, hunger, and brokenness. Lord, let them find you. Draw them nigh to you. They have the opportunity to encounter the serenity, affection, and delight of the Lord. Oh Lord, let them meet their maker and see what difference Jesus makes in their life, in Jesus's name! God bless you! Amen!

JANUARY 12

DREAM!

God communicates to us through His Spirit, His Word (the Bible), and the Prophets' mouths. Through dreams, God communicates with us as well.

Joel 2:28 says, And it shall come to pass afterward, that I will pour out my spirit upon all flesh; and your sons and your daughters shall prophesy, your old men shall dream dreams, your young men shall see visions:

Genesis 15:1 After these things, the word of the LORD came unto Abram in a vision, saying, Fear not, Abram: I am thy shield, and thy exceeding great reward.

Genesis 46:2 And God spake unto Israel in the visions of the night, and said, Jacob, Jacob. And he said, Here am I.

Praise God! Our God has a unique approach to revealing His plan. God does not discriminate when it comes to dreams, regardless of age or faith. Even though they were not Israeli kings, Pharaoh and Nebuchadnezzar both had a dream. Dreams can be pursued by any nation, people, or age.

During one night, I had a dream where two snakes came out of a fence and tried to bite me and two of my family members. A car accident occurred the following night, involving our vehicle and two drunk drivers. I've recently come to America and only have a vague understanding of my dreams. Following the car accident, they made an effort to pursue us, which was an alarming situation. Thankfully, in the dream I had, they attempted but failed.

When a dream or vision comes to you, be attentive. If you're struggling to comprehend, turn to prayer and ask God for clarity. Share your dreams with people who can interpret them. Through dreams, God is communicating and either warning or informing you.

There was a dream that the king of Egypt, Pharaoh, had.

Genesis 41:2 And, behold, there came up out of the river seven well-favored kine and fatfleshed; and they fed in a meadow.3 And, behold, seven other kine came up after them out of the river, ill favored and leanfleshed; and stood by the other kine upon the brink of the river.4 And the ill-favored and leanfleshed kine did eat up the seven well-favored and fat kine. So Pharaoh awoke.5 And he slept and dreamed the second time: and, behold, seven ears of corn came up upon one stalk, rank and good.6 And, behold, seven thin ears blasted with the east wind sprung up after them.7 And the seven thin ears devoured the seven rank and full ears. And Pharaoh awoke, and, behold, it was a dream.

JANUARY 12

What's the reason behind having the same dream twice?

Genesis 41:32 And for that the dream was doubled unto Pharaoh twice; it is because the thing is established by God and God will shortly bring it to pass.

If God intends something, he will use a dream as a double means of communication. Acting wisely is crucial considering the future revealed in the dream.

The Bible says: Proverb 24:3 Through wisdom is a house built, and by understanding it is established:

Let's seek God's guidance for not only a dream but also the wisdom to act on future revelations. When someone has a horrifying dream and reaches out to me for prayer, I rebuke the enemy's scheme. I use the blood of Jesus to shield myself and call upon angels for protection. In the name of Jesus, we possess the power and authority to bind, blind, confuse, and dismantle their plan. Remember, the real world is the spirit world. God's Spirit will make known the plans of the evil spirit world.

Some nights ago, I had a dream where the walkway was surrounded by water under a dark night sky. There were several chameleons in stunning colors that I saw on one side. On the other side, a giant Scorpion fighting with people. That day, I came across a video that showed the numerous challenges Christian schools in India are facing. They mentioned Jai Esuram in the video. In the Indian language, Jesus is known as Esu, not Esuram. I realized that Satan was planning to wage war against God's chosen ones. The idol worshipers of India were color-changing chameleons in my dream. Innocent Christians who teach the truth are targeted by scorpions to inflict harm.

It is difficult to comprehend every dream. Satan's deceptive plan is revealed to us by God, so that we may pray against it. Our mission is to enlighten individuals about the fact that Jesus is the only genuine deity. If they don't want to accept the truth, they are free to exit Christian Schools. Only God is aware of everything. The power of God's hand is immense. God's warning has been revealed, calling for prayer and fasting by wise individuals to counteract Satan's deceptive plan. The success of Satan's plan should be prevented in the Christian life.

The mind will be greatly influenced by a dream sent by God. Make sure to give special attention to the Dream received from God.

It provides an escape from Satan's destructive scheme. We are grateful, Lord, that you have chosen to communicate with us through a dream.

LET US PRAY

Dear Lord, make us alert, wise, and always on guard. Transform us into fearless warriors capable of battling demons disguised as chameleons, scorpions, lizards, and snakes. We appreciate the authority you've given us to resist any type of infestation, even if it challenges the truth. Let God give us victory. The mighty angels sent by God protect His people from harm and danger. May the eyes of those individuals be opened by the Lord Jesus. Cause them to have a change of heart. Please put love for Jesus in their hearts. Our prayers extend beyond Christians in India to all those suffering around the world. Satan employs various strategies to undermine Christianity. Lord Jesus, make us ready to encounter you. The Lord is on the way to receive His people. Can anyone beat Jesus? No, He is mighty in battle. Get ready in Jesus's name. Amen! God bless you!

JANUARY 13

SIMPLE WAYS OF GOD!

By following God's guidance, we can easily solve and resolve our problems. Do not seek help from any other sources. We must obey, as His prophets have affirmed. Do not question or analyze the instructions given by God. We can't comprehend it. It is beyond the understanding of our carnal mind. Going against His ways results in chaos permeating our lives. The enemy that opposes us is our carnal mind.

Roman 8:7 Because the carnal mind is the enemy against God: for it is not subject to the law of God, neither indeed can be.

Submit yourself to God and obey His commands.

Naaman, who was a leper, served as a captain in the Syrian army. He was told that there was a prophet in Israel who could heal him of his leprosy. Unfamiliar with Jehovah God, he disregarded the prophet's guidance. Despite being a brave and experienced captain, he struggled to follow God's command.

When he was instructed to seek out Elisha the Prophet, *2 King 5:10 And Elisha sent a messenger unto him, saying, Go and wash in Jordan seven times, and thy flesh shall come again to thee, and thou shalt be clean.*

The Prophet gave a simple directive, but his mindset was twisted. Give him your ear and listen to what he's saying.

11 But Naaman was wroth, and went away, and said, Behold, I thought, He will surely come out to me, and stand, and call on the name of the LORD his God, and strike his hand over the place, and recover the leper.

Can you actually believe this? He has already determined the way in which it could have been executed. Really? He refused to follow the Prophet's instructions. Not just that, he was upset and decided to go back. God's voice must be obeyed, no questions asked.

Naaman had a lesson to learn; he was a captain doesn't mean he can direct God.

Isaiah 55:8 For my thoughts are not your thoughts, neither are your ways my ways, saith the Lord. 9 For as the heavens are higher than the earth, so are my ways higher than your ways, and my thoughts than your thoughts.

We should be grateful for the wise individuals who are not afraid to give us advice when we are lost.

JANUARY 13

2 King 5:13 And his servants came near, and spake unto him, and said, My father, if the Prophet had bid thee do some great thing, wouldest thou not have done it? How much rather then, when he saith to thee, Wash and be clean? 14 Then went he down, and dipped himself seven times in Jordan, according to the saying of the man of God: his flesh came again like unto the flesh of a little child, and he was clean.

Follow God's instruction without questioning or arguing.

I endured a relentless attack from a malevolent spirit and fought for several days. I experienced torment from a demon. I spoke with a prophet and his prophecy turned out to be accurate. I described the torment I endured from this devil. Your area has been infiltrated by a wandering spirit he sent, which is causing you torment. His request was for me to anoint a new handkerchief or material with Holy oil. Pray over it, cut it into 2"x2" pieces, bury it in four corners of your house, hang it on entrances/exits, and place it on bedroom windows. Believing in the Prophet has been a lifelong conviction of mine. The Prophet is essential for life to prosper. It is his responsibility to provide information from a higher authority. Certain positions have been called and appointed by God to carry out His work on earth.

All attacks were eradicated as I followed the guidance of the Prophet. The evil spirit lost its power when the anointed cloth made contact with it. When we say something is 'destroyed', it means it cannot be restored. You seem to have understood it perfectly. If you're experiencing the same patterns, anoint your home. Place pieces of prayer cloth on the ground, on doors, and on windows. Witness the immense power of destruction through anointing.

Ephesians 4:11 And he gave some, apostles; and some, prophets; and some, evangelists; and some, pastors and teachers;12 For the perfecting of the saints, for the work of the ministry, for the edifying of the body of Christ:

If I desire success, I must rely on the Prophet ordained by God.

2 Chronicles 20:20b Jehoshaphat stood and said, hear me, O Judah, and ye inhabitants of Jerusalem; Believe in the LORD your God, so shall ye be established; believe his prophets, so shall ye prosper.

Defeat enemy attacks by obeying without hesitation. I engage in the practice of anointing schools and laying prayer clothes on the ground. Almost every month, I make sure to place recently anointed prayer cloths in my yard. I anoint both the exterior and interior of my house with oil. We are constantly engaged in spiritual warfare. Just engaging in reading and meditation alone won't yield results. We require your immediate action. Perform the task to observe the outcomes. Your idea and God's will clash. Discover an unknown adversary by following God's guidance, who possesses all knowledge. Good news, you don't see Satan and his cohort; just do what I did. You and your family will experience freedom, deliverance, and healing. Discover the promises in God's word and experience the results by obeying them. The Bible is meant to be both read and applied in life. Without work, faith is lifeless.

Obeying the word leads to a life-changing transformation. Inner transformation results in outer transformation. Witnessing healing, miracles, deliverance, and supernatural phenomena is possible through a simple act of obedience. Spend your time improving compliance instead of going to church. Your situation can only be changed by the Lord. In the Bible, there's a solution for every trial and trouble you experience. Seek out the Prophet who was sent by the Lord. Be cautious because the Bible warns about false prophets. God Bless you!

LET US PRAY

Lord, please give us an obedient heart. Your ways will give great deliverance, healing, victory, and much more. Lord Jesus, your learning comes from obedience.

Help us obey, so we know as well. We can, too, if we listen and do as it says. Our God's only aim is to help us, not cause harm. So let our hearts trust and believe in your instruction. By obeying your instructions in the name of Jesus, we offer you glory, honor, and praise. Amen! God Bless you!

JANUARY 14

WAGES OF SINS ARE DEATH!

The Bible, the Word of God, has been tested seven times and stands forever. If you follow the word, you'll experience abundant, overflowing joy.

A life filled with peace and triumph, both in this world and beyond.

The Bible in Romans 6:23 says the wages of sin is death.

But if you abide by the laws of Jesus, then you will live forever in heavenly place. Eve's intentional sin resulted in eternal death for the family and the destruction of humankind. Cain killed Abel. Who was responsible for 's death? His mother, Eve.

Jezebel's sin resulted in death for her and her family. Your children will be blessed if you choose to live for God.

Revelation 2:20 Notwithstanding, I have a few things against thee because thou sufferest that woman Jezebel, which calleth herself a prophetess, to teach and to seduce my servants to commit fornication, and to eat things sacrificed unto idols. 21 And I gave her space to repent of her fornication, and she repented not. 23 And I will kill her children with death, and all the churches shall know that I am he which searcheth the reins and hearts: and I will give unto every one of you according to your works.

God has no tolerance for sin. He is without sin. His blood was given to redeem you from eternal death in a never-ending fire.

God's commandments take precedence over the customs and rituals of the country. The key is to accept and follow God's words without question. Religious churches, people, and organizations conveniently eliminate God's laws and commandments for their own convenience. Religions can be a gateway to embracing false beliefs. Religion causes followers to be blind and deaf to other perspectives. Religion is a modern-day gathering of serpents, distorting the truth.

When you witness Jezebel's spirit in a position of power, stay alert and expect judgment. The offspring of religious, rebellious women are subject to God's wrath. In the house, a wife overrides the husband. When Jezebel overrides God's laws and commandments in church or country, chaos is inevitable. Be careful of spirit! Through her treachery as a murderer, she will bring harm to the kingdom, church, or home. Don't forget, the church is not the physical structure.

Athaliah, Jezebel's daughter, became the queen of Judah through marriage. The royal bloodline was ended by Athaliah's actions. Friends don't sin. Heartache, chaos, and eternal death in hell are the consequences of the sins of mother or father.

Disturbing news reaches us: children are being abducted, murdered, sexually assaulted, and mistreated. Why? The mother is a foolish and negligent sinner. Her choice to live an immoral, unrighteous, and ungodly lifestyle is causing confusion within the family. The father shares the same lack of responsibility.

The news has taken a turn for the worse. Imprisonment alone cannot contain the consequences of sin; eternal punishment in the lake of fire awaits.

Do you think no one saw you doing evil? Watch the news about how a wicked woman allures a man, and the man pays the wages behind the bar and still doesn't repent, then ends up in hell. We need a godly law in operation. Do not feel sorry for this kind of person; pray for them. Do not play with fire. You sin in the middle of the night in darkness and think no one knows,

The Bible says, Psalms 139:12 Yea, the darkness hideth not from thee; but the night shineth as the day: the darkness and the light are both alike to thee.

Furthermore, you'll have to endure all sicknesses and diseases, resulting in a miserable life.

Seek repentance, seek forgiveness, and avoid self-righteousness.

Psalms 103:3 He forgives all your sin; He heals all your diseases.

As soon as your sins are forgiven, your disease is gone. It is considered a sin for a woman to have a relationship with a married man. There is no difference in sinfulness between the two. Sin involves cheating, adultery, and various other transgressions. Don't hold others responsible if your children or you end up dead. On the day of judgment, this sin will bring death upon your soul. Modify your conduct by acknowledging your humility before God. It pains me when a nation permits the freedom to commit adultery. Do you consider yourself superior to the law of God? God created His laws to be followed, not questioned. The intention behind his laws is to bring you blessings. It stands above any kind of authority. The Word of God is not taken into account by rebellions. The sin of pride results in a fall, reducing it to dust once again. Embracing pride results in emptiness, depression, and downfall.

Seek humility through prayer to God.

Chronicle 10:13 So Saul died for his transgression which he committed against the LORD, even against the word of the LORD, which he kept not, and also for asking counsel of one that had a familiar spirit, to inquire of it;

A few people take pride in attending church. Does devotion make them perfect? No, be humble; seek God in your sickness. God will show you which sin causes your illness. Go in water and wash away all your sins in Jesus's name. The blood of the lamb is hidden under the name of Jesus, which will wash away sins. Don't question; just submit.

Chronicles 16:7 And at that time Hanani the seer came to Asa king of Judah, and said unto him, Because thou hast relied on the king of Syria, and not relied on the LORD thy God, therefore is the host of the king of

Syria escaped out of thine hand. 12 And Asa in the thirty and ninth year of his reign was diseased in his feet until his disease was exceeding great: yet in his disease, he sought not to the LORD, but to the physicians.

Sin is deceiving and will blind you. It is a pleasure for a moment, don't be overconfident.

Learn of a humble and great man of God, and see how they feel about themselves in the presence of God.

Job 42:5 I have heard of thee by the hearing of the ear: but now my eye seeth thee. 6 Wherefore I abhor myself and repent in dust and ashes.

James 4:10 Humble yourselves before the Lord, and He will exalt you.

1 Peter 5:6 Humble yourselves therefore under the mighty hand of God, that he may exalt you in due time:

Romans 3:23 For all have sinned, and come short of the glory of God;

You and I are sinners. Is there a big or small sin? All sin will be punished if you don't repent and wash in the blood.

Roman 6:23 For the wages of sin is death, but the gift of God is eternal life through Jesus Christ our Lord.

Be humble and Say, Lord, wash me in your blood. I am made of flesh, and there is nothing good in my flesh.

Roman 7:18 For I know that in me (that is, in my flesh) dwelleth no good thing: for to will is present with me; but how to perform that which is good I find not.

So please pray that the blood of the lamb takes away our sins. The Bible says to go in the water in Jesus's name to wash away your sins. We have a gift of eternal life in His name.

Religion makes us blind and deaf, but the Lord gives truth and sets us free from the lie and deception of sin.

LET US PRAY

The Lord grants us a repentant spirit to acknowledge our sins. May we be granted wisdom and understanding by the Lord's word to perceive the effects of sin. May the Lord touch you with healing and deliverance. May your path always be filled with divine direction, protection, and guidance. May his spirit of healing and miracles bring cure to all your diseases! In the name of Jesus, may the Lord bless us and free us from the power of sin and sickness. In Jesus' name, Amen God Bless you!

JANUARY 15

YOU ARE UNLIMITED!

There is no boundary for your blessings; the only limit is your mind. Through faith in God, all things are possible, and you can receive what you believe. Put the Word of God in your mind and heart. Express your thoughts verbally, demonstrating trust and belief in the circumstances.

Back in 2015, God used an angel to open an enormous door, declaring it impossible for anyone to close it. Also, I cannot close it. So, as God spoke by the mouth of the prophet, I went to India to preach and teach the Gospel. My travels took me to India and Dubai for three months.

Part of my visit included visiting churches in South Gujarat. During my visit to Gujarat, I went to a worship service that was filled with people and had no available seating. Sunday afternoon, I visited the Pastor's house. It's a house. I was honored to have the opportunity to meet his family. I noticed that the pastor was trapped and overwhelmed by fear, doubt, and worry while we were praying. Don't forget, the shepherd is the target of Satan's arrow.

A large number of people abandoned false gods and goddesses in favor of the One True God. Because of their faith, humility, and devotion to the truth, Jesus is visiting the poor and performing incredible miracles. Their need for help was desperate. Individuals are trapped by the shackles of darkness. As they entered God's presence, Jesus was granting them freedom. Why wouldn't anyone want to have faith in this wonderful God? Upon seeing the immense gathering, I urged the Pastor to create a bigger space for worship, teaching, and training. He stated that we were financially insufficient. Was money mentioned by me? For the past 23 years, I haven't worked, and God has faithfully provided for me as He promised. I was called by God to work in His field and He promised to provide for me. God used my voice during the prayer for the Pastor to convey the message of building a more significant location and promised to provide.

The Pastor showed obedience to the prophecy. Upon hearing God's message from me, he began constructing a project. In my perception, the devil employed doubt, fear, and worry to obstruct his mind. As I laid my hand, the anointing of Jesus shattered the presence of the evil spirit. There was no room for doubt or fear in his mind. At a later time, the Pastor contacted us and confirmed that we had completed the construction of the place for worship, teaching, and prayer. Within the next two months, the praying and worship center will be both debt-free and fully prepared. According to the Pastor, the act of laying hands on me removed my worries and fears. According to him, we created it through prayer and praise, and it is completely debt-free.

Your mind is hindering your progress. God stated that there are no limits to what can be achieved.

Philippians 4:13 I can do all things through Christ which strengtheneth me.

JANUARY 15

You can do anything through Jesus.

John 14:12 Verily, verily, I say unto you, He that believeth on me, the works that I do shall he do also; and greater works than these shall he do; because I go unto my Father. 13 And whatsoever ye shall ask in my name, that will I do, that the Father may be glorified in the Son. 14 If ye shall ask anything in my name, I will do it.

Through belief, you can achieve a complete transformation in Christ. He is waiting for your belief and declaration. If you have no doubt, speaking will bring you what you desire. Pay no attention to the situation or the environment. Believe and experience the power of God firsthand. The mountain must be moved, sickness must be expelled, and poverty must be eradicated. No problem is great; no valley is deep for our God. Nothing, not even the ocean, can hinder your mind. Let the living words of God and the powerful testimonies fill your mind. Do not worry; how will they climb mountains? How do they manage to move through both the ocean and rivers? How did they become whole and establish their kingdom? Their mind was free from distractions and filled with Christ. Prioritize the well-being of your mind, my friends. Put the helmet of salvation on your head.

What does salvation mean? The biblical meaning is to save, assist in trouble, rescue, liberate, and release.

Today, liberate your mind by downloading information that is verifiable. If you allow unwanted things in your mind, like watching, reading, and hearing nasty things that you should not, it will work against you. By reading worldly material or contemplating negative thoughts, you provide Satan with an opportunity to harm you. When going through trials, especially when you are sick or facing challenges, Satan will bring it back to your memory. The devil brings negativity to your memories and tries to undermine your faith. The likeness of Christ is seen in a mind that is filled with the Word of God. Your brain is of utmost importance. Protect yourself by wearing a helmet.

Ephesians 6:17 And take THE HELMET OF SALVATION, and the sword of the spirit, which is the word of God.

Isaiah 59:17 He put on righteousness like a breastplate And a helmet of salvation on His head; And He put on garments of vengeance for clothing And wrapped Himself with zeal as a mantle.

1 Thessalonians 5:8 But let us, who are of the day, be sober, putting on the breastplate of faith and love; and for an helmet, the hope of salvation.

The presence of positive thoughts is connected to the hope for salvation.

Roman 5:5 And hope maketh not ashamed; because the love of God is shed abroad in our hearts by the Holy Ghost which is given unto us.

Receive the Holy Ghost. He is the teacher, the source of comfort, the guide, the provider of power, and the divine presence within you.

Program your mind computer with God's Word.'s Word. Get ready to unlock the unlimited potential of your mind. Your life will be enriched and overflowing with blessings. You will receive abundant blessings from God.

LET US PRAY

Lord, please protect our minds with the proper armor. Never let us be without the special armor of God.

Give us true teachers to know how to battle against unseen Satan, a prince of the air. Our minds become a battleground as Satan attacks with negative thoughts, worry, and confusion. May Jesus bless and protect our minds, keeping them in perfect soundness. Lord Jesus, bless us with the Helmet of salvation to shield our minds. In Jesus' name, Amen God Bless you!

JANUARY 16

GOD'S WAY OF COMMUNICATION!

The lifeline of every relationship is built on communication. By communicating with God, we can expect Him to do the same. There are several methods through which God speaks to us.

In the morning, I woke up to find myself in a dream. My dream took me to a nation with a predominantly Muslim population. The door to the room was not open. Both my mom and I slept in different beds, but we were in the same room. Out of nowhere, a sudden change occurred. During my dream, I had the impression that I had reached the end and a Muslim man was sleeping next to me. A wave of fear washed over me. However, in my dream, I found myself preaching about Jesus to the man sleeping beside me. I experienced a sense of safety and security as well.

One part of the dream ended, and a new chapter began. I thought two men had already come yesterday, so I assumed they wouldn't return today to bother me. Right before nightfall, I was about to shut the door, but I ended up being slightly delayed. While attempting to close it, I witnessed a group of youngsters approach and forcefully push the door, causing it to open. I witnessed myself delivering a sermon to a group of youth. It was clear to me that they were eager to know more about Jesus.

During this time, Christians were being attacked by radical Muslims everywhere. I had a moment of thinking it was a dream as I prayed against violence towards Christians. Destruction and bombing of churches, cities, and homes occurred during this period by radical Muslims. I have a habit of touching Muslim nations on the map and offering my prayers for them, which I still do. My prayers are for Lord Jesus to grant Muslim countries visions and dreams and to save them. Pray for God to meet them in the same way He met Paul on the road to Damascus. All roads transform into the road of Damascus, as I claimed. Fear overwhelmed me when I saw Muslims in my dream. I started rebuking the devil. I pleaded with God to spare me from such terrifying nightmares. Being in a Muslim nation wasn't my preference, but I'm okay with offering prayers for them.

Sunday morning was when the dream took place. At church, the pastor singled me out, Sister Elizabeth, and prophesied that I would be taken by God to Muslim nations where I would initiate a great revival. He stated that you would be traveling to Indonesia.

Despite my shock and initial belief that it was a bad dream, it was not. It was God talking to me; I praise God that I have the true prophet in my life; the prophet tells the future.

ELIZABETH DAS

Through years of prayer, I have gained knowledge about Indonesia. My prayers are informed by knowledge. My area of study is Indonesia, a country with Sharia law, aiming to introduce Blasphemy Law. There are separate laws in different Muslim nations to address blasphemy.

In the dream, I was glad that they didn't come to harm me, but their interest was in knowing about Jesus. Muslim men slept next to my mom and me in the same bed in the first dream. There was no touching or harming involved whatsoever. I was given a sign from God, assuring me that I have everything under control.

The media presents a narrative in which Indonesian Muslims are frequently reported to be involved in the rape and physical assault of pastors in churches. I received a divine burden from God to pray for those people during that specific period. This has been a significant burden that I've been praying for. This beautiful creation is utilized by the Lord. Those who find the truth should also find Jesus and recognize that God's belief is in giving life, not taking it away. Muslims, once they find the truth, can become extraordinary Christians.

Communication from God often comes through dreams.

You don't have to seek answers or information from fake psychics or spirit mediums. Approach either God or His appointed prophet.

Observe how God communicates with His people via prophets.

2 Chronicle 20:20b Hear me, O Judah, and ye inhabitants of Jerusalem; Believe in the LORD your God, so shall ye be established; believe his prophets, so shall ye prosper.

2 Chronicles 7:14 If my people, which are called by my name, shall humble themselves, and pray, and seek my face, and turn from their wicked ways; then will I hear from heaven, and will forgive their sin, and will heal their land.

I am happy that I belong to a church where prayer is important and where there is a genuine prophet. It's not difficult to build the building, but building a praying church is a different story. Those who have repented, been baptized in Jesus's name, and received the Spirit are considered the dwelling place of God in the New Testament. The building is not the Church, but you are.

When saints pray and focus on Jesus' mission, they are connecting with God. The building must be called the house of prayer, not a church. The presence of God results in healing, deliverance, and freedom from addiction, bringing you peace and joy. Keep in mind, you represent the Church, not the physical edifice. The temple of the Lord resides within your body.

Isaiah 56:7 Even them will I bring to my holy mountain and make them joyful in my house of prayer: their burnt offerings and their sacrifices shall be accepted upon mine altar; for mine, house shall be called a house of prayer for all people.

If you do not see the prayer in the building, it is the robber 's house. Let the Lord disrupt the tables of money-changers and sellers. Instead of finding yourself in the Church, you are actually in the house of Robbers.

Mark 11:17 And he taught, saying unto them, Is it not written, My house shall be called of all nations the house of prayer? but ye have made it a den of thieves.

Jeremiah 7:11 Is this house, which is called by my name, become a den of robbers in your eyes? Behold, even I have seen it, saith the Lord.

Matthew 21:13 And said unto them, It is written, My house shall be called the house of prayer, but ye have made it a den of thieves.

Dreams, prayer, prophets, and the Word of God serve as channels for God's communication with us. Establish a direct connection with God. Remain cautious and don't be deceived by religion, false prophets, and false teachers. God desires to communicate with us but on His terms, not ours. Surrender yourself to Him and devote your life. When you submit to Him, He will appoint you as a laborer in His vineyard. Cultivate the faith of a child, pursue Him relentlessly, abide by God's Word, not human-made beliefs.

Seeking a connection with God through His word and being guided by His Spirit. Allow the Holy Spirit to lead and teach you. Watch what unfolds. If someone is there to pray to, then there is a higher power to respond.

LET US PRAY

Oh, Lord God of Abraham, Isaac, and Israel, speak to us when we pray. Bless us with many great blessings. Isaac prayed to God, the God who answered his prayer for a wife and blessed him with twins. O God of Israel, you transformed Jacob from a deceiver to someone completely different by changing his name. I pray to God to change each and every one who is listening. Lord, communicate with us through dreams, prophets, and your Word, and bless us individually. God's promises provide us with a steadfast foundation to stand upon. Lord, grant them the fulfillment of their dream. May the Lord expedite all promises concerning us in Jesus 'name. Amen! God Bless you!

JANUARY 17

YOUR MIND!

Who do you see as your enemy, your mind, or the devil? When your mind is focused on carnal matters, it becomes an enemy to your well-being. Today's lesson focuses on the mind as our adversary and the power of God's Word to transform our lives.

God's Word is found in the Bible. To lead a prosperous life, we have been provided an instruction book by God for His creation. To have a friendship with God, we need to store the Word of God in our minds and hearts. I don't want you to just read, but to truly live by the manual of life's Bible. If you remember this book, you will conquer tests and trials.

Years back, my family came across a Korean brother. I received a request from my brother to seek out a Korean brother who can provide a healing prayer for my condition. I injured my back while working at the post office during that period. He pointed at my leg and told me to look at it. The lengths of the legs were not equal; one was shorter than the other. Then, he examined my spine, which had been moved out of alignment in the middle. I wasn't aware of the reason behind my weak legs since I didn't have an MRI on my middle spine.

I didn't know what was causing the leg weakness and lack of communication between the upper and lower body. According to the Korean Brother, the reason for my debilitation was the displacement of my spine. Through prayer, the spine returned to its original position. His prayer was for a leg and hand to grow. Upon witnessing this miracle, I found a newfound sense of balance while walking. Nevertheless, my legs were weak. Once I recovered, I began walking and my muscles grew stronger. Brother James' ministry was elevated when I personally witnessed a miracle. I was no longer reliant on a wheelchair.

A lot of people struggle to comprehend the root of their life's problems. The source of their trouble is the devil residing in their thoughts. By speaking with the demon within, the Korean brother obtains all the necessary information. I found this to be completely new and mind-blowing.

I constantly strive to surpass the extraordinary achievements of Jesus.

John 14:12 Verily, verily, I say unto you, He that believeth on me, the works that I do shall he also do; and greater works than these shall he do; because I go unto my Father.

Jesus is the manifestation of the Word. He fulfilled everything mentioned in the Bible. He fulfilled the roles of creator, provider, healer, deliverer, and savior. I once asked my Korean brother for advice on how to reach this level. During his testimony, he stated that I identified as an atheist and had no belief in gods. Christianity

JANUARY 17

became real to me when I received the Holy Spirit one day. He claimed to have prayed to receive all the spiritual gifts from God in order to prove its authenticity to others. His goal was to go around healing and delivering individuals possessed by demons with the ultimate aim of glorifying God. The brother stated that I have been reading the Bible nonstop, from morning until night. According to him, he nearly lost his business, his house, and exceeded his credit card limit. A Korean sibling confessed to being so ravenous to God that he couldn't set the Bible aside. He said, during that time; the miracle was uncountable. The Korean brother claimed that he is guided by the Holy Spirit in his learning.

1 John 2:20 But ye have an unction from the Holy One, and ye know all things. 27 But the anointing which ye have received of him abideth in you, and ye need not that any man teaches you: but as the same anointing teacheth you of all things, and is truth, and is no lie, and even as it hath taught you, ye shall abide in him.

I remember when I moved to Dallas; I did not know many people, so I read the Bible from morning to night, and I noticed I had a different anointing. My mind was full of the Bible.

The Bible says the word will judge you.

John 12:48 He that rejecteth me, and receiveth, not my words, hath one that judgeth him: the word that I have spoken, the same shall judge him on the last day.

As you study, that book will test you. If you learn to drive, you study the book that teaches driving laws. If you drive without knowledge, you jeopardize your and others 'lives. Similarly, if you are driving your life not knowing dos and don'ts, it can lock you up.

The Bible says the carnal mind is your enemy.

Roman 8:7 Because the carnal mind is enmity against God: for it is not subject to the law of God, neither indeed can be.

A natural man is carnal.

Ephesians 2:3 Among whom also we all had our conversation in times past in the lusts of our flesh, fulfilling the desires of the flesh and the mind; and were by nature the children of wrath, even as others.

The mind is capable of thinking, acting, and reacting in sexual, lustful, lascivious, libidinous, lecherous, and licentious ways.

The human race, by nature, is full of evil. Those who are focused on worldly desires lack the teachings of the Bible. Take the time to understand your mind, as it can be troublesome if left unchecked. It's your responsibility to program your mind's computer with the Word of God.

During my time in Dallas, I had the pleasure of meeting an elderly lady who shared with me her accomplishment of finishing the Bible in a mere two months. I am aware that it takes a lot of time to read the entire Bible. She mentioned that we competed in a Bible reading contest. She mentioned that I used up every moment and managed to finish it within a span of two months. I heard about a practice where individuals would read the Bible for twenty-four hours straight, or until they reached the end.

Roman 7:25a. I thank God through Jesus Christ our Lord. So then, with the mind, I serve the law of God.

When the Word became flesh and walked on the earth, He performed miracles because He contained all the Word within Him.

The Word of God is necessary to conquer the enemy within your mind. If you dedicate every minute of your life to reading the word, your craving for worldly things will cease in a week. There isn't any space available for it. There's a lot of talk about addiction and pornography. Why would you choose to poison your mind with something deadly? It is having a devastating impact on our society.

When judgment day comes, every book of the Bible will be open to pass judgment on you. What excuse will you come up with? Keep in mind that all excuses are lie.

ADD, ADHD, Schizophrenia, bipolar, PTSD, etc., are mental problems labeled by Satan and considered poisonous to the mind. Those who commit rape, lying, murder, theft, adultery, and fornication have evil intentions within them. Don't invite negativity into your life by allowing harmful influences to enter your mind. Reading and obeying God's Word is more important than attending church. Not knowing the Bible means you have no understanding of your duties, benefits, and what is allowed or prohibited. Abiding by the word ensures a life free from trouble. The Word of God is the sole weapon against the enemy in our minds.

Be ready for a life-changing experience that will revolutionize your mind, actions, thoughts, lifestyle, communication, and vision.

John 15:7 If ye abide in me, and my words abide in you, ye shall ask what ye will, and it shall be done unto you.8 Herein is my Father glorified, that ye bear much fruit; so, shall ye be my disciples.

LET US PRAY

Lord, we bind all evil thoughts and imagination in the mighty name of Jesus and cast them in hell. The Lord put a powerful hunger and thirst for the Word of God! May the Lord give you understanding and wisdom through His Word. Lord, lead and guide you by His Word. Allow the Word of God to be your light and lantern, preventing any missteps. May the Lord make you healthy by taking His Word into a Spiritual Diet. May the Lord give spiritual health by eating His Word as food; in Jesus's name Amen! God Bless you!

JANUARY 18

A BLESSING HUNTER!

Strive for Blessings! Individuals in this world search for fulfillment. If only they understood that Jesus is the only way to satisfy desire.

Jacob and Esau, both twins, held contrasting beliefs about their priorities. Their profits and setbacks were in line with their interests. One received his birthright by the grace of God, and the other lost it by a minute, second, or maybe an hour. The way God granted blessings to the firstborn was highly regarded by Jacob. How Esau acquired the firstborn blessing was of no importance to him. Esau pursued pleasure for his body and rejected God's path.

When God calls us to serve His Kingdom, it entails living the life He has demonstrated to us. It's a calling to walk and talk in a particular manner!

The significance of being the firstborn diminishes if you disregard your responsibilities. If you receive something valuable, make sure to handle it with care. Make sure to guard and stay alert to God's calling upon you. Hold onto the blessings God has given you, don't let them slip away.

In the present day, we encounter all kinds of human attributes. It's up to us whether we take heed with sincerity or are neglectful and careless.

Esau understood that he was entitled to the "Double Portion" according to Jewish law for being the firstborn. He recognized the meaning of being holy to God and the prohibition against handling God's holy possessions. God views the firstborn as His possession. They are summoned to fulfill the Holy ceremonies and are acknowledged by both their family and God. God's Laws are absolute, and He treats all individuals impartially without showing favoritism.

Deuteronomy 21:17 But he shall acknowledge the son of the hated for the firstborn, by giving him a double portion of all that he hath: for he is the beginning of his strength; the right of the firstborn is his.

Due to his lack of appreciation, Esau was negligent in handling his birthright blessings. All Esau cared about in that moment was filling his stomach, indulging in his carnal desires. Noticing his brother's weakness in his physical condition, Jacob took advantage of the situation by selling him stew in exchange for the birthright, and Esau agreed to the arrangement. Esau placed greater importance on his fleshly desires rather than the blessings.

ELIZABETH DAS

It's time for a reality check. We are able to observe the characteristics, personalities, and values of the two brothers. It's a character with an opposite personality! If you act foolishly out of jealousy, you risk losing the blessings in your life. Fulfilling the requirements of God's Word grants access to His blessings. As children of God, we are granted entitlement to them. Jacob coveted the blessing of the firstborn and usurped it from his brother due to his higher regard for its meaning.

Genesis 25:29 And Jacob sold pottage: and Esau came from the field, and he was faint: 30 And Esau said to Jacob, Feed me, I pray thee, with that same red pottage; for I am faint: therefore was his name called Edom. 31 And Jacob said, Sell me this day thy birthright. 32 And Esau said, Behold, I am at the point to die: and what profit shall this birthright do to me? 33 And Jacob said, Swear to me this day, and he sware unto him: and he sold his birthright unto Jacob.

Reuben, Jacob's son, also acted foolishly. Here comes another individual who lacks caution and shows negligence!

1 Chronicle 5:1 Now the sons of Reuben the firstborn of Israel, (for he was the firstborn; but, forasmuch as he defiled his father's bed, his birthright was given unto the sons of Joseph the son of Israel: and the genealogy is not to be reckoned after the birthright.

If victory and the prize are what you seek, dedicate yourself to exercise and practice. Stay alert and be mindful of your lifestyle choices. Consecrate yourself and stick to God! Focus on Him, and don't move out of the Will of God! Be diligent and take heed of your calling! Don't lose your blessings!

According to the LORD, these are His words:

Exodus 4:22 And thou shalt say unto Pharaoh, Thus saith the Lord, Israel is my son, even my firstborn: 23 And I say unto thee, Let my son go, that he may serve me: and if thou refuse to let him go, behold, I will slay thy son, even thy firstborn.

God's love for Israel is expressed through my firstborn son.

To the Lord, the Firstborn is sacred and has consecrated themselves to serve God.

The firstborn son in the Old Testament holds more significance than just being the heir. That means he is set apart as God's possession. He must be given to the Lord.

Exodus 22:29 Thou shalt not delay to offer the first of thy ripe fruits, and of thy liquors: the firstborn of thy sons shalt thou give unto me. Because he is the Lord's possession, he must be redeemed.

Exodus 13:12 That thou shalt set apart unto the Lord all that openeth the matrix, and every firstling that cometh of a beast which thou hast; the males shall be the Lord's. 13 And every firstling of an ass thou shalt redeem with a lamb; and if thou wilt not redeem it, then thou shalt break his neck: and all the firstborn of man among thy children shalt thou redeem. 14 And it shall be when thy son asketh thee in time to come, saying, What is this? that thou shalt say unto him, By strength of hand the Lord brought us out from Egypt, from the house of bondage: 15 And it came to pass, when Pharaoh would hardly let us go, that the Lord slew all the firstborn in the land of Egypt, both the firstborn of man, and the firstborn of beast: therefore I sacrifice to the Lord all that openeth the matrix, being males; but all the firstborn of my children I redeem.

The firstborn child also carries responsibilities and is accountable to the father for their siblings. Reuben ripped his clothes in despair when he couldn't locate Joseph, the son of his father Jacob.

The Firstborn Received the Kingdom:

Chronicles 21:1 Now Jehoshaphat slept with his fathers, and was buried with his fathers in the city of David. And Jehoram, his son, reigned in his stead. And their father gave them great gifts of silver, and of gold, and of precious things, with fenced cities in Judah: but the kingdom gave him to Jehoram; because he was the firstborn.

God wants to give you so much; hunt for it. Avoid being satisfied with just a small amount, pursue every excellent gift.

I identify as a Christian and believe in inheriting God's promises. God has made promises to all, but there are conditions attached. Earth serves as your testing ground, where you will exhibit and substantiate your pursuits, losses, or gains, whether they bring curses or blessings. Certain individuals claim to be Christian but fail to remember that neglecting their responsibilities can result in losing their salvation, healing, and blessings. Practice both diligence and sincerity. Discover blessings by faithfully following God's commandments and laws as written in His Word. Pay close attention to keeping them with all your heart.

LET US PRAY

Dear God, help us be obedient to your Word with a sincere heart. God, help me surrender to you completely. To surrender completely to Jesus and receive the blessings and promises found in the Holy Bible. May the Lord discover your sincerity and genuine love for God, and may all blessings be unleashed upon you! In Jesus's Name, Amen! God Bless you!

JANUARY 19

ACCOUNTING IN THE KINGDOM!

Let us see how the accounting system works in the Kingdom of God. Who gives us? Of course, God!

2 Peter 1:3a According as his divine power hath given unto us all things that pertain unto life and godliness

We come naked, but God clothes us; we get up hungry, but God won't let us go to sleep starved.

Job 1:21 And said, Naked came I out of my mother's womb, and naked shall I return thither: the LORD gave, and the LORD hath taken away; blessed be the name of the LORD.

Who paid the first tithes? Abraham, and see His blessings.

Hebrews 7:2a. To whom also Abraham gave a tenth part of all.

Genesis 14:19 And he blessed him, and said, Blessed, be Abram of the most high God, possessor of heaven and earth:20 And blessed be the most high God, which hath delivered thine enemies into thy hand. And he gave him tithes of all.

And so... *Genesis 13:2 And Abram was very rich in cattle, in silver, and gold.*

Instruction from Jehovah God to pay tithe.

Tithes are Holy.

Leviticus 27:30 And all the tithe of the land, whether of the seed of the land, or of the fruit of the tree, is the Lord's: it is holy unto the Lord.32 And concerning the tithe of the herd, or of the flock, even of whatsoever passeth under the rod, the tenth shall be holy unto the Lord.

Malachi 3:8 Will a man rob God? Yet ye have robbed me. But ye say, Wherein have we robbed thee? In tithes and offerings.9 Ye are cursed with a curse: for ye have robbed me, even this whole nation.10 Bring ye all the tithes into the storehouse, that there may be meat in mine house, and prove me now herewith, saith the Lord of hosts, if I will not open you the windows of heaven, and pour you out a blessing, that there shall not be room enough to receive it.

If you give first fruits of all income for His service, then you will be surprised to see the increase and protection of God.

One advantage of paying tithes is you get divine protection, shield, refuge, and hedge.

Malachi 3:11 And I will rebuke the devourer for your sakes, and he shall not destroy the fruits of your ground; neither shall your vine cast her fruit before the time in the field, saith the LORD of hosts.

I met a pastor once; he said I thought I was excused for paying tithes and offering to God since I am a pastor. The Pastor was withholding what rightfully belonged to the Lord. With his money going towards medical expenses, he found himself needing extra funds to meet his other financial obligations. Once he found out he couldn't get away with it, he started giving tithes. He realized that the children had stopped being sick. Find out where and how to give tithes and offerings. Support the laborer toiling in God's field - the impoverished, the widowed, the orphaned, and the hungry.

I used to have a strong desire to work to pay tithes. I obtained a job and started providing aid to the poor, individuals with leprosy, widows, and orphans. That was the most blessed time to just give to God. When I reflected, I discovered the abundance of blessings from God in my life. How can you not afford to pay what belongs to the Lord?

The New Testament expects pastors to be both leaders and laborers. They go out and work in God's field. Where is the field? In India, my mom and brother would regularly give money to people who came to our house and performed prayers for us. We provided support to God's servants working in the field. They go places on hot, cold, or rainy days to pray, visit, and comfort others.

Jesus said:

Luke 10:7 And in the same house remain, eating and drinking such things as they give: for the laborer is worthy of his hire. Go not from house to house

1 Timothy 5:18 The laborer is worthy of his reward.

Upon being called by God for ministry, I was assured that He would provide for me. He gave his word to support and reward his employees, acknowledging that they deserve to be compensated for their work. I never face financial problems, even with my meager earnings. The faithfulness of God is unwavering.

In the past, I would go around and pray with a brother who had an abundance of spiritual gifts. I was healed and able to walk again after he prayed for me. Because I had already given tithes, offerings, and missions to the church, I didn't think I needed to give him an offering. It is said by my brother that one must never approach God without making an offering. My brother shared a Bible scripture with me and convinced me that the Korean brother is a worker of God who deserves to be compensated. God's blessings are activated through your giving to His workers. Understand that the building is not the designated church. You embody the church. Support laborers directly, rather than giving to a specific denomination, organization, or non-denominational church. You'll be able to perceive the distinction.

1 Samuel 9:7 Then said Saul to his servant, But, behold, if we go, what shall we bring the man? For the bread is spent in our vessels, and there is not a present to bring to the man of God: what have we? 8 And the servant answered Saul again, and said, Behold, I have here at hand the fourth part of a shekel of silver: that will I give to the man of God, to tell us our way.

ELIZABETH DAS

I see people aren't afraid to spend money on nails, hair, restaurant vacations, clothes, drugs, alcohol, cigarettes, and medicine, but they will pay nothing to the laborer of God. In addition to that, they anticipate you to cover their meal and leave. Consequently, they lost the blessings granted to them by God.

Recognizing the worth of a laborer: I used to have trouble accepting help from people, even though I was working for God. A female friend believes that refusing a donation for your services will result in missing out on her blessings. She described how you are formed from dirt and explained that by planting offerings in your ground, I can receive blessings multiplied by thirty, sixty, or a hundred times. The scripture became clear to me at that moment. By rejecting what they wanted to give, I hindered their blessings. Keep in mind that in this dispensation, there are workers known as pastors, apostles, teachers, prophets, and evangelists. Jesus, fulfilling the roles of a pastor, teacher, or prophet, didn't use the pulpit for his teachings. He revealed to us that he flipped the table and got rid of them. In this era, individuals with titles bestowed by God are workers, actively engaged in casting out demons, healing the sick, preaching the Gospel, and baptizing whenever they come across water. Don't mistake the building for something else. Building is no longer allowed in this era.

Matthew 13:8 But other fell into good ground, and brought forth fruit, some a hundredfold, some sixtyfold, some thirtyfold.

Can you please specify what you want and how much?

Luke 6:38 Give, and it shall be given unto you; good measure, pressed down, shaken together, and running over, shall men give into your bosom. For with the same measure that ye mete withal, it shall be measured to you again.

Each of us is blessed in our unique way. Our lives are filled with God's abundant blessings. My usual method of worldwide ministry involves phone calls, hospital visits, or home visits.

During one of my missionary trips, an extraordinary incident occurred. The prophecy was made by my Pastor, who is also a prophet. A woman visited me and placed the money inside an envelope. I stored it and completely forgot. On the third day, the Lord asked me to check her contribution. I was busy, so I said, ok, I will. After the Lord's third reminder, I decided to check the money. At first, I took an envelope and kneeled in prayer for it. Based on my knowledge, I offer her a fourfold blessing. After the Lord denied it, I prayed for her to receive a hundredfold blessing. The Lord said no to that as well. I simply stated that I didn't know anything else. I inquired of the Lord, seeking His advice on how to bless her. The Lord said to bless her without limits. That was something I had never been familiar with. Want to hear the best part? She has been blessed abundantly by God and doesn't need to work. Let me tell you about this lady who has always believed in my prayers and received amazing blessings. Not just her, but everyone who knows her contacted me for prayer.

The act of giving brings blessings. If God were to hire you as a laborer, He would also take care of you. To fulfill a need, the Lord knows how to employ a crow or widow. I ensure that I plant my tithe, offering, and missions in the right place to receive the Blessings. I dedicate my work to the Lord and make offerings to numerous workers.

1 Timothy 6:10 We know that For the love of money is the root of all evil:

The act of giving to the kingdom of God removes all affection for money.

LET US PRAY

May the Lord bless you and make you rich with His blessings. May you receive the revelation from the Lord about the value of giving, as all scriptures need to be understood. The Lord makes us cheerful givers. Our Lord loves a cheerful giver. Appreciate what you have and witness the divine generosity. The more you give, the more you will be given. Request the Lord to guide you in giving generously and abundantly. We are grateful for your generosity in giving blessings where there is no space to receive them. I hope God provides you with a financial investor to support the kingdom. We pray for our nation to be blessed in the name of Jesus. Amen! God bless you!

JANUARY 20

WHAT MAKES DIFFERENCE?

What leads to a transformation in a nation, town, religious institution, or residence? It's the leadership that is righteous, honest, and God-fearing that brings about change. Your character is shaped significantly by your political and spiritual leaders, parents, and teachers. Obeying the Bible, praying, and using the name of Jesus can bring about a substantial change. If your leaders remove everything mentioned above, it would destroy your society, country, self, and family. We are headed towards the downfall of society.

Let's investigate the occurrences of a prosperous and well-regarded king or queen. King Solomon received a promotion and was filled with wisdom from God. King Solomon lost his way, abandoned God, caused his kingdom to fail, and died without finding redemption. Regrettably, he died without being able to find his path. Can you never lose your salvation once you've been saved? Once you find the truth of the Word of God, be diligent and sincere, and carefully consider every action you take. It has to be on the truth of God's Word.

1 King 11:4 says, "For it came to pass, when Solomon was old, that his wives turned away his heart after other gods: and his heart was not perfect with the LORD his God, as was the heart of David, his father." Nehemiah said in Nehemiah 13:27, "Shall we then hearken unto you to do all this great evil, to transgress against our God in marrying strange wives?"

In the previous verse, Nehemiah mentioned Solomon's sin. yet among many nations was there no king like him, who was beloved of his God, and God made him king over all Israel: nevertheless, even him did outlandish women cause to sin." (Nehemiah 13:26)

The Book of Judges is about the falling and rising of a ship without sailors and a people without righteous leaders.

Judges 2:7 says, "And the people served the LORD all the days of Joshua, and all the days of the elders that outlived Joshua, who had seen all the great works of the LORD, that he did for Israel."

The Bible reports the nations served the Lord under the leadership of Moses and Joshua. These influential leaders brought the people of Israel to the promised land, whom God used for deliverance from slavery. These leaders had unconditional love for God. God is still looking for devoted people. People with integrity who will stand up and trust in God. God says in His Word, "My eyes go to and fro looking in the heart who can do all I say."

JANUARY 20

When your home gets a television, movies, video games, and other media entertainment, it makes one so busy that it is easy to forget God. To forget His Word, prayer, and Bible reading until one gets divorced from God. As spouses and children, we need attention so the family does not drift apart. God loves your fellowship, so you do not drift away from Him. If you love God, as He said, with all your heart, mind, soul, and strength, then you have a one hundred percent guarantee that your children and their children are blessed beyond measure.

When you love God the way you should, you will not spend your money on drugs and alcohol, cigarettes, or ungodly things. Godly leadership is essential! A spiritual leader has a vital role in your life and will make a difference.

Judges 2:13 says, "And they forsook the LORD, and served Baal and Ashtaroth. 14 And the anger of the LORD was hot against Israel, and he delivered them into the hands of spoilers that spoiled them, and he sold them into the hands of their enemies round about so that they could no longer stand before their enemies." And Verse 18 of that same chapter tells us, "And when the LORD raised them up judges, then the LORD was with the judge, and delivered them out of the hand of their enemies all the days of the judge: for it repented the LORD because of their groanings by reason of them that oppressed them and vexed them."

God's establishment of America and its rise to greatness as a nation is attributed to the people's foundation in the Word of God, prayer, and the name of Jesus. America's decline began in the 1960s when it banned prayer in schools, legalized abortion (leading to over 60 million terminated pregnancies), and now faces jeopardy to the name of Jesus and the gospel. Our nation is currently dealing with poverty and mental health problems. Everywhere you look, there is chaos due to the overflowing jails and prisons.

Modern-day America can be compared to Israel, as both have corrupt leadership, churches, and politicians. Our faith should be in the Word of God, not in corrupt leaders of corrupt churches. Invite the Holy Spirit into your life, open your Bible, and allow the Lord to guide you through His Word. Watch what unfolds. Seek God's guidance and let Him be your leader. America's focus has shifted to strange and false gods. The divine leaders, both political and spiritual, who established this country have passed away. Nevertheless, present-day leaders are giving in to corruption, witchcraft, and various malicious activities. We should offer prayers for the appointment of adequate leaders. We need to reintroduce the Bible and prayer into our schools, homes, and lives. Please pray for spiritual leaders as they minister to the people. Pray against leaders who deceive and manipulate others for their own interests in power and wealth. Once again, let the Lord Jesus become the God of this nation. We can receive the Holy Spirit if we all decide to turn to God, repent, and be baptized in the name of Jesus to have our sins washed away. This Spirit will lead us and direct us towards the truth. He will be the much-needed spark to ignite change in our lives.

It's time to eliminate the impurity in our lives, families, and country by rejecting false idols.

Nehemiah 13:28-30 reads, "And one of the sons of Joiada, the son of Eliashib, the high priest, was son in law to Sanballat the Horonite: therefore I chased him from me. 29) Remember them, O my God, because they have defiled the priesthood, and the covenant of the priesthood, and the Levites. 30) Thus cleansed I them from all strangers, and appointed the wards of the priests and the Levites, everyone in his business."

LET US PRAY

Lord, bless our country and us with spiritual leaders who are guided by the Spirit and fear God. Make our streets safe again by restoring our lives. May God bless you with exceptional spiritual leaders in the name of Jesus. Amen! God Bless you.

JANUARY 21

LET US STAND FOR JESUS!

If we don't have a firm belief, we are easily swayed by anything. "Praise God!" Peter Marshall quotes. Standing firm requires both unyielding determination and a steadfast decision. A strong backbone and a healthy spine are necessary for standing.

The original path of righteousness is being abandoned by many. Their attention shifted to the concerns of the world, resulting in increased busyness. The future generations were not taught the ways of God and Jesus Christ. Neither of those two generations is capable of raising their children to be righteous. Today's generation is heavily involved in substance abuse, and suicide, and lacks responsibility. Parents and grandparents fail to recognize the importance of teaching the Word of God. You are responsible for your children's downfall. Home is where you'll ultimately be defeated, regardless of your accomplishments.

Some people take a detour and navigate their way around forbidden things. Your failure with your children means you have to raise your grandchildren. Because you did not uphold God's unchanging Word, you disrupted the harmony within the family. Our tactics and agenda have successfully deceived numerous grandparents and parents. Give your full attention and sincerity to God's unchanging, original ways.

Children have been failed by society's inability to correct their behavior. They are no longer capable of exerting power and authority to discipline their kids. Many don't stand on 'what thus saith'. If we had taken the right actions, society wouldn't be demanding rights for their errors. In the present day, individuals have a distaste for being corrected. Love and accept me as I am. Although I may lack spiritual sight and hearing, please refrain from correcting me. Allow me to share something with you. You're as lost and fallen as Satan. How does the sinner achieve cleansing through confessing sins while you do not? They went against their own beliefs and actively fought them. To sum it up, I am defiant, resentful of divine authority, and refuse to obey. Nevertheless, I am worthy of complete approval. Accept me for who I am. Who is responsible for the failure of the country, family, and people? We did. We didn't stand in the same way as Daniel, David, Moses, and Joshua. The consequence is either your head or your life on the line. Some were killed for their commitment to doing what was right. Paul was beheaded and Peter was hung upside down by an immoral homosexual society in Rome. Why? They accurately communicated the truth and provided a clear definition of Christ and His mission. They possessed complete knowledge and comprehension of their beliefs. The reason why no one, including the harsh emperor, can change is because of that.

A majority of the Roman emperors, specifically 14 out of 15, engaged in homosexual relationships. This kind of mindset will leave you with no chance, my friends. This sin marks the end of any possibility of redemption. Reading a book of Romans is like today's news.

ELIZABETH DAS

Roman 1:28 And even as they did not like to retain God in their knowledge, God gave them over to a reprobate mind, to do those things which are not convenient.

Don't be deceived by false doctrine—teach the truth instead. What does the term doctrine refer to? Doctrine means established or respected teaching (viewed as reliable, time-honored) or instruction. (From Bible Hub)

Ephesians 4:11 And he gave some, apostles; and some, prophets; and some, evangelists; and some, pastors and teachers; 12 For the perfecting of the saints, for the work of the ministry, for the edifying of the body of Christ: 13 Till we all come in the unity of the faith, and of the knowledge of the Son of God, unto a perfect man, unto the measure of the stature of the fulness of Christ: 14 That we henceforth are no more children, tossed to and fro, and carried about with every wind of doctrine, by the sleight of men, and cunning craftiness, whereby they lie in wait to deceive

What leads to the downfall of society? When teachers, prophets, and religious leaders become corrupted. Spiritual and religious authorities committed adultery with the Word of God. The delivery of the Word of God should remain pure and unchanged. A personal interpretation should never exist. Society becomes confused, sick, and unholy, then falls away from God when you slack in doing it.

That is why John warned:

1 John 4:1 Beloved, believe not every spirit, but try the spirits whether they are of God: because many false prophets are gone out into the world.

Stand on the teachings of Lord Jesus.

Aim for the unadulterated, sacred voice of God through the Scriptures. Strive for purity, righteousness, and holiness. Find joy in living a healthy and wholesome life.

2 Chronicles 16:9 God's eyes go to and fro to see whose heart is perfect towards Him.

Your heart is the origin of life. Be cautious not to confuse it with a country. The surroundings provide freedom for sin. It goes uncorrected by everyone. Could you paint a picture of Joseph, Daniel, and Esther's way of living? Even though they were surrounded by different cultures, they remained righteous in their actions. We must live exactly as the Lord commands.

There will be no alteration to the Book of God. If we don't stand for the truth, we'll be susceptible to everything that surrounds us. There are deceptive falsehoods surrounding us. A beautiful package concealing an evil entity. A seductive trap. The trash in the gift bags. Escape from it.

Where are you today? In prison, on the streets, behind bars, jobless, confused, worried? Is your home eating you up? Your home is beautiful and big, but there is no peace. You have a big TV and liquor. Your regular church attendance hasn't brought you the peace you seek. The use of drugs and divorce can cause immense harm to you and your children.

You have been actively seeking out false teachers and prophets who offer no direction for your futile lifestyle. Is God less important to you than your flesh? Where are you dedicating your time, money, and life? Does life bring sorrow? The source of power is truth. Remain steadfast in the truth, which is found in the Word of God.

2 Timothy 3:5 Having a form of godliness, but denying the power thereof: from such turn away.

Without a dedication to truth, titles and positions lose their significance. We need to live honestly.

Folks turn to God, repent, and live for Jesus!

1 Peter 2:9 But ye are a chosen generation, a royal priesthood, a holy nation, a peculiar people; that ye should shew forth the praises of him who hath called you out of darkness into his marvelous light: 10 Which in time past were not a people, but are now the people of God: which had not obtained mercy, but now have obtained mercy.

LET US PRAY

Dear Lord of Heaven, grant us the spirit of repentance and show the highest mercy. Give us true teachers and prophets. Give us the heart to follow your laws, statutes, and commandments. Let the Holy Spirit be our guide and teacher. The Holy Spirit guides us towards righteousness and gives us strength to defend the truth. God, please bless us with the boldness and bravery that Daniel possessed. Help us love you like David, have the humbleness of Moses, and be light for those who are lost and in darkness. May the Lord grant us understanding of His Word and grant us an obedient heart to follow you! Be blessed, and your children rise and bless you. May the Lord shine upon you and give you peace in Jesus 'name. Amen! God Bless you!

JANUARY 22

YOUR SIN WILL HAUNT YOU!

Failure to eradicate sin can lead to a terrifying experience.

Roman 6:23 For the wages of sin is death.

The consequences of sin include the sting of death. Sinners will be dragged out of the earth by a sting. The gift of God is repentance, which unveils your true nature. If not, you might mistakenly believe everything is okay.

The great news is that we remain sinners until we find forgiveness from God. Only God has the power to sever the string that pulls you towards hell. God's mercy extends to His creation, providing them with the truth. May we humbly admit our faults and implore the Lord's guidance, recognizing our sinful nature.

The act of putting on flesh allowed Him to give life through blood.

Leviticus 17:14c for the life of all flesh is the blood thereof:

Hebrews 9:22b and without shedding of blood is no remission. Baptism offers access to blood. If you baptize in the name of Jesus, baptism becomes a burial for sinners.

Acts 22:16 And now why tarriest thou? Arise, be baptized, and wash away thy sins, calling on the name of the Lord.

Blood is the only way to remove sin, as death is tied to sin. Blood is the carrier of life.

Leviticus 17:11a For the life of the flesh is in the lamb's blood, which is hidden under the name of Jesus. That is why all Jews and newly converted gentiles were added to the church following the Book of Acts at the beginning of three centuries. They were all baptized in the name of Jesus to remit their sins.

Despite Cain killing his brother Abel, his blood continued to live on. It was crying.

Genesis 4:10 And he said, What hast thou done? The voice of thy brother's blood crieth unto me from the ground.

Who will be the judge on your final day? Who has the authority to determine if you go to heaven or hell? Jesus will sit on the throne.

JANUARY 22

Accepting His Way allows the Lord Jesus to deliver.

Cain was questioned by God, who wanted to know where Abel was. Cain said, am I my brother's keeper? God convicted Cain by letting him know I knew where Abel was. Cain's lack of an acceptable sacrifice meant that he did not have a relationship with God.

Had Cain known God, his story could have been different had he confessed his sins. He passed up the opportunity to come clean about what he did. The act of confessing holds great significance.

1 John 1:9 If we confess our sins, he is faithful and just to forgive us and cleanse us from all unrighteousness.

God will cleanse and absolve you once you acknowledge your wrongdoing.

A certain woman was plagued by a lying spirit and had a constant habit of lying. She grew tired of it and decided to confess. Following that incident, she never told a lie again. Friends, don't hesitate to confess if you're involved in lying, stealing, jealousy, or any other sinful behavior. Your sins will be wiped clean by God, removing all traces of unrighteousness. If you don't, your life will be plagued with misery and curses. Confess solely to the Lord Jesus, please.

The opportunity for Cain to confess slipped away.

Genesis 4:11a, 11 And now Art thou cursed from the earth 12 When thou tillest the ground, it shall not henceforth yield unto thee her strength; a fugitive and a vagabond shalt thou be in the earth.

Number 32:23 But if ye will not do so, behold, ye have sinned against the LORD: and be sure your sin will find you out.

No one is offended by sin except God.

In the absence of her husband, a woman had the urge to engage in sinful behavior. Joseph had a personal relationship with his God. The law of God resided within His heart. People who sin are ignorant of God's existence. They think they can get away with sinning without anyone noticing. These individuals lack spiritual vision.

Joseph was a devout man who feared God. He chose not to use his power and position for personal gain. He had no interest in what the woman had to offer. He understood that sin was not directed towards the master or woman but towards God. You are constantly being watched by God. What did Joseph flee from woman or immorality? Truly, from Sin!

Genesis 39:9 There is none greater in this house than I; neither hath he kept back anything from me but thee, because thou Art his wife: how then can I do this great wickedness and sin against God?

You'll be followed by sin. This thing will sting you and leave a lasting impression.

I received a call from a friend one day regarding her son's past transgression. This sin was tormenting him. He shared details with me about it. I understood that God was revealing to him the seriousness of sin. I described the situation while he admitted it and made no attempt to conceal it. Through confession, the atheist has received forgiveness from God. And he was clean from that sin. When I prayed for him, a sense of peace settled within. Please accept God's wa's ways. Sin affects everyone in the same way, regardless of who they are.

Go into your room, confess to God, and say, "Lord, I did this, and this is wrong, and I renounce."

Make a list of committed sins and present it to God with a repentant heart. Embrace the opportunity to have your sins cleansed and forgiven through His plan, in the name of Jesus.

LET US PRAY

May the Lord grant you the eyes to see the seriousness of sin. May you baptize in Jesus name and wash away your sins. May the Lord declare you innocent on judgment day. Let His blood wash all your sins and cleanse you. In Jesus' name, the Lord grants you the courage to confess sins and discover forgiveness, peace, blessings, and the joy of the Lord. Amen! God bless you!

JANUARY 23

JESUS GIVES THE KINGDOM KEY, WHICH HAS A REVELATION OF HIM.

You can't give your house, car, or office keys to someone unless you know them.

God will say to strangers, I don't know you. Only after knowing Jesus 'identity did he entrust Peter with the key to building the church. He is Not Jesus Joseph, but a Messiah. According to the Bible, according to Peter, Jesus was the avenging Jehovah they had been waiting for.

Is. 35:3-7 says to heal the lame, to open blind eyes, heal the sick and heal the broken heart.

As per the prophecy of Isaiah 9:6, this is the God who came in the form of a male child. Jews have long awaited this promised redeemer, knowing that the blood of animals cannot absolve their sins. They sought the sinless blood of the creator, thus He manifested in human form and was symbolized as the lamb of God. They knew Jehovah must take human form to shade the blood. God is a spirit, and to shade the blood, He must put on flesh.

Paul was knowledgeable in all Torahs and an observer of the law of God. He followed the first commandment, affirming the existence of only one God.

Deuteronomy 6:4 Hear, O Israel: The Lord our God is one Lord: 5 And thou shalt love the Lord thy God with all thine heart, and with all thy soul, and with all thy might.

There is only Jehovah as God, no other. Jesus is not God, so why are Jews preaching Jesus? Do you think God will permit Him to utilize his knowledge for His kingdom?

You can't be employed by the King if you do not know the King's identity.

Paul later said,

1 Corinthians 2:8 Which none of the princes of this world knew: had they known it, they would not have crucified the Lord of glory.

Psalms 24:10 Who is this King of glory? The Lord of hosts, he is the King of glory. Selah.

Paul, too, had an encounter with the King of Glory on the Damascus Road, whom he had been persecuting. In Hebrew, Jehovah spoke to Paul at Damascus RD, clarifying that Jesus is Jehovah's savior.

A revelation of Jesus is essential for anyone who wants to preach about him. There is widespread confusion in the world due to people preaching about Jesus without a clear understanding of His identity. Jesus has not called them, but they have called themselves. Numerous snakes have spread chaos by preaching about hell within various organizations, denominations, and non-denominations. Jesus is not operating through them. It's wonderful to learn the Bible by following Jesus 'footsteps as an example.

Acts 19:11 And God wrought special miracles by the hands of Paul:

Acts 15:12 Then all the multitude kept silence, and gave audience to Barnabas and Paul, declaring what miracles and wonders God had wrought among the Gentiles by them.

The Lord supports and empowers those who possess the revelation of Jesus. In the name of Jesus, we witness the manifestation of His might, power, knowledge, and authority. Is it possible to work without being aware of the authorities? Remember, this is the kind of work that deserves recognition from the King. King Jesus arrived as a servant, but not as a servant within His kingdom. He had a temporary role, with numerous prophecies mentioned in the Book of Prophets. Give importance to understanding why and what to prioritize in this era.

First, love Him as one true God walking in the flesh to receive the key to open the treasure. I do desire nine gifts of the Spirit to continue to give fame to the name of Jesus as God in the flesh. All you need is revelation and commitment. Refrain from the desire for power to receive business and money. It is not for personal gain but the service for the creation of the creator. The Lord gave Himself love for His creation. One crucial virtue, we should have love as He does.

John 14:21 He that hath my commandments, and keepeth them, he it is that loveth me: and he that loveth me shall be loved of my Father, and I will love him and will manifest myself to him.

In the New Testament, revealing Jesus as one Jehovah God in the flesh is a must.

John 14:15 If ye love me, keep my commandments.

The bottom line: He has a treasure for those who love Him. He has mansions; He has eternal life, abundant life on earth and in heaven.

The revelation comes as you keep walking, seeking, asking, knocking, and continuing in the Word of God. I am sure it is easy for those whose eyes are fixed on God and His work.

I keep seeking God for all situations and problems. The Lord loves to give His keys to open the wealth of knowledge, wisdom, understanding, blessings, riches, and power. It comes from God alone. Many are looking at God for the wrong purpose.

In this dispensation, the Lord said, my follower who knows me will do supernatural things since I am working through them.

JANUARY 23

Mark 16:20 And they went forth, and preached everywhere, the Lord working with them, and confirming the word with signs following. Amen. 17 And these signs shall follow them that believe; In my name shall they cast out devils; they shall speak with new tongues; 18 They shall take up serpents; and if they drink any deadly thing, it shall not hurt them; they shall lay hands on the sick, and they shall recover. 19 So then, after the Lord had spoken unto them, he was received up into heaven and sat on the right hand of God.

By witnessing the work, signs, and wonders of the Lord, one can identify His disciples. This is the result of having a relationship with the Lord Jesus. Experiencing this is only possible if you have the revelation of Jesus and are committed and called.

To achieve the desired outcome, it is important to understand each scripture and fulfill its requirements. Looking for forgiveness for your transgressions? The key is to baptize in Jesus's name and experience the complete package of new creation, like on the day of the garden of Eden. Through water Baptism, a brand new, purified conscience will be formed by the Lord. How wonderful it is to finally have the truth! This is the answer to breaking free from the devil's lies, sickness, and heartache and finding deliverance in the name of Jesus.

God wants obedience and submissiveness and doing as it says.

Matthew 7:22 Many will say to me in that day, Lord, Lord, have we not prophesied in thy name? and in thy name have cast out devils? And in thy name done many wonderful works? 23 And then will I profess unto them, I never knew you: depart from me, ye that work iniquity. 24 Therefore whosoever heareth these sayings of mine, and doeth them, I will liken him unto a wise man, which built his house upon a rock:

This scripture emphasizes that knowing Jesus is more important than being able to perform miracles, healing, and other signs and wonders. Salvation cannot be maintained without the revelation of Jesus, even when authority is exercised.

Luke 12:32 Fear not, little flock; for it is your Father's good pleasure to give you the kingdom.

Peter came into possession of the key after having a revelation about Jesus's identity.

Matthew 16:15 He saith unto them, But whom say ye that I am? 16 And Simon Peter answered and said, Thou art the Christ, the Son of the living God. 17 And Jesus answered and said unto him, Blessed art thou, Simon Barjona: for flesh and blood hath not revealed it unto thee, but my Father which is in heaven. 18 And I say also unto thee, That thou art Peter, and upon this rock, I will build my church; and the gates of hell shall not prevail against it. 19 And I will give unto thee the keys of the kingdom of heaven: and whatsoever thou shalt bind on earth shall be bound in heaven: and whatsoever thou shalt loose on earth shall be loosed in heaven.

Obeying the teachings of His disciples, prophets, and apostles is crucial for receiving the revelation. In this current time, the Lord commanded us to persist in the teachings of disciples.

Acts 2:42 And they continued steadfastly in the apostles' doctrine and fellowship, and in the breaking of bread, and in prayers.

Ephesians 2:20 And are built upon the foundation of the apostles and prophets, Jesus Christ being the chief cornerstone.

Pay attention to the scriptures. Jesus came to set an example and shed blood. Blood has life, so He gave life to us.

LET US PRAY

Lord, we are grateful for the love you have shown in Calvary. We want to walk on your path to find the truth and have eternal life. Your word needs revelation. Each word can reveal if we obey your voice. Many false teachers and prophets have started denomination and non-denomination for personal benefits. Lord, let us stick to your word and the doctrine of apostles and prophets. We need a revelation from the Spirit of God, as you did to Paul and Peter in Jesus's name. Amen! God bless you.

JANUARY 24

WAY TO ESCAPE!

We are familiar with the appropriate actions to take in the event of earthquakes, fires, or emergencies. Whenever God declares an emergency, there is always a solution. Only God knows the way to escape.

Genesis 6:5 And God saw that the wickedness of man was great in the earth and that every imagination of the thoughts of his heart was only evil continually. 6 And it repented the Lord that he had made man on the earth, and it grieved him at his heart. 7 And the Lord said, I will destroy man whom I have created from the face of the earth; both man, and beast, and the creeping thing, and the fowls of the air; for it repenteth me that I have made them.

He planned to wipe out ungodly immoral sinners from the face of the earth. Noah and his family were saved when they were given the plan to build the Ark. It's quite remarkable, don't you think?

Genesis 6:8 But Noah found grace in the eyes of the LORD.

Noah built the ark. It nearly took a century. Throughout that period, he preached a message of repentance to the world.

In the time of Noah, people veered off course and behaved in an ungodly manner.

Matthew 24:38 For as in the days that were before the flood they were eating and drinking, marrying and giving in marriage, until the day that Noe entered into the ark, In God's eyes, Noah was a righteous and unblemished man. Noah walked with God. Noah and his family were rescued by God.

Genesis 7:4 For yet seven days, and I will cause it to rain upon the earth forty days and forty nights; and every living substance that I have made will I destroy from off the face of the earth

2 Peter 2:5 And spared not the old world, but saved Noah the eighth person, a preacher of righteousness, bringing in the flood upon the world of the ungodly;

Before eliminating them, God observes the bitterness of sin. The warning from God is to repent. He pays attention to the categories of sins, how serious they are, and the consequences they bring. Next, He carries out His judgment.

Genesis 7:11 In the six hundredth year of Noah's life, in the second month, the seventeenth day of the month, the same day were all the fountains of the great deep broken up, and the windows of heaven were opened. 12

And the rain was upon the earth forty days and forty nights. 13 In the selfsame day entered Noah, and Shem, and Ham, and Japheth, the sons of Noah, and Noah's wife, and the three wives of his sons with them, into the ark;

Once more, we witness the consequences of sin as God's punishment unfolds. Before passing judgment on Sodom and Gomorrah, he spoke with Abram. Does God care? Yes, He does. This is the reason He communicated with Abraham. God speaks to those who are righteous, not those who sin.

Genesis 19:29 And it came to pass, when God destroyed the cities of the plain, that God remembered Abraham, and sent Lot out of the midst of the overthrow when he overthrew the cities in which Lot dwelt.

God is righteous. In His judgment of the earth or individuals, God is bound by the laws He set to judge His creation. The qualities of God are righteousness, justice, and truth. The Lord informed Abraham of the plan before finishing off the sinners in the land. Abraham makes a plea for them.

Genesis 18:23 And Abraham drew near, and said, Wilt thou also destroy the righteous with the wicked? 25 That be far from thee to do after this manner, to slay the righteous with the wicked: and that the righteous should be as the wicked, that be far from thee: Shall not the Judge of all the earth do right?

First, he rescued a righteous man named Lot, and then he destroyed the sinners and their city. God delivers righteous judgment.

The Lord delivered righteous King David from the wicked, rebellious King Saul. He rescued David from numerous trials and tribulations.

By sending His angels, He saved Daniel from the lions by closing their mouths. God abides by the precepts and laws He has established. God plans to defy Earth's natural laws and take action. I am grateful that God can righteously redeem all destructive natural plans. He is capable of saving you from fire. The fire couldn't harm Shadrach, Meshack, and Abednego thanks to God's protection.

Daniel 3:19 Then was Nebuchadnezzar full of fury, and the form of his visage was changed against Shadrach, Meshach, and Abednego: therefore he spake, and commanded that they should heat the furnace one seven times more than it was wont to be heated.

He possesses the power to walk on water, divide the ocean, and transform the sea into solid ground. God knows how to rescue the righteous and prevent them from any harm or danger.

I found it perplexing to read the end-time prophecy in Matthew 24, Luke 17, 21, and Mark 13. I asked God, Lord; you always delivered people from slavery, sicknesses, war, and trouble. Can you explain the plan to rescue us during the end time? There certainly is at least one. I need assistance in finding a way to avoid an unbearable end time. I cannot envision the catastrophe and distress unless He unveils it to me, just like He did with Noah, Abraham, and other devout followers of God.

In the scriptures about the end times, there is a list of disasters, such as earthquakes occurring in different places. Pleasure and truce breaking are what people are after. The sinful existence we observe resembles the era of Noah, Sodom, and Gomorrah. Sin is running wild on the planet. There is a lack of righteousness.

JANUARY 24

Examine these chapters, analyze, search, and reflect on the way people lived back then. Daniel has talked about what will happen at the end time.

Daniel 12:4 But thou, O Daniel, shut up the words, and seal the book, even to the time of the end: many shall run to and fro, and knowledge shall be increased.

I sought guidance from God on how to survive the upcoming unbearable period.

1 Peter 3:20 Which sometime were disobedient, when once the longsuffering of God waited in the days of Noah, while the ark was a preparing, wherein few, that is, eight souls were saved by water. 21 The like figure whereunto even baptism doth also now save us (not the putting away of the filth of the flesh, but the answer of a good conscience toward God,) by the resurrection of Jesus Christ:

In this time, Water Baptism is the means of escape. In the name of Jesus, baptism can wash away your sins.

Acts 2:38 Then Peter said unto them, Repent, and be baptized every one of you in the name of Jesus Christ for the remission of sins, and ye shall receive the gift of the Holy Ghost.

Take the time to examine the Book of Acts, which offers the New Blood Covenant for the forgiveness of our sins.
Prayer is another weapon that holds great power.

Matthew 26:41 Watch and pray that ye enter not into temptation: the spirit indeed is willing, but the flesh is weak.

Luke 21:35 For as a snare shall it come on all them that dwell on the face of the whole earth. 36 Watch ye therefore, and pray always, that ye may be accounted worthy to escape all these things that shall come to pass, and to stand before the Son of man.

LET US PRAY

Lord, help us be ready. Save us from the snare of this earthly existence. Deliver us from the world system. The Lord gives us the spirit of prayer. I pray you go in the water in Jesus 'name and experience a mighty surgery in conscience. Let the power of sin detach from our soul, spirit, and body. Lord bless you in Jesus's name. Amen! God Bless you!

JANUARY 25

DO YOU HAVE ROOM FOR ME?

The Spirit of God seeks a dwelling place within your body.

John 4:24 God is a Spirit

1 Corinthians 6:19 What? Know ye not that your body is the temple of the Holy Ghost which is in you, which ye have of God, and ye are not your own?

Jesus, bearing the highest name, was the embodiment of the Spirit of Jehovah on earth. Baby Jesus couldn't find a place to have his birth. If you hear the Lord Jesus knocking, open your heart's door. Open the door for Him to perform mighty deeds through you. If you give permission, will He be able to enter?

Revelation 3:20 Behold, I stand at the door, and knock: if any man hear my voice, and open the door, I will come in to him, and will sup with him, and he with me.

Our bodies serve as the temple for God's Spirit in this era, not the constructed edifice we know as 'the church.' There was a time when God's Spirit dwelt in the temple of Jerusalem. When the temple's service was corrupted, and people lost the righteous way, the Spirit of God came out. He wants to use your body as a temple if you have repented and cleansed yourself by baptizing in Jesus 'name. Do not defile the temple where God's Spirit dwells. Please make some room for Him.

1 Corinthians 3:16 Know ye not that ye are the temple of God, and that the Spirit of God dwelleth in you?

God, your creator, is gentle. He needs your permission, your approval. He never made His creations like robots. He gave them free will.

When Jesus was walking on earth, He dwelt amongst the disciples. Jesus finished His job of sacrificing to shed blood and came again as the Holy Spirit. His spirit can live in you if you have washed the sins in His blood.

John 14:16 And I will pray the Father, and he shall give you another Comforter, that he may abide with you for ever; 17 Even the Spirit of truth; whom the world cannot receive, because it seeth him not, neither knoweth him: but ye know him; for he dwelleth with you, and shall be in you. 23 Jesus answered and said unto him, If a man loves me, he will keep my words: and my Father will love him, and we will come unto him, and make our abode with him.

JANUARY 25

This again says one Spirit of God, the Holy Spirit in you. After the resurrection, Jesus became a spirit again.

God always wants to be with His creation. He created humans to have a relationship with us. Like a father wants a relationship with his children. Fathers and mothers long to live with their children forever. Don't we see that in the Bible? Jacob, Abraham, and Isaac stayed with their sons. Sure, we are living in a mixed-up, crazy world. Children have nothing to do with their parents. The lost generation also has nothing to do with their heavenly Father.

God can work supernaturally if you allow Him to come and stay within you.

The Bible says in the Amplified Bible,

1 Corinthians 12:4 Now there are [distinctive] varieties of spiritual gifts [special abilities given by the grace and extraordinary power of the Holy Spirit operating in believers], but it is the same spirit [who grants them and empowers believers]. 5 And there are [distinctive] varieties of ministries and service, but it is the same Lord [who is served]. 6 And there are [distinctive] ways of working [to accomplish things], but it is the same God who produces all things in all believers [inspiring, energizing, and empowering them].

Same Spirit, same Lord, and same God, since one God is doing all. God's spirit played a different role in rescuing His creation in different dispensations. His new position also had a new title fitting the role.

At this end-time, His Spirit works by indwelling within our body. Lord Jesus will do mighty works through you if you let Him in.

Zechariah 4:6 Then he answered and spake unto me, saying, This is the word of the Lord unto Zerubbabel, saying, Not by might, nor by power, but by my spirit, saith the LORD of hosts.

I will win the battle through the Spirit of God if I yield to it.

Anyway, the real world is the unseen spirit world. There are many types of spirits, so be careful not to open to evil spirits. The Spirit of Truth is God's Spirit.

Remember, allow the Lord to come in when he knocks. You must covet so the spirit can do mighty things through you.

1 Corinthians 12:31a But covet earnestly the best gifts: According to 1 Corinthians 12:8-10, desire and ask God to come to have His office within. Let the Spiritual Gifts, which are knowledge, wisdom, miracles, faith, healing, various tongues, interpretation of tongues, discerning of spirits, and prophecy, operate through you. These gifts are of His Spirit. It is the same Lord, God, and spirit, but it does unique work through you. You become the office of the Spirit God. He will administer the rest. When you do not see spiritual gifts in operation, it means the same Lord, same spirit; same God is absent. The spirit is not there to perform all this work.

I attended (for five years) the sanctuary where miracles are normal. The pastor will call people out and give all information like MRIs, X-rays, or other diagnostic machines. I have been around many spirit-gifted saints and have seen legs and arms grow. Demons will give information and see many miracles. I attend a century called Eagle's Nest Church. Pastor operates through all nine gifts. The pastor has allowed Jesus to come and sup. The Holy Spirit will give all the information, like the name of the grandchildren, phone number, house number, and other details. At first, I couldn't understand, but I know now that the Spirit of God is in him and did all. I understand this is what God wants to do to edify His only church. By giving nine gifts of Spirit, He will enable you to do supernatural work. You become His residence, and He will do the rest.

Paul was just a man, but the living God in him administered special operations. God was letting people know he loves and cares for them. God not only gives information but knows how to fix your problem. He loves you, and if you allow Him, He can do great and mighty things. God desires to heal broken hearts, sicknesses, and diseases and expel demons. God gives divine guidance and direction for the future. God gives divine prosperity. Jesus does not want His people to be bewitched by pharmacists practicing drugs on His creation.

Jesus is asking you if he can live in you. Please make some room…

Lord Jesus says, "Your body is my temple, my house. I don't want Satan to come into your body and spend all your money, your health, or your wealth. I am here for you. Just let me in." Lord Jesus needs a room in your temple. Your body is God's residence.

LET US PRAY

Heavenly Father, Lord, and Savior give us love for the gifts of the spirit. Put a desire for all spiritual gifts so I can become a fruitful and blessed vessel for Jesus. Mary said, "So be it." Let us say, "Yes, Lord, come in, sup with me." I will allow you to come and do all. I want to give you glory and praise in Jesus 'name! Abode in me, Lord, in the name of Jesus, Amen! God Bless you!

JANUARY 26

YOUR ASSIGNMENT IN THE KINGDOM!

There is a purpose behind God's creation of man. God assigns tasks that are neither difficult nor impossible to complete. God entrusted Adam with the task of tending to the Garden of Eden. The creation of man was not without a purpose. Our failure to remember, discard, or be attentive can cause us to become lost. We prioritize our plans above God's plans. Once you are hired by an employer, job descriptions cannot be overridden. You give your utmost effort to perform the job they hired you for. Keeping a job is contingent on your actions.

Should you be hired to preach the gospel but have intentions to harm your boss and steal money, the repercussions will be unfortunate and sorrowful. Eli, the high priest, was given the responsibility of supervising the Israelites and imparting God's Torah to them. Eli is obligated to observe it and pass on the knowledge of observation to everyone. God's word treats everyone equally, without favoritism. No personal benefit based on family, nationality, race, or appearance. Don't let bribes cloud your judgment. Pay attention to what God says. The Bible represents God. God can be found in the Bible.

Keep in mind, the authority has a defined set of tasks outlined in their job description. We need to read what it says.

Ephesians 4:11 And he gave some, apostles; and some, prophets; and some, evangelists; and some, pastors and teachers.

Why? What is their responsibility to enjoy, go gulf, fish, vacation, eat, and drink? No. They discipline us as Jesus did. Go work on the field as Jesus did.

12 For the perfecting of the saints, for the work of the ministry, for the edifying of the body of Christ:13 Till we all come in the unity of the faith, and the knowledge of the Son of God, unto a perfect man, unto the measure of the stature of the fulness of Christ:

But, watch out if they're failing to complete their assignment. The outcome will be identical, regardless of whether they resemble Priest Eli, Kings like Solomon and Saul, or Esau: comply or lose it. You have the freedom to make your own choices.

1 John 4:1 - Beloved, believe not every spirit, but try the spirits whether they are of God: because many false prophets are gone out into the world.

ELIZABETH DAS

You may say, what is my calling? Preach the gospel by evidence of casting a demon out, healing the sick, and baptizing them in the name of Jesus. Watch your actions. Seek the kingdom of God first. His kingdom is in heaven and on earth if you let him by allowing Him. The people of Israel rejected God's kingship. Don't do that. Submit yourself. Do as it said. Life could be just like in the Garden of Eden, beautiful. All things will be added. Roads, highways, and bridges of your relationship with God and blessings will be repaired. They will know you as peculiar people, Chosen generations.

You will see the miracles. Your God will work if you listen to Him.

Joshua 23:10 One man of you shall chase a thousand: for the Lord your God, he it is that fighteth for you, as he hath promised you.

Matthew 7:15 - Beware of false prophets, which come to you in sheep's clothing, but inwardly they are ravening wolves.

Take care of your assignment. Read the Bible, and learn through the Holy Spirit by believing and obeying. Don't think pastor, priest, king, or any human race is an excuse.

You may ask why these people haven't been judged even though they are not walking, living as thus saith the LORD.

It's crucial to remember that if God assigns tasks and people rebel, they will remain in those positions until they pass away or are eliminated. Despite facing rejection, King Saul maintained his status as king until he passed away. So is King Solomon; Eli died at 98 years old. Until that Eli worked as a high priest. Occasionally, this is what you come across. Since they have rejected God, God does not work through them and rejects them. The choice is always in the hands of humans, and they bear the consequences of straying.

Allow me to tell you a short story. There was a time when a farmer attended church. The poor farmer offended the people of that church. His attire was unpleasant, and he took someone's seat and parked in their usual spot. The church members were angered and behaved poorly towards him. A farmer approached God, expressing concern about the unfriendliness of church people towards him. Which church did God ask him about? He provided God with all the details about the church. Jesus said he didn't know because he hadn't been to that church before. So, folks, go where God goes. If He is there, you will see all He promises to happen in the church.

What are you going to do for God? God gave us a calling and assignment to us. He is also continuously looking to fill every position. While departing from the earth, Jesus finished His mission and gave us an assignment. Mark 16... go preach the gospel with the power of His Infilling Holy Ghost. He was giving us a job to continue the projects of healing the sick, casting out demons, healing a broken heart, and setting captives free from the hands of Satan.

What are you doing? Jesus never made disciples, so they could sit on pews, eat, and think I am saved. Jesus was hard-working, and so were His disciples. Are you followers of Jesus or followers of so-called churches and pastor organizations?

There's an assignment waiting for you. He taught his disciples and then departed, instructing Terry to remain until receiving the Spirit. Why? The purpose of Jesus 'coming is to complete all tasks. It's the Power of Spirit; as we were told in Acts 1:8 Holy Spirit will give you power, and Zechariah 4:6, by thy Spirit. Don't try to impress others with your titles, degrees, or knowledge. The test for Jesus's workers is that a sign will accompany them. They possess the power to speak in unknown languages, expel demons, resurrect the dead, and restore health to the sick. If that's what they claim, then accept it as true. If that's not the case, then avoid counterfeit products. God is not manifesting His power through them. That church doesn't have Jesus. Fulfill your responsibilities and do what you were hired to do.

Luke 4:18 The Spirit of the Lord is upon me because he hath anointed me to preach the gospel to the poor; he hath sent me to heal the brokenhearted, to preach deliverance to the captives, and restore of sight to the blind, to set at liberty them that are bruised,

and this is your job now.

LET US PRAY

I pray the Lord anoints you for His kingdom, so you work for Him with signs and wonders. Jesus is glorified as King and Lord because people's hearts are free. I pray you hear at the entrance of the pearly gate, job well done. In Jesus's name. Amen! God bless you.

JANUARY 27

"POWER OF THANKFULNESS"

Thank you" are marvelous words. When you say "thank you," it changes the game. The opposite of "thank you" is unthankfulness, complaints, murmur, and careless attitude.

The Lord said that your complaint and murmuring came to my ear. Thankful people will never lose salvation. What is salvation? The word 'salvation' is healing, victory, help, and deliverance.

The Lord delivered Hebrews from slavery and liberated them from harsh people. Rather than expressing gratitude, they overlooked the pain and suffering and instead murmured and complained.

Numbers 14:27 How long shall I bear with this evil congregation, which murmur against me? I have heard the murmurings of the children of Israel, which they murmur against me. 28 Say unto them, As truly as I live, saith the LORD, as ye have spoken in mine ears, so will I do to you: 29 Your carcases shall fall in this wilderness; and all that were numbered of you, according to your whole number, from twenty years old and upward, which have murmured against me, 30 Doubtless ye shall not come into the land, concerning which I sware to make you dwell therein, save Caleb the son of Jephunneh, and Joshua the son of Nun.

Your words and attitude make all the difference. They were unable to reach the stunning promised land filled with milk and honey, despite their journey. The story is so heartbreaking! The Lord blesses us and remains faithful to His promises when we appreciate His goodness and show gratitude.

"While you have not yet reached the finishing line, work hard with diligence and tenacity!" — Ernest Agyemang Yeboah.

Finish well! Conclude positively!

True thankfulness originates in the heart, not just in speech.

Psalm 100:4 Enter into his gates with thanksgiving, and his courts with praise: be thankful unto him, and bless his name.

Begin prayer by expressing gratitude rather than complaining. Thanksgiving involves making sacrifices. Despite feeling tired from the ordeal, express gratitude as you enter His presence. You will have God's complete attention. His ear is ready to hear from you. He will gladly assist you and offer his blessings. Try it. For a few years, I would do that whenever I became seriously ill.

JANUARY 27

There was a time when I went through a severe and testing trial. Due to my illness, I was confined to a wheelchair. I endured years of sleepless agony, going without rest for almost two full days and nights. Before beginning my early morning prayer, I always take a moment to check my heart. I wanted to make sure my heart was pure, and I'm grateful. The Lord is my healer, He will make me walk and bring me out of a fiery trial. While enduring this trial, I had to remember to be grateful. In the morning, my first words are a prayer of thanks to the Lord for this trial, as it will eventually lead me to walk and run. There have been numerous instances where I've collapsed. I couldn't find any relief anywhere in my body. It was over the roof. I can't remember anything and I'm unemployed. Despite everything, I never gave up hope and appreciation.

I stood firm on the promise that God gave me.

Proverb 4:12 When thou goest, thy steps shall not be straitened; and when thou runnest, thou shalt not stumble.

It's common to hear people complaining about their clothes, food, and appearance. What is that? Who bestowed upon you everything? Go check what's happening outside. No one pays attention to people sleeping in filth and wearing dirty clothes. Why? Losing what you have is a possible consequence of being unthankful.

Those who express gratitude are cherished by God.

Experience the transformative power of a heart that is thankful.

Luke 17:12 And as he entered into a certain village, there met him ten men that were lepers, which stood afar off: 13 And they lifted up their voices, and said, Jesus, Master, have mercy on us. 14 And when he saw them, he said unto them, Go shew yourselves unto the priests. And it came to pass, that, as they went, they were cleansed. 15 And one of them, when he saw that he was healed, turned back, and with a loud voice glorified God, 16 And fell down on his face at his feet, giving him thanks: and he was a Samaritan. 17 And Jesus answering said, Were there not ten cleansed? but where are the nine? 18 There are not found that returned to give glory to God, save this stranger. 19 And he said unto him, Arise, go thy way: thy faith hath made thee whole.

What is the meaning of "whole"? It meant utterly perfect in body, soul, and spirit. Completely safe, peaceful, and sound.

In the past, we had a tradition of sharing testimonies. That service has taught me a great deal. During testimony time, individuals will speak about the goodness of God. I observed the people of God dancing and showed gratitude to the Lord. You must give thanks to God. Don't forget to express gratitude to anyone who assists you. This word has a magical effect that makes people want to do even more for you. Just as God did, he made man whole and complete by expressing gratitude upon his return.

We need a thankful generation who can say, "Lord, I thank you for the freedom to worship, an abundance of food, and great provision. How can I thank you enough for what you have done for me?"

Once you express gratitude to God, you'll notice positive transformations within yourself. Change your attitude, change your surroundings, and heaven will pour you a blessing. May we receive from the Lord a heart that counts blessings, uncovering the power found in thankfulness. God Bless you!

LET US PRAY

O Lord, bless us with a heart of thanksgiving, so that we may experience fullness and completeness. May God grant us deep understanding to recognize and comprehend that He is aware of our struggle. Leprosy, blindness, poverty, sickness, or any trouble amounts to nothing. Let us enter with thanksgiving in our hearts when we wake up with thanksgiving on our lips. Lord, we are grateful for the blessing of our jobs and family. We are grateful for a real God. May the Lord Jesus keep you safe, sound, and complete in Jesus 'name. Amen! God bless you!

JANUARY 28

I ATTACH THE REWARD TO YOUR ACTIONS!

Imagine the earth as a stage, where you can play the role of a good or bad person. The choices you make shape your future. The impact of your actions extends to future generations, bringing either blessings or curses. The influence of our actions is more substantial than the devil's speech. Your actions will determine the outcome.

In terms of excitement, the Bible is comparable to an action book. Multiple examples are provided in written warnings to illustrate the consequences of your actions. It's a book that God authored and 40 people transcribed over various eras and places. It took 1500 years to write. In the book, you'll find genuine narratives about people who either did the right thing or the wrong thing. Your actions will dictate your destiny. Don't forget, you are the real actor/actress called to the stage of Earth. Your legacy will never fade away. Your actions are documented in a book located in heaven. On judgment day, God will open it to pass judgment on you. It will be impossible to deny because there will be a record of your actions.

Want to be a popular actor? Follow David's example in your words and actions. David said, "Don't touch God's anointed. Who can escape from God?"

In God's grand production, individuals are chosen to exhibit love, desire, and sincerity in their roles. God selected different individuals to assume the roles of prophet, shepherd, king, fool, murderer, and preacher. It's determined by the emotions within your heart. The Bible contains numerous examples recorded by God.

There are individuals who go through life unaware of the Creator and His plans. They don't know God. They forget to act and react correctly. Their lives may continue, but they are marked by hopelessness and monotony, leading to tragic tales.

Earth is your stage, and the Bible is your script. If you choose the right role by looking at His laws, precepts, and His commandments, God will admire you. If you are greedy, you will show in your actions. But it is the Lord who stays true to His word. A promise giver has an open book at your reach. Reach and choose your script and act.

Hebrews 12:1 Wherefore seeing we also are compassed about with so great a cloud of witnesses, let us lay aside every weight, and the sin which doth so easily beset us, and let us run with patience the race that is set before us, 2 Looking unto Jesus the author and finisher of our faith; who for the joy that was set before him endured the cross, despising the shame, and is set down at the right hand of the throne of God.

Jesus will start writing as you act. He is the author.

Seek your role, pleasing God. He will use you in His drama and also reward you. You measure the success of Hollywood and Bollywood actors by the money they make. Don't be fooled by their wealth. Earth is a stage where you act to be chosen. You see movie stars and the money they make, the car they drive, and the house they live in and die like a fool. I would instead choose the role of righteousness that I receive permanent retirement in heaven. It is eternal peace, health, joy, comfort, and much more for playing a role in suffering for truth on earth.

Your action has a reward.

Hebrews 11:6 But without faith, it is impossible to please him: for he that cometh to God must believe that he is, and that he is a rewarder of them that diligently seek him.

Wow! Your children will inherit rewards for your actions!

Psalms 37:25 I have been young, and now am old; yet have I not seen the righteous forsaken, nor his seed begging bread.

The best role is the role of the righteous. I have seen children begging for bread. They are the children of the unrighteous. People make a lot of money but always lack money. Why? Because they chose the wrong role.

A man who chooses the role of adultery loses his soul. He acted like a fool.

Proverb 6:32 But whoso committeth adultery with a woman lacketh understanding: he that doeth it destroyeth his own soul. 33 A wound and dishonor shall he get; and his reproach shall not be wiped away.

Esau always played the role of the fool, even in picking wives.

His mother (Rebekah):

Genesis 27:46 And Rebekah said to Isaac, I am weary of my life because of the daughters of Heth: if Jacob takes a wife of the daughters of Heth, such as these which are of the daughters of the land, what good shall my life do me?

Ruth 1:16 And Ruth said, Intreat me not to leave thee, or to return from following after thee: for whither thou goest, I will go; and where thou lodgest, I will lodge: thy people shall be my people, and thy God my God:

Ruth chose the role of a virtuous woman.

Ruth 3:11 And now, my daughter, fear not; I will do to thee all that thou requirest: for all the city of my people doth know that thou art a virtuous woman.

Ruth was the great-grandmother of King David, and the Messiah came through David's lineage. She made a wise decision in choosing her role. She displayed great acting skills while on Earth. Also, Mary, Esther, and many great women chose their roles wisely without being afraid of laws, society, and the shame of death.

The most complex role ever played was by God, putting on flesh and acting like a human. He took suffering, sorrow, rejection, spitting, and whipping and received that greatest prize.

Luke 22:42 Saying, Father, if thou be willing, remove this cup from me: nevertheless not my will, but thine, be done.

As Jesus chose this role, let us read what the Bible says about Him.

Philippians 2:5 Let this mind be in you, which was also in Christ Jesus: 6 Who, being in the form of God, thought it not robbery to be equal with God: 7 But made himself of no reputation, and took upon him the form of a servant, and was made in the likeness of men: 8 And being found in fashion as a man, he humbled himself and became obedient unto death, even the death of the cross. 9 Wherefore God also hath highly exalted him, and given him a name which is above every name: 10 That at the name of Jesus every knee should bow, of things in heaven, and things in earth, and things under the earth; 11 And that every tongue should confess that Jesus Christ is Lord, to the glory of God the Father.

All your actions can be categorized as either positive or negative, credit or debit, and blessing or curse.

Be cautious when selecting your role and action as it comes with both blessings and curses. God's reward and judgment apply to everyone, without exception. May we make wise decisions? Ask for wisdom when you wake up. What actions can I take to honor you today, Lord? Show me the way to righteousness and guide my actions to be holy.

LET US PRAY

Dear God in heaven above, who shows mercy to the thousand generations. Lord, I ask you to bless your people with wisdom, knowledge, and understanding from above. Help your people, Lord, to choose right and not be deceived by their surroundings. Let nothing from the world fool us. Today, we choose to honor the unseen God who provides visible rewards. His blessings are visible. His mercy, peace, and hope are to be ours as we choose the role of the righteous. Lord, write your word in our hearts and minds to be like Christ. May the Lord grant your petitions and give you the role of blessings for you, your children, and a thousand generations after you, in Jesus 'name. Amen! God Bless you!

JANUARY 29

DIRT!

Dirt serves as a representation of our human flesh. Humans were created by God from the dirt. Out of the earth, clay or dirt is the human flesh made. When men die, they go back to the dirt again. You do not know whose flesh you brought in when you bring dirt into the house. Dirt has a significant connection with our life.

Shoes are not allowed in many Asian cultures when entering homes. To enter the house, idol worshipers remove their shoes. Growing up in India, I learned to take off my shoes when entering a Hindu home.

I once received a call from India, where someone sought my help for spiritual matters. The story they described to me was astonishing. It was a Christian home with a constant attack from the demons of the mother and daughter. That house is where they were buried after being killed. When I say Christian home, I am specifically referring to a religious Christian household.

The house was constructed on that piece of land. The place is now occupied by its new owner. Chaos reigned in the lives of everyone in that house. They had no information whatsoever about the woman and her daughter buried beneath their land. There was an ongoing assault on every individual member. The people residing in that house experienced oppression, depression, mental illness, and possession. The family faced a horrific challenge.

Some family members relocated to other nations from that house. Two family members shared the same house. The couple was experiencing terrifying torture. Nighttime was the most difficult time. They would be targeted and physically attacked by those spirits. The evil spirit is air or pneuma and cannot hurt unless it comes into the body. However, it must be a fallen angel, as they possess the capability to mimic our appearance and perform tasks just like us. The family was scared, leading to sleepless nights.

When I called, they informed me that they'd seen and heard a woman with a little girl.

In that location, they couldn't find the spiritual support they needed from Christians. People desire assistance but reject the truth. Their coworker was knowledgeable that someone within a Muslim mosque would be able to assist. A friend recommended seeking assistance from a Muslim clergy member, and they agreed. I don't know the specific name for this type of mosque. The Muslim spiritual leader instructed them to sweep their house, gather the dirt, and place it on a blank white paper. And they did. A Muslim spiritual leader sets fire to a paper with dirt in front of this couple. Wording came out on burnt paper, "I will go, but first I will destroy you, then leave." We know Satan comes to steal, kill, and destroy. I wouldn't find it surprising if the spirit wrote something on the burnt paper.

JANUARY 29

It was confirmed that the dirt belonged to the buried woman and her daughter. This sentence on the burning paper was written by them.

Have you ever had the experience of a demon climbing up from your feet? Yes, always, since the moment we stepped on dirt. Why dirt? Our existence is a result of God making us from dirt. It's common for spirits to appear when we bring dirt into our homes.

Genesis 2:7 And the LORD God formed man of the dust of the ground, and breathed into his nostrils the breath of life, and man became a living soul.

Genesis 3:19 In the sweat of thy face shalt thou eat bread, till thou return unto the ground; for out of it wast thou taken: for dust thou art, and unto dust shalt thou return. 20 All go unto one place; all are of the dust, and all turn to dust again.

When a person dies, they become dirt again. Wow, the Bible is a true book of knowledge!

Ecclesiastes 12:7 Then shall the dust return to the earth as it was: and the spirit shall return unto God who gave it.

1 Corinthians 15:47 The first man is of the earth, earthy

A man was created by God from the dirt. That's the reason why the soil hears everything you say. The dirt will be a powerful witness on the day of judgment.

Matthew 10:14 And whosoever shall not receive you, nor hear your words, when ye depart out of that house or city, shake off the dust of your feet.

Luke 9:5 And whosoever will not receive you, when ye go out of that city, shake off the very dust from your feet for a testimony against them.

They used dirt in the time of Moses. Does it have the power to witness if the wife did wrong?

Numbers 5:11 And the Lord spake unto Moses, saying, 12 Speak unto the children of Israel, and say unto them, If any man's wife goes aside, and commit a trespass against him, 13 And a man lie with her carnally, and it be hid from the eyes of her husband, and be kept close, and she be defiled, and there be no witness against her, neither she be taken with the manner; 14 And the spirit of jealousy come upon him, and he be jealous of his wife, and she be defiled: or if the spirit of jealousy come upon him, and he be jealous of his wife, and she be not defiled: 15 Then shall the man bring his wife unto the priest, and he shall bring her offering for her, the tenth part of an ephah of barley meal; he shall pour no oil upon it, nor put frankincense thereon; for it is an offering of jealousy, an offering of memorial, bringing iniquity to remembrance. 16 And the priest shall bring her near, and set her before the Lord: 17 And the priest shall take holy water in an earthen vessel; and of the dust that is in the floor of the tabernacle the priest shall take, and put it into the water: 18 And the priest shall set the woman before the Lord, and uncover the woman's head, and put the offering of memorial in her hands, which is the jealousy offering: and the priest shall have in his hand the bitter water that causeth the curse: 19 And the priest shall charge her by an oath, and say unto the woman, If no man has lain with thee, and if thou hast not gone aside to uncleanness with another instead of thy husband, be thou free from this bitter water that causeth the curse: 20 But if thou hast gone aside to another instead of thy husband, and if thou be defiled, and some man have lain with thee beside thine husband: 21

Then the priest shall charge the woman with an oath of cursing, and the priest shall say unto the woman, The Lord make thee a curse and an oath among thy people, when the Lord doth make thy thigh to rot, and thy belly to swell; 22 And this water that causeth the curse shall go into thy bowels, to make thy belly to swell, and thy thigh to rot: And the woman shall say, Amen, amen. 23 And the priest shall write these curses in a book, and he shall blot them out with the bitter water: 24 And he shall cause the woman to drink the bitter water that causeth the curse: and the water that causeth the curse shall enter into her, and become bitter. 25 Then the priest shall take the jealousy offering out of the woman's hand, and shall wave the offering before the Lord, and offer it upon the altar: 26 And the priest shall take an handful of the offering, even the memorial thereof, and burn it upon the altar, and afterward shall cause the woman to drink the water. 27 And when he hath made her to drink the water, then it shall come to pass, that, if she be defiled, and have done trespass against her husband, that the water that causeth the curse shall enter into her, and become bitter, and her belly shall swell, and her thigh shall rot: and the woman shall be a curse among her people. 28 And if the woman be not defiled, but be clean; then she shall be free, and shall conceive seed. 29 This is the law of jealousies, when a wife goeth aside to another instead of her husband, and is defiled; 30 Or when the spirit of jealousy cometh upon him, and he be jealous over his wife, and shall set the woman before the Lord, and the priest shall execute upon her all this law. 31 Then shall the man be guiltless from iniquity, and this woman shall bear her iniquity.

Make sure you keep dirt out of your home. The key to success is knowledge. Some areas are known as cursed lands. Why? The act of practicing witchcraft is done by them. Some families engage in witchcraft. God's curse falls upon those who engage in witchcraft, as well as the land and families involved. God wants nothing to be built there. Our efforts are being hindered by the cursed ground in that area. Your flesh, composed of dirt, will serve as evidence against you. There is life within the dirt.

The brain of a computer is made from sand, in the form of computer chips.

Revelation 13:1 And I stood upon the sand of the sea and saw a beast rise up out of the sea, having seven heads and ten horns, and upon his horns ten crowns, and upon his heads the name of blasphemy.

In biblical terms, the sea represents a nation or region, while the sand represents the people. Dirt will be utilized by the devil.

Today, we need accurate knowledge of God to act and live a free life. Our minds and eyes need to be freed from the blindness inflicted by the devil. God is the answer, not Satan. Remaining in His truth results in freedom.

LET US PRAY

Dear Lord, as your word says, "And ye shall know the truth, and the truth shall free you." So the Lord blesses us with the truth. Teach us the truth.

We need your guidance to move forward, as your word is the only truth we have. May we be blessed with deep spiritual comprehension and be freed from religious obstacles and misleading doctrines. Lord, let your Holy Spirit teach us. Holy Spirit, please touch every life. The spirit of truth comes to refresh us and give us all understanding so we live with truth in Jesus 'name. Amen! God bless you!

JANUARY 30

DO NOT FAIL GOD!

Humans were created by God for fellowshipping with Him. In the New Testament, God is referred to as a groom who desires a bride. Earth was created to fill it with obedient people and maintain a continuous connection. The only way for heavenly messages to reach Earth is through us. A newsperson, media specialist, and broadcaster are needed for Heaven's broadcast. Rather than fake news, God only needs a straightforward message. The only option is to be willing to hear and follow. The key to success is listening and obeying. Numerous people hear His voice and experience visions and dreams. Prophets are the means through which many hear His Spirit and His written Word in the Bible. When you get a message, it's necessary to respond. To share the message with others via live-streaming, you must transform into media. Deuteronomy 29:29 The secret things belong unto the LORD our God: but those things which are revealed belong unto us and to our children forever, that we may do all the words of this law.

Just imagine if everyone started living and teaching God's commandments and precepts with sincerity. What might be the result? His people are spared from police, jail, divorces, famine, plague, or hell.

God used Jesus Christ as the conduit for imparting His laws, commandments, precepts, and grace.

John 1:17 For the law was given by Moses, but grace and truth came by Jesus Christ.

Exodus 31:18 And he gave unto Moses when he had made an end of communing with him upon mount Sinai, two tables of testimony, tables of stone, written with the finger of God.

The law of Moses was meant to be followed, not violated.

Hebrews 10:28 He that despised Moses' law died without mercy under two or three witnesses

Had Adam and Eve obeyed, we would be left with just one law: not to consume the fruit of knowledge of good and evil. If that were the case, we wouldn't have any concerns. Adam and Eve's lack of caution and refusal to obey resulted in their loss of the garden and separation from God. Who doesn't meet God's expectations? We are the modern version of Adam and Eve! Instruction is important. We are obligated to follow all the guidelines stated in the Bible.

Instead of directing our anger at Adam and Eve, let's examine our behavior. Why not explore His laws? What is the word of the Lord for you? Begin examining your shortcomings and make amends by obeying His commandments. Following God's laws will result in blessings for us and future generations.

There was one condition attached to God's call to dress the garden of Eden.

Genesis 2:17 But of the tree of the knowledge of good and evil, thou shalt not eat of it: for in the day that thou eatest thereof thou shalt surely die.

Their actions were the complete opposite. What does this mean for us? Do you think we resemble Adam and Eve in the present day? By eating the forbidden fruit, they were expelled and cursed. Following God leads to blessings while disobeying leads to judgment.

Saul was chosen to be a king, but he did not pass any of the tests. Was his removal the only action taken? The subsequent generation lost their kingship after King Saul. Who did not meet God's expectations? King Saul!

King David was righteous in all his actions except for his sins with Bathsheba and the murder of her husband. Judgment was passed on to him, even though he expressed remorse.

2 Samuel 12:10 Now, therefore, the sword shall never depart from thine house; because thou hast despised me, and hast taken the wife of Uriah the Hittite to be thy wife. 11 Thus saith the LORD, Behold, I will raise up evil against thee out of thine own house, and I will take thy wives before thine eyes, and give them unto thy neighbour, and he shall lie with thy wives in the sight of this sun. 12 For thou didst it secretly: but I will do this thing before all Israel, and before the sun.

Your dietary guidelines were given by God. The reason has been scientifically proven without a doubt. Remember, God is not science. The creator, God, is full of knowledge. While not advised, his warning does provide accurate information. He knows what is best. Do you drive in the opposite direction on a one-way street? Are you willing to plunge into the water without any knowledge of swimming? Is it common for you to leap off the roof? You may answer, "No, that is crazy." You may say, "I do not believe in committing suicide." Why are you committing suicide? Do you know it's for eternity? Hell will be the soul's eternal destination.

A warning comes from above to deliver us; the Lord came to deliver us. God uses Nathan since he was the prophet at the time. He wasn't afraid. Do you understand the potential outcomes of pronouncing judgment? Prophet Nathan showed no fear, even though the king had the power to kill. He fulfilled his duty by God's command. Obey God's commands if He asks you to. No need to question it, just do it because it's the highest authority.

It's possible to lose the given authority.

The same applies to the king; he is not an excuse. The Lord promotes him. The promotion comes from the Lord!

Psalm 75:6 For promotion cometh neither from the east, nor from the west, nor from the south. 7 But God is the judge: he putteth down one, and setteth up another.

Be humble. What is to be 'humble'? To listen to authority, to obey. The title of the most humble man was given to Moses. Why? He followed God's instruction, that's why. It's the requirement to establish God's plans, agendas, lordship, and monarchy. Stay patient and you'll see how amazing God is!

The Hebrews and Egyptians both witnessed the miraculous, judgmental, and powerful plague. A slave and master both saw nothing but the supernatural in operation. Through his humility, Moses exhibited majestic power from above.

Rebellion is simply another word for pride. Like Lucifer, it will be rejected and discarded.

Isaiah 14:12 How art thou fallen from heaven, O Lucifer, son of the morning! how art thou cut down to the ground, which didst weaken the nations! 13 For thou hast said in thine heart, I will ascend into heaven, I will exalt my throne above the stars of God: I will sit also upon the mount of the congregation, in the sides of the north: 14 I will ascend above the heights of the clouds; I will be like the most High.

Proverb 9:10 The fear of the LORD is the beginning of wisdom: and the knowledge of the holy is understanding.

The failure is a reminder that they overlooked the need to operate with high power. It is wise to have knowledge of Him and follow His commands. His decision remains constant.

Psalm 14:1 The fool hath said in his heart, There is no God. They are corrupt, they have done abominable works, there is none that doeth good. 2 The Lord looked down from heaven upon the children of men, to see if there were any that did understand, and seek God. 3 They are all gone aside, they are all together become filthy: there is none that doeth good, no, not one. 4 Have all the workers of iniquity no knowledge? who eat up my people as they eat bread, and call not upon the Lord. 5 There were they in great fear: for God is in the generation of the righteous.

Make sure you don't let God down. Be a reliable parent to your children. You have the option to take your own life in the way you choose. To receive promotion and blessings for yourself and future generations, pay heed to the voice of God as it is revealed in His Word. Don't forget to drive on the right side. Live your life guided by a deep reverence for God. Shift your focus towards moving in the right direction. Be humble.

1 Peter 5:6 Humble yourselves therefore under the mighty hand of God, that he may exalt you in due time:

LET US PRAY

Lord, please give us a humble heart. Create in us a clean heart. Fill us with a renewed spirit. We need direction from on high. Lead our lives and navigate us towards a heavenly destination. Life happens once; eternity is forever. Grant us a divine revelation. Block our surroundings so that we can focus on you. Bless our children and us, so we are head, first, and above. May the Lord give you crazy favor in Jesus 'name, Amen! God bless you!

JANUARY 31

BIBLE IS A MIRROR OF YOUR SPIRIT!

A mirror allows us to see our reflection. A mirror has beneficial effects. We enhance our looks by fixing our faces, combing out hair, dressing up, and so on. When we see our reflection, we take the necessary steps to appear attractive and presentable. Our existence extends beyond the physical body to include a spirit. To understand our spirit's state, we need a mirror. Your spirit's condition can be examined through the Bible, like a mirror.

John the Baptist came from above to confront our trespasses and find the solution for our spirit. Despite looking unattractive on the outside, a pure spirit can radiate beauty from within.

John, the Baptist, said, "Generation of vipers." What was he talking about? He did not see how others saw him as religious, paying tithes and offerings, praying, and being self-righteous. John was talking about spirit conditions, and it wasn't good. That is why he said, "Generation of vipers." A viper is a serpent that is a deceiver and is false.

Matthew 12:34 O generation of vipers, how can ye, being evil, speak good things? for out of the abundance of the heart the mouth speaketh. 35 A good man out of the good treasure of the heart bringeth forth good things: and an evil man out of the evil treasure bringeth forth evil things. 36 But I say unto you, That every idle word that men shall speak, they shall give account thereof in the day of judgment. 37 For by thy words thou shalt be justified, and by thy words, thou shalt be condemned.

Could you define a viper? A venomous serpent possessing large fangs that can hinge. Also, hidden spiritual meaning is the spiteful, false, or treacherous person.

Can you trust these people? This kind of person brings the kingdom of God down to dust. Dispensation changes when people of God forget to take inner care. No matter how great they look, how much knowledge they have, or what position they hold in a church or synagogue, you do not have to know the person but discern the spirit operation behind them. John the Baptist confronts synagogue leaders who have dangerous, poisonous spirits.

John the Baptist sought to transform dishonest individuals by directly confronting them. He met Hebrews face to face and tackled their poor spiritual condition in the eyes of God. He described them as a poisonous snake in the eyes of God, he told them.

Why did he choose to use a harsh tone when speaking to the Israelites? The topic of discussion for John the Baptist was the condition of the spirit. Even though they looked good from the outside, paid tithes, and

JANUARY 31

studied laws, precepts, and commandments, the condition of their spirit was dangerous. They forgot they needed to take care of their spirit.

2 Corinthians 7:1 Having therefore these promises, dearly beloved, let us cleanse ourselves from all filthiness of the flesh and spirit, perfecting holiness in the fear of God. 2 Receive us; we have wronged no man, we have corrupted no man, we have defrauded no man. 3 I speak not this to condemn you: for I have said before, that ye are in our hearts to die and live with you.

As you know, our society is all about looks. You could spend all the time and money looking good on the outside yet looking horrible inside. You may be like the snake, unreliable, adulterer, fornicator, liar, wicked, proud, ungodly, greedy, and lover of self, but try to doll up and deceive others. Our beauty is deceiving. If looks attract you, you could meet with a snake, murderer, rapist, fighter, or wicked enemy to your soul.

That is why the Bible is warning us.

Proverbs 31:30 Favour is deceitful, and beauty is vain: but a woman that feareth the Lord, she shall be praised. 31 Give her of the fruit of her hands; and let her own works praise her in the gates.

People are cautious about face-lifting, looks, style, wrinkles, etc. They like to correct everything, like the color of their hair, eyes, and nails. All face and body products must be visually appealing. Dermatologists make billions of dollars to make people look beautiful on the outside. Money is nothing if it is for their looks. After doing everything for their appearance, they are still pitiful, depressed, and never content or satisfied. Why? Because they are sick inside. Why are many committing suicide? If your look is an answer, why are so many going crazy and killing themselves?

Go check yourself in the mirror called the Bible, and do what it takes to look beautiful inside. Many spiritual remedies are there. Put in action what the Word of God instructs. The best detergent is to wash sins in the blood of the Lamb and receive His Spirit. All confusion about the look and torment of the enemy that leads to destruction will be removed. As we know, the problem is the person you see in the mirror. You need to confront yourself and take action through the Word of God.

1 Corinthians 2:10 But God hath revealed them unto us by his Spirit: for the Spirit searcheth all things, yea, the deep things of God. 11 For what man knoweth the things of a man, save the spirit of man which is in him? even so the things of God knoweth no man, but the Spirit of God. 12 Now we have received, not the spirit of the world, but the spirit which is of God; that we might know the things that are freely given to us of God. 13 Which things also we speak, not in the words which man's wisdom teacheth, but which the Holy Ghost teacheth; comparing spiritual things with spiritual. 14 But the natural man receiveth not the things of the Spirit of God: for they are foolishness unto him: neither can he know them, because they are spiritually discerned. 15 But he that is spiritual judgeth all things, yet he himself is judged of no man.

The Lord lets you see how beautiful you are through the mirror called the Bible. We are made in God's image.

2 Corinthians 5:17 Therefore if any man be in Christ, he is a new creature: old things are passed away; behold, all things are become new.

A converted Muslim lady was put in jail for accepting the truth. She was reading the Bible! The inmate asked her why she was reading the Bible. As she started giving Bible study, they understood that this wasn't simply a book but an actual book for guidance for life. The Christian convert lady said the Bible is the mirror. At first, they laughed at her, but then they learned that it was a mirror. The Word of God convicted the situation and gave the remedy to be set free from all spirits.

The Bible is divine, not human, in origin. It will do great work to change the inner look to bring outer change. Open the Bible and see yourself through the word. More reading will bring a mighty change in your life. Amen! Start reading every page of the Bible.

LET US PRAY

Lord, make all things new. Lord, we put on a new man, which is after God. We are created in righteousness and true holiness. We put on Lord Jesus Christ by baptizing in Jesus's name. Our outward man perishes, yet the inward man is renewed daily. Please grant us, according to the riches of your glory. We are strengthened with your might by the Spirit in the inner man, in Jesus 'name. Amen! God bless you!

FEBRUARY

FEBRUARY 1

LORD, SET THE CAPTIVE FREE!

Isaiah 61:1 The Spirit of the Lord GOD is upon me; because the LORD hath anointed me to preach good tidings unto the meek; he hath sent me to bind up the brokenhearted, to proclaim liberty to the captives, and the opening of the prison to them that are bound;

The Bible says that the purpose of Jesus to come in the flesh was to set the imprisoned free. When Jesus was on earth, He spoke to those money-milking religious leaders, saying I set my people free whom you have kept under the bondage of tradition and religion. He said I would pay for what it takes. They are my creations, and you cannot restrain their life by keeping them under your man-made rules, customs, and regulations. He talks straight to those religious leaders of the synagog.

Luke 4:18 The Spirit of the Lord is upon me because he hath anointed me to preach the gospel to the poor; he hath sent me to heal the brokenhearted, to preach deliverance to the captives, and recovering of sight to the blind, to set at liberty them that are bruised,

That day in the synagog fulfilled the prophecy spoken by

Isaiah 42:7 To open the blind eyes, to bring out the prisoners from the prison, and them that sit in darkness out of the prison house.

What is the meaning of captive? A captive is a prisoner inmate, abductee, confined, or locked up. Your freedom disappears if I imprison you. So when you are held captive by whoever, your ability to move or act freely is closed. Praise God! God put on flesh and dwells among His creation for the time being for a reason. To set the captive free is one of the reasons. Freedom is a marvelous experience. Freedom is what God gives us. Many individuals are detained, either in prison, or jail, or restricted to their homes. These individuals are subject to restrictions. Nevertheless, people are also constrained by numerous forms of spirits. Drugs, alcohol, cigarettes, sex, adultery, lies, and all sorts of demon operations constrain God's creation. Devil held captive with the chain of darkness. Egyptians enslaved Hebrews, demonstrating how people can oppress one another. The slave longs for freedom, and it is only through God Almighty that they can be liberated from captivity.

Psalm 126:1 When the Lord turned again the captivity of Zion, we were like them that dream. 2 Then was our mouth filled with laughter, and our tongue with singing: then said they among the heathen, The Lord hath done great things for them. 3 The Lord hath done great things for us; whereof we are glad. 4 Turn again our captivity, O Lord, as the streams in the south.

FEBRUARY 1

My first powerful experience with freedom was in the '80s when I came to the USA. I was hungry and thirsty for the Lord. I was sick and tired of religion. Religion is an illusion. My religion bound me. Go to church not finding the truth, and despite that, I always go to listen to other teachers. I knew there was so much more that God offers. Where is it? I desire it. My marvelous experience when I went under the water in the name of Jesus was to wash away my sins. In the beginning, I fought against this valid baptism with false religious teachings which had bound me. I was angry that I wanted to say no, but the Lord said, you baptize, and the preacher did. Oh my God, I came out so free, light like a feather; I felt I could fly and walk on water in that light. The verse says, Baptize in Jesus 'name, and your sins will be forgiven, which is what happened when I was baptized in Jesus's name.

Acts 2:38a Then Peter said unto them, Repent, and be baptized every one of you in the name of Jesus Christ for the remission of sins;

This truth set me free from religion, false teachers, and prophets. The false doctrine held my mind captive. It was an omnipotent experience when I went underwater in Jesus's name. I was astounded. I have come against the devil; you stop the book of Act by one scripture,

Mathew 28:19, and remove the name where the blood is hidden. You are a liar. I started searching for the truth, and the more I found the truth through revelations, the more I experienced freedom. I am thankful to God that His mercy prevails. How great is the experience of freedom? No more religion! I've visited many places where they try to make me believe that this is the end-all-be-all.

Do not seek anymore; just sit under our false teaching. There is nothing more than this. Let me milk you, and you keep your mouth shut. I don't trust religious authorities. There is more and more and more. Stay away from religion, hypocritical teachers, and deceptive prophets. Seek God. He will lead you, be humble. You'll find liberation from religious beliefs. My past was dominated by religion, but now I have found freedom. I used to think that it was relatively simple to overcome addictions to cigarettes, alcohol, and drugs, but much more difficult, if not impossible, to break free from religion. Why? Your actions, such as reading the Bible, avoiding sin, praying, fasting, and paying tithes, make you think you are not sinning. Hmmm. What we perceive as sin may not align with God's perspective on sin. Two contrasting things! Praise God! His commission will persist as long as true teachers and prophets are willing to fight against the deceitful antichrist spirit of Satan. Remember, you go where their commission is what Jesus entrusted to them, not a social club or just fellowship. Our mission is to set others free through His truth.

LET US PRAY

O Lord, our people are imprisoned in countries by the chains of religion, tradition, and language.

Nahum 1:13 For now will I break his yoke from off thee, and will burst thy bonds in sunder.

Lord, break the yoke off of them, burst the bonds in sunder

Psalm 107:14 He brought them out of the darkness and the shadow of death, and brake their bands in sunder. Lose us from spiritual darkness, customs, false teachers, false prophets, and bondages of lie and deceit.

Psalm 146:7 Which executeth judgment for the oppressed: which giveth food to the hungry. The LORD looseth the prisoners.

ELIZABETH DAS

Deliver us from the power of poverty, sickness, sin, from the lie of the devil. The Lord loses all prisoners in the mighty name of Jesus. You are free from all bondage of generational curses of pressures, arthritis, leprosy, heart attack, blindness, alcohol, diabetes, and afflictions of cancer in the mighty name of Jesus. May the Lord anoint you with His Holy oil and Holy Spirit in the Name of Jesus. Let Lord Jesus set you free. You are free in Jesus 'name! Amen! God Bless you!

FEBRUARY 2
EXAMPLE!

According to Jesus, he will give you an illustration to follow.

1 Peter 2:21 For even hereunto were ye called: because Christ also suffered for us, leaving us an example, that ye should follow his steps:

John 13:15 For even hereunto were ye called: because Christ also suffered for us, leaving us an example, that ye should follow his steps:

Who is Jesus? What's the reason for following His example?

The Bible says, 1 Timothy 3:16 And without controversy great is the mystery of godliness: God was manifest in the flesh,

He is the Spirit God put on flesh to shed the blood and pay the price. He came to do the significant work of defeating the devil. The Bible says God is a spirit, and spirit has no Blood. He clothed himself in human flesh.

Acts 20:28b to feed the church of God, which he hath purchased with his own blood.

God in spirit form took on a physical body to acquire the church through His bloodshed. They sacrifice the lamb Jesus and let His blood flow to pay the price for our sins. There was no sin in the Blood of Jesus. We need the sinless lamb to sacrifice for the cost of our sins. He carried His blood to the Holy place in heaven to redeem us from our sins. Remember, Blood has life. Our blood has sinned.

God loved us and gave an example of His love by laying down His life for us. The example we have is to show love for one another.

Lord Jesus gave an excellent example of how one should follow Him. Jesus in the flesh worked and delivered people from all kinds of sickness, diseases, and brokenness. Despite his righteousness, he dedicated himself to teaching and praying. There was no fault found in Him. To fulfill the plan of God, He died in our place.

He chose different people of the walk, vocation, and ages to follow Him. He gave them the power to do what He wanted to establish His mission. His mission was not to start powerless churches but to call them to carry on what He planned to continue.

ELIZABETH DAS

Luke 9:2 And he sent them to preach the kingdom of God, and to heal the sick.

He dispatched followers to put His teachings into practice.

Matthew 10:8 Heal the sick, cleanse the lepers, raise the dead, cast out devils: freely ye have received, freely give.

Are you continuing His mission or starting your own with a different name and brand label? Are you attending the church and believing I am following Jesus?

During my time in India, I consistently shared my testimony about Jesus with my Hindu friends. They bombarded me with arguments. I had nothing to prove that Jesus is real since I did not experience all the good things the Bible says. What good is your product if you cannot prove it? If you say He can heal, then prove me by healing. If he can raise, let me see some dead rising and deliverance, I would like to see the demon-possessed free.

I had a very argumentative college friend. She always argued with me on this Bible subject. She was one of the college friends who had vehement opposition. I was not disappointed but sought truth to prove to her that Lord Jesus is the only God, but I didn't have power. I never gave up on seeking Him in His power and might.

A day came when I received baptism in the name of Jesus. The weight of a colossal mountain was lifted from my shoulders when I received forgiveness for my sins. The extraordinary power of God is in operation when you use the name Jesus in baptism. It amazed me to feel that lightness and freedom through the saviors' mercy. Then I received the Holy Ghost. It was yet another incredibly powerful experience. The presence of His Spirit in me made me feel like I was nobody. I am like a dot, a tiny dot. You think you are nothing in the presence of our great God. At work, a coworker asked if I had received the Holy Ghost. I was surprised! How did she become aware that I received the spirit of God? She said I could tell seeing the change on your face.

Wow! I have seen the surgery happening in Jesus' name water baptism. Ugly sinners, high on a drug, as they are baptized or receive the Holy Ghost, the significant change comes from within and without.

I wanted to testify to the entire world about my experience. Everyone should know that Christianity is true. Experience yourself since I can't explain the feeling. As per the New Testament, I was born into a Christian family without having a firsthand experience of God. I understood individuals should hunger, thirst, seek, ask, and seek to have all. I am glad I am not a follower of anyone but Jesus. Thank God my parents knew the Lord, but I must follow Jesus.

I was excited. I wanted to turn the world upside down. I wanted to proclaim, Hey, this is real; try the true God and His love.

It was my turn now to follow His example.

Once, God, in His mercy, allowed me to go to India. There I met a lady. She said, did you receive the Holy Spirit? I see the light on your forehead.

During this journey, I met many Hindu friends. I testified to them of receiving the Holy Spirit. I have the power of God in me. One friend said there was a demon in my house. She asked if I could help her. Now, this is my chance to witness. I purchased a Bible for her and instructed her to read it aloud, teaching her about spiritual warfare prayer. Well, the previous night, I slept at her house. Early in the morning, I woke up to noise. I saw her ugly, angry face looking at me, and her hand started growing, came toward me, and disappeared. It became her son's figure then and the same, pointing his hand toward me, and his hand started growing toward me and disappeared. I closed my eyes to make sure I was awake. One afternoon, I was discussing with non-Christian friends my spiritual experience in the US. I was testifying, and one of my friends said, there is a demon in my house; it bothers me a lot. There is no peace in my home. I said I saw it last night; She asked what it looked like. I said it had your and your son's face. She said we fight like cats and dogs; we don't get along. The devil does all this fighting, killing, and disrupting our family. We do not see a spiritual being, so we think it is the one being used. The Bible says I came to give peace, not agitation, distress, or conflict.

She was tired of the demon but did not know what to do. She had the intention to offer food, but her mother-in-law prevented her. Well, I said would you do what I asked you to do? Now this visit was different. God already filled me with the Holy Ghost. So I was laying a hand on people for them to receive healing and deliverance. Devil manifested; many healing in a family, even she experienced healing. She was without excuse. She was desperate for help. I taught her to plead the blood of Jesus in-house and read the Bible out loud. Bind the demon, break its power in Jesus 'name, then command the demon to get out.
It works!

Hallelujah! She did what I taught. Wow! She was free and sent me the letter, telling me the devil was gone from my house. Well, it was a letter-writing era.

I tried to connect her with some people, but as you know, we do not have enough laborers who follow Jesus's example. Sheep require the follower of Jesus's example, not the church. Cast out the demon, heal the sick. Pray for people who continue to follow Jesus's example, not the followers of the churches, organizations, pastors, people, or denominations. He came to give an example. If you and I follow His standard, this world will find light, peace, healing, deliverance, truth, and salvation in Jesus 'name. This is the time of gentiles. How beautiful!

LET US PRAY

Lord Jesus, open our understanding that we follow your example. Lord, we seek freedom and salvation for the entire world. Lord, help us obey and not argue. Help us seek because we will find the faithful Savior. Let you be our way, truth, and life to take us to heaven for eternity. We have nobody but your example to follow. Help us, Lord, in Jesus 'name. Amen! God bless you!

FEBRUARY 3

TREASURE IN EARTHEN VESSELS!

The Bible is full of treasure; all riches are in this book. Once you open it, you can't put it down. I carry many Bibles as I visit places, hospitals, and homes so I can give. I purchase many Bibles to give to those who do not have them.

The Bible is a treasure to own. Many have told me they go to church but never read the Bible or just a little. Some do not own a Bible. I buy the KJV Bible in bulk and carry it in my car. I know all their problems are because of the need for more truth in the world. Truth can set them free. But you need to read to know what is available. I had a spiritual encounter where God conveyed the concept that the Word is God and God is the Word. Read the Word if you want to know God.

Colossians 2:3 In whom (Jesus) are hidden all the treasures of wisdom and knowledge.

Jesus hid all the treasures of knowledge.

The Bible is the book of Jesus. The Bible hides knowledge and wisdom in this book. Nowadays, many theologians know the Word without its application. The application of knowledge is called wisdom. Knowledge and wisdom go together. Like you have a car and do not know how to drive.
Do not entangle yourself on earth with earthly affairs. It will steal your soul.

Matthew 6:19 Lay not up for yourselves treasures upon earth, where moth and rust doth corrupt, and where thieves break through and steal: 20 But lay up for yourselves treasures in heaven, where neither moth nor rust doth corrupt, and where thieves do not break through nor steal: 21 For where your treasure is, there will your heart be as well.

Hidden things are only evident if the Lord intervenes in that matter.

Isaiah 45:3 And I will give thee the treasures of darkness, and hidden riches of secret places, that thou mayest know that I, the LORD, which call [thee] by thy name, [am] the God of Israel.

I know God. I acknowledge Him in all my ways. Jesus is the answer to all trials, sicknesses, and problems. Only He has the knowledge and wisdom to get us out of it if we seek. It is peace of mind that God has all our worries. We do not know how, but we know the Lord does.

Isaiah 33:6 And wisdom and knowledge shall be the stability of thy times, [and] strength of salvation: the fear of the LORD [is] his treasure.

The treasure is hidden within the pages of the Bible. Your power and help book, the book of victory, healing, success, and much more. Your father in heaven has given you to guide and not to misguide. It is a book of life and treasure. Book to live a successful life on earth.

As we know, the greatest is peace and contentment. You can have it all, but if you do not have peace, it is almost impossible to enjoy life. Only Jesus can give peace. Life has many storms. The storm comes not to stay, but in all storms, we need peace.

John 14:27 Peace I leave with you, my peace I give unto you: not as the world giveth, give I unto you. Let not your heart be troubled, neither let it be afraid.

I was visiting India, and my friends 'parents opened their house for me. My friend's mom said, Please do not go anywhere, but stay with me, so I did.

Luke 10:5 And into whatsoever house ye enter, first say, Peace be to this house. 6 And if the son of peace is there, your peace shall rest upon it: if not, it shall turn to you again.

My friend's mother would go in the night for their Hindu meeting, where the Hindu saints or Sadhu would read from their religious books. Many ladies were attending, and this man read and explained from their Hindu book. All the ladies were in search of peace.

Once, I offered to lay a hand and pray. She allowed me to pray. As I lay hand and prayed, she witnessed, I never experience the peace till you lay your hand on me. She was amazed! She was almost 60 and never had experienced the peace of God. I did as the word of God instructed and applied. My knowledge became a treasure. Through the power of the Spirit of God, I can bring her peace when I lay hands.

After this experience, the whole family wanted me to stay with them. They were Hindu, but something they found was beyond. It was peaceful and healing. I ministered to them almost every day, and all lined up for prayer. They wrote every word I spoke in prayer and asked me to teach them how and what to say when they pray. It was a time of revival in a family.

I have the Holy Spirit. It is the treasure in my body.

The Bible says God made a body of dirt,

2 Corinthians 4:7 But we have this treasure in earthen vessels, that the excellency of the power may be of God, not of us.

We can live above and beyond if we have the Spirit of God with knowledge. Knowledge of truth gives us victory, healing deliverance, riches, and success. Many people have the Holy Spirit, but don't know how to use it.

While visiting India in 2015, I met many people and am still connected with them. Every day I teach the Word. They also will tell me about the outcome of using this treasure hidden in the promises of the Word.

A Lady named Haley testified about her work. She did not get a sewing machine in the morning. She waited two hours to start her work while the other coworkers finished two hundred pieces. She was 200 pieces ahead by the evening when she started working on the machine

She said I took the Word of God and claimed for my situation. Run with God's word; it boosts where you apply.

Zechariah 4:6b Not by might, nor by power, but by my spirit, saith the Lord of hosts.

Haley prayed, Lord, let your spirit do all my work. By 4 PM, she was ahead of them by a few hundred pieces. She cashed her promises given in the word by praying and claiming. Do the same and see the power hidden in over five thousand promises of God! Treasure is hidden. Stand on the Word by proclaiming, claiming, and believing. The application, which is the wisdom of knowledge, is called treasure.

Many are against you in battle, but you can win if you stand on the Word and claim it. It is good anytime and for anyone; only you have to claim it.

I teach the new convert. They are faithful and depend for the Lord. They pray for every situation. Call on God, and stand on the Word. Wow. Then they testify the answer to their prayer to coworkers or other families. They see victory, healing, and deliverance and trust in the Lord Jesus. In Jesus is a hidden treasure.

Your testimony is the most potent weapon. It gives the hearer the validity of treasure hidden in the Bible, follows directions, and claims it. Many don't know what they have, and it is hidden. Once you receive it by claiming it, it will become visible. Testify and be light of this hidden treasure.

LET US PRAY

May the Lord reveal to you all your promises. It is for you. Claim it and be free. Decree and declare to get the victory, healing, deliverance, and all you need. Lord, give your creation a believing heart to have knowledge and wisdom of hidden treasure. May the Lord give you all that belongs to you in Jesus's name. Amen! God bless you!

FEBRUARY 4

THEY KNEW HIM NOT!

Have you ever thought about why the Lord chose the system of the word, prayer, Priest, Levi, and now Apostle, pastor, teacher, prophet, and preachers? Altogether, we stay connected with the almighty God throughout every generation. We are applying the word of God in life situations to see the effect of it. The word of God is not for debate or to memorize. God's system connects us with Him for provision, protection, and blessings. Remember, it is all about God and not about anyone.

Lord came to His chosen people, a descendant of Abraham to whom He promised the land. He went to the people to whom the Torah from heaven was delivered. He came to the people for whom he picked true prophets like Samuel by replacing Eli and King David by replacing King Saul. So He can lead and guide people of God's nations. He wanted the world to know that He is a miracle worker, a promise keeper, only true God. But in the end, what happened?

John 1:11 He came unto his own, and his own received him not.gain rejection!

Are your rulers and authority like this?

John 7:48 Have any of the rulers or the Pharisees believed in him? Do you mean no one from temple leaders and authorities believed in Jesus whom they worshiped? How did they become blind, and what caused them blindness?

Have mercy! People in temple services, from Aaron to the coming of Jesus, were mind-blowing scenarios. The following scriptures describe them.

John 12:37 But though he had done so many miracles before them, yet they believed not on him: 38 That the saying of Esaias the prophet might be fulfilled, which he spake, Lord, who hath believed our report? and to whom hath the arm of the Lord been revealed? 39 Therefore they could not believe, because Esaias said again, 40 He hath blinded their eyes, and hardened their heart; that they should not see with their eyes, nor understand with their heart, and be converted, and I should heal them.

Why did God have to send John the Baptist, who had the spirit of Elijah? Because corrupted rulers were blocking God's work.

What is the situation today? God's service is done in the Temple in Jerusalem back then versus church services in an era of God's dispensation today. His spirit must operate spiritual work. There should not be any personal interest unless you are completely blind and deaf, as Isaiah says.

ELIZABETH DAS

Let me share my experience.

Years ago, I attended a particular church. There was much favoritism, bias, and unrighteousness that I saw. I came from India, so I believed my position must be respected. I was blind since I thought church authority was the most trustworthy and righteous. Even though I saw and experienced it, I still trusted the title and believed they couldn't be wrong. I felt everything they said, thinking it had to be from God. But my spirit did not agree. Later in the years, they started backsliding in their heart. Jesus said follow me, and the devil started hundreds of new denominations and non-denominations; what is that?

All that they taught wrong became right. I started seeing the pressure against righteous, indirect, and direct opposition and knew it was real. I told myself to wake up. You either please them or receive harassment and beaten up for standing for the truth. I could not get out until God got me out.

I started praying and fasting more and more just to survive. I started seeing the spiritual world. Remember, it is not the outer force, but the inner force that will ruin you. Only God knows what happened, but that church becomes a man's follower. It doesn't matter what title they hold, King, Ruler of Synagog, priest, pastor, or high priest; after all, they are human. God made them of clay called humanity. If church authority changes, run from them under the Holy Ghost's direction.

I noticed I came home from the church oppressed. I shared this with a church sister who was a prayer warrior. One early morning we came to church to pray. I went to the front, and she went back to pray. I stood at the altar, put my hand on the podium, and prayed, Lord, put righteous here. Guess what? I saw a man sitting on the pulpit who looked exactly like the pastor. He got up and pushed me. I went backward and almost fell. Now, who would believe me if I told them? Once you turn the eyes away from God and make them human worshipers, they become blind and deaf. Many knew but had no guts to come against church authorities.

I have experienced much evil in the church as it was going toward darkness. Once the prayer is removed and watered down the fasting, then you have your agenda. You only can convince people, but not God. The form of religion is dangerous. God's work will never be destroyed by outer force but by inner force.

After prayer, I shared my experience with my prayer partner, and the same day, she shared what she saw. She saw an arrogant blond woman in a silky dress touching everywhere. She turned her face. Her face was like a lizard's. Wow! A spirit of Jezebel! Now, remember, we both were alone in the church.

I know about the spiritual world. As you know Spiritual World has many beings. People who die lost become a demon called Pneuma. The demon has no power unless going into the body. Remember the legion demon who wanted to go into the swine?

Now fallen angels, unholy angels, cannot come into your body. They are a powerful spiritual entity. They work as generals or overseers for the devil. This angel can do so many supernatural things. It can take any form, shape, and look. Fallen angels can move items around and do mighty things. Just like God's Holy Angel can do many things. That morning, God told me to go on fasting, and my friend said God asked her to fast as well. I said, let's do it, or there is no way we can survive. God has the right direction. We must follow His way of victory.

God started with Moses until the rejection of God's monarchy by asking for the king was mind-boggling. The situation was the same when the Lord Jesus came onto the earth—rejecting God again and following blind leaders. The teacher will bring great calamity and destruction when a position is filled with an unrighteous, power-hungry, jealous, greedy priest, preacher, or pastor. Open your eyes. Who are you following, God or Satan-operated authority? Wake up. We serve the mighty God who said I would share my glory with no man. Remember, you follow authority as long as you are following God. If not, then run from them.

So how can you be secured in this situation? Just believe in the unchangeable Word of God, which has been tried seven times and will not change. Listen to the Spirit of God; He will lead and guide you. Pray and fast; you will be safe with Him.

LET US PRAY

I pray, Lord, open our eyes and ears, so we see and hear His voice. May the Lord give divine intervention to you and your family's souls! We can escape from times like this with His righteousness. Lord, give us direction by His Spirit. Give you true prophets and teachers in Jesus's name. Amen! God bless you!

FEBRUARY 5

ARE YOU CHARGED UP?

What happens when you pray? When you pray, your spirit connects with God's Spirit. God will supply energy power, and you will be charged up again. You can charge up if you pray. The flesh needs to connect with God to charge.

The Bible says, first, pray. Prayer connects us to the Spirit of God. With that, you can work.

1 Thessalonians 5:17 pray without ceasing.

If you have a phone or any electronics, it needs a connection with electricity to charge. After charging, you can use it again. Your body, spirit, and soul must also be charged to work for the Lord.

Jesus being God, He prayed? Why? The flesh needs to charge up to get help or to work.

Psalms 65:2 O thou that hearest prayer, unto thee shall all flesh come.

If you need help from God, you must connect your body and soul Spirit with Him. Prayer is that connection.

Luke 3:21 Jesus also being baptized, and praying; the heaven was opened.

If the phone is charged, it can connect with the world via the internet. Praying it will set you to connect with the heavenly or spiritual realm.

Matthew 14:23a And when he had sent the multitudes away, he went up into a mountain apart to pray:

Remember, the flesh needs to charge up. Jesus prayed to charge up after He sent out a multitude. Just like the battery needs to recharge again after use.

That is why you need to pray. All flesh must pray. If not charged, then you would not know the direction of God. God in heaven gives us guidance and help.

We must know different kinds of prayer. I will talk about some of them.

1 Timothy 2:1 I exhort, therefore, that, first of all, supplications, prayers, intercessions, and giving of thanks, be made for all men; 2 For kings, and for all that are in authority; that we may lead a quiet and peaceable life in all godliness and honesty. 3 For this is good and acceptable in the sight of God our Saviour;

FEBRUARY 5

There are many types of prayer. There is a prayer where the Spirit of God will intercede for the unknown matter.

Roman 8:26 Likewise, the spirit also helpeth our infirmities: for we know not what we should pray for as we ought: but the spirit itself maketh intercession for us with groanings which cannot be uttered. 27 And he that searcheth the hearts knoweth what is the mind of the spirit, because he maketh intercession for the saints according to the will of God.

God in heaven above knows our flesh has a limitation. If His Spirit charges us up, it will search like internet searches. This all is available if you charge up by praying connection with God.

Acts 4:31 And when they had prayed, the place was shaken where they were assembled together; and they were all filled with the Holy Ghost, and they spake the word of God with boldness.

Charge up, pray, get connected, and see what happens.

2 Chronicles 7:1 Now when Solomon had made an end of praying, the fire came down from heaven, and consumed the burnt offering and the sacrifices; and the glory of the LORD filled the house. 2 And the priests could not enter into the house of the LORD, because the glory of the LORD had filled the LORD'S house.

When I was very sick from 1999 through 2003, I prayed day and night. One evening, I completed my first audio recording and put a CD in a player to play. It was a Bible teaching CD. I went backward in my motorized wheelchair to listen. I saw the house was gone and could not find the wall or kitchen. It was a scary moment; I thought I had lost my vision. But in the thick cloud, I saw Jesus smiling at me.
God descended into a thick cloud in my house.

1 King 8:11 So that the priests could not stand to minister because of the cloud: for the glory of the LORD had filled the house of the LORD."The LORD has said that he would dwell in thick darkness.

By charging through prayer, you get connected with the Holy God. No other way but by worship!

Jesus knew the trial was hard and unbearable, so He charged up ahead of time.

Luke 22:41 And he was withdrawn from them about a stone's cast and kneeled down, and prayed 43 And there appeared an angel unto him from heaven, strengthening him.

The flesh can block you from connecting with God. It has a limit to see so far. Flesh gets tired, worried, fearful, and confused seeing a situation. As you connect with heaven, it will charge your flesh and spirit to revive, gain strength, and victory. Disciples fell asleep and failed the trial, even though Jesus asked them to pray. What about us? Do we pray without ceasing? Do we pray first?

Daniel plugged in three times a day and charged up to stay connected.

Daniel 6:10 Now when Daniel knew that the writing was signed, he went into his house; and his windows being open in his chamber toward Jerusalem, he kneeled upon his knees three times a day, and prayed, and gave thanks before his God, as he did aforetime

That is why God used Daniel since he was charged up. He had power beyond measure through prayer connection.

Daniel 1:20 And in all matters of wisdom and understanding, that the king inquired of them, he found them ten times better than all the magicians and astrologers that were in all his realm.

People who connect with God know heavenly activities. Our help comes from God only if you learn to connect. Who would not like the help, victory, strength, healing, and joy of salvation?

Please be charged up by the prayer. Get connected with heaven to intervene in all problems, and see what happens. All our Christians, home, and family pray as it says in the Bible. Then what can happen? Righteous prayer works wonders in heaven to bring revolution to the earth.

Revelation 8:3 And another angel came and stood at the altar, having a golden censer; and there was given unto him much incense, that he should offer it with the prayers of all saints upon the golden altar which was before the throne. 4 And the smoke of the incense, which came with the prayers of the saints, ascended before God out of the angel's hand. 5 And the angel took the censer, and filled it with the fire of the altar, and cast it into the earth: and there were voices, and thunderings, and flashes of lightning, and an earthquake.

Can you visualize the charging with prayer? If not, you see gangs, killing, shooting, jail, a prison filled up, divorcing, darkness, depression, kidnapping, lies, deception, and all kinds of sin over the land. First, pray, pray without ceasing to charge up.

LET US PRAY

The Lord gives us a spirit of prayer, an understanding of prayer to pray. Help us teach our children and their children to pray without ceasing. Prayer will charge us, empower us, refresh and restore us. Lord, help us reschedule our life and order in your ways and plan. We are weary, losing hope, and dying in despair. Help us remove all business and start again by reconnecting and charging our life in Jesus's name. Amen! God bless you!

FEBRUARY 6

GOD IS IRREPLACEABLE!

God is Irreplaceable, meaning He is valuable, priceless, unrepeatable, incomparable, and unique.

Satan's all wishes are to

2 Thessalonians 2:4 Who opposeth and exalteth himself above all that is called God, or that is worshipped; so that he as God sitteth in the temple of God, shewing himself that he is God.

Notice what the devil is doing from the beginning? The devil labels his name on God's products and tries to make others believe he did all. I have experienced the same. Someone stamped their name when I worked overseas or even in the US after I finished. I spent my time and money, and it does not mention my name anywhere. They put their name and photo on my work. If one has a question about how they can contact me? It is God's work, and glory only goes to God. The Devil does precisely like that.

Remember, people who like to get glory are unaware of God's greatness. If they know God, then they will always give God glory.

At the place I was fellowshipping in Dallas when people get healed, get word of knowledge, prophecy, or deliverance, the pastor turns around and says, it was Jesu who did this, not me. In the beginning, I thought I and everyone knew Jesus could do all and no one else. Why does the Pastor have to keep saying, Jesus did this? But now I understand the Pastor has many gifts of the Spirit and God entrusts him with all since he gives God glory.

I want to share important information. I mean any organization; the devil wants you to get their title and name when you join the company. Why? So your labor can make money for them by labeling their name. Also, they go around and use your work by saying we started this church, a company, an orphanage, a school, or a hospital. Wait on God, Don't go after the crumbs. Trust God; He will supply your needs.

When God took away my job in the year 2000, He clearly said you take the little-retired check and not the other option I had where I get double. So I obeyed His voice. Seeing I was not getting enough to pay house notes. So in my calculation, I did not have enough money to pay other utilities, food, and all other bills. But God said you work for me, and I will take care of you. I heard this certainly. He was hiring me to His vineyard. He was taking all my responsibilities. I never look for another way but for God's provision. I have witnessed that from 2000 to now; I have not worked but for the Lord. The Lord has provided me.

According to Philippians 4:19 But my God shall supply all your need according to his riches in glory by Christ Jesus.

Promises given through His Word and His promise to take care of me brought peace and assurance.

Earthly benefits, money, prosperity, wealth, and position have replaced our faith in God. I see people who want to work for God and constantly worry about money. You work for Jesus only if you have faith. He will supply as He has promised.

There was a time when I struggled to pay bills and was worried. When I get busy with the kingdom, I do not remember my problem. He comes through on time. I see the most significant problem: people sell their more enormous blessings for crumbs. If people depend on The Lord, the provision will come from His riches, not crumbs. Do not settle for less.

I got many offers from church organizations with their condition. They said that if you do exactly what we ask, we will help you. Really? Who gave me the spirit of healing, prophecy, miracle, the power to cast demons out? God gave, not them. I was not looking for crumbs.

Daniel had an order not to worship His God for 30 days but for King Darius. Daniel did not worship Darius, the King. Well, the King promoted him to his province.

Daniel 6:3 Then this Daniel was preferred above the presidents and princes because an excellent spirit was in him, and the king thought to set him over the whole realm.

Now a stumbling block and temptation were set up against Daniel to demote to remove. Daniel refused to worship the king. Daniel knew,

Psalm 75: 6 For promotion cometh neither from the east, nor from the west, nor from the south. 7 But God is the judge: he putteth down one, and setteth up another.

Daniel never wavered in his faith! Daniel knew his God and had a direct relationship with Him. As you sell or compromise yourself for the country, positions, jobs, promotions, churches, organizations, or government, you have replaced God for them. Daniel was single-minded. If you compromise for the crumb, little money, or any favor, then you have replaced God. That's what the lying devil says; I will take His seat and be like most High.

Isaiah 14:14 I will ascend above the heights of the clouds; I will be like the most High.

Devil is a trickster. All his plans are destructive. I know it is tough to live for God, but He has only called the one who is bold and courageous and made up his mind.

They crucified the lust.

Galatians 5:24 And they that are Christ's have crucified the flesh with the affections and lusts.

Do you see? How does God want you to follow Him? Look at Jesus. Zero in your gaze at Jesus. Help, promotion, strength, and provisions come from God. The trial prepares your testimony if you respond in spirit, but compromising with your flesh has destruction and demotion.

Remember, God will pay all your labor off in heaven. John the Baptist had nothing. Jesus has no place to lay

His head. To others, He said, seek my kingdom, and I will give you free for what you are toiling. You will receive it all without replacing me. The devil's offer comes with toiling and death.

Matthew 6:34 Take therefore no thought for the morrow: for the morrow shall take thought for the things of itself. Sufficient unto the day is the evil thereof.

When Jesus sent out people, did they lack anything?

Luke 22:35 And he said unto them When I sent you without purse, and scrip, and shoes, lacked ye anything? And they said, Nothing.

If you know God, you will be fearless. But if you sell yourself for money or favor to any church, organization, job, or profession, then remember you are their slave. You work, and they will take credit to make money by putting on their brand label. In return, they will give you crumbs. Glory goes to God by depending on Him.

I want my supply from heaven. There is a mansion in heaven. I never worry about them taking credit for my labor since the Bible says:

1 Timothy 5:18b "The laborer is worthy of his reward."

Joseph was on top. He did not give an inch to the devil and was not afraid of prison or being sold as a slave.

Friends, Jesus is your provider. He alone gets all glory.

Matthew 6:19 Lay not up for yourselves treasures upon earth, where moth and rust doth corrupt, and where thieves break through and steal: 20 But lay up for yourselves treasures in heaven, where neither moth nor rust doth corrupt, and where thieves do not break through nor steal Heaven is real, and so is God. Do not depend on anyone but Jesus. He has called, then He governs all your needs, not some, but all.

I have labored day and night in the vineyard of God all these years. I am a witness that He is the only one who is trustworthy.

For Moses, King David, Daniel, Peter Paul, and many who depended on Him gave glory to His might and power. They never compromised or crumbs. I know it is so true. Jesus is an unchanging God. I see everything around me is changing. The trial prepares your testimony if you respond in spirit, but compromising with your flesh has destruction and demotion. Decide your destiny and where you want to spend the rest of eternity. He is not replaceable, as many may think. There is a God who shows you supernatural power. He will promote you where you can only replace yourself. Wait on Irreplaceable God Jesus.

LET US PRAY

Lord, help us keep our eyes on Jesus. Let us see two fish multiply. The supply of manna from heaven, oil, and flour's miracle. In famine, dry land gave 100 times more crops. Lord, we need you and your provision. Please give us all that belongs to us to provide you with glory and you alone. We want an Irreplaceable Jesus for our provision in Jesus 'name. Amen! God bless you!

FEBRUARY 7

THE BODY IS THE CARRIER OF THE SPIRIT!

What is Spirit? The basic meaning is wind. Breath is also a basic word for spirit.

Spirit needs the body. If there is nobody for the spirit, it becomes powerless. There is a beautiful spirit called the Holy Spirit, and evil spirits are called evil spirits. Spirit governs our natural world. You are carrying either the Holy Spirit or the evil spirit.

Once I saw the preacher was casting the evil spirit out. He requested to please leave if you are not born again. Because the spirit will need the body to carry on its work. The Evil Spirit works under Satan's stealing, killing, and destruction.

James 2:26 For as the body without the spirit is dead, When the spirit leaves the body, the flesh is dead. If a person dies lost, then the spirit goes under Satan's control. Satan will use those spirits against its family members.

That is why you need the Holy Spirit baptism so God can do His work through you. God also needs the body since He is the Spirit. Yield to the Holy Spirit, please.

For example, if the demon of alcohol enters someone's body, it will make the person drink. Formerly, the demon had a body, now craving alcohol, drugs, food, water, etc. He needs a body to satisfy the craving.

One time I heard that an alcoholic father died, and the demon of alcohol entered his son's body and made him an alcoholic. Same with the cigarette, drug, lie, sex, murder, anger, schizophrenia, bipolar, and strange spirit will work as they enter the body. The evil spirit is a destructive force. By entering, one's body carries on its work. Do not yield the wrong spirit.

Nowadays, we are ignorant of the spirit world. Satan is having a revival in churches. Ignorance is the weapon of Satan against us.

Hosea 4:6 My people are destroyed for lack of knowledge: because thou hast rejected knowledge, I will also reject thee, that thou shalt be no priest to me: seeing thou hast forgotten the law of thy God, I will also forget thy children.

When Jesus was on earth, evil spirits knew Him and witnessed; we know who you are.

Mark 1:24 Says, Let us alone; what have we to do with thee, thou Jesus of Nazareth? Art thou come to destroy us? I know thee who thou art, the Holy One of God.

Spirit makes your body alive, *John 6:63 It is the spirit that quickeneth; the flesh profiteth nothing: the words that I speak unto you, they are spirit, and they are life.*

Quickeneth means to make a living.

It is evident when you cast out demons of alcohol, drugs, lies, and killing flesh; then a person will be free. The body is a carrier of spirit. Spirit needs the body.

Psalm 1:1 Blessed is the man that walketh not in the counsel of the ungodly, nor standeth in the way of sinners, nor sitteth in the seat of the scornful.

When you keep company with an ungodly, sinner, or scornful, their spirit will jump on you, just like you do not keep bad mango with good. The body needs to get rid of waste, and evil spirits by obeying the instructions given in the Bible. Pray and fast; fast correctly as instructed in the Bible, no food, no water. No shortcut. Lord Jesus did not take a shortcut.

When my friend went to the hallway in my house, she said she felt a chill. So I prayed, Lord, whatever spirit entered here must get out of my house. After praying, I played a Bible CD in-house. In my dream, I saw a demon of an Arab man walking out of the door and looking to another part of the house but could not enter. Sometimes people come to our place; unknowingly, they carry spirits. And they leave the house, dropping the spirit. I have many experiences with spirits.

I have the habit of anointing my house with holy oil daily. The anointing will break that spirit. Oil represents the Holy Spirit. The Bible is a working-out book. Before, the priest used to anoint, and now we are the priest of the Lord, having His Spirit in us. We must anoint our body, home, food, water, land, tree, school, office, cars, etc. I go around anoint, schools, parks, malls, stores, and every place where I go. The evil spirit's job is to work for the devil, who knows how to steal, kill, and destroy.

John 10:10 The thief cometh not, but for to steal, and to kill, and to destroy:

If they do not cast these demons out, they will do what it says in the Bible, steal your money, kidney, mind, city, county, and life. A good nation becomes poor. How and why? Because they allow false gods, goddesses, witches, warlocks, Satanists, psychics, and other media to reject the Holy Spirit. These demons will swamp the country to destroy it.

Only God knows the truth. Do not go to familiar spirits, witches, or warlocks for help and information. They are working for the Devil, called the kingdom of darkness.

Do you want to be cursed? The family they do devilishly and evil will be destroyed. God will deliver them to Satan for destruction.

2 Chronicles 10:13 So Saul died for his transgression which he committed against the LORD, even against the word of the LORD, which he kept not, and also for asking counsel of one that had a familiar spirit, to enquire of it;

God knows the demon provides no remedy. It will provide information without a solution. Only your heavenly Father can help if you allow Him. Do not go to the wrong medium.

2 Chronicles 33:6 And he caused his children to pass through the fire in the valley of the son of Hinnom: also he observed times, and used enchantments, and used witchcraft, and dealt with a familiar spirit, and with wizards: he wrought much evil in the sight of the Lord, to provoke him to anger.

Leviticus 20:6 And the soul that turneth after such as have familiar spirits, and after wizards, to go a whoring after them, I will even set my face against that soul and will cut him off from among his people.

Leviticus 20:27 A man also or woman that hath a familiar spirit, or that is a wizard, shall surely be put to death: they shall stone them with stones: their blood shall be upon them.

God never changes. God has accurate information to stay away from evil. If you get help from the dark kingdom, you will be destroyed. The spiritual world is something that I deal with. I know some who are connected with evil spirits. I have observed their end, which was sad and wrong. They think they are winning. Remember, we have the power to bind evil spirits, destroy them, and cast them out. God is greater in His power. He came to give an example so we could follow. Now He wants to stay in our body as the Holy Spirit. The Holy Spirit has mighty power, the legions of the evil spirit.

There is a doctrine of Satan, teaching that you have the Holy Spirit when you accept the Lord Jesus as your savior. God wrote it in the book of Acts. You will speak in the tongue when you receive the Holy Spirit. God created your body for His residence. The Holy Spirit will make a great living in you. Allow and yield to the Spirit of God and see what it does through you.

John 14:12a Verily, verily, I say unto you, He that believeth on me, the works that I do shall he do; and greater works than these shall he do;18 I will not leave you comfortless: I will come to you.

Acts 1:8 But ye shall receive power, after that the Holy Ghost is come upon you: and ye shall be witnesses unto me both in Jerusalem, and in all Judaea, and in Samaria, and unto the uttermost part of the earth.

LET US PRAY

May the Lord give you the heart to serve Him! May the Holy Spirit live in your body. Allow the Spirit of God to do mighty through you. Let this world know that the Holy Spirit is the only power we need. I pray that we all follow the book of Acts church, not false teachers and prophets. Let the Lord empower us through His Spirit. Lord, give everyone the nine gifts of the Spirit. Spirit does all-powerful work through us. We need the Gift of the Spirit to edify the church. Please grant your Spirit, Lord, in Jesus's name. Amen! God Bless you!

FEBRUARY 8

DO YOU WONDER WHAT HAPPENED TO PEOPLE?

What brought a significant change in Christianity? Is it Hollywood, Bollywood, media, games, or worldly music? I worked with different cultures, colors, nationalities, and countries. I noticed the drastic change among Christians, cities, and nations. What happened?

I traveled to India a few years ago and was shocked. I met the same people with a significant change. I mean, the person I knew is no longer the same. Many become liars, stealers, tearers, gossipers, fighters, or a person filled with jealousy and pride, etc., you name it. I could not understand what had happened to them. They all want to look like movie stars. They all think they are a millionaire but can't spend a penny on others. These people have no interest in God, but they go to their denomination building and hold influential positions. Little promotions made them arrogant and prideful. Divorce and adultery in a married couple are common in the religious world.

I thought, who would like to go to these places to visit?

I started questioning God about what brought such a drastic change to the nation. I asked the Lord, what happened? I found the missing part, called repentance of sins. Sin disconnects us from God. We must know what sin is in the eyes of God. God hates sin. That is why the first thing John Baptist said. If you want your relationship with the Creator to be restored, then

Mathew 3:2 And saying, Repent ye: for the kingdom of heaven is at hand.

After that came, Jesus said,

Matthew 4:17 From that time Jesus began to preach, and to say, Repent: for the kingdom of heaven is at hand.

Then Jesus picked 12 men and taught them what to preach.

Mark 6:7 And he called unto him the twelve, and began to send them forth by two and two; 12 And they went out, and preached that men should repent.

What did Peter say on the day of Pentecost?

Acts 2:38 Peter replied, "Repent and be baptized, every one of you;

Once you repent of all your sins, the broken bridges of your relationship with God will be repaired. If you do not repent of your sins, then according to the Word of God,

John 8:24 I said therefore unto you, that ye shall die in your sins:

What is sin? Sins are mentioned in the following scriptures you have to repent of,

Galatians 5:19 Now the works of the flesh are manifest, which are these; Adultery, fornication, uncleanness, lasciviousness, 20 Idolatry, witchcraft, hatred, variance, emulations, wrath, strife, seditions, heresies, 21 Envyings, murders, drunkenness, revellings, and such like: of the which I tell you before, as I have also told you in time past, that they which do such things shall not inherit the kingdom of God.

Every day I pray against sin and to stay clean within. I wash in the blood. I have also been baptized in Jesus' name to wash away my sins in the blood. Under the name of Jesus is the blood of the Lamb. Blood will remit our sins. I also take communion every day for the forgiveness of my sins. Communion should be wine, not grape juice, and unleavened bread.

If not, then remember, Romans 6:23 For the wages of sin is death;

Here, death is the eternal death of our soul in hell because of sin. The flesh is mortal, but the soul is immortal.

Sin will cause sickness in your body,

Psalm 103:2 Bless the Lord, O my soul, and forget not all his benefits:3 Who forgiveth all thine iniquities; who healeth all thy diseases;4 Who redeemeth thy life from destruction; who crowneth thee with lovingkindness and tender mercies;

Sin will give the free pass to Satan to kill, steal, and destroy you. Repent is meant to turn away from your sins. Have you heard people say, I am born like this? That is my nature; I cannot change. It does not give you a license to sin. All have sinned, so we all need to repent of each sin and get cleaned up by baptizing in Jesus' name, and we will have a new conscience.

1Peter 3:21 The like figure whereunto even baptism doth also now save us (not the putting away of the filth of the flesh, but the answer of a good conscience toward God,) by the resurrection of Jesus Christ:

People who are spiritually blind think everyone else is terrible but themselves. Because they attend religious church, pay tithes, and warm up a seat, they are good. Jesus came to let us know what sin is and what it costs Him. It costs Him His life, which is in the blood. He shed His blood by crucifying.

1 John 3:8 He that committeth sin is of the devil; for the devil sinneth from the beginning. For this purpose, the Son of God was manifested, that he might destroy the devil's works.

Repentance is a gift from God by acknowledging the truth.

2Timothy 2:25 In meekness instructing those that oppose themselves; if God peradventure will give them repentance to the acknowledging of the truth;

Romans 2:4 Or despisest thou the riches of his goodness and forbearance and longsuffering; not knowing that the goodness of God leadeth thee to repentance?

Jesus gave the spirit of repentance to Israel.

Acts 5:31 Him hath God exalted with his right hand to be a Prince and a Saviour, to give repentance to Israel, and forgiveness of sins.

Acts 11:18 When they heard these things, they held their peace, and glorified God, saying, Then hath God also to the Gentiles granted repentance unto life.

If we have a similar spirit like Jeroboam, power, and position hungry, then we will also remove the teaching of God.

1 Kings 12:31 And he made an house of high places, and made priests of the lowest of the people, which were not of the sons of Levi. 13:33 After this thing Jeroboam returned not from his evil way, but made again of the lowest of the people priests of the high places: whosoever would, he consecrated him, and he became one of the priests of the high places.

These false teachers and prophets are tare, raising goats and not sheep.

2 Peter 2:1 - But there were false prophets also among the people, even as there shall be false teachers among you, who privily shall bring in damnable heresies, even denying the Lord that bought them, and bring upon themselves swift destruction.

Matthew 7:15 - Beware of false prophets, which come to you in sheep's clothing, but inwardly they are ravening wolves.

2 Timothy 4:3 For the time will come when they will not endure sound doctrine; but after their own lusts shall they heap to themselves teachers, having itching ears; 4 And they shall turn away [their] ears from the truth, and shall be turned unto fables.

False teachers and prophets will bring darkness.

1 John 4:1 Beloved, believe not every spirit, but try the spirits whether they are of God: because many false prophets are gone out into the world.

Do not miss a step called repentance, which is the acknowledgment of sin in the eyes of God. The devil does not give you freedom; sin has a chain of darkness. You will be taken to hell by this chain, where there is no light and no way out.

John 1:17 For the law was given by Moses, but grace and truth came by Jesus Christ.

Repentance is a 180-degree turn against your former walk and talk. David's sin of adultery killed Uriah, Paul killed many Christians, and Peter denied Jesus. After all, they repented and found His mercy and grace. A woman anointed Jesus's feet. Simon considered her a sinner, but she repented.

Luke 7:47 Wherefore I say unto thee, Her sins, which are many, are forgiven; for she loved much: but to whom little is forgiven, the same loveth little. 48 And he said unto her, Thy sins are forgiven. 50 And he said to the woman, Thy faith hath saved thee; go in peace.

Be bold and courageous to come to the altar of God no matter where you are. Repent and ask God to forgive your sins. All will turn around. Amen!

LET US PRAY

The Lord who came not to preach the easy gospel. But the good news of salvation is the deliverance from sin. Sin results in sickness and poverty. Please give us the spirit of repentance. Bless us with salvation. May the Lord give us true prophets and teachers to lead sheep beside the still water. May the Lord give us many laborers to work God's agenda! Repent of all our sins. May the Lord God meet us at the road of Damascus to confront us of our self-righteousness! May the Lord send us bold prophets like John the Baptist and Nathan, who are not afraid of any power but the power of God and say this is wrong, and thou art the man. Lord, give us the spirit of repentance and freedom from sins, in Jesus's name. Amen! God bless you!

FEBRUARY 9

CONSISTENCY IS OMNIPOTENT!

What is the definition of consistency? It is uniformity, regularity, and stability. The Bible says Daniel prayed three times a day. He was consistent!

Omnipotent? Omnipotent meant all-powerful, almighty, supreme. omni=all Potent=powerful

Daniel 6:10 Now when Daniel knew that the writing was signed, he went into his house; and his windows being open in his chamber toward Jerusalem, he kneeled upon his knees three times a day, and prayed, and gave thanks before his God, as he did aforetime.

Because of His constancy and stability, Daniel was ready to meet God in any condition. God also proved that He is omnipotent. He rescued Daniel from the mouth of the Lion.

Would you hire an employee who does not show up at work regularly, even though they may have the best of the best skill? Let us see Solomon. God chose him, a very skillful and wisest king.

But in the end,

Nehemiah 13:26 Did not Solomon, king of Israel, sin by these things? Yet among many nations was there no king like him, who was beloved of his God, and God made him king over all Israel: nevertheless, even him did outlandish women cause to sin.

Remember, keeping first things and staying in order with God will prove God as omnipotent and all-powerful.

In a personal career, employment, commerce, and dealing need uniformity. So does an operation of Omnipotent power need uniformity?

Psalm 102:27 But thou art the same, and thy years shall have no end.

Hebrews 13:8 Jesus Christ the same yesterday, and today, and forever. God has power over everything. He is consistent. We have choices to make. Our choices impact our future and generations after us. David was consistent in his worship. David prayed three times a day. In his trouble, God delivered him.

No one could overthrow King David. No external or internal forces can work against consistent people.

How can you call someone who hardly prays? Maybe they are in the movie, golfing or doing everything else but praying. I do not think anyone would call me if my prayer life had no constancy.

Psalms 55:17 Evening, and morning, and at noon, will I pray, and cry aloud: and he shall hear my voice.

We do not have to look for the sun, moon, or seasons. God is there to take care of day and night with daylight and night light. Dependable employees get the promotion; if not get fired. God is looking for those who stay connected with the Lord. We lose connection by choosing other things.

Malachi 3:6 For I am the LORD, I change not; therefore ye sons of Jacob are not consumed.

Psalms 102:27 But thou art the same, and thy years shall have no end. If you know He is the same all the time, you will not get depressed, despairing, worried, and wondering. First, let us pray and pray without ceasing. Nothing is more important than consistency in our lifestyle, talking, and walking with God. Man lies, but not God. His uniformity and regularity are from the beginning to eternity.

Numbers 23:19 God is not a man that he should lie; neither the son of man, that he should repent: hath he said, and shall he not do it? Or hath he spoken, and shall he not make it good?

Abraham had stability in his walk with God. He never questioned why, what, and when. He said, yes, Lord, I am ready. The Lord proved His power.

Genesis 12:2,3 And I will make of thee a great nation, and I will bless thee, and make thy name great, and thou shalt be a blessing:

Because of David's continual walk with God, David received the promise of the Messiah to come through His bloodline.

Psalms 72:17 His name shall endure forever: his name shall be continued as long as the sun: and men shall be blessed in him: all nations shall call him blessed.

Remember, you have an assignment from God as you turn to God. You also can achieve blessings if you are consistent in your calling. If you follow His laws and commandments, you will have special promises because you are reliable in caring for God's business.

I know a pastor who has many spiritual gifts since his walk with God is constant. I have seen him in the valley. Now it is the other way around. He is on top of the mountain. His sons stopped taking drugs and are now settled down. His grandchildren are winning many trophies, but no place to put them. Grandchildren are number one in academics, music, and games. How do these grandchildren achieve blessings? His wife said since Grandpa goes around and prays for people, people receive healing deliverance in Jesus 'name.

Your consistency receives blessings for you and generations after. Be constant in your assignment from God. Pray without ceasing, preach the gospel, cast out the demon, and heal the sick to see your reward.

Above all, I choose God. He has brought me out of many trials and troubles. He entrusted me with many spiritual gifts. I can keep these spiritual gifts as long as I have a stable and steady walk and talk with God. You can receive all promises and show the World that God is omnipotent by walking steadily in His Word.

FEBRUARY 9

LET US PRAY

Our Lord of Heaven gives you consistency in your godly walk and holy lifestyle. May you be the mighty prayer warrior; pray without ceasing. May the Lord find you faithful in all assignments. The Lord needs the laborer willing to hear and carry on God's command. May the Lord find the trust for Him within us. The Lord does all, but He needs someone faithful in His affair on the earth. Lord, I am available. Lord, make me faithful in Jesus 'Name. Amen! God Bless you!

FEBRUARY 10

CONTINUE THE LORD'S MISSION!

Jesus has shown the way to follow Him. Thank you, Lord. The most outstanding example He gave was walking on the path to show us what it takes to start and continue His mission on earth. If we follow the path of Jesus, people will find life through the truth.

Redemption of a soul is the plan and thought in His mind. He never took the shortcut. He did it all the way.

The word of God can come alive if we put it into action. If not, then it is powerless. Quicken means Made alive, To become active. Quickening means giving life. When you do as scripture says, the Word comes alive. Many preach about prayer, but what happens if they practically start praying? If we fast as it is written in the Word, the demon oppressed and possessed will be set free.

Let us see what Jesus says in the following scripture. As we know, the Word of God can come alive only if we do it.

Matthew 17:14 And when they were come to the multitude, there came to him a certain man, kneeling down to him, and saying, 15 Lord, have mercy on my son: for he is lunatic, and sore vexed: for oftimes he falleth into the fire, and oft into the water. 16 And I brought him to thy disciples, and they could not cure him. 17 Then Jesus answered and said, O faithless and perverse generation, how long shall I be with you? how long shall I suffer you? bring him hither to me. 18 And Jesus rebuked the devil; and he departed out of him: and the child was cured from that very hour. 19 Then came the disciples to Jesus apart, and said, Why could not we cast him out? 20 And Jesus said unto them, Because of your unbelief: for verily I say unto you, If ye have faith as a grain of mustard seed, ye shall say unto this mountain, Remove hence to yonder place; and it shall remove; and nothing shall be impossible unto you. 21 Howbeit this kind goeth not out but by prayer and fasting.

There are many kinds of battles. We can win all battles if we learn the Word application.

Jesus said we wrestle not against flesh and blood.

Ephesians 6:12 For we wrestle not against flesh and blood, but against principalities, against powers, against the rulers of the darkness of this world, against spiritual wickedness in high places.

If this is the battle, then we all have to be praying with much fasting. Is our Shepherd Jesus doing what He preached and taught?

FEBRUARY 10

Let us see the Bible statement of Jesus fasting,

Mathew 4:2 And when he had fasted forty days and forty nights, he was afterward an hungered.

Now let us see some examples of Jesus praying for different places, occasions, and people.

Luke 5:16 And he withdrew himself into the wilderness, and prayed. Our Shepherd prayed for us.

John 17:9 I pray for them: I pray not for the world, but for them which thou hast given me; for they are thine.

Matthew 26:39 And he went a little farther, and fell on his face, and prayed,

Mark 1:35 And in the morning, rising up a great while before day, he went out and departed into a solitary place, and there prayed.

Praise God, our Shepherd Jesus, came in the flesh to let us know that Word alone has no power, but it will come alive if we practically put it into action. Do not just preach. Practice what you preach. We must continue doing what the Lord showed us. Lord proved by doing the Word, and the Word came alive.

Matthew 20:28 Even as the Son of man came not to be ministered unto, but to minister, and to give his life a ransom for many.

Hallelujah, We have organized our group and prayed daily: our group fasts one week each month and regular weekly fasting. We follow in our Lord's footsteps to continue His mission.

We prayed all night as the Lord prayed all night. Every day we pray early in the morning, praying without ceasing. If we do exactly what He said, we will have the chance to win. We have seen people being delivered, set free, and chains being broken. In our all-night prayer, we intercede. We pray for nations and situations. One dear lady was bound for many years with sickness and disease. She was utterly delivered and set free. So, friend, only Jesus can do it if you are willing. If you allow Him to be His yielding vessel. Go in prayer, and meet Him for direction.

I desire to establish God's plan. What an excellent plan! He has never stopped loving His creation. Father wants His children to be healed, set free, and enjoy freedom from drugs, alcohol, sicknesses, and diseases. His mission can be established if He finds one who would listen to Him. Satan established churches and organizations.

As you know, God has an agenda, and Satan also has a plan. Satan's agenda is to stop, block, and hinder the way of God once you follow God and continue in His ways.

He will do the rest. Only He needs someone who has an ear to hear, eyes to see, and loves to work for God. Lord said I would give you my Spirit to do miracles, healing, Word of knowledge, wisdom, supernatural gift of faith, prophecy, tongue, interpretation of tongue, and discerning the Spirit. If you want to continue God's mission effectively, ask for all gifts possible. I have seen some operate in God's given gifts to establish His mission.

To continue the mission of God on earth requires all your attention, dedication, and with your submission. May the Lord give us many who can do what He has left under our trust. Just say Yes, Lord! Amen!

ELIZABETH DAS

LET US PRAY

Our heavenly Father, as you came to set the captive free, heal the broken heart, and heal the sick, help us continue your mission. As you gave us the authority and assignment, we desire to fulfill your mission. Lord, if we do not lay our hand, they will not know that Jesus heals. So, help us lay hands on the sick so that they are to be healed. Lord, we know our God came to set the captive free. So Lord, help us fast and free to cast the demons out. Lord, many are heartbroken, so help us reach our broken hearts. Lord, comfort those broken-hearted. Your mission continues if we have the laborers. Lord, send us more laborers. Harvest is plenty, but laborers are few. Lord, make us one. We want your anointing; anoint us with the Holy Ghost and Power in Jesus's name. Amen! God Bless You!

FEBRUARY 11

SATAN'S MISSION IN THE CHURCH.

Satan's mission in the church, yes, you heard me right. There is a mission for Satan in the church. Satan has a mission in your city, state, and country. We hear this statement, don't we? But God is mighty. He can overthrow the power of Satan. He defeated Satan on Calvary. Yes! At their tables, he also turned down priests, who are now called pastors, as well as high priests, who are now known as superintendents or bishops.

Matthew 21:12-13, And Jesus went into the temple of God, and cast out all them that sold and bought in the temple, and overthrew the tables of the moneychangers, and the seats of them that sold doves, And said unto them, It is written, My house shall be called the house of prayer, but ye have made it a den of thieves.

You are getting my point. The same spirit is working in the churches. Remember, those people physically died, but the spirit behind them did not. It took another form in the era of the Gospel. It became religious and rejected JESUS. Lord Jesus was a Jehovah God whom they sought. They sought Him, or they sought power, position, and money. They were religious, not spiritual.

Let me explain the difference between religious and spiritual. Cain was religious, and Abel was spiritual. Cain brought the offering and was not accepted, but Abel brought what Jehovah God accepted. Do you know this kind of person who was Cain? How far was he from Abel?

He was right next to him, his brother. Now you know they are your brothers, sisters, mom, and dad. But you are in denial. Why? Because you do not want to believe that my sister or brother can sell me as a slave like Joseph's brother. My sister and Mom would not destroy my marriage as Jezebel did. Wake up!

Don't be blinded by religious actors and actresses playing different roles behind the pulpit and holding titles and positions. Please read the Bible; it says to look for their fruits. Watch the sign following them.

Religious people will lie and not fear God. Religion is a powerless organization of Satan to deceive us. It brings divisions among the groups. No matter where they go, they contaminate everything.

Proverbs 16:28, A froward man soweth strife: and a whisperer separateth chief friends.

God called religious people fools, not friends, family friends, pastors, or saints. Do you see these kinds of people coming to your family? Shut the doors on them!

They are tare. Fruit gives title to the tree. Look for the fruits.

Proverb 10:18 He that hideth hatred with lying lips, and he that uttereth a slander, is a fool.

Proverb 11:13 A talebearer revealeth secrets:

They separate husbands from wives and families. But they always talk about Jesus. Be careful of religious people. They cannot stand spirituality. Cain could not stand Abel. They are not too far from you. They could be your own family or come as friends to you or your family.

Proverbs 16:28 A froward man soweth strife: and a whisperer separateth chief friends.

Jesus tells religious people as tares. Satan has put them in the building they called the church so he can accomplish his mission.

Matthew 13:38 The field is the world; the good seed are the children of the kingdom; but the tares are the children of the wicked one; The enemy that sowed them is the devil; the harvest is the end of the world; and the reapers are the angels. As therefore the tares are gathered and burned in the fire, so shall it be at the end of this world.

Goat and sheep. You wait until the end to see the judgment of God.

Matthew 13:41, The Son of man shall send forth his angels, and they shall gather out of his kingdom all things that offend, and them which do iniquity; And shall cast them into a furnace of fire: there shall be wailing and gnashing of teeth.

Who was constantly coming against the apostle Paul? They were religious men and women. All who fought with Paul were the religious group. God's people, Israel, had a spiritual queen named Jezebel. Jezebel was religious and had many false prophets. How can you doubt who masked themselves as an angel of light? How to recognize Jezebel's spirit? First, they are manipulative, and second, they see the fruits they produce.

1 Kings 18:22, Then said Elijah unto the people, I, even I only, remain a prophet of the LORD; but Baal's prophets are four hundred and fifty men.

This religious woman had a mission to come against the prophets of God. She wanted to kill Elijah, the prophet.

1 Kings 19:2, Then Jezebel sent a messenger unto Elijah, saying, So let the gods do to me, and more also, if I make not thy life as the life of one of them by to morrow about this time.

Have you seen the religious leaders 'wives? They are super religious and very dangerous. Are you confused about being friends with them? Jezebel had a daughter, and she married a certain King. Her name was Athaliah,

2 Kings 11:1, And when Athaliah the mother of Ahaziah saw that her son was dead, she arose and destroyed all the seed royal.

Some religious spirit comes to the children from their parents. The Bible is a book that tells the truth. It reveals the personality of religious and spiritual people. You must have seen or met as many of these people as I have. No matter who they could be. Please stay away from them! They will destroy you. They are not your friends, family, or your leader. As the Lord said, they are tare, fools, and hypocrites.

They have their father's mission, which is to steal, kill, and destroy. See their fruits, and do not be deceived.

LET US PRAY

Lord, give extra protection to you, your family, children, and grandchildren. May the Lord provide you with protection and the spirit of discernment.

May the Lord keep you from harm, danger, tare, fool, and talebearers. Scripture says in 1 John 4:1 Beloved, believe not every spirit but try the spirits whether they are of God: because many false prophets are gone out into the world. Lord, this is the end time. Please give us true teachers and prophets to keep us from harm and danger, in Jesus 'name. Amen! God bless you!

FEBRUARY 12

SPEAKS BLESSINGS OVER YOURSELF

Your words have a creating power. If you can see the spirit work created by your words, you will arrange your vocabulary carefully. You will think before you speak. If the power of the Words of God boosts your words, then your words can create what you spoke. God's words are established for eternity. Heaven and earth can pass away, but not God's word. You can inherit every promise and rejoice in the Lord if you know how to.

Psalms 119:11 "Thy word have I hid in mine heart, that I might not sin against thee."

If you dislike trouble, then speak about what you like to gain. Being able to go out and come in is a blessing for me. I have his power to tread down the enemy. I live in his shadow. Jesus Is my shepherd, and I am well taken care of. You start your day by speaking positively, not by what you see or feel. Many times, you may wake up feeling sad or sick. Maybe you have a family situation but as you speak positive words, your words will start creating as you are talking. You rewrite your day no matter what you see. Do not fall into your mouth trap. Just speak. I walk by faith and not by sight. I believe what I don't see. I do not believe in what I see.

This will bring glorious victory, healing, and belief. Our Word has a trap of seeing. So, if you have the Word of God in your mouth, they save you.

1 Peter 3:10 For he that will love life, and see good days, let him refrain his tongue from evil, and his lips that they speak no guile,

You are creating your life. Do you want a good life? Like a millionaire? Then, to say it, I am a rich child. I am a child of King Jesus. He supplies all my needs. From his abundance, he owns heaven and earth; he provides me with his abundance; he has an addition and multiple programs for my provision, and I am blessed.

Proverb 21:23 "Whoso keepeth his mouth and his tongue keepeth his soul from troubles."

Ephesians 4:29" Let no corrupt communication proceed out of your mouth, but that which is good to the use of edifying, that it may minister grace unto the hearers."

What Is corruption? Corrupt means to change from good to bad, defile or pollute, and entice from good and allure to evil. If you speak badly, it will depart and change the pleasant situation to bad. The word of God teaches us what to speak and what not to speak.

Proverb 10:19 "In the multitude of words wanteth not sin: but he that refraineth his lips is wise."

Pick words exactly how you would like to see the results. Believe that It Is happening as you speak. Do not speak what you see. Say I am blessed; God got my back; he is my protector. I will come out of this sick bed, walk, and have his mercy and grace.

Matthew 12:37 "For by thy words thou shalt be justified, and by thy words, thou shalt be condemned."

Jesus Is the judge. So you say I am wrong, but I want your mercy, not judgment.

Confess fault and ask for forgiveness. Learn to speak, which can change your world, trial to testimony, war to victory, poverty to abundance.

Psalms 119:11 "Thy word have I hid in mine heart, that I might not sin against thee."

Go to the holy ghost teaching college, take a deep breath, and say, holy spirit put the words in my mouth so I speak the right words. The holy spirit will take over.

Isiah 54:17 "No weapon that is formed against thee shall prosper, and every tongue that shall rise against thee in judgment thou shalt condemn. This is the heritage of the servants of the LORD, and their righteousness is of me, saith the LORD."

God Is righteous, so we inherit all that he said. I cash His promises by speaking and believing in my heart. I have seen a significant victory. His words are good all day and night. I see weapons of doubt, situations, fear, house, and family situations where problems arise.

Job 15:6 "Thine own mouth condemneth thee, and not I: yea, thine own lips testify against thee."

This is so powerful. What a life-learning lesson. So speak positively. Say, I am going to have a good day. I am a king's kid. He has mercy and grace for me. I am head. I am first. I am above. I am highly favored. Since my supply comes from the Lord, I am rich. I am healed. Jesus paid for my sins through stripes. My children are mighty men and women of God.

Proverb 15:4 "A wholesome tongue is a tree of life: but perverseness therein is a breach in the spirit."

The Bible says Jesus healed people through His Words, Jesus Is the counselor; we can be His counselor if we speak gentle and sensible words. Words can heal or can give deep wounds.

Psalms 34:13 "Keep thy tongue from evil, and thy lips from speaking guile."

Proverbs 18:21 "Death and life are in the power of the tongue: and they that love it shall eat the fruit thereof."

If you say, "I am catching a cold," wait and see; it will happen. I am afraid then you will. "I am upset," you will.

If I am not wise, then see what you become. But as you say, "I can do all things by Jesus." He will enable you, strengthen you, then it will happen, as you said. When you speak as King David spoke, "My help cometh from the Lord, he anoints my head with oil, my cup rennet over, I am secured in Him." Then, all that you said will start happening in your life. You will say, "My God! How great thou art! Hallelujah!

Psalms 35:28 "And my tongue shall speak of thy righteousness and thy praise all the day long."

LET US PRAY

Lord, my God, help us speak the truth of the Word. Help us to talk about health, prosperity,O and blessings. Speak, I see I am a new creature.

Old things have passed away. The newness of life has resurrected me. I am made in your image. I am the handiwork of God. My life is hiding In you. I know I am safe and sound. I am blessed above and over. In Jesus's name. AMEN! God bless you!

FEBRUARY 13

WE NEED HUMBLE LEADERS.

Pray that the Lord gives us humble leaders. What is the definition of humble? Modest means were submissive and meek.

The Bible says in Numbers 12:3 (Now the man Moses was very meek, above all the men which were upon the face of the earth.)

Humble will take the order and carry on. God never has to worry. If anyone wants to establish a kingdom, business, or company, they need a person who can do as instructed. God called Moses to take the Israelites to the promised land. Since Moses was a humble man, it was a big task to lead six hundred thousand men on foot beside women and children. He did exactly what God commanded him. Even in the contrary situation, he stood for the Lord. So not Egyptian, but the surrounding country saw that the God of Hebrews was powerful. He is real. They were afraid of Jehovah God. Why? A humble leader will lead in the leading of the Lord Almighty.

Joshua 5:1 And it came to pass, when all the kings of the Amorites, which were on the side of Jordan westward, and all the kings of the Canaanites, which were by the sea, heard that the LORD had dried up the waters of Jordan from before the children of Israel, until we were passed over, that their heart melted, neither was there spirit in them anymore, because of the children of Israel.

Moses waited to hear from the Lord in all situations. Moses never over-ridded God. Waiting, listening, and obeying God is the way to succeed.

Isaiah 48:17 Thus saith the LORD, thy Redeemer, the Holy One of Israel; I am the LORD thy God which teacheth thee to profit, which leadeth thee by the way that thou shouldest go.

God wants to connect with his people and show the world that He is real. He is the creator and the savior. How can he do this? Well, God needs someone humble, like Moses. God needs someone to carry on instruction in every good, bad, or contrary situation. Never question his leading and guiding. What is the opposite of the humble? Proud! Proud will not hear but suffer consequences and rule without thinking. Pharaoh is an example of a proud king.

Exodus 10:3 And Moses and Aaron came in unto Pharaoh and said unto him, Thus saith the LORD God of the Hebrews, How long wilt thou refuse to humble thyself before me? Let my people go, that they may serve me.

A man saw calamities and plague but did not want to submit to the Lord. Even servants were wiser and humbler than Pharaoh. This is the best example of not listening to the authority of heaven.

Exodus 10:7 And Pharaoh's servants said, How long shall this man be a snare unto us? Let the men go, that they may serve the LORD their God: knowest thou not yet that Egypt is destroyed?

Why do people of God suffer? Same reason: They refuse to hear God and obey. Humble will abide by but proudly think they know all. Lord's plan is for now and the future. Remember, it may not make sense now, but it will. Remember, learn to wait.

Psalms 106:13 They soon forgat his works; they waited not for his counsel:

The Kings of the Northern Kingdom dropped humbleness, failed God's people, and lost the nation of Israel in the war in the year 722.

2 Chronicles 7:14 If my people, called by my name, shall humble themselves, and pray, and seek my face, and turn from their wicked ways; then will I hear from heaven, and will forgive their sin, and will heal their land.

This scripture is to do and not to call, not to memorize, but you need to humble yourself and pray. History repeats itself since the leader gets in a hurry. I do not want you to open the word, not to connect with God. Why were families and nations destroyed? For the same reason, there is no humble leader. May God send a leader who is godly and fears Him, so that our land may have peace.

1Timothy 2:1 I exhort, therefore, that, first of all, supplications, prayers, intercessions, and giving of thanks, be made for all men; 2 For kings, and for all that are in authority; that we may lead a quiet and peaceable life in all godliness and honesty. 3 For this is good and acceptable in the sight of God our Saviour;

We need healing in our marriage, family, land, and children. How? The only way is if you listen to God. If we humble ourselves and listen and do as he commands, there is security, protection, and prosperity. Jesus said, "My sheep are without a shepherd." The spiritual authority will connect you with God. Pray for Godly, Humble leaders in the spiritual and secular world; pray for God-fearing leaders.

Proverbs 29:2 When the righteous are in authority, the people rejoice: but when the wicked beareth rule, the people mourn.

David was a Godly humble leader. His victory was a reason for taking counsel from God and obeying him.

Samuel 30:8 And David enquired at the Lord, saying, Shall I pursue after this troop? Shall I overtake them? And he answered him, Pursue: for thou shalt surely overtake them, and without fail recover all.

Samuel 5:19 And David enquired of the LORD, saying, Shall I go up to the Philistines? Does wilt thou deliver them into mine hand? And the LORD said unto David, Go up: for I will doubtless deliver the Philistines into thine hand.

2 Samuel 21:1 Then there was a famine in the days of David three years, year after year; and David enquired of the LORD. And the LORD answered. It is for Saul and his bloody house because he slew the Gibeonites.

So, all your success and defeat voice you are hearing. David was not dependent on his smartness or anyone but the Lord. God needed a man who could do the most challenging task and set the captives free from the slavery of the Egyptians. God is mighty and powerful. He needs someone to carry on his command to establish an earthly plan, agenda, and program. Moses was a humble man whom God used to establish the great kingdom of Israel in the year 1300-1200. Later, the proud leaders of Israel ignored God, and they destroyed his counsel and Israel in the year 722. Proud and arrogant leaders destroyed 722

B.C. Families, cities, countries, and. Jesus, being humble, came with a grand plan to heal, deliver, and set the captive free. Lord Jesus gave sinless blood and bought back what Satan had stolen from humanity in the Garden of Eden. It is available if you repent, wash sins away in Jesus 'name, and receive the Holy Spirit.

The prideful religious leaders seek to prevent the carrying on of Jesus' mission, which began with the Holy Ghost's power in 120 disciples. That is why we see destruction everywhere. Lord, give us a humble heart to do what you ask in Jesus's name.

LET US PRAY

Lord, make us humble. James 4:6 But he giveth more grace. Wherefore he saith, God resisteth the proud, but giveth grace unto the humble. Lord, give us your grace and mercy. 1 Peter 5:6 Humble yourselves under God's mighty hand that he may exalt you in due time. James 4:10 Humble yourselves in the sight of the Lord, and he shall lift you. Lord bless our home, city, state, and nation. We need your mercy and guidance so we can have a peaceful life. Give us humble leaders in Jesus 'name. Amen! God bless you!

FEBRUARY 14

WE ARE PILGRIM AND STRANGER

Earth is where your journey starts. Earth, where you need a guideline to be successful, just like anywhere you travel on land. You need a map, guide, or tour bus to take you around. Otherwise, you will get lost. The Bible says you are a pilgrim and stranger.

What is Pilgrim? A traveler or wanderer, especially in a foreign place. Stranger meant in experience or visitor or newcomer. Yes. Earth is where you have never been before, and you need help from one who has experienced it, and that is God. Have you traveled to any nation or place for a few days? You know you will not stay there. You carry the necessary items only. Every day, you are preparing to move on.

The Bible says 1 Peter 2:11 Dearly beloved, I beseech you as strangers and pilgrims, abstain from fleshly lusts, which war against the soul Knowing you're passing by, stay away from what God warned you against. Calling up Adam and Eve was not permanent on Earth. They were pilgrims and strangers as well. Beware! Beware of yourself. You have eyes, flesh, and pride that can misguide you as it did to Eve and Adam

1 John 2:16 For all that is in the world, the lust of the flesh, and the lust of the eyes, and the pride of life, is not of the Father, but is of the world.

Sin separated us from God. Satan was not the cause of sin but the flesh. First, as Eve saw, she desired that is the lust of the eye. Second, her flesh desired to eat, which is a lust for flesh, and third, she wanted to be like God, which is the pride of life. Adam and Eve's sin separated humanity from their creator, God Almighty.

Ephesians 2:12, That at that time ye were without Christ, being aliens from the commonwealth of Israel, and strangers from the covenants of promise, having no hope, and without God in the world:

God cared for his people and came up with a grand plan. Abraham was the father of faith. God showed us that he can bless us if we hear and obey, even though we are pilgrims and strangers on earth. When God asked Abraham to move out of his kindred, did he argue? No.

Genesis 12:1 Now the LORD had said unto Abram, Get thee out of thy country, and from thy kindred, and thy father's house, unto a land that I will shew thee:

He did as God asked him, as instructed, his generation after him. This is where we fail God. We need to remember to teach our children.

FEBRUARY 14

Train your children as pilgrims and strangers and nothing else. Introduce the maker as a guide and how to listen to his voice and obey.

Psalms 25:5 "Lead me in thy truth, and teach me: for thou art the God of my salvation; on thee do I wait all the day."

Do you cry out as David and others did? You must ask for direction from God in times of need.

Psalms 39:12 Hear my prayer, O LORD, and give ear unto my cry; hold not thy peace at my tears: for I am a stranger with thee, and a sojourner, as all my fathers were.

Our life is a shadow. How long have you seen shadow? Our life is like a vapor, flower, and grass in the field. We can understand these expressions; they are just for a moment. So is our life compared with eternity.

Chronicles 29:15. For we are strangers before thee, and sojourners, as were all our fathers: our days on the earth are as a shadow, and there is none abiding.

Corinthians 5:1 For we know that if our earthly house of this tabernacle were dissolved, we have a building of God, a house not made with hands, eternal in the heavens.

God is our creator, and Father has great mercy and love for us. God put on flesh and introduced his Kingdom; his plan redeemed us so we could reach that mansion. He is preparing an eternal residence for you and me. Jesus is not earthly but as.

1 Corinthians 15:47 The first man is of the earth, earthy: the second man is the Lord from heaven. Jesus witnesses for his Heavenly Kingdom,

John 18:36. Jesus answered, My kingdom is not of this world: if my kingdom were of this world, then would my servant's fight, that I should not be delivered to the Jews: but now is my kingdom not from hence.

To teach this heavenly place, we must follow his way.

Hebrew 11:16 But now they desire a better country, that is, an heavenly: wherefore God is not ashamed to be called their God: for he hath prepared for them a city.

If you know the truth, you will act and live on earth like passengers. Abraham, Isaac, and Jacob did not have any problem leaving one place and going to another as directed by God. Have you seen people live on earth like they are going to stay forever? But what did Jacob say when he was about to finish the journey on earth?

Genesis 47:9 And Jacob said unto Pharaoh, the days of the years of my pilgrimage are an hundred and thirty years: few and evil have the days of the years of my life been, and have not attained unto the days of the years of the life of my fathers in the days of their pilgrimage.

Many evils came to Jacob, and do not live as long as his ancestors did. Jacob said it was just a journey. He moved from place to place, but all good. Take inspiration from David's example and learn to cry out when you confront trouble.

Psalms 39:12. Hear my prayer, O LORD, and give ear unto my cry; hold not thy peace at my tears: for I am a stranger with thee, and a sojourner, as all my fathers were.

I remembered, one time in a prayer meeting, a prophetess spoke to me, pack, you are moving." I did not know what she was talking about. Before the injury, I fixed up my house. I had no job when she was saying you are moving. I thought about this health condition. Where? Years and years ago, I decided never to move to Texas. I heard an evil report about this state. Well, a year passed, and another friend who heard the prophecy said it was not God. I said it would happen. The same day I heard that other family members were moving, and they were planning to take us. They traveled to different places to find a suitable location. In one prayer meeting, the prophetess said Texas is the state. Do you remember? I said there is no Texas that exists on my map. I did not want to move to Texas. I've been here in Texas for 17 plus years, AMEN.

And your responsibility is to teach your children and children's children as God commanded Abraham,

Genesis 18:19 For I know him, that he will command his children and his household after him, and they shall keep the way of the LORD, to do justice and judgment;

To teach them is your job as a parent, grandparent, teacher, pastor, and whatever you are called, and also to live like pilgrims and strangers. Praise God; we are going to the most beautiful place. If we prepare ourselves.

Isaiah 35:8 "And a highway shall be there, and a way, and it shall be called The way of holiness; the unclean shall not pass over it; but it shall be for those: the wayfaring men, though fools, shall not err therein."

Hebrew 12:28 Wherefore we receiving a kingdom which cannot be moved, let us have grace, whereby we may serve God acceptably with reverence and godly fear:

LET US PRAY

I pray, oh, Lord, as your word teaches that we are pilgrims and strangers, so we are. Please teach and guide me to do and not deviate from you. Don't be sidetracked by anyone or even by ourselves. Let your word be the light and a lamp to our feet. So we stay on the correct path on earth. Keep us from temptation. So we do not fall into the trap of the devil. Lord, let us find the way which leads us to eternity in heaven. We want to spend our time with you. We love you, and thank you for loving us, in Jesus 'name, AMEN. God bless you.

FEBRUARY 15

DO NOT BE DECEIVED

Are you familiar with the phrase "now you are saved" being used when people become members of a church? Their belief is that salvation is attained through activities like sitting on the pew, paying tithes, and joining the tea party. Don't be deceived. Even those who preach or hold a different role in the church believe they are saved. Being born again and living righteously is your ticket to salvation upon leaving this world. Don't forget, Jesus is the one who saves! To be saved, you must follow Him. If you hear the words "well done" upon entering heaven, it means you have been saved.

In Matthew 25:21, "His Lord said unto him, Well done, thou good and faithful servant: thou hast been faithful over a few things, I will make thee ruler over many things: enter thou into the joy of thy Lord.

When the Lord separates you from goat and sheep, many wrong teachings of false teachers and prophets deceive you. Wake up if you become a choir leader. You are just a cheerleader unless you're fasting and praying for direction from the Lord. Remember, Judas was still going with two and two; his spiritual condition was sad and wrong.

Matthew 7:22 "Many will say to me in that day, Lord, Lord, have we not prophesied in thy name? and in thy name have cast out devils? And in thy name done many wonderful works?

What omniscient God says about all who are busy in the ministry and forget to come in God's presence for renewal? I do not know you; depart from me.

Just like when your car needs gas, you need to pump in. Similarly, you must pump in the Holy Spirit and come in his presence. Many kill time just by staying active in church and forgetting about the Lord's assignment. Plan your vineyard to dress. Ordinarily, churchgoers find someone like them to go out and eat with when the time is finished. You are working for the church by holding positions. Sitting in a nice chair in an auditorium or pulpit does not give you a ticket to heaven. Our calling is to prepare for God's army, not a church agenda. Go back to basics, and study words. Refrain from being satisfied with a brief lecture that fits your life.

Go back to Jesus 'teaching in the Word of God. Go back to Paul. Do not be bewitched by false teaching. Being a true teacher of God, Paul taught Galatians truth, but they also went astray from Paul's teaching.

Galatians 3:1, O foolish Galatians, who hath bewitched you, that ye should not obey the truth, before whose eyes Jesus Christ hath been evidently set forth, crucified among you? Are you so foolish? Having begun instant spirit, are you now made perfect by the Flesh?

Are you learning from the teachings of Jesus, Paul, Peter, and other true apostles? How had they been instructed to different churches? Check it out.

Are you casting the demon out? Healing sick, visiting widows, orphans and all that Jesus did,

John 9:4 I must work his works that sent me, while it is day: the night cometh, when no man can work.

Jesus will be glad if people follow in his footsteps. I have seen the certain spirit of the World, and Hollywood has settled into the building. People say the church is not God but people.

It has contaminated Christianity. What does the Bible say about our contamination?

2 Timothy 4:3 For the time will come when they will not endure sound doctrine; but after their lusts shall they heap to themselves teachers, having itching ears;

Galatians 6:7-9 Be not deceived; God is not mocked: for whatsoever a man soweth, that shall he also reap. For he that soweth to his flesh shall of the flesh reap corruption, but he that soweth to the Spirit shall of the Spirit reap life everlasting. And let us not be weary in well doing: for in due season we shall reap if we faint not.

What is mock? False to mimic or imitate or to laugh at. Remember how Satan deceived Eve?

Genesis 3:1. Now the serpent was more subtil than any beast of the field which the LORD God had made. And he said unto the woman, Yea, hath God said, Ye, shall not eat of every tree of the garden?

Satan takes our focus from God's instruction, commandments, and teaching. Are you questioning God's instruction? Who does not like to stand on a pulpit? No one wants to get dirty.

Luke 21:8, And he said, Take heed that ye be not deceived: for many shall come in my name, saying, I am Christ; and the time draweth near: go ye not therefore after them. But when ye shall hear of wars and commotions, be not terrified: these things must first come to pass; but the end is not by and by.

Friend, the time is near. Do not be deceived, and be prepared to meet your maker. Stay away from the wrong crowd.

Matthew 7:15. Beware of false prophets, which come to you in sheep's clothing, but inwardly they are ravening wolves.

What are pernicious ways to be careful of churches 'highly dangerous or destructive agenda?

2 Peter 2:1 But there were false prophets among the people, even as there shall be false teachers among you, who privily shall bring in damnable heresies, even denying the Lord that bought them, and bring themselves swift destruction. And many shall follow their pernicious ways; because of whom, the way of truth shall be evil spoken of. And through covetousness shall they with feigned words make merchandise of you: whose judgment now of a long time lingereth not, and their damnation slumbereth not.

When you go to your Father's mission, as Jesus did, you will hear welcoming words from the Lord. Remember, God chose you for his field to dress and not to go about the programs. Do not be so busy with religious agendas. Check with the word of God. Truth has power not a church agenda. Let us see how Jesus has described his church.

Matthew 25:31 When the Son of man shall come in his glory, and all the holy angels with him, then shall he sit upon the throne of his glory: And before him shall be gathered all nations: and he shall separate them one from another, as a shepherd divideth his sheep from the goats: And he shall set the sheep on his right hand, but the goats on the left. Then shall the King say unto them on his right hand, Come, ye blessed of my Father, inherit the Kingdom prepared for you from the foundation of the world: For I was an hungered, and ye gave me meat: I was thirsty, and ye gave me drink: I was a stranger, and ye took me in: Naked, and ye clothed me: I was sick, and ye visited me: I was in prison, and ye came unto me. Then shall the righteous answer him, saying, Lord, when saw we thee an hungered and fed thee? Or thirsty, and gave thee drink? When saw we thee a stranger, and took thee in? or naked, and clothed thee? Or when we saw thee sick or in prison and came unto thee? And the King shall answer and say unto them, Verily I say unto you, since ye have done it unto one of the least of these my brethren, ye have done it unto me.

Follow only those missions if you want to enter his Kingdom. Many are called, and few are chosen.

1 Corinthians 1:8 Who shall also confirm you unto the end, that ye may be blameless in the day of our Lord Jesus Christ.

I want to be blameless, as my whole desire is to spend eternity with Lord Jesus.

LET US PRAY

May the Lord speak to you through visions and dreams. May the Lord wake you up and find you working for him in his vineyard. May the Lord give you strength, peace, and comfort. Lord, help us be ready. Let our land be filled with oil, in Jesus 'name. Amen. God bless you.

FEBRUARY 16

ARE YOU SEEKING GOD?

I know you will say. Oh yes, I attend church. I read the Bible. I also do what pastor says, etc.

No! My question is, are you seeking God? I'm not talking about going to mom, dad, friends, or family.

Jeremiah 29:13 And ye shall seek me, and find me when ye shall search for me with all your heart.

Why do we have to seek God?

Jeremiah 29:11 says, "For I know the thoughts that I think toward you, saith the LORD, thoughts of peace, and not of evil, to give you an expected end.

See, only the Heavenly Father wants you to have a peaceful, prosperous life. When you get an answer from God, do it without pausing, arguing, or questioning. If people seek God, who is Alpha and Omega, beginning and ending, first and last, then the chapter of their life will be different.

Your life will be successful, favored, and blessed like King David, Abraham, Moses, and Queen Esther, who sought God. Seek God who is an omniscient, all-knowing, omnipotent, all-powerful God; your life on earth can be the most successful because your life story's writer, director, and producer is God.

How can God do this? Only if you seek, as said in the Bible.

Matthew 6:33 But seek ye first the kingdom of God, and his righteousness, and all these things shall be added unto you.

The Bible says you seek God and his righteousness first, not after you mess up and can't bear it anymore. Not after we screw your children up, and you cannot sleep. Not after your marriage goes wrong and your health is down the hill. Under God's direction, life can be triumphant, prosperous, bouncing, wholesome, and successful. Explicit, straightforward instruction is given in the Bible to seek God.

God has a way and information for you. Do not go psychic, tarot card, familiar spirit, or any medium. Do not just open the Bible and pick Scripture and think this is my answer. Especially never to religious family members.. They are lost. Why don't you seek God? I always wake up early in the morning, around 3:00 am and latest, 3:50 am, to seek God, pray, and worship God. Regularly, weekly, and monthly long fasting. Why?

FEBRUARY 16

The Bible says in Psalms 63:10. O God, thou art my God; early will I seek thee: my soul thirsteth for thee, my flesh longeth for thee in a dry and thirsty land, where no water is; To see thy power and glory, so as I have seen thee in the sanctuary.

What happened to Rome? How had they become homosexual? The last sin is where God's judgment kicks in. Romans went after games. There was a day when there was no God in their memory. If you do not know God, then how can you seek him?

Roman 3:10 As it is written, There is none righteous, no, not one: 11 There is none that understandeth, there is none that seeketh after God. If you seek God for your day, then your day will be directed by God. I know Satan has the plan to destroy your day and future. So God has the plan to bless and protect you. He has taken responsibility for us to protect. But you must come in his presence and get direction from the Lord.

Psalm 63:7 Because thou hast been my help, therefore in the shadow of thy wings will I rejoice. 8 My soul followeth hard after thee: thy right hand upholdeth me. 9 But those that seek my soul, to destroy it, shall go into the lower parts of the earth. 10 They shall fall by the sword: they shall be a portion for foxes. 11 But the king shall rejoice in God; every one that sweareth by him shall glory: but the mouth of them that speak lies shall be stopped.

Are you so busy that you have forgotten about God? He is a tiny part of your life and not your life. Attending a building, you may say church, but having no personal relationship with God. Many position holders in churches and organizations have different lives as they close their doors. They are like Eli choosing children over God, like Judas greedy for 30 silver coins, like Cain, jealous, prideful, and a liar. Like King Saul, he is rebellious and stubborn. Be careful. Go to God. He is real.

Proverb 8:17 "I love them that love me; and those that seek me early shall find me."

Matthew 7:7 "Seek, and ye shall find."

When I had cancer, I sought God. I cried out to him. When I went for a checkup for the fourth time, they could not find cancer. How great thou art,

Jeremiah 17:14 Heal me, O LORD, and I shall be healed; save me, and I shall be saved: for thou art my praise.

Stand on the word of God. The only thing Satan has done is to distract us. I have found what God said.

Isaiah 55:8 "For my thoughts are not your thoughts, neither are your ways my ways, saith the LORD. For as the heavens are higher than the earth, so are my ways higher than your ways, and my thoughts than your thoughts."

Oh my God! How beautiful that is! So do not compromise it. Seek that higher planning thought that our God has. Run from those wicked who come against you and destroy you.

Remember, they will be your family, friends, or whatever is around you. You remember Abraham had a promise.

Genesis 15:5 "And he brought him forth abroad, and said, Look now toward heaven, and tell the stars, if thou be able to number them: and he said unto him, So shall thy seed be."

Genesis 22:17 "That in blessing I will bless thee, and in multiplying I will multiply thy seed as the stars of the heaven, and as the sand which is upon the sea shore, and thy seed shall possess the gate of his enemies."

The devil heard this promise to Abraham and hindered them. But the Lord is a deliverer. Isaac prayed, and God set the womb free to produce a baby.

Genesis 25:21 "And Isaac intreated the LORD for his wife, because she was barren: and the LORD was intreated of him, and Rebekah his wife conceived."

The devil never gives up. I am a witness to that watch. What happened to Rebecca?

Genesis 25:22 And the children struggled together within her; and she said, If it be so, why am I thus? And she went to enquire of the LORD. 23 And the LORD said unto her, Two nations are in thy womb, and two manner of people shall be separated from thy bowels; and the one people shall be stronger than the other people, and the elder shall serve the younger.

Promises of God can be hindered, blocked, or stopped by the devil. That is why you have to seek God for deliverance, healing, and salvation. Destroy that stealer, killer, and destroyer to get an inch in your life, family, finances, children, and grandchildren. Seek God.

Isaiah 55:6 Seek ye the LORD while he may be found, call ye upon him while he is near:

LET US PRAY

Lord God, let us be ahead of the game of our life. Lord, help us seek your face and get direction from you. Help us seek you for our children and their future. Help us so we seek God for help against kidnappers, molesters, drugs, alcohol, divorces, and gangs. Lord, teach us how to aspire to you. We thank you for being our only protector, defender, and lover of our soul. God, thank you for allowing us to come into your presence. May you find the Lord as you seek His grace and mercy in Jesus 'name. Amen! God bless you.

FEBRUARY 17

GIVE BIRTH TO THE GODLY NATION

Our God, being the Creator, knows all. His words that he has written for the evidence of fact we should know and understand. Also, we can understand God as just, holy, and righteous. There is no fault in his judgment. God said what he meant and what he meant, he said. The Creator of the womb knows the creation.

Isaiah 44:24, Thus saith the LORD, thy redeemer, and he that formed thee from the womb, I am the LORD that maketh all things; that stretcheth forth the heavens alone; that spreadeth abroad the earth by myself;

To know the Lord as the Creator of Heaven and the Earth is the beginning of fear.

Proverb 9:10, The fear of the LORD is the beginning of wisdom: and the knowledge of the holy is understanding.

God, who makes all things and the womb, knows you before you were formed. God has given you every will. So, choices are yours even though God created us. Rebekah knew there was something wrong in her womb. She felt the war in her womb. They manifested a personality in her womb. She did not know that she had two nations in her womb. She went to God to enquire.

Genesis 25:23, And the LORD said unto her, Two nations are in thy womb, and two manner of people shall be separated from thy bowels; and the one people shall be stronger than the other people; and the elder shall serve the younger.

Who were these two nations? Esau is Edom and Jacob is Israel. What does God want us to see? God is not talking about twin brothers. He is talking about the personalities of twins. God is providing us with two personalities.

By the character and nature of these two sons of Isaac, God is telling us not to blame him. As God spoke, so was it. We see the careless son and the careful son. Choosing God can cost lives, and Jacob took a risk. Jacob took the time to cook a meal to enjoy and satisfy his hunger.

But over a tasty meal, he chose God. He decided to do a blessing over his belly. But his heedless brother Esau minded the stomach over blessings. Esau despised the birthright. See, God saw this before Esau and Jacob were born. God allowed Esau to be blessed by letting him come first.

But Jacob did everything to achieve what he lost in the womb. Boys were against each other in the womb to come out first. Jacob lost his firstborn blessing by birth, but Jacob had made up his mind to pay for it. He won!

Jeremiah 1:5, Before I formed thee in the belly I knew thee;

If you decide to get the blessing and decide. You can change God's mind, and so is people's mind. Remember Canaanite women.

Matthew 15:22, Have mercy on me, O Lord, thou son of David; my daughter is grievously vexed with a devil.

Jesus did not want to help her, then she went one step further.

Then she worshiped him, saying, "Lord help me!" Jesus said, "I came to help my people, not a Canaanite dog." She said that if you consider me a dog, give me cramps. See! Her persistence. She changed God's mind.

Matt 15:28 Then Jesus said to her, "Oh woman, great is thy faith, be it unto thee even as thou wilt." And it made her daughter whole from that very hour.

See, her daughter was not just healed but whole. Whole means mind, body, spirit, and soul healed, delivered, sound, and set free. God needs a personality like Jacob and persistence like a Canaanite woman. It is worth trying. Do not think he will not bless you. That is why Jacob became the father of the nation. People who know God have the determination to get God.

Remember, God knows your heedless and careless personality as well. Ask God to bless the womb, nation, people, and character in the womb. Satan worshipers do all evil works over mom's womb. Be careful!

Psalms 58:3 The wicked are estranged from the womb: they go astray as soon as they are born, speaking lies.

God shows personality and spirituality. So that we can understand God, who is just and righteous, he has to do precisely what he says. Anoint the womb and bless by reading the word of God to your unborn baby. Protect your baby. Jacob's mother did.

I thank God for my godly mother, who was righteous. She protected us from evil and kept us right. I appreciate holy mothers who can perceive wrong from right to keep us from harm.

A few days ago, I received a phone call from Fresno. A pregnant lady was very sick. She kept going back to the hospital. The doctor said it is a high risk. But as I started praying against the demon attack, she and the baby were completely healed. In that instant, she experienced complete healing. See, learn to attack, and counterattack.

Abraham was not just a father of a nation, but nations.

Genesis 17:1 And when Abram was ninety years old and nine, the Lord appeared to Abram, and said unto him, I am the Almighty God; walk before me, and be thou perfect. 2 And I will make my covenant between me and thee, and will multiply thee exceedingly. 3 And Abram fell on his face: and God talked with him, saying, 4 As for me, behold, my covenant is with thee, and thou shalt be a father of many nations. 5 Neither shall thy name any more be called Abram, but thy name shall be Abraham; for a father of many nations have I made thee.

The Devil wanted to abort this promise. But Moses entreated the Lord. Moses convinced God. Moses stood in the gap between God and stiff, stubborn, and rebellious Hebrews.

Exodus 32:11 And Moses besought the Lord his God, and said, Lord, why doth thy wrath wax hot against thy people, which thou hast brought forth out of the land of Egypt with great power, and with a mighty hand? 12 Wherefore should the Egyptians speak, and say, For mischief did he bring them out, to slay them in the mountains, and to consume them from the face of the earth? Turn from thy fierce wrath, and repent of this evil against thy people. 13 Remember Abraham, Isaac, and Israel, thy servants, to whom thou swarest by thine own self, and saidst unto them, I will multiply your seed as the stars of heaven, and all this land that I have spoken of will I give unto your seed, and they shall inherit it forever. 14 And the Lord repented of the evil which he thought to do unto his people.

People who recognize God receive the blessing. We must stand in the gap and intercede for nations. God can protect, bless, and keep the nation. Recognize God and do what it takes to receive a blessing for you and the generation after you. David, the great king, recognized God's greatness and repented each time to stay on God's blessing track. It is God's word that if you do what it takes, God bless you to inherit the earth.

Psalms 37:22, For such as be blessed of him shall inherit the earth; and they that be cursed of him shall be cut off.

God has a great plan to give us the Kingdom of heaven.

Luke 12:32 "Fear not, little flock; for it is your Father's good pleasure to give you the kingdom."

LET US PRAY

Lord, the mighty God, help us to have a bull dog determination to follow you. Help us, O Lord, to hold the hand of an unchangeable God. Help us walk humbly to do justly and love mercy. So we are worthy to inherit the nation and Kingdom. Lord, you are righteous and holy. Help us walk before you perfectly like Abraham, Isaac, and Israel. To receive the blessing of nations in Jesus 'name. Amen! God bless you.

FEBRUARY 18

LEARNING FROM THE HOLY SPIRIT

We will have a new daily lesson if we learn to hear the Holy Spirit. The Holy Spirit is a wonderful teacher. You will be in awe, living in a miracle land. You will have what you desire. It's a subject every day. The teacher will be the Holy Spirit God because God is spirit. There is one God. Jesus is the flesh manifestation of the spirit, God,

John 16:13 Howbeit when he, the spirit of truth, is come, he will guide you into all truth: for he shall not speak of himself; but whatsoever he shall hear, that shall he say: and he will shew you things to come.

I used to drive home late from work. One night, the police stopped me. The Holy Spirit was saying, "Do not open the door." Policeman asked me to open the door, but I did not. I rolled down the window just a little. The police officer said, "you look familiar." I said, "No, I don't." He said, "Where are you coming from?" I said, "from work."

"Are you nurse?" I said, "no. I work in the post office."

He smiled and said, "Ok, go." Who was that?

Thank God. The Holy Spirit taught me what to do. We know we all go to school and college. We learn and observe others. Learn and some never. But it is everyday learning for me.

Similar dreams of the two individuals can have different meanings. I had two calls come, and both had almost identical dreams. But the meaning of dreams was different. While praying in the tongue, the interpretation came that one was fearful but not the other person who had a similar dream. God has an additional remedy for both individuals. I prayed against the fear and asked God to give her courage and boldness. Amen!

Please ask for help from the Holy Spirit, and He will guide you to all truth in Jesus 'name.

Roman 8:26, Likewise the Spirit also helpeth our infirmities: for we know not what we should pray for as we ought: but the spirit itself maketh intercession for us with groanings which cannot be uttered.

It is beautiful to learn if you have a teachable spirit. Now, over-smart people do not need God's teaching since they know all but humble will. God will direct them, and they have no problem leaning on God. Their liars, deceiver, and gossiper friends will direct evil. They like to hear what they want to hear. Have you seen many go to church, read the Bible, pray, and fast? But some learn, and some never. Even in your own home, you may have many kids and the same parents but the same situations, some good and some bad. When

Moses, a humble, teachable man, was leading the Hebrews out of slavery. Did Hebrew ever learn? No! God said they were stubborn, stiff necks. Of course, there will be some exceptions.

Exodus 32:9 And the LORD said unto Moses; I have seen this people, and, behold, it is a stiff-necked people:

If you see all miracles, read the word, and still do not want to learn and understand. Do you know what the result will be? Do you flunk class?

Hebrew stayed 40 years in the same class and failed repeatedly. Your teacher, God, has great patience.

Leviticus 26:41 And that I also have walked contrary unto them, and have brought them into the land of their enemies; if then their uncircumcised hearts be humbled, and they then accept of the punishment of their iniquity:

God has to teach them hard. You do not learn to believe and obey. Then see that you do not receive any promise. Promises are conditional. Do not add foolishly. Hebrew did and saw what God said.

Numbers 14:30, Doubtless ye shall not come into the land, concerning which I sware to make you dwell therein, save Caleb the son of Jephunneh, and Joshua, the son of Nun.

Remember what God promised them.

Exodus 6:8, And I will bring you in unto the land, concerning the which I did swear to give it to Abraham, to Isaac, and to Jacob; and I will provide it with you for a heritage: I am the LORD.

These people saw the miracle and wonderful work but never learned. God says I took your diseases; I want to heal a broken heart. I want to cast out demons. But look around. How many are dying, sick, possessed, broken-hearted? Why? We are spiritually deaf, hard of hearing, and stubborn for this reason.

2 Timothy 3:7 Ever learning, and never able to come to the knowledge of the truth.

I counsel and pray for many people who call me. Teach over and over, saying the worst is the Holy Spirit-filled people.

Remember, the Lord was not walking with Heathen but with Hebrews; he wanted to bless them. In the same situation, He came to us as the Holy Spirit to dwell and do work. But we do not allow him. We are no better than Hebrews; I get tired and want to tell them not to go to this church where God is not working miracles.

Jeremiah 32:33 And they have turned unto me the back, and not the face: though I taught them, rising up early and teaching them, yet they have not hearkened to receive instruction.

God is teaching us to heal, deliver, and set free; you are being trained just the opposite. The Holy Spirit is behind bars. You kidnap the Holy Spirit and put it under house arrest.

Ephesians 4:30 And grieve not the holy Spirit of God, whereby ye are sealed unto the day of redemption.

Nowadays, we must ask God to give spirit-led leadership, not spirit-filled. Many are filled but not led. They tried to stop me from ministering, but I said, get me behind, Satan.

ELIZABETH DAS

I came to seek God, no religion. I had a religion and was sick of it. It would help if you had the boldness and courage to stand against all religious authorities trained not to believe and not to practice, which is available to us. I hate to say it, but we have trained many wimp, weaklings, and ineffectual churchgoers. I get tired of council religious people.

They are confused and deceived by listening to God and attending religious churches. Good news! It is your fault and no one. The Bible says the Holy Spirit will lead you and guide you to all truth. The Holy Spirit will teach you, comfort you, and empower you. Why are you letting a human figure who is not the role model of Jesus misguide and mistreat you?

Hebrew 5:12 For when for the time ye ought to be teachers, ye have need that one teach you again which be the first principles of the oracles of God; and are become such as need milk, and not of strong meat.

Christianity is real. It is open to all who are open to it. Be open-minded and see this salvation of God. What is salvation? It meant healing, deliverance, and redemption. Take a class from the Holy Spirit.

Psalms 25:12. "What man is he that feareth the LORD? Him shall he teach in the way that he shall choose.

Psalms 32:8 "I will instruct thee and teach thee in the way which thou shalt go: I will guide thee with mine eye.

Psalms 71:17 "O God, thou hast taught me from my youth: and hitherto have I declared thy wondrous works."

Get hungry for a healthy spiritual diet. So you will be a healthy Christian. The Bible is the word of God. It is true, powerful, and reliable. What do you need to do in order to fulfill your responsibility of believing and obeying? God said, if you seek, knock and ask, then I will let you find, open and give. Where are you seeking in the church or denomination, or organization box? He is not there anymore. Remember the spirit came out of the temple? You are the temple. Now, Let the spirit teach and guide you. God only wants you to sit and relax.

Take a high mountain ride with the Lord and see the wonderland. You will see lame walk, the blind see, the demon-possessed be set free, and the dead rise. Please let us learn as the holy spirit teaches us, Hallelujah! You, your children, and your city need peace. See what Isiah says,

Isiah 54:13 And all thy children shall be taught of the LORD; and great shall be the peace of thy children.

If we learn and walk under the holy spirit's teaching, people will see God's mission as he was walking and practical teaching to people. People will run to us for this outstanding knowledge of God. The teaching of the holy spirit is to give power to the creative words spoken by your mouth to manifest. All you have to do is to believe and say. It will manifest by the power of the holy ghost.

Micah 4:2 And many nations shall come, and say, Come, and let us go up to the mountain of the LORD, and to the house of the God of Jacob, and he will teach us of his ways, and we will walk in his paths: for the law shall go forth of Zion, and the word of the LORD from Jerusalem.

FEBRUARY 18

LET US PRAY

That O Lord, open our ears to learn as spirit teaches us. Let your spirit teach us. Thank you for giving us the holy spirit as our teacher. Make us understand as it teaches. Please help us be excellent teachers to others. Let us teach our children and grandchildren to obey and serve this great living God whose desire is to bless us, protect us, and keep us from harm and danger. In Jesus 'name. AMEN!! God bless you!

FEBRUARY 19

YOUR WORDS ARE THAT POWERFUL!

God said let there be light, Let there be a firmament amid the waters, Let the waters under the heaven gather together unto one place and let the dry land appear, Let the earth bring forth grass, the herb yielding seed. The fruit tree yielding fruit after his kind, whose seed is in itself, let there be lights in the heaven's firmament to divide the day from the night, and let them be for signs, and seasons, and days, and years:

Genesis 1 And God spoke in existence to great whales and every living creature that moveth, which the waters brought forth abundantly, after their kind and every winged fowl after his kind. The earth brings forth the living creature after his kind, cattle, and creeping thing, and beast of the earth after his kind:

God said it was good. G created by the Spoken Word. Another day, God asked me to call a particular person and ask her to sit outside and read the Bible aloud. She said I prayed loud but not Bible reading. May the Lord help us see what happens when we read the Bible out loud over places. Try it; no matter who you are, it is the Word of God. God honors His word and promises. Many read words slowly so no one hears the word.

I was at the hospital to pray over a young Indian man. His father-in-law flew to the US to visit his son-in-law. I always go with the Word of God, which is the Bible. Only one could stay in the ICU room. Seeing no one inside the room, I sat on a chair and read the Bible. The father-in-law was looking inside through the glass door. I asked if he would read the Bible aloud as I entered the room. He agreed. On the next visit, the elderly father-in-law said, I had never read the Bible, but the Bible is fascinating to read. He asked for another Bible. His Father-in-law said this is an old Bible, so please buy me a new one, and I did. I right away bought him a rainbow Bible.

Never take lightly or gamble the word of God. Word has the power to establish what it is spoken for. Yesterday, the sister in Lord Pena said, I had an accident, but I said thank you, Lord.

1 Thessalonians 5:18 In everything give thanks: for this is the will of God in Christ Jesus concerning you.

I was glad the word came out of her mouth. She was a little injured and had no medical insurance, but we prayed. The word of God spoken out of your mouth gives the promised word a creating power. As you talk, you are creating the remedy, healing, deliverance, and miracle.

I remain confident and positive while shopping, trusting that I'll find what I need. There is something God has in store for me. He always provides me with a reasonable price. Many said it never occurred to me. Learn the technique. Promised word of God needs a faith ingredient to quicken it. If you speak the word by faith, it creates what you are expecting.

God spoke for light and darkness to come into existence. God did not create birds but brought them to existence by His word. So you speak what you desire and see what happens. See what and how the people are talking and receiving. When they speak negatively, there is a negative effect. Words are powerful, either negative or positive. It is your thinking, knowledge, and confidence in your God.

Daniel 11:32b the people that do know their God shall be strong, and do exploits.

Read the Word; the Word does the work. A miracle only happens when you speak what you desire.

God did many miracles by the hand of Moses, but the Hebrews were afraid when they saw Egyptians pursuing them. Moses comforted the Hebrews by speaking the word.

Exodus 14:13 And Moses said unto the people, Fear ye not, stand still, and see the salvation of the Lord, which he will shew to you to day: for the Egyptians whom ye have seen to day, ye shall see them again no more forever. 14 The Lord shall fight for you, and ye shall hold your peace.

The Lord honors what you say. You are the one who brings the matter into existence by speaking.

28 And the waters returned, and covered the chariots, and the horsemen, and all the host of Pharaoh that came into the sea after them; there remained not so much as one of them.

How beautiful! Do not scream, cry, and fear, wait on the Lord for healing, deliverance, and salvation is on the tip of your tongue. God has given His creation the authority to claim, redeem, and give life to each promise given by your creator. Do you know your creator and His might and power? Do you know His knowledge and wisdom? Do you know his riches and glory? If not, then you will never progress. You cannot get what you desire. Lack of knowledge is the deadly enemy of humans; you will die hungry, sick, oppressed, possessed, hurt, and much more. May the Lord fill us with the word spoken by God. His word needs the boosting of faith. It has mountain-moving power and life-saving strength. Word has a supernatural mind-boggling creative force.

I pray for people on the phone and see the result is beyond imagination. Teach others the word, and use the word in your conversations; the word will open others 'eyes when it fulfills.

Isaiah 55:10 For as the rain cometh down, and the snow from heaven, and returneth not thither, but watereth the earth, and maketh it bring forth and bud, that it may give seed to the sower, and bread to the eater: 11 So shall my word be that goeth forth out of my mouth: it shall not return unto me void, but it shall accomplish that which I please. It shall prosper in the thing whereto I sent it.

What is the problem? Why don't we see the works of God in operations? Simply, people do not know the promises of God. It came out of God's mouth and not yours or any human's. Believe and see; it will establish your spoken word force behind the promised word in the Bible.

I have seen many who always speak negatively. I am poor, don't have money, and cannot give. They are still poor, do not have, and always lack. But the same token is the one who always speaks powerful words rather than a different story. I am using President Trump's words, very positive, big, and great, and we see the result of it. We see His life. I pay attention to His word, and His faith force has brought significant results in the US. Amazingly, our word needs the knowledge of the almighty before we speak with confidence. Open the Word of God. Pray to the Lord to bring word back to practice in our home, school, and our individual lives in Jesus's name! Amen! God Bless You!

LET US PRAY

Heavenly Father, the creator of all we see and feel; we give you glory and honor. Your knowledge is beyond but provides us with the imagination for the things we want to bring to existence. Our faith needs knowledge. Lord, please supply it. Lord, what a wonderful God you are. Our Creator shares all He owns and has given us great knowledge. It is your Word. To Know word is to know treasure, riches, and power. Lord, the one who claimed the healing by speaking it to existence. Not only that, they became witnesses in the world. It is no longer limited to Israelites but through the blood to Gentiles. Your blood, which is hidden under your name, does the cleansing of sins if we go in the water by pronouncing the name of Jesus. The name of Jesus has swallowed up all the Old Testament names of Jehovah. This name has the blood of the Lamb; the Saviors blood has life-giving power to all who obey the word In Jesus 'name! Amen! God bless you!

FEBRUARY 20

THE KINGDOM OF GOD IS HIDDEN

The word of God is a treasure. If you read and understand with the help of the Holy Spirit, it is priceless. In the 80s, when I came to the United States, I was searching for Jesus.

I went to many churches in Los Angeles. In a few years, we moved to West Covina, California, and started going to different churches there. I was very disappointed. I felt parched but never gave up.

As Matthew 7:7 says, seek, and you will find.

When I was in India, I took bible study from Seventhday Adventists and Jehovah's Witnesses and attended Methodist Church. I also read the Bible many times. I was not ready to give up. One day while talking to a lady, she gave me two numbers of churches and asked me to try these churches. So I called.

I was praying for a church. To my great surprise, I had two numbers on my dresser, but one disappeared. So just one left. I called the pastor. He offered Bible study. Since we needed help in the family, we accepted. We needed help but only wanted it from the Lord Jesus and no other sources. Mom rejected many offers from other religions. We have a true God, and he will help. I read in the scripture, "this kind does not come out but by prayer and fasting." So I did.

As the pastor started teaching different subjects, but with baptism, I was shaken up.

I read the Bible many times but have never seen that baptism is only in the name of Jesus. As I heard the voice telling me to be baptized, I was not ready to accept, but I did. I obeyed the voice. It was a unique first experience in my life. This scripture just came alive.

As it says, your sins will be gone. Yes, it was. And I felt lighter than a feather. I can walk on water. The truth will set you free; the devil has to target the truth alone.

I was shocked; I said, devil, you cannot hide the truth from me. I was happy to have such a wonderful experience.After that, I started studying the Bible Day and night. I kept the Bible in hand reach. As scripture says, It is hidden, yes! It is.

Matthew 13:44 Again, the Kingdom of heaven is like unto treasure hid in a field; the which when a man hath found, he hideth, and for joy thereof goeth and selleth all that he hath, and buyeth that field.

When people move to the United States, they have many dreams, not just one. But after finding this truth, I was just focusing on the truth. I don't know how and why I could not see this truth before. Yes, of course, it was hidden, right? My joy was overwhelming. Now I am confident to declare that Christianity is true. It offers salvation, healing, and deliverance. I shared my experience with all.

Matthew 13:45 Again, the Kingdom of heaven is like unto a merchant man, seeking goodly pearls: 46 Who, when he had found one pearl of great price, went and sold all that he had, and bought it.

Exactly! I also got rid of false teaching. The Bible was coming alive as it says false teachers and false prophets. Yes. Now I can see the difference. Giving labels such as Church, pastor, Prophet, and cross on a building meant nothing. I was not upset but joyful. I have a choice to seek, and I did.

Matthew 13:47 Again, the Kingdom of heaven is like unto a net, that was cast into the sea, and gathered of every kind: 48 Which, when it was full, they drew to shore, and sat down, and gathered the good into vessels, but cast the bad away.

See, I took Bible study from all denomination groups, but when I found the truth, I knew what to eliminate. I started translating, making videos, teaching, and reaching out to all who would receive them. I did all that I could to let others know the truth. As I reached out to many, many accepted; started working. It delivered and healed many. I never stopped working to reach out to the lost.

Matthew 13:23 But he that received seed into the good ground is he that heareth the word, and understandeth it; which also beareth fruit, and bringeth forth, some an hundredfold, some sixty, some thirty.

Loyal people seek the word of God by praying and fasting; then, they will receive seed on good ground.

Matthew 13:33 Another parable spake he unto them; The Kingdom of heaven is like unto leaven, which a woman took, and hid in three measures of meal, till the whole was leavened.

Living through the Word of God is a contagious lifestyle. Your righteous lifestyle will influence others. Living on Earth is like being a traveler. Why are you seeking wealth, fame, and money? All you want is the Kingdom and his righteousness. All you desire is right there. Learn God by doing and applying it. Word will come alive as you

apply, do, and see how it quickens. No one can learn the word by sitting on a bench and listening year after year.

Matthew 6:33 But seek ye first the Kingdom of God, and his righteousness, and all these things shall be added unto you.

Paul says I was walking, contrary to what he was seeking. When it was revealed, it became most important, and had no fear even dying.

Philippians 3:7 But what things were gain to me, those I counted loss for Christ. 8 Yea doubtless, and I count all things but loss for the excellency of the knowledge of Christ Jesus my Lord: for whom I have suffered the loss of all things, and do count them but dung, that I may win Christ, 9 And be found in him, not having my own righteousness, which is of the law, but that which is through the faith of Christ, the righteousness which is of God by faith:

Seek God; the truth is powerful. You are a traveler; you will spend life or death eternally. Life on Earth is limited. The flesh is mortal. But the soul is immortal.

Your soul is under your possession. Mend the way, change priority, turn, take the road of righteousness, and love the truth. You will find the Kingdom where you will find peace and joy in all you desire.

LET US PRAY

I pray in the name of Jesus. That Lord gives you the hunger and thirst for the word of God. Lord, show us the truth. We want to be free and set others free. Please give us the boldness and courage to receive the Kingdom. Teach us to overcome all obstacles. Let all weapons stop; block and hinder, be removed, and cast down to hell. We know that the Kingdom of God is not meat and drink but righteousness, peace, and joy in the Holy Ghost. Lord, fill us with the Holy Ghost in Jesus 'name, AMEN. God bless you.

FEBRUARY 21

GOD DOES SURGERY

We know that the doctor does surgery on the table, putting us to sleep. He gives anesthesia after surgery. When you come back to your senses, you will experience pain and need a painkiller. In the spiritual world, anointed saints lay hand then you fall. Have you seen this? I have.

I also fell many times when anointed Saints laid hands on me. God does the surgery when you are lying on the floor, just like a doctor does when you are lying on the table. When anointed people pray over you, then the spirit does the surgery.

God performs surgery when you are on the floor, lying down. When you are asleep, God also does surgery on your body. Remember, ignorantly, Saul was slaughtering disciples. God had to do some surgery on his eyes and heart so he could see what he was doing. Saul loved God and waited for God to come as Messiah. But did not know that Jesus was the God in the flesh as a Messiah. He did not know that Jesus was the hope of 12 tribes.

Paul was a devout Pharisee who knew there was but one God. He did not want to worship Jesus, knowing he was the son of Joseph.

Acts 26:7 Unto which promise our twelve tribes, instantly serving God day and night, hope to come. For which hope's sake, king Agrippa, I am accused of the Jews.

See, this was their hope for the Messiah. Prayer Warrior cried out for help. In Damascus, God came down and did some surgery on Saul. Jesus changed his heart thinking and also his name, Saul, to Paul.

Acts 9:3 And as he journeyed, he came near Damascus: and suddenly there shined round about him a light from heaven: 4 And he fell to the earth and heard a voice saying unto him, Saul, Saul, why persecutest thou me? 5 And he said, Who art thou, Lord? And the Lord said, I am Jesus whom thou persecutest: it is hard for thee to kick against the pricks. 6 And he trembling and astonished, said, Lord, what wilt thou have me to do? And the Lord said unto him, Arise, and go into the city, and it shall be told thee what thou must do. 7 And the men which journeyed with him stood speechless, hearing a voice, but seeing no man. 8 And Saul arose from the earth; and when his eyes were opened, he saw no man: but they led him by the hand, and brought him into Damascus. 9 And he was three days without sight, and neither did eat nor drink.

God did surgery on the floor; his eyes, heart, thinking, and life needed mighty surgery from heaven above. Thank you, Lord. The story of Paul changed after the surgery.

FEBRUARY 21

Galatian 1:23. But they had heard only, That he which persecuted us in times past now preacheth the faith which once he destroyed.

They're talking about Paul. He destroyed the faith, but now he's preaching the same story.

God's surgery will bring change in life, heart, thinking, healing, deliverance, and salvation.

The change will be inside out, upside down, even a change in your look. Many years ago, I was going through some problems but did not understand. Once God told me to open a small booklet called Daily bread to read, I did. When I saw the word anxiety, God said, you have anxiety, I said, "Lord, I am not worried or afraid. While the next day was Sunday, I came from church, and God said, "Look in the dictionary for the meaning of anxiety.

So I did. I said precisely this is the way I feel; I go to sleep and wake up feeling the same. I did not understand why and did not know how to explain to someone to get help. Anxiety meant a nervous disorder marked by excessive uneasiness and apprehension. They are a group of mental illnesses, and the distress they cause can keep you from carrying on with your life normally. I work in the evening. Sunday was my day off, so I went to sleep early. I love to wake up early to pray. So I woke up at 5 AM to Pray. I heard in my spirit asking me to go back to sleep. I started reasoning. This cannot be God, so I tried to pray.

Again, I heard I should go to sleep. Now I heard someone saying do not ignore God's voice. He does have a strange agenda. Do not try God to fit in yours. So I said, God, I'm going to sleep, which I do not like, but if I am wrong, please forgive me. I fell asleep and had a dream; in my dream, men touched my head in a dream. I saw the neck down part and not the face. I woke up anxiety-free. I was very happy to be free but excited that I had learned to hear and obey God's voice. I thought God would never ask you to go to sleep when you are praying. But God had dispatched an Angel to do surgery. He wanted me to stay sleeping as the doctor gave us anesthesia to stay and sleep for surgery.
Wow that is Very exciting. To hear his voice.

Matthew 17:15, Lord, have mercy on my son: for he is lunatick, and sore vexed: for ofttimes he falleth into the fire, and oft into the water.

Mark 9:25 When Jesus saw that the people came running together, he rebuked the foul spirit, saying unto him, Thou dumb and deaf spirit, I charge thee, come out of him, and enter no more into him. And the spirit cried, and rent him sore, and came out of him: and he was as one dead; insomuch that many said, He is dead. But Jesus took him by the hand, and lifted him up, and he arose.

See, Lord did the surgery, making him sleep on the floor. That boy got his deliverance. God sends healing and deliverance while you are sleeping. I have heard. When a sick person sleeps a lot it means the body is healing during their rest. When Jesus said to Romans, "I'm the look what happened"

John 18:6. As soon then as he had said unto them, I am he, they went backward, and fell to the ground.

Revelation 1:17 And when I saw him, I fell at his feet as dead. And he laid his right hand upon me, saying unto me, Fear not; I am the first and the last:

People are slain in the spirit or falling in the spirit in the presence of Almighty God in

Number 24:4 He hath said, which heard the words of God, which saw the vision of the Almighty, falling into a trance, but having his eyes open:

Bellam also received the message as falling on the ground in the presence of God, where God's spirit overtakes us.

God is taking control when he puts you to sleep. His work has a mighty outcome without pain. And pay no beep medical bills. I know when God's presence comes.

He anoints us and breaks chains and yolks and sickness and diseases. And he is a mighty surgeon and a creator. He let Adam fall into a deep sleep to create his helpmate Eve and take his rib.

Genesis 2:21 And the LORD God caused a deep sleep to fall upon Adam, and he slept: and he took one of his ribs, and closed up the flesh instead thereof; And the rib, which the LORD God had taken from man, made he a woman, and brought her unto the man.

It's when the Lord causes you to sleep that all of this happens. In a dream, God communicates with us. God provided Pharoah, Jacob, and Nebuchadnezzar with a prophetic vision to uncover His plan. During our sleep, God reveals in our sleep.

Thank you, Lord; I believe surgery only happens in the presence of God or people who are anointed by the Holy Spirit and the power of God. Amen.

LET US PRAY

I pray. May the Lord do great surgery in a time like such. We need more surgeries by God. We need deliverance, healing, and salvation by surgeon Jesus. We need Saul to Paul's experience. May Lord help lunatics, and ADHD, ADD, Schizophrenia, and Autistic today. I pray that the Lord gives us the mighty anointing of the Holy Spirit and Power. Lord, give us the power to be workers, where God be the surgeon, work through us in Jesus's name. Amen! God bless you.

FEBRUARY 22

MY PEOPLE HAVE FORGOTTEN ME DAILY

My people have forgotten me daily. How has it happened? By Misguiding spirit. We worship and pray to many idols. How? We, our jobs, and everything we put before God become idols. How many people among us want to pray? We are not discussing praying to God five or three times as Daniel did. We can only be connected with God, our creator, by speaking and listening to Him.

We cannot be connected with God by going to prayer breakfasts or watching Christian movies. Going to church for a few hours and sitting or holding a position in church does not connect us to the Lord.

All these activities do not connect us with God but disconnect us from God. Connection with God is like having the Internet. Disconnection with God is not having the Internet.

Do you understand? We have many connections, but the most important is a connection with God. We feel lost, insecure, worried, hurt, and sick. We have police, a security system, a powerful military, and a protection system, yet we face significant problems. We are not secure unless we have security from God. Today, God is replaced by a 911 call or other security system.

Jeremiah 2:32. Can a maid forget her ornaments, or a bride her attire? Yet my people have forgotten me for days without a number.

Why many promises to secure you, and still you are not, because it does not connect you with God?

Jeremiah, 13:25, This is thy lot, the portion of thy measures from me, saith the LORD; because thou hast forgotten me, and trusted in falsehood.

Do you see weeping and crying everywhere? Mental stress, nightmares, and finding no help. You are lost, apart from how you would have been delivered from the lion's den, tiger's mouth, fiery furnace, prison jail, and enemy weapons. The supernatural help of the Lord is out by misleading and misleading spirits, taking the true Bible out of home, life, school, and organization, and having all troubles, but we are still not understanding. We still wonder what the cause is. We have just lost the path of God and the connection with God. God should not be last, but first and foremost,

Jeremiah 3:21. A voice was heard upon the high places, weeping and supplications of the children of Israel: for they have perverted their way, and they have forgotten the LORD their God.

False teachers and prophets fail God. Shooting and killing show the absence of God. Where are those people who can see Satan's destructive agenda? One call can stop all spiritual darkness through Jesus. We need someone who can stand fearlessly, find the most profound, darkest work of the enemy, and come against it. Take the key from Satan and say to him, "You lost." God's people have no taste or desire for God. There is no hunger and thirst for God, a form of godliness. We forgot to pray and to travail. A travailing spirit gives birth to ministry. God is waiting for our call. He has an army of angels to help us, but no one is calling. Call the police! Is this our solution? Screaming and blood shading are everywhere. What happened? Can anyone say let us pray and fast? God has a solution. People are lost without a true, righteous shepherd.

Ezekiel 34:2 Son of man, prophesy against the shepherds of Israel, prophesy, and say unto them, Thus saith the Lord GOD unto the shepherds; Woe be to the shepherds of Israel that do feed themselves! Should not the shepherds feed the flocks? Ye eat the fat, and ye clothe you with the wool, ye kill them that are provided: but ye feed not the flock. And as for my flock, they eat that which ye have trodden with your feet; and they drink that which ye have fouled with your feet.

Shepherd has no time for hurting, depressed, oppressed, and possessed sheep. How sad! People go psychiatric.

Can a psychiatrist help? Is drug an answer? Satan is using people to shed blood. Do you hear God's voice? Are you busy eating, drinking, golfing, buying, shopping, and vacationing? See where your Bible is. No one wants to teach the truth. Teach the word just enough to get the business going.

Do not come here to get help. We use Jesus, so our money keeps coming. We do not know what oppression, possession, deliverance, or illness are. Do not burden us with your problems since we have doctors. Yes, we get money from you. So, we can buy many houses, cars, and all luxury equipment and be happy. We are blessed. Really? Are you truly blessed or cursed? Is your city blessed or cursed? I remember in California, where I lived, I went around and knocked on doors and witnessed.

I stood at the DMV and passed Bible tracts, praying the night. Praying early in the morning, and that is why my city had peace. Many schools had a fence, but not in the city where I lived. I did what it took. Once in the night prayer, I saw a witch who came to my city. I prayed for her out. I stood in a psychic place and cursed it out. Do you know it never opened? No place for Satan. The Bible has become a multimillion business everywhere. Watch and pray over your town, city, and nation.
Jesus came to set captives free.

Possession by demons, cancers, sicknesses, drugs, alcohol, and divorces can afflict individuals. The devil got all now; why? People have gotten prideful and prayer-less. Just enough to know the scripture to be fooled. Jesus started healing and deliverance. He healed broken-hearted while the church denomination took people's eyes away from God and turned their faces toward them. Blocked them in the name-brand boxes so tight that they could not see or hear anyone but them. Talk about Jesus, but stop the work of Jesus. The name is ok, but do not get connected with him. Jesus will come, and we will lose our Kingdom.

John 11:48. If we let him thus alone, all men will believe on him: and the Romans shall come and take away both our place and nation.

We should connect no rulers with Jesus.

FEBRUARY 22

John 12:42. Nevertheless among the chief rulers also many believed on him; but because of the Pharisees they did not confess him, lest they should be put out of the synagogue:

Call 911, and wipe the blood, but do not want to call on Jesus. Where do you help cometh? 911? Government? Thank the devil. He did an excellent job of bringing revival among false teachers and pastors to shut down anyone who called on Jesus. Thank the devil that he made leaders so blind and deaf that when people need help, they do not know how to pray. They show false and fake sympathy. The criminal will be put to death. Devil will be praised to prayers, topper.

What happened? How did they get disconnected from God? Some buildings they called churches will disturb you if you pray there. Some Pastors never pray and even teach on that subject. Show starts, I mean, church starts with the same program.

Everyone comes to watch a beautiful show. No worry if anyone healed, delivered, or whatever. Give money to God. Which God? Our business keeps going as long as we disconnect you from Jesus. No one gets saved by attending church; remember, the building is not the church. By finding God, you get saved. So seek God. He is waiting for you, like a prodigal son, to return, lost coin to be found, and lost sheep to be found.

I understand you are disappointed, but you must step out of the all-man-made agenda. Seek God. Look where he can be found. Ask David, Jehoshaphat, Daniel, and others who said, "I called upon the Lord, and he helped me." God is the one you need to connect with. Prayer is communication with God.

Prayer is a simple talk with the creator. Prayer is a connecting network with the heavenly Realm: Call on Jesus.

All connections on Earth will not work. So, disconnect from them. See how many hospitals are there, but still, many are sick. God said I would put all sicknesses and more. Why? You have lost your connection with the life-giver, healer, deliverer, and savior. Disconnection from God has filled prisons, jails, crazy houses, mental institutes, Police departments, judges, and advocates. If we had kept Jesus first by praying first and praying without ceasing, all confusion would have disappeared. First, connect with Jesus. Love Jesus with all your heart, mind, soul, and strength. You will stay connected all the time. Time is so bad. As the Bible says, they will hate you if you know the Lord. Where God used to be, and the devil was out. But now the devil has taken over, and God is out. In some places, I could not teach the truth. Why?

Remember, they say, do not listen to Jesus. Satan hosts the Bible to target the truth and mocks you. When you cry, he loves it. He is happy that you are blind and deaf enough to fool you. Satan uses the Bible to destroy the truth by introducing religion. What a shameful situation. We know Jesus heals; we cry for insurance and pay insurance. What happened? Can't you seek God? Where? On your knees? Do not go to the den of thieves. They do not know what Jesus can do. There is no time for him. They worry about money. Be careful. Disconnect yourself from them. Connect with God, find true teachers and prophets who know how to connect with God. God is waiting to hear your cry and comfort you with open arms.

LET US PRAY

Lord, give us the desire to seek you. Help us connect with you so we find a solution to all problems on Earth, in Jesus 'name. Amen. God bless you.

FEBRUARY 23

JESUS IS THE HOPE OF SALVATION.

Jesus is the name that stands above all previous names as Jehovah God fulfilled His role. Jehovah God was known by different titles as he performed different acts. Jehovah was known as Nissi, Alroi, Alshedai, Adonai, and Yahweh Shalom.

But Yahweh put on flesh to shed blood; he came by the beautiful name of Jesus. It became the saving name for the world. Why name Jesus? Angel revealed the hidden name to the parents, Mary and Joseph.

Matthew 1:21 And she shall bring forth a son, and thou shalt call his name JESUS: for he shall save his people from their sins.

Jesus in Greek is Yeshua, which means Yahweh saves or is salvation. Saves means Heals, delivers, and saves. This name is above all other titles he had. The last act of Jesus was greater.

The name Jesus has the authority to heal, save, set free, and deliver. God as creator and Father, did what it took for his creation. What causes sickness?

Sin is the cause of all sicknesses. Do not believe all the labels and words the doctor gives to your sicknesses. Just repent of all your sins. Go in water to wash away sins in Jesus 'name.

Jesus's blood will apply to your sins, and you will be forgiven of all your sins, and you will be healed. You become a new creature. All things passed away. Wow! I loved the name of Jesus since I understood the meaning of this name and experienced forgiveness and healing.

Philippine 2:9 Wherefore God also hath highly exalted him, and given him a name which is above every name:

One day all knees will bow to his name. One day you will know Jesus as a mighty God and have no choice. Why not today?

Philippians 2:10 That at the name of Jesus every knee should bow, of things in heaven, and things in earth, and things under the earth; authority and power are given under auspicious names if we use the sacred name of Jesus with reverence. We will see the unexpected outcome.

Luke 10:17, And the seventy returned again with joy, saying, Lord, even the devils are subject unto us through thy name.

FEBRUARY 23

Matthew 1:23 Behold, a virgin shall be with child, and shall bring forth a son, and they shall call his name Emmanuel, which being interpreted is, God with us.

When you say Jesus, his name is above all God's titles. Satan knows the power and authority in this name. I met some Hindu ladies who have been converted to Christianity. I was interested to know what convinced them to turn to Jesus. As you know, Hindus believe in over 33 million gods and goddesses.

I will give them names so you understand. Lady Lily had a daughter who was suffering from cancer on her lips. She went to many witch doctors, gods and goddesses. Nothing happened. So, she gave up. Lady Gigi, who had just converted, informed Lily.

Why don't you pray to Jesus? He will take care of your problem. Lilly said, I do not believe in your Jesus, and I will not pray since I am tired of all these so-called gods and goddesses and witch doctors. I lost my son, husband, and money going after all these gods, witch doctors, and goddesses. Gigi said, Just try Jesus. Gigi showed her leg.

See, my leg was paralyzed and dried up. Now my leg is extended. It has life and blood circulation. Gigi continued we had no money for food, but since I turned to Jesus, we have food and peace. Lily said OK, I give your Jesus three days. In three days, cancer disappeared from her daughter's lips.

She was surprised! Jesus healed her daughter completely! So she removed all the photos of gods, goddesses, and idols from her home. The devil was mad and fought with Lily.

Her fan from the ceiling fell and cut her ear off.

She said, Jesus, I put scotch tape, and tomorrow when I wake up, let it be heal. The next day her ear was healed. Hallelujah! Lily and all her daughters are serving Jesus. Jesus is a healer. All other gods and goddesses could not help but Jesus; he is a hope of salvation. He is a healer. He took your sins on his back by taking a stripe where the blood came and paid the price of each sickness and sin. How wonderful is Jesus?

Gigi told me her husband could not afford ₹10 for food. Since Gigi turned to Jesus, Jesus became her provider. Jesus blesses her finances. Gigi says her husband gives her ₹100 daily for food. We have so much money that we have motorbikes and gold and help other family members.

No one can argue, not even Devil, what authority and power we have in the powerful saving name of Jesus. When we turn to Jesus, he takes the reins of our life. Sit back! Jesus is in charge of your journey on earth. No worries about tomorrow.

Provision, sickness, diseases, and whatever you need while passing by this earth.

Romans 15:13 Now the God of hope fill you with all joy and peace in believing, that ye may abound in hope, through the power of the Holy Ghost.

Jesus will take you to your beautiful destiny since he has higher and better plans and thoughts for you.

Jeremiah 29:11 For I know the thoughts that I think toward you, saith the LORD, thoughts of peace, and not of evil, to give you an expected end.

People live hopeless lives till they find Jesus. Jesus solves all problems and takes sorrows and worries. Restores refills and refreshes them. Experiencing the healing and deliverance of Jesus is not enough. Living for Jesus authorizes full benefits. All your wondering place to place for hope and a tiring journey in a dark, hopeless world will be over. That is why I have given my life to Jesus.

I work day and night so that someone finds healing, deliverance, and salvation.

This beautiful gospel is interesting to me. He is still in the healing, deliverance, and savings business. I have seen many being healed and delivered.

I have seen it. God has done mighty things as we call for our salvation. God has the power to do anything that you ask; just keep your hope in Jesus.

Hebrews 10:35 Cast not away therefore your confidence, which hath great recompence of reward.

We go through many physical, family, financial, emotional, and mental health trials. But trusting Jesus brings us out of all accusations, lies, and allegations of the enemy. We will see victory and deliverance through our God. I never lost hope since I knew he would bring salvation,

Isaiah 41:10 Fear thou not; for I am with thee: be not dismayed; for I am thy God: I will strengthen thee; yea, I will help thee; yea, I will uphold thee with the right hand of my righteousness.

Do not go anywhere. Just bring your petition to Jesus.

Psalms 54:4 Behold, God is mine helper: the Lord is with them that uphold my soul.

Psalms 34: The righteous cry, and the LORD heareth, and delivereth them out of all their troubles.

If you are going through any trials or trouble, do not give up or give in to the enemy. He will come on time. Your prayer has power but also requires patience for timing.

Psalms 37:5 Commit thy way unto the LORD; trust also in him; and he shall bring it to pass.

LET US PRAY

I pray, may the Lord bring light on your dark path. May the Lord grant you a petition and fulfill your heart's desire. May Jesus get peace, provision, and pathways of success by giving you an understanding of his ways and truth. May all your burdens be removed, and God give you his lighter burden. Lord, keep and guide and bless you in Jesus's name. Amen. God bless you.

FEBRUARY 24

LIFE-GIVING POWER IN THE BLOOD.

1 John 3:16 Hereby perceive we the love of God, because he laid down his life for us:

God laid down his life for you and me. Lamb symbolizes Jesus. God put on flesh temporarily to shed blood.

Acts 20:28. Take heed therefore unto yourselves, and to all the flock, over the which the Holy Ghost hath made you overseers, to feed the church of God, which he hath purchased with his blood.

God has purchased us with his blood. God, being our Father and Creator, loved us. That is why he paid the price of his blood to purchase our life by giving his blood.

Why does God have to shed blood? Jesus is God in the flesh.

Leviticus 17:11 For the life of the flesh is in the blood: and I have given it to you upon the altar to make an atonement for your souls: for it is the blood that maketh an atonement for the soul.

The reason is that he gave his blood for my penalty in hell. Blood has life. If you remove the blood from the body, your flesh will die. Life is in the blood. Adult body requires 0.2 to 1.5 gallons or 4.5 to 5.0 litres. Blood is a living thing. It never dies.

Genesis 4:10 And he said, What hast thou done? The voice of thy brother's blood crieth unto me from the ground.

Do you see? How is Abel's blood crying out to God? A killed or murdered person can testify against the killer and murderer to God. The blood of righteous Abel has no power to take away our sins. Righteous Abel has his father's sinful blood. Remember, blood is from Father's side and never from the mother's.

Hebrew 12:24, And to Jesus the mediator of the new covenant, and to the blood of sprinkling, that speaketh better things than Abel.

Since the blood of Jesus has no sin, sin has a sting of death, which is eternal death in hell. Blood is the only source of life for our eternal death in hell.

2 Corinthians 5:21, For he hath made him be sin for us, who knew no sin; that we might be made the righteousness of God in him. We need sinless blood. God voluntarily put on flesh and shed his blood to take away our sins.

Hebrew 9:12. Neither by the blood of goats and calves, but by his own blood he entered in once into the holy place, having obtained eternal redemption for us.

Our sin cost God his life. The Bible says God came in the flesh.

1 Timothy 3:16, And without controversy great is the mystery of godliness: God was manifest in the flesh.

Many Bible versions have removed God and put the word 'He ' to create confusion. But it is one God put on flesh for a redemption plan.

God is sovereign. He can do it anytime without any outer help. Life is in the blood. We need blood to escape the eternal punishment in hell. A sinful Man needs saving sinless blood.

Hebrews 9:22 And almost all things are by the law purged with blood, and without shedding of blood is no remission.

Our sins cost Jesus his life, which is in the blood.

Matthew 26:28 My blood of the New Testament, which is shed for many for transmission of sins.

Jesus himself said that my blood is what you are going to need for the remission of your sins. That is why we go underwater in Jesus 'name. Why? Baptism is not a ritual. Baptism Is for the washing away of our sins. Blood is hidden under the name of Jesus.

Ephesians 1:7 In whom we have redemption through his blood, the forgiveness of sins, according to the riches of his grace;

Jesus wants you to know that he did all it took to help you. So you have the power to live on Earth through his blood. His blood will speak when Satan comes like a flood. Living Blood will say for you that you are righteous.

Jesus's blood will speak that you are not guilty. Hallelujah! I remember this true story.

A woman Satan worshiper met two Pentecostal ladies discussing with her that all Satan worshippers are fasting and praying to destroy churches. Blood serves as a testimony for our righteousness, as confessed by Satan worshippers in conversation.

They were praying and fasting to Satan to send demons to make churches fall financially and pastors to fall into adultery. When you go in the water in the name of Jesus, as the book of Acts churches says, your sins are remitted, and your consciousness is purged.

Hebrews 9:14 How much more shall the blood of Christ, who through the eternal Spirit offered himself without spot to God, purge your conscience from dead works to serve the living God?

1 Peter 3:21, The like figure whereunto even baptism doth also now save us (not the putting away of the filth of the flesh, but the answer of a good conscience toward God,) by the resurrection of Jesus Christ:

Biblical definition for purge is to clear from guilt or moral defilement as to purge one of guilt or crime. You purge away sin to clear from accusation or the charge of a crime, as in the ordeal as Jesus gave his blood on the

Heavenly holy altar. He went and took away the key to hell and death.

Revelation 1:18 I am he that liveth, and was dead; and, behold, I am alive for evermore, Amen; and have the keys of hell and death.

Blood gave us access to the holy of holy places; what we lost in the Garden of Eden, Jesus bought back through his blood. We can boldly enter his throne room by using his blood on our sins.

Ephesians 2:13 But now in Christ Jesus ye who sometimes were far off are made nigh by the blood of Christ.

Adam and Eve hid them when they sinned. Sin is the transgression of the law. Stay away from what God says no. Their relationship with God was broken.

Isaiah 59:2 But your iniquities have separated between you and your God, and your sins have hid his face from you, that he will not hear.

Thank the Lord, for he did all just for his creation. What we have to do is to repent of all our sins. And take his name in baptism to wash away our sins. We can have a new life.

2 Corinthians 5:17 Therefore, if any man be in Christ, he is a new creature: old things are passed away; behold, all things are become new.18 And all things are of God, who hath reconciled us to himself by Jesus Christ, and hath given to us the ministry of reconciliation;19 To wit, that God was in Christ, reconciling the world unto himself, not imputing their trespasses unto them; and hath committed unto us the word of reconciliation.

LET US PRAY

May God help us to do what it takes to get forgiveness which is in Jesus's name. Through water baptism in the precious name of Jesus, the blood we receive purifies us from our sins. May, Lord, give us that humbleness to find the way, the truth, and eternal life, that caused God his life. May the Lord bless you with eternal life in Jesus's Name. Amen! God bless you.

FEBRUARY 25

GUN HAS REPLACED THE BIBLE.

Give your children a Bible, or the Devil will give them a gun. Is the weapon a replacement for the Bible?

Is this the way you want to live? Introducing your children to police, psychiatric, karate, kid word, dancing, swimming, meth, music, and games where there is no true help. Whose report do we hear? Police, News media relayer, or God. Satan brings the pulpit down to his level. Where demon-possessed lawyers, cheaters, prostitutes, druggies, alcoholics, adulterers, and sinners do not feel uncomfortable. Tell me simple faith and love. Bible says God's way is narrow with all restrictions to go to heaven.

God took time to write 66 books to show us a righteous way.

Eternal life, prosperity, and security are created by false teachers and prophets who walk in the flesh and not in spirit. Like Eve, Adam Esau, and King Solomon, King Saul died lustfully without receiving promises.

1 Timothy 4:8 For bodily exercise profiteth little: but godliness is profitable unto all things, having promise of the life that now is, and of that which is to come.

Jochebed's mother taught Moses, Merriam, and Aron the truth. Living in Egypt, she did not budge from her faith. She did not look for simple faith. A mother-father is the teacher. Do not rely on Sunday school teachers, teachers, or the country you live in.

When you give birth to your children, you must know that the place called Earth has a devil, fallen unholy angels, and demons with a great agenda. Satan plans to misguide, kill, steal and destroy.

The parents do not take time to guide their children, and that is why they and their children become a victim of Satan.

Jochebed being a daughter of Levi, knew the ways of God. She taught her kids since there was no operant church, synagogue, or Sunday school. Her faith, wisdom, dedication, and zeal demonstrate in her children's life. God used Moses since he was a hearer and doer. God used Moses to bring the Hebrews out of great slavery.

They fought with Pharaoh and introduced the word Jehovah God as a deliverer and a mighty God. A spiritual, Godly woman took all her time keeping her children safe and sound from Satan's killing, stealing, and destroying tactics. Jochebed gave birth to the best children who brought the heavenly commandments, laws, and precepts.

FEBRUARY 25

Deuteronomy 4:7 For what nation is there so great, who hath God so nigh unto them, as the LORD our God is in all things that we call upon him for? 8 And what nation is there so great, that hath statutes and judgments so righteous as all this law, which I set before you this day? Is this the way our nations are?

Are you secured with security systems, owning a gun, and automated power? Or do you put your trust in the God of the Bible? Can a gadget help to guard you in distress and trouble? David, Daniel, people of God called on Him, and God sent them help.

Psalms 18:6 "In my distress I called upon the LORD, and cried unto my God: he heard my voice out of his temple, and my cry came before him, even into his ears."

We live in a world where there is a real battle, but we do not know the solution. We need true teachers and followers of God like Moses, Joshua, and David.

Psalms 55:16 "As for me, I will call upon God; and the LORD shall save me."

We are going through a most critical time shooting, killing, sickness, suicide, and divorces. Prison jails are full and fear everywhere.

Do we have any Jochebed, Ester, Merriam, Moses, or Joshua? We need someone who can take us back to the law and commandments of God. Anytime I hear someone sick right away, they run to the doctor. The doctor prescribes medicine, and without any hesitation, they take it.

Why not seek God rather than a doctor, psychiatrist, police, and other sources where there is no help? Is there anyone who practices the word of God?

Does anyone know to call on God when shooting, killing, and someone is hurting? Can anyone do as Jesus said, anointing and praying? Mom and Dad used to pray all night for prison doors open to the rescue. I am so hurt that all these possessed and oppressed people need someone to cast down their demons and call on God.

Devil in them uses their hand and mind and leaves them behind the prison door.

He goes out to look for someone to kill more. Do you understand? Devil is the one who uses the hand, feet, and mind. How about raising children to know the life-giving word of God?

Your children can become the light to many. Teach them to swing the sword of the word of God, to destroy the plan and strategy of satan. Satan has taken our Christian Country and cities. Why?

Because there is some belief in simple faith, what is that? God's word is not a buffet. Take what fits your life and throw out what is inconvenient to your flesh.

We find blind leaders who are lost in agreeing on what we like. Hell is real and hot. No light, just darkness, screaming torment, and no way out. Someone ready to give life for faith or fool to compromise. The pleasure of the world has become their first and foremost.

Did Jesus take a short way, or did he empty all? Suffer all the way? Are you falling by taking a cross, or have you already thrown it away? Why? Is there anyone who understands all gone astray? Does no one understand? God said I am the answer. Living in the true word of God is the answer.

Deuteronomy 30:15-16, 19 See, I have set before thee this day life and good, and death and evil; 16 In that I command thee this day to love the LORD thy God, to walk in his ways, and to keep his commandments and his statutes and his judgments, that thou mayest live and multiply: and the LORD thy God shall bless thee in the land whither thou goest to possess it. 19 I call heaven and Earth to record this day against you, that I have set before you life and death, blessing and cursing: therefore, choose life, that both thou and thy seed may live.

Be spiritual and choose life and blessings.

1 Corinthians 2:14 But the natural man receiveth not the things of the Spirit of God: for they are foolishness unto him: neither can he know them, because they are spiritually discerned.

We hear news which is no more good news. News has made people insensitive. Please give your children the Bible and teach them the word as it is. You will be blessed, and so will your children. Be healthy and blessed.

Revelation 22:19 And if any man shall take away from the words of the book of this prophecy, God shall take away his part out of the book of life, and out of the holy city, and from the things which are written in this book.

LET US PRAY

Lord, give us knowledge, wisdom, and understanding to raise our children like David, Moses, Joshua, and Esther. Bold and courageous to stand alone to prove the power of God in a critical time like such. We need light through your words. We need your spirit to teach, guide, and empower us. Lord, use our hand to cast out demons. He'll seek and comfort others and not shoot and kill. We are going through a time when simple faith, the Devil's doctrine, failed God. Help us find the right path and truth in Jesus's name. Amen. God bless you.

FEBRUARY 26

GOD, INCREASE MY CAPACITY.

If you have a small cup, then you receive so much only. Liquid capacity of a gallon, litter, and other measurement carries, respectively. According to the capacity of the container, you can carry the liquid. Same way God can give the Holy Spirit, faith, and spiritual miracles according to our faith capacity.

Matthew 9:29 "According to your faith be it unto you".

You are a vessel that has a measure of faith. There is a fourfold blessing, a tenfold blessing, and an unlimited blessing.

Well, to receive all, we need to have a different capacity.

Isaiah 44:3 "For I will pour water upon him that is thirsty, and floods upon the dry ground: I will pour my spirit upon thy seed, and my blessing upon thine offspring":

God has a bigger measurement to give us. It all depends how much we allow. Just follow the steps as instructed by God.

Malachi 3:10 "Bring ye all the tithes into the storehouse, that there may be meat in mine house, and prove me now herewith, saith the LORD of hosts, if I will not open you the windows of heaven, and pour you out a blessing, that there shall not be room enough to receive it".

During the dispensation of Law, we brought tithes and offerings to the temple but now we don't have a temple so give those who are working as laborers 30, 60, hundred, and unlimited blessings in return. Remember when he wants to bless you, keep unlimited capacity as prophet asked women to go get the vessel borrowed, not little.

2 King 4:3 "Then he said, Go, borrow thee vessels abroad of all thy neighbours, even empty vessels; borrow not a few".

Your mind designs are limited or limitless. God wants to keep blessing as long as you allow.

2 King 4:6 And it came to pass, when the vessels were full, that she said unto her son, Bring me yet a vessel. And he said unto her, There is not a vessel more. And the oil stayed.

The oil stayed as they limited having no more vessels. God has no limit.

John 3:34, "For he whom God hath sent speaketh the words of God: for God giveth not the Spirit by measure unto him".

God can give gifts of spirit, and healing as you allow. He can give how much you open up. God is an unlimited, omnipotent God.

Ephesians 1:19 And what is the exceeding greatness of his power to us-ward who believe, according to the working of his mighty power.

His mighty power can work through us as we permit God.

John 14:12 Verily, verily, I say unto you, He that believeth on me, the works that I do shall he do also; and greater works than these shall he do; because I go unto my Father.

How and what Jesus did when he was walking on this earth.

John 21:25 And there are also many other things which Jesus did, the which, if they should be written every one, I suppose that even the world itself could not contain the books that should be written. Amen.

So the God of heaven has done so much and said you can do greater things. Can I do greater? Yes, and that's what I am looking for. When we see earthquakes, tsunamis, hurricanes, and tornadoes, we see God's power in operation. Hebrews could not believe after seeing the great work of plague and deliverance from the cruelty of Pharaoh. The great and mighty God acted based on their capacity to believe in this wonderworking miracle.

Every step we take; we must know that we are enabling or disabling God. How much and what do we want from God? How much is your capacity? No matter what God does still you can limit or release to perform his act. Let us see what Hebrew did.

Exodus 17:3 And the people thirsted there for water; and the people murmured against Moses, and said, wherefore is this that thou hast brought us up out of Egypt, to kill us and our children and our cattle with thirst?

We stop our Miracle, Blessing, and promises, by forgetting what he is capable of doing.

Psalms 106:13 They soon forgat his works; they waited not for his counsel: But murmured in their tents, and hearkened not unto the voice of the LORD.

Humans forget God and his works as they face different situations and problems. God wants us to remember his mighty work by hearing and remembering his work.

Numbers 14:22 Because all those men which have seen my glory, and my miracles, which I did in Egypt and in the wilderness, and have tempted me now these ten times, and have not hearkened to my voice; 23 Surely they shall not see the land which I sware unto their fathers, neither shall any of them that provoked me see it: 24 But my servant Caleb, because he had another spirit with him, and hath followed me fully, him will I bring into the land whereinto he went; and his seed shall possess it.

Here Caleb received the promise as he allowed God to bless him.

A lady said if I touch His garment, I will be whole. Whole means mind, body, soul, and Spirit healed and sound. Whole means complete. Not defective or imperfect, restored to health and soundness. She knew the man restored in her region from the legions of demons. She can also receive healing from blood issues if she touches the Lord Jesus's garment. You create a negative or positive atmosphere respectively with your confidence. Our words give God or the devil a platform to produce or fail.

Before leaving Earth God promised his spirit and nine gifts of Spirit to do work. He said I will give you different gifts as you covet. Gifts of spirit are to edify the church (remember you are Church) Also will increase the believers as they see the miracles, healing, prophecy, healing of heart, discerning spirit, message and supernatural information for the situation.

Gifts of the spirit are available to all as you give the place by asking and desiring for the purpose of edifying the Church of God. It is all up to us to allow or to disallow. All depends on what you are seeking to do with gifts.

1 Corinthians 12:31, But covet earnestly the best gifts:

Covet meant too long for. To desire very much. The purpose of God is the same. To continue the mission that he started.

Luke 4:18 The Spirit of the Lord is upon me because he hath anointed me to preach the gospel to the poor; he hath sent me to heal the brokenhearted, to preach deliverance to the captives, and recovering of sight to the blind, to set at liberty them that are bruised,

Ask God for greater, go wild in your imagination.

Jeremiah 33:3 Call unto me, and I will answer thee, and shew thee great and mighty things, which thou knowest not.

Do not put God in people in boxes of religion. It will limit God and his purpose, and allow the Holy Spirit to teach, guide, and empower you to do the impossible. Ask God to increase your capacity. To carry his spirit since he is capable of doing impossible, supernatural, celestial, miraculous, and incredible.

LET US PRAY

Lord God whose purpose is to do wonders for his people makes us partaker of it. Incredible God helps us to believe in the impossible so others can be blessed. Break us, lose up all limiting, stopping, unbelieving factors from us. May the Omnipotent God be magnified on this earth. Let God of heaven be blessed as we allow ourselves to be his unlimited vessel in Jesus's name. Amen! God bless you.

FEBRUARY 27
SET YOUR PRIORITY IN ORDER.

We all have a to-do list, but if we want to be blessed, then we should keep our program in God's order.

Bible says first,

1 Timothy 2: I exhort therefore, that, first of all, supplications, prayers, intercessions, and giving of thanks, be made for all men; 2 For kings, and for all that are in authority; that we may lead a quiet and peaceable life in all godliness and honesty. 3 For this is good and acceptable in the sight of God our Saviour; 4 Who will have all men to be saved, and to come unto the knowledge of the truth.

Every morning I wake up before 4:00 AM. I get connected with God. I know Satan works in the night to destroy the day. Before I met my day, I meet God and ask him which is the safest route. I intercede for others. What a great job assigned to us! What a wonderful thing!

Being human, we can come before His throne room to get security, direction, protection, and blessings. Let me tell you, God is real. I always wanted to be rich through his blessings.

Proverbs 10:22 The blessing of the LORD, it maketh rich, and he addeth no sorrow with it.

He knows how to multiply and add. God wants us to get connected with Him first, then get our day protected, blessed, and prosperous. Make God in charge. God wants his children to check in with him to get direction.

Every day is a gift. As it says, give us Our Daily Bread. Manna came every day.

So by inviting God every day to be an overseer, it makes the day blessed and prosperous. He reassures us, I will give you what you need as I have promised in the Garden of Eden. But first, take care of my vineyard. You dress it as I have commanded you to do so. God has a map. If we follow His map of instruction, then what a peaceful life we will have.

Leviticus 26:6 And I will give peace in the land, and ye shall lie down, and none shall make you afraid: and I will rid evil beasts out of the land, neither shall the sword go through your land.

Exodus 23:22 But if thou shalt indeed obey his voice, and do all that I speak; then I will be an enemy unto thine enemies, and an adversary unto thine adversaries.

FEBRUARY 27

Are you afraid of swords, guns, kidnappers, gangs, cheaters, liars, or wicked? Get your life in order, as the word of God says. Learn from a book called the Bible and find the way you have lost.

If darkness is in your way, then get everything in order. Pray with given authority. Pray with the knowledge. It is our job to keep God's authority above us. He will keep us on the right path when we do not know what to do. Otherwise, there is chaos, uproar, and havoc will be in our land. Remember, we are not here to work for material things, but God. Our priority should be to guard our souls against hell.

Abraham had his priority in order, as he was called. God's plan for him to come out of his kindred, and he did.

The test of Mount Moriah was the key to success. He passed the test. God is real. He wants to keep us in order. So we have peace, protection, and riches.

Genesis 13:2 And Abram was very rich in cattle, in silver, and in gold. So was Isaac, as he kept priority in order.

Genesis 26:13 And the man waxed great, and went forward, and grew until he became very great:

Psalms 112:1-3 Praise ye the Lord. Blessed is the man that feareth the Lord, that delighteth greatly in his commandments. 2 His seed shall be mighty upon earth: the generation of the upright shall be blessed. 3 Wealth and riches shall be in his house: and his righteousness endureth for ever.

See, people go after wealth. But if they know the key to wealth will change their life story. If we seek God, then he will not keep any good things from us. He is a supplier in abundance. I loved to get connected with God before the sun rises. I continue seeking the way of God during the day.

In the year 1999, I had an accident. I went through a physical trial. According to God, it was a fiery trial. And God assured me I will come out as gold, and I did! Praise the Lord! My God knows how to test and how to bring them out of a trial to make a person qualified.

He did to Abraham, Job, and many others who were called for his Kingdom. God told me when He called me for His service, "I will take care of you, work for me as I am taking your job away". At this trial, I didn't know what he was thinking. For my life, I wanted his will. I was not worried so much about the supply. I learned God's faithfulness while walking Him.

I enjoy living for God. I have given my life 100% to God. Knowing only Jesus can bless me and not my salary. During my trial, I thought I am glad I have fixed up my house, now nothing to worry about extra expenses. My retirement pension was not enough to pay house notes. All that I figured out was impossible. He made it possible through His divine power. I had many questions in my mind. Thank God He proved me wrong by moving me in His magnificent plan. I wasn't getting enough money to sustain my expenses, but Oh Hallelujah, what a great God.

Do not ask how I paid the other bills. Later he gave me a brand new house which is bigger and better. I never have to worry about tomorrow. And if I did as a human, then I told myself that the Lord is faithful. He will supply every time he meets my needs. I never tried to help God out but trusted him. I know he said; "You work for me and I will take care of you. That is comfort. I have never asked for monetary help, having no job, and a little retirement Check.

Matthew 6:33, But seek ye first the kingdom of God, and his righteousness; and all these things shall be added unto you.

Lord supplied all when He sent me out. The Lord provided for my trip, food, and accommodation. Keeping priority right, we experience the Bible's promises to come alive. I see people always complain. They make so much money, still empty. They receive crazy income, which I've never seen in my life. But I live beautifully and also helped people with my meager check.

All over the world, I work as a minister. I see miracles, healing, and people being saved every day. I work for God and serve him every day. In many places I go, probably they never knew I came and prayed as they were in a coma. Praying on the phone when they do not know who I am. Keeping our priorities in the right order is the key to success and receiving a blessing for ourselves and for the generation to come.

God is a promise keeper. He shows mercy to1000s generations. Keeping your priority will keep blessings flowing. Because God wants to help those whose priority is messed up.

In Haggai 1:6 Ye have sown much, and bring in little; ye eat, but ye have not enough; ye drink, but ye are not filled with drink; ye clothe you, but there is none warm; and he that earneth wages earneth wages to put it into a bag with holes.

Nowadays, people work morning to evening and work many jobs. In the end, they die of cancer, heart attack, and many other illnesses. How sad! How simple to keep our priorities on track and receive what we are seeking from God?

I always wanted blessings from God for me and my family. That is the only thing we can keep for eternity. Remember, all you have on earth is going to be burned as the earth will be burned. Set your priorities in order. Keep God's order as your priority. When it ends well, everything is fine.

LET US PRAY

May our Lord Jesus bless you with wisdom, knowledge, and understanding through his word. Quicken us through your Word. Let our lives be in His priority plan. Let God's agenda be ours. Give us a supernatural calculator which has adding and subtraction only. May the Lord give us the highest blessing. We want this world blessed through us, in Jesus 'name. Amen! God bless you.

FEBRUARY 28

ACTION HAS AN ATTACHMENT.

Our action has an attachment to blessings or curses. Every action of a person decides their tomorrow. Many felt they had a right to act and react wrong, but be careful. Having a position will dare you to do unjust, but leave the revenge in the hand of God. Some think that I'm young so I can abuse my elderly. Set your preference in order. You arrived or were promoted just for a test. No one gets a permanent position. Your action has an attachment. Don't be surprised if you see grief and sorrow if you have not acted wisely and righteously.

The Bible says our work does not save us. We cannot receive salvation by works. But the sinless blood of the savior has life, and Lord Jesus gave it for us. It does not mean that we live whatever and however. The Bible has many don'ts and do's and wills for or against.

Ten Commandments never changed. Follow commandments, teach against lie, adultery, stealing, etc.

As we know, Enoch,

Hebrews 11:5 By faith Enoch was translated that he should not see death; and was not found, because God had translated him: for before his translation he had this testimony, that he pleased God.

David was the man of God's own heart, but he committed adultery and murdered a man. It brought him great judgment. His action has an attachment to serious punishment in his bloodline.

2 Samuel 12:10 Now therefore the sword shall never depart from thine house; because thou hast despised me, and hast taken the wife of Uriah the Hittite to be thy wife.

King David's Child died, and his son Absalom took his concubine. David did it in secret, and Absalom did it in the open. Your sins have an attachment to the result. David attached curses, sickness, and sorrows to his descendants.

Teach your children righteousness so they are blessed. Do not abuse the power against someone whom you dislike. It is a matter of eternal judgment of life and death, and curse and blessing. It is a serious matter, right? Pray that God brings God-fearing spouses into your family. Be a good example to your children. I have seen parents use children against in-laws if they dislike them. Be careful, teach them to love, to be kind and helpful. You generate curses and blessings in their life. Remember, they will suffer consequences. Teach your child the correct way so they receive blessings and you as well. God is serious about his statutes, commandments, and laws. Get serious, otherwise, you are playing with fire.

Eli as a priest harms his own descendants. Not taking heed and correcting his children, according to the laws of God. What a curse he attached to his offspring. Have you seen wicked lineage, cursed to die with sickness and diseases? Sin has curses that attach to your issues.

2 Samuel 2:31 Behold, the days come, that I will cut off thine arm, and the arm of thy father's house, that there shall not be an old man in thine house. 32 And thou shalt see an enemy in my habitation, in all the wealth which God shall give Israel: and there shall not be an old man in thine house for ever. 33 And the man of thine, whom I shall not cut off from mine altar, shall be to consume thine eyes, and to grieve thine heart: and all the increase of thine house shall die in the flower of their age.

See, Eli's action has an attachment to calamities. It is going to follow Eli's offspring. Now you understand, to fear the Lord, and do what he has asked. Be careful of your actions. I know the life story of Brother in the Lord. His name is Mr. Min. He prayed for me and I received healing. His life is an example of being blessed. Many of his family members told him to forget the hard labor he was doing for Jesus. He did not have enough money so he went around to pray. His car broke down many times when he went out to pray and came home late at night. His children will hear a comment from other rich family members against their father. But Brother Min did God's work without expecting in return. After some years, I saw the blessing start flowing. God turned all around, all grandchildren taking first place in all activities in school. All the children are married and hold good jobs, brother Min and his wife have a good marriage. Children and grandchildren are doing great. All blessings came because of good, godly actions. There is an attachment to your actions. His wife says these blessings are because of Grandpa going around and praying for people. The rich brother and their children have lost everything. His brother's children were on drugs, some divorce, wife died of illnesses. Blessings are attached to your actions. Righteousness gets attached to all provisions, privileges, and benefits for them and for thousands of generations.

Psalms 37:25, I have been young, and now am old; yet have I not seen the righteous forsaken, nor his seed begging bread.

1 Chronicle 16:14 He is the LORD our God; his judgments are in all the earth.

Matthew 5:5 Blessed are the meek: for they shall inherit the earth.

Deuteronomy 12:28 Observe and hear all these words which I command thee, that it may go well with thee, and with thy children after thee forever, when thou doest that which is good and right in the sight of the LORD thy God.

The Bible says fear of the Lord is the beginning of wisdom. Fear knowing Lord Jesus is alive and has no variants in him. God is holy, righteous, and true. Decide today that you leave a blessing for your children. Mary, Rehab, Joshua, Moses, and Queen Esther brought blessing, deliverance, and birth to the Kingdom by their actions. We are the door for all our offspring, for God's blessing to continue for thousands of generations.

If we take the right actions.

Psalms 5:12 For thou, LORD, wilt bless the righteous; with favour wilt thou compass him as with a shield.

We must take heed and be careful about our actions because every action has an attachment.

FEBRUARY 28

LET US PRAY

Oh Lord, please show us a righteous way, so we inherit the blessings for us and our children.

Lord, we want to inherit all your blessings. We can receive your promises if we walk in your ways, laws, and commandments. Show us your plan of success so we and our family will be blessed. We want a shield and protection from you. We want to continue in blessings for generations after us, in Jesus 'name. Amen! God bless you.

FEBRUARY 29

FEW ARE CHOSEN!

Many are called, but few are chosen!

Matt 22:14 For many are called, but few are chosen.

God chooses who chooses him over everything. Ruth chose the God of Naomi, so God blessed her. He turns her into a widow to marry. He came through her lineages. The purpose of the heart is to be watched. Loving God can be shown in our looking, eating, and having.

2 Pet 1:10 Wherefore the rather, brethren, give the diligence to make your calling and election sure: for if ye do these things, ye shall never fall:

Be diligent and add faith, virtue, knowledge, temperance, patience, godliness, kindness, and charity. Our desire to have GOD or things to show off? Our desire shows what is in our hearts. David got good blood and has goodly godly choices. So God gave her health and wealth blessings beyond and above. God chooses if we choose him over the nation, our kindred, and our family. He loves those who love HIM. Set your affection on things above, not on things on the earth. Learn how the creator moves and how creation benefits.

Do you know you can mortify your affection and desire for this world by fasting and praying? When you say no to the things of the world and continue watching where you are and how you are keeping your eyes will help you deny obstacles to your spiritual growth. Our choices make God get attracted toward us or turn His face away from us. Life has a lesson to learn from Lord Jesus, other Biblical characters, and the surrounding people.

1 Corinthians 6:9 Know ye not that the unrighteous shall not inherit the kingdom of God? Be not deceived: neither fornicators, nor idolaters, nor adulterers, nor effeminate, nor abusers of themselves with mankind, 10 Nor thieves, nor covetous, nor drunkards, nor revilers, nor extortioners, shall inherit the kingdom of God. 11 And such were some of you: but ye are washed, but ye are sanctified, but ye are justified in the name of the Lord Jesus, and by the Spirit of our God.

All your life, we have to decide. It is not one time but every day a new situation, problem, and matter to decide.

Proverbs 14:12 - There is a way which seemeth right unto a man, but the end thereof are the ways of death.

FEBRUARY 29

It is always your choice, no one but yours. Daniel prayed 3 times. Three Hebrew slaves chose not to worship idols. Esther fasted three days and nights without food or water. Moses chose not to desire Egypt and its position. People who choose the word of God to practice end up having what they desire, but better and higher.

Jeremiah 29:11 For I know the thoughts that I think toward you, saith the LORD, thoughts of peace, and not of evil, to give you an expected end.

When you are thinking of God, He has shown in His word through statutes, laws, commandments, and precepts. He is also thinking and making your path toward prosperity, success, protection, and wealth. The choices and decisions you make determine the hidden conditions of God's blessings.

What is God showing us by putting the forbidden tree in the garden of Eden? Do we have to choose what to do?

Deuteronomy 11:26 Behold, I set before you this day a blessing and a curse;

Life has all freedom but misuses freedom of choice can have an eternal good or bad effect. Have you seen all this trouble God took to instruct us through the word of God using many prophets, teachers, priests, High priests, apostles, evangelists, pastors, preachers, and the Holy Spirit to lead us to the Blessings of God? He blessed His creation when He created them. All you have to do is decide to please God and He will chase you to bless you.

We grew up around people, school friends, neighbors, family members, and cousins. We see the decision they make brings either chaos or success in their life. Deciding to have friends is also an open door to trouble or success. Your choices leave a legacy of good or bad effects on the world and bloodline. Today, decide to pay attention in making the right decision where Lord Himself can say you are good and faithful and enter your rest.

Lord has so much not on earth but for eternity. You should not decide on a temporary solution. Do not fear taking over your heart and mind to divert your life to destruction. It is the Lord who protects, helps, promotes, provides, and gives success, but only one condition is for you to make the right decision. How easy it is to be fooled by the choices we make. Life on earth is temporary, our physical life is temporary and life is short. We get blinded by the things we see, feel taste, and pride in life. If you reach heaven then you know what Lord was talking to you and what He has stored for you. When the Lord said something, remember He already knows what He has blessed and kept on yonder. Let the obstruction of eyes be the obstacle of your flesh and pride. It is either God or Devil. It is over hell or heaven. It is either Blessings or curses, and either life over death.

What a serious matter! It is a job to make life decisions and not just live a day at a time. Now, do you understand why the Lord said to choose blessing and life? Your making a plan without the instruction of God can lead you to a total darkness abode where there is no exit door.

You also choose your life by making choices in your life. Some will be called wise and some fool. Your chores will make you que on right or left according to the choice you made. You can be called a sheep or goat.

Lord has a mapquest and if you connect with the network of the Holy Spirit then He will guide, lead, teach, empower and strengthen you to reach your destiny.

When choosing you over a rebellious person like Eli, King Saul or Adam and Eve know that there is the right thing you are doing and choosing the right path. It is not you but the Lord is taking you higher.

LET US PRAY

Lord, we are grateful for giving us the freedom to choose. We ask for your direction, counseling, and wisdom to choose. Lord, we do not want torepeat the past. We know your spirit leads and guides. So, the Holy Spirit leads and guides us to all the truth. We gird up with your righteousness. We can be the light and a good example of the follower of Christ. Lord help your creation in Jesus's name. Amen! God bless you.

MARCH

MARCH 1

ARE YOU PUZZLED?

Do you question every trouble and problem you see in the world today? Are you looking for solutions and finding no answers about what to believe or whom to believe? Let me encourage you to think and stand on the solid ground of the Word of God, the Bible. From the beginning, the Bible is God's accurate and infallible word. Please read, quote, stand on, and testify about its significant power. The devil hates when you testify of the greatness of God and the power in His Word. Testifying of Jesus will bring many souls to Him. Your testimony is the Blood of Jesus against the Devil. The devil trembles at the Blood of Jesus. The Blood is under the name of Jesus. Life-giving power is in the Blood of Jesus. The devil quiets down, mentioning the name of Jesus and the Blood of Jesus.

Revelation 12:11 tells us, "And they overcame him by the blood of the Lamb, and by the word of their testimony; and they loved not their lives unto the death."

What are you allowing Jesus to do through you today? Don't tell them about your church, but tell them about Jesus and what He can do. What you hear in the news today is shootings, killings, raping, drugs, kidnapping, accidents, movies, makeup, Hollywood celebrities, etc. Jesus gave authority and power to His disciples. Are you a disciple of Jesus?

Mark 6:13 "And they cast out many devils, and anointed with oil many that were sick, and healed them.14a And king Herod heard of him; (for his name was spread abroad:)"

Luke 10:17 "And the seventy returned again with joy, saying, Lord, even the devils are subject unto us through thy name."

Is this happening around you? Do you see miracles, healings, and the power of God in operation? If not, then it is available. Just seek the truth, anointing, and power.

The Bible says in Hebrew 13:8 "Jesus Christ the same yesterday, and today, and forever."

Please seek Jesus to find the power to continue His task, project, and assignment. The devil did another great job of getting rid of prayer in most buildings; you called them a church. What about your personal life since you are the temple of God? Without prayer, we are disconnected from God. You do not hear from Him if you do not call on Him. Remember, we are limited. The flesh can get connected with God only by prayer, which is talking to Him. Even Jehovah God in the flesh prayed when His Spirit came in the body of Jesus.

MARCH 1

Matthew 14:23 says "And when he had sent the multitudes away, he went up into a mountain apart to pray: and when the evening was come, he was there alone.

Mark 1:35 And in the morning, rising up a great while before day, he went out, and departed into a solitary place, and there prayed." Get connected with Jesus.

Another thing the devil will tell you is just believe and have a simple faith. This false doctrine is what the churches and organizations teach and preach. Once you accept this lie, you only know about Jesus as much as they teach you. Religion, denomination, or non-denominational can never become a true replacement for God. You connect with God by opening your heart, mind, and mouth. Find a cave, mountain, closet, bedroom, or car, and talk to Him. He is your God. Don't get limited by what someone teaches you. Seek God for yourself. Start talking to God.

He will respond to you. God has given you teachers and prophets, but you also have the Word and Holy Spirit to confirm if they are true. God has given offices to people with a title to carry on His mission. The assignment of these offices is to make us perfect in God's doctrine; that is His teaching. Make sure they are called by God, or did they call themselves? Giving oneself a title does not mean God has ordained that person.

Ephesians 4:11 tells us, "And he gave some, apostles; and some, prophets; and some, evangelists; and some, pastors and teachers;"

I tell you that all of your fear, worry, sicknesses, and confusion are the outcome of being disconnected from God. Daniel, Joseph, Moses, and Joshua kept their connection with God, and God did the same.

Why is there so much confusion and trouble when you claim your God is real? Can He do anything supernatural for you? Can you prove it to me? Where is His peace, protection, and power to heal and deliver His creation?

We have taken the shortcut. There is no shortcut, friend. Jesus is the way. Prayer to Jesus is the solution. Do not look around, down, or in any direction. Look up, be humble, and follow God. The redeemer is as close as the mention of His name, Jesus.

While studying the end times, I asked the Lord some questions. Lord, the Bible says time will be bad; it was never before and will not be after. Lord, there has to be an escaping way. He gave me this scripture,

In Luke 21:36 "Watch ye therefore, and pray always, that ye may be accounted worthy to escape all these things that shall come to pass, and to stand before the Son of man."

Your government, religious leaders, or no one has an answer but the Lord. Let the Lord do His job. Bring all tragedy and problems to Jesus. Can you be humble enough to kneel before Him? He will protect you and give you peace. Jesus is the answer to all the chaos, disorder, and havoc. Pray, turn from all wrong ways, and make Jesus your way.

Mark 13:33 tells us, "Take ye heed, watch and pray: for ye know not when the time is. 34 For the Son of Man is as a man taking a far journey, who left his house, and gave authority to his servants, and to every man his work, and commanded the porter to watch. 35 Watch ye therefore: for ye know not when the master of the house cometh, at even, or at midnight, or at the cockcrowing, or in the morning 36 Lest coming suddenly he find you sleeping. 37 And what I say unto you I say unto all, Watch."

I had a dream years ago. In this dream, I was preaching the gospel on the streets of America. Suddenly someone started shooting at me. I was fearless and saw bullets bouncing back. Wow! That was Sunday, so I went to fellowship that morning, and the preacher looked into my eyes and said God would protect you from the bullets. You will be bulletproof; it will bounce back. Daniel, Joseph, David, and all who trusted the Lord have seen the power of His deliverance. We will see more incredible things happening these days and times if we connect with the Lord. I said to communicate with the LORD. Pray; prayer is the answer to escape tribulation.

2 Chronicles 7:14 tells us, "If my people, which are called by my name, shall humble themselves, and pray, and seek my face, and turn from their wicked ways; then will I hear from heaven, and will forgive their sin, and will heal their land."

Do not look to the churches but to the Lord. A gun, the police, and the hospital are not the answer, but getting connected with the wonder-working power in Jesus is the answer.

LET US PRAY

Lord Jesus gives us humbleness to bring back the operation of the Holy Spirit in our lives. Bring prayer and the Word of God back into our lives.

May the Lord give us a believing heart to believe in Jesus. Jesus is the only answer to all the chaos we are facing. Jesus is the protector, not the gun. May Jesus hide you under His wings and cover you with His Blood. Jesus blinds the enemy and confuses them that they never find the target. May the Lord release His ministering Angels to the service of His creation in Jesus's name! Amen! God Bless you!

MARCH 2

TOILING OR WITH EASE?

Toiling is one curse for transgressing God's commandment. God created Adam and Eve and blessed them. The blessing of God makes our lives easy, worry less, and relaxed. The curse is just the opposite to it. Once a friend commented, where is Eve? Let my hand be on her. Yes, but where are you today?

Walking with God in obedience, we can have much peace and joy since He cares for all our needs and provisions. Toil means wearisome, sweat, hardship, slavery, and stress.

Genesis 3:17 And unto Adam he said, Because thou hast hearkened unto the voice of thy wife, and hast eaten of the tree, of which I commanded thee, saying, Thou shalt not eat of it: cursed is the ground for thy sake; in sorrow shalt thou eat of it all the days of thy life; 18 Thorns also and thistles shall it bring forth to thee; and thou shalt eat the herb of the field; 19a In the sweat of thy face shalt thou eat bread, till thou return unto the ground;

All blessings have the power to remove slavery and toiling on earth. Lord, help us work under your direction to escape weariness and disappointment. Have you seen people work hard all day in the sun? Nowadays, people work hard. Have you ever thought about why we work hard, have not enough, and are always tired? Sweating is a curse. If you accept direction from God, your day and night sweating and hard labor can do it in no time with powerful results. Pray for your laboring to be fruitful. Let the Lord be in your boat, so the storm ceases.

Peter, with other fishermen, toiled all night, and the result was a disappointment. But as they followed the voice of God, they found fish in abundance. Lord knew where and how to bless you. It is not man but God. It is not your hardship, sweating, and slavery, but by harkening and obeying His voice. Hearing the voice of God will turn into a stress-free life.

Luke 5:4b he said unto Simon, Launch out into the deep, and let down your nets for a draught. 5 And Simon answering said unto him, Master, we have toiled all the night, and have taken nothing: nevertheless, at thy word, I will let down the net. 6 And when they had this done, they inclosed a great multitude of fishes: and their net brake.

Why is our life so miserable? What causes our life so hard and results in disappointment? We discard His word as Eve and Adam. That is why we continue in the curse. The Word of God is the direction of easy, toil-free, and peaceful life.

Every situation and every life problem can be resolved if we learn to hear His voice and obey. Life can be most enjoyable if we hide His word in our hearts for direction. A wise man takes advice and counsel from the Lord to avoid toiling, discouragement, and stress.

Sounds like wise King David. David knew God and always waited for His direction. As David obeyed and revered God's direction, we saw a mighty victory throughout. A great and successful king's victory was not through his might or power but in the order of the Spirit of God.

2 Samuel 5:23 And when David inquired of the LORD, he said, Thou shalt not go up; but fetch a compass behind them, and come upon them over against the mulberry trees. 24 And let it be, when thou hearest the sound of a going in the tops of the mulberry trees, that then thou shalt bestir thyself: for then shall the LORD go out before thee, to smite the host of the Philistines. 25 And David did so, as the LORD had commanded him; and smote the Philistines from Geba until thou come to Gazer.

You can have a victorious life if you let God be God. God's direction makes little sense but needs trust, total trust.

Studying all Kings of Israel, I noticed that the one who returned with victory took the counsel of God. They had great peace and quietness, wealth, provision, and prosperity. God fought the battle, as God is the man of war. Who is mighty like God? No one! Under the Lord's direction, they will preserve us from an enemy. God will keep a cloud of darkness in between. God will hide us from the enemy. There will be a light of fire and a cloud to protect us from heat and darkness. The Lord will be a shield and buckler. Are we hearing Him today, or are we the modern-day Adam and Eve? Do you want to relax and enjoy your life by listening to what He says in His Word? Do you want to be blessed?

Let us see what God says in His word.

Matthew 6:28 And why take ye thought for raiment? Consider the lilies of the field, how they grow; they toil not, neither do they spin: 33 But seek ye first the kingdom of God, and his righteousness; and all these things shall be added unto you. 34 Take therefore no thought for the morrow: for the morrow shall take thought for the things of itself. Sufficient unto the day is the evil thereof.

If you hear and obey the voice of the Lord, then,

Psalms 128:2 For thou shalt eat the labor of thine hands: happy shalt thou be, and it shall be well with thee.

Invite Jesus in your storm, chaos, home. He will give you divine peace, protection, and provisions. Life can be easy, restful, and peaceful. The absence of the voice of His commandment can bring all toiling, slavery, and sweating. His voice will result in rest, victory, and amazement if you harken. Why are you stepping out without His guidance? It distressed disciples on a ship. Their life was in jeopardy, but inviting the savior on board the vessel brought peace. God has power over a storm. He can quiet the storm down and rescue you from Satan. Satan is a prince of the air. He brings a storm, but God brings peace.

Mark 6:48 And he saw them toiling in rowing; for the wind was contrary unto them: and about the fourth watch of the night he cometh unto them, walking upon the sea, and would have passed by them 51 And he went up unto them into the ship, and the wind ceased: and they were sore amazed in themselves beyond measure, and wondered.

Wow! Destruction to construction, ruin to raise, death to life. What a wonder-working God! Joseph had a hardship in Egypt, but when God blessed him, he forgot all about slavery, disappointment, and hardship.

Genesis 41:51 And Joseph called the name of the firstborn Manasseh: For God, said he, hath made me forget all my toil and all my father's house.

LET US PRAY

Lord, mighty God, come in our stormy lifeboat, give amazing peace and tranquility. Let your ear open to God's loving counsel to bless you. Lord releases His plan of success and brings us an expected end. May the Lord put a desire in your heart to seek His kingdom and righteousness to have all joy, peace, and protection in Jesus's name. Amen! God Bless You!

MARCH 3

GIVE ME THE TRUTH!

Why only the truth only? There is nothing as powerful as truth. God is behind the Truth. God almighty will support you if you are telling the Truth. But the opposite to truth is falsehood, lie, and untruth.

Psalm 9:17 The wicked shall be turned into hell, and all the nations that forget God.

You can escape from hell.

John 8:32 And ye shall know the truth, and the truth shall make you free.

The truth was Israelite did not know they were in bondage. They argued with Jesus, claiming they were not slaves. But indeed, they were the slaves of Satan. They were the slaves of sin.

False teachers and prophets have bewitched people. The truth is, your company can be dangerous even if they claim to be Christians. Truth is, you have to know and confess that you are a sinner and can be saved by Jesus Christ. Truth is, your salvation is a process, a work in progress by you recognizing the seriousness of sin. Many are misled by church authority into believing that church attendance, being born into a Christian family, knowledge of the Torah-Bible, or holding a church position can save them. Truth is, continue in the truth of the Word for the way out of all bondages, sins, and wrongs. The truth is sinners need the savior's blood, baptism in Jesus's name, and infilling of the Holy Spirit. Allow the Holy Spirit to guide you to all truth. Truth is, the Holy Spirit has no lie. Revelation is, Satan is a liar and father of lies since lies were first found in Satan. Truth is Satan is an author of confusion.

Truth is what Jesus said.

John 8:44 Ye are of your father the devil, and the lusts of your father ye will do. He was a murderer from the beginning, and abode not in the truth, be-cause there is no truth in him. When he speaketh a lie, he speaketh of his own: for he is a liar and the father of it.

Strong's concordance definition of truth is, in fact, certainly, everything as it was.

Jesus said in John 14:6 that he is the truth.

God, please give me the truth. People will ask for a new car, good job, plane, houses, or children, but I ask God to give me the truth. Truth is a powerful weapon for deliverance. Deliverance from an enemy, poverty, any addictions, or whatever you need to be delivered from. Truth has the power to deliver us from the lion,

MARCH 3

tiger, fire, sicknesses, hell, and diseases. Truth can put us in trouble, but truth can deliver us out of trouble. Truth is the most powerful missing element today. People like to hear sugar-coated lies and deception. People love the facade, however, they know the truth. They will not harm themselves. Truth is the way of God, but the sugarcoated facade is the religious way of Satan. Make sure it is clear in your mind that Jesus is the truth. Truth is, life with-out Jesus is life without light. The fact is, a confused person dies lost if they do not find the truth. Every-thing that you are looking for is in the word of God. His Spirit releases from heaven's truth. The Bible says the Holy Spirit is the truth. Love the truth, hold on to the truth and stand on the truth, which is the Word of God.

What is the truth?

John 18:37b Jesus claimed to be a truth that I should bear witness unto the truth. Every one that is of the truth heareth my voice.

The pilot was interested to know the truth.

John 18:38a Pilate saith unto him, What is a truth?

Are you wandering from place to place, confused? But when you find the truth, your wandering will be over. You know that there is nothing beyond the truth.

What is the truth? God is ONE is the truth; gods are not millions. The truth is, you cannot create gods, but One God created you and can give you life. The truth is, you can carve statues or idols but cannot put life in them. God created heaven and earth is the truth. The truth is, God can heal and deliver. The truth is God is the only one who is supernatural.

Exodus 8:18 And the magicians did so with their enchantments to bring forth lice, but they could not: so there were lice upon man and upon beast. 19 Then the magicians said unto Pharaoh, This is the finger of God:

Truth is, God knows the cause of illnesses is sin. Why did He take 39 stripes? There are 39 categories of sickness resulting from sins. Jesus, the mighty God, paid all so you have freedom from sickness. Truth is, the blood came out of stripes to pay the sins. The blood of a sinless savior is the only remedy for salvation. Truth is sin will cause death in hell, but life-giving blood will redeem you from hellfire. Truth is when you ask the elder to pray by anointing oil, then any sin involved will be forgiven and you will be healed.

I haven't taken medicine for healing and curing illnesses. I called someone who has the Holy Spirit to pray over me when I am sick.

James 5:15 And the prayer of faith shall save the sick, and the Lord shall raise him up; and if he have committed sins, they shall be forgiven him.

Hell is real and so is heaven. Only Jesus is the way to heaven. Truth is, the truth is out of churches that are building. That is why you do not see healing and deliverance. Why do we see drugs, gangs, divorces, suicide, shooting, wickedness, cancer, prison-jail full, oppression, and possession? The reason is the truth is not welcome in religious churches. The fact is, you need two or three scriptures to make a doctrine to practice. Truth is, you need two or three witnesses to establish any doctrine. Truth is adding to or subtracting from the word that will remove its power.

It has proven the power and validity of truth by one who practiced the truth. Truth is Queen Esther, Mary, Joseph, Moses, Joshua, Isaiah, Jeremiah, Paul, disciples, and ancient churches continued in the truth. They proved the power of deliverance, healing, opening blind eyes, deaf ears open, the lame walk, and many great miracles. Loving the truth is to love yourself. Loving the truth is the Loving God.
Your tradition is dangerous.

Mark 7:13 Making the word of God of none effect through your tradition, which ye have delivered: and many such like things do ye.

Truth delivered by Lord Jesus Christ and disciples discontinued in it.

Luke 18:8b Nevertheless when the Son of man cometh, shall he find faith on the earth?

Lord, sanctify us. What is sanctification? To cleanse, purify, or make holy.

John 17:17 Sanctify them through thy truth: thy word is truth.

Truth is, we need the Word authored by God Almighty to find our way on earth. The truth is, the Lord is still in favor of humanity to show them grace and mercy. What about you? Do you care for truth or self like Eve and Adam?

LET US PRAY

Oh Lord God of Abraham, Isaac, and Israel, who knew one true God Jehovah, please help us. Lord, help us know the truth of the Messiah, who was Jehovah God in the flesh as Jesus Christ. Lord, give us a revelation. Give us love for truth, since your word says I will reveal who loves me. Yes, Lord, we want the truth since all scriptures need revelation. Lord, show us the truth to be delivered from hellfire. Thank you for the truth in the Word of God. Give us the Holy Spirit to teach and guide in Jesus's name. Amen! God Bless you!

MARCH 4

POWER OF PRAISE!

We praise God, knowing what He has done for us. We know the Lord alone brings us out of all trials and troubles. He gives us victory and deliverance. Every time we praise Him, His presence comes into our midst, and an enemy runs.

Definition of Praise from KJV dictionary Appreciation is bestowed on a person for his virtues or worthy actions, on admirable actions themselves, or anything valuable; appreciation is expressed in words or songs.

Praise is the idea of giving thanks and honor to one who is worthy of praise.

I remember my story of working in the post office. I prayed a lot since the place was very dark. Many times I had dreamed of snakes at the workplace. One time I had dreamed of Snake Valley. I dreamed of a snake jungle that was impossible to clear up. All the snakes were hanging everywhere. As I worked there, I saw people's actions and reactions toward each other. You do not see demons and Satan, so you blame the person who used the snake, which is the devil.

I came from India, where we do not believe in demon existence. I was not ready to acknowledge the existence of demons, evil spirits, fallen angels, and Satan. I was afraid of monsters. I did not know that evil spirits could harm Christians. We had no teaching on demons or Satan. Our knowledge of the spiritual world, which is the real world, was very little.

When I moved to the US, I started attending Pentecostal Church. They were teaching nothing but the Spirit World, and I also began having experiences after that. One time I spoke to God, Lord, I prayed a lot, but demons sucked my spiritual energy out at the workplace. I feel weak. I prayed daily, fasted twice a week, and once a month, I went straight for three days and nights without water and food. Still entering the Post Office building, I experienced spiritual energy drained.

Doing all these still, there was no result. Nothing was moving. As I kept seeking, one day, the Lord said you praise me for half an hour, speak in tongues for half an hour, lay your hand on your head and pray in the tongue for half an hour. I did for the time I worked in the post office. That helped me a lot. Remember, seeking an answer by praying and fasting is not in vain. That is the time your answer will come. The Bible says we must seek, and seeking is a task. Sometimes people will talk and complain to friends or families instead of talking to the Lord. Talking to spirit-filled saints will help find direction if they can pray for the situation.

I did not understand His Ways, but I did what he asked me without fail. I attended a conference once. Preacher asked us to worship and praise the Lord, and we did. Then the preacher started teaching on the subject of praises. I was glad to be there. That day I understood what praises do.

He explained Psalms 149. The preacher said, see what happens as we praise the Lord,

Psalm 149:4 For the Lord taketh pleasure in his people: he will beautify the meek with salvation. 5 Let the saints be joyful in glory: let them sing aloud upon their beds. 6 Let the high praises of God be in their mouth, and a two-edged sword in their hand; 7 To execute vengeance upon the heathen, and punishments upon the people; 8 To bind their kings with chains, and their nobles with fetters of iron; 9 To execute upon them the judgment written: this honor have all his saints. Praise ye the Lord.

As praises go up, the blessings come down. Well, Satan desires to chain us with darkness, sicknesses, depression, fear, worry, doubt, and name it. But as you praise God with song, word, dance, and music, all Satan's nobles and kings assigned over the city, county, state, or country who puts forth a fetter of iron goes back to them. Their chains return to them. Praises are a reversal program of God against Satan's agenda. Verses 7 and 8 are the key. That is the secret of praising God. The presence of God comes and takes over your battle. We also invite God's spirit by praising Him.

Psalms 22:3 But thou art holy, O thou that inhabitest the praises of Israel.

King David had this key of praise since he was always in battle. His life was in jeopardy since Satan knew David was threatening the kingdom of darkness. When you are a threat to the kingdom of darkness, then, believe me, you will be a target for the enemy. He will come against you, but using the weapons of praise, his chains, and iron fetters will return to the devil. Satan and his army will be chained back, and you will be free. We quote the scripture, "no weapon form against us can prosper." It is only if we know how to reverse back to the enemy. We must understand what the correct key for reversing is. Your word can be praised or by the Word of the Bible. Praise Him with the loud musical instrument. Praise by dancing. Remember, David danced while bringing the ark of God. Michael criticized David and had no children.

2 Samuel 6:16 And as the ark of the LORD came into the city of David, Michal Saul's daughter looked through a window, and saw king David leaping and dancing before the LORD; and she despised him in her heart. 23 Therefore, Michal the daughter of Saul had no child unto the day of her death.

People will criticize you when you praise the Lord, but do not worry. They will lose their blessings. I heard someone saying in a Pentecostal church; it is not nice for elderly ladies to jump and dance. I can worship at any age. You can worship God at any age. It is your relationship. I have seen people never receive blessings since they never learned the greatest key to praising. As you praise, your family problem will be taken care of. The devil cannot stand when you praise God. God uses people for His work. That is why the devil stops and hinders them by chaining us to problems and troubles. But oh, if you know how easy it is to tear his kingdom down. By going wild in your praise and worship. Take liberties to do so. There is no age limit.

Many times I wake up feeling tormented, sick, and chained. As I perceive the attack from Satan, I turn on some music and get lost in praising the Lord. Praise and worship are not in the church alone but all the time, every day. Praises bring in the wonder-working power of God into the room. I get freedom, and guess what? As the Bible says, it chained the Devil up. Hallelujah! Praise the Lord!

MARCH 4

LET US PRAY

The Lord gives us the revelation of praise. Give us victory, healing, and deliverance through praise. Lord, fill our hearts and mouths with praise. Lord, as we praise, let us see the defeat in the enemy's camp and victory in our life. As praises go up and blessings come down. You alone are worthy of all praise and none else, so we praise you in Jesus's Name. Amen! God Bless You!

MARCH 5

LEARN TO SEEK GOD!

The Bible says if you seek me, you will find me! What and why do we seek? We seek the things we do not have. We seek if we have lost something. You do not seek what we already have. Does it make sense? It is evident from the Bible that If We seek, then we will find it.

The Bible says in Matthew 7:7c seek, and ye shall find;

Also, you find the higher way of God by seeking Him.

All that God has is blessings. His ways and plan are to bless and keep you all the way.

Psalm 119:2 Blessed are they that keep his testimonies, and that seek him with the whole heart.

The definition of Seek from strong concordance is to search for, desire, and inquire about giving God glory.

Seeking may require physical or spiritual involvement. Seeking help from the secular world will not be the same as God would. If you seek God for the situation, then you will find the supernatural result. Remember, He has created Angels to help. The angel will come and help if you seek help through God.

Amos 5:14 Seek good, and not evil, that ye may live: and so the Lord, the God of hosts, shall be with you, as ye have spoken.

You can seek through a different medium as King Saul went to a familiar spirit. Many go through a medium like Tarot cards, Psychic, magicians, or astrologers. This will all answer, but God has the solution to avoid trouble. Going to another medium will have punishment without remedy. The Bible says to seek God early. They have changed this scripture. The devil does not like us to seek God early. If we wake up early to seek, our day and work will be smooth. Satan's plan, tactic, and net to catch us will be destroyed.

Psalms 63:1 O God, thou art my God; early will I seek thee: my soul thirsteth for thee, my flesh longeth for thee in a dry and thirsty land, where no water is.

All situations and problems can be solved if we seek through omniscient God. Our life can be victorious and joyful. Lord's answer comes with the solution. Indeed, God knows all, and despite that, we go to Him last. We go to God when we get stuck and have no remedy left.

MARCH 5

Psalms 34:4 I sought the Lord, and he heard me and delivered me from all my fears. 10 The young lions do lack, and suffer hunger: but they that seek the Lord shall not want any good thing.

In the late 90s, I had a back injury. I only knew the healing through the Lord. Now, this was my test, not knowing how and what will be the result. The Lord wanted me to see an orthopedic. Well, I don't particularly appreciate seeing a doctor. Somehow Lord connected me with the doctor who respected my belief. The doctor never forced me to take medicine. All his reports were truthful, with no one to be blamed. During that period, I kept seeking God. One day, He said He would heal me in two steps. First, I will walk and then run.
God gave me the Promise.

Proverb 4:12 When thou goest, thy steps shall not be straitened; and when thou runnest, thou shalt not stumble.

My mind could not comprehend His ways, but I believed. One day, walking out of the workplace, Lord said, you will never return here again. In my fiery, painful trial, I walked very close with an attentive ear to His voice. My coworkers questioned, knowing me. Liz is a good Christian. Then why is she going through this? Yes, we do not go by our karma, which is our work, but with the plan of God. There was a day I lost my job. After some years, one day, my miracle of the first part came true. Mr. Min prayed for me, and I started walking. He had many gifts. As he prayed, my leg and hand grew, and my spine returned to the place. After healing, God allowed me to attend one of my coworkers' father's funerals, where I met my past coworkers. It surprised them to see me walking. As I left after the funeral, they went to a restaurant. All my coworkers were around my friend Chen asking what happened and how Liz healed since she does not take medicine. My friend Miss Chen told them she took me to the Korean brother Min who has healing power from Jesus. Miss Chen told them how my leg grew and my spine returned. It was an excellent time for joy to be the witness to the Lord. The Lord is faithful, even if it takes time. He alone gets glory among the heathen. Seeking God will show His supernatural power.

The devil is doing a marvelous job of replacing God's stripes, miracles, and healing. Some people on earth will give no one glory but the Lord.

All who sought God found the way out of trouble, sicknesses, battle, and personal situation. Make Him your counselor. I always seek God's counsel, no matter how small or big the issue. I never take the case in my hand to get dirty. To take revenge is the Lord's, and glory belongs to Him alone. God has solutions for all our problems. He uses the person who knows how to yield His Spirit. Hannah and Isaac sought God for the child, and God gave them. David always sought the Lord for each step he took. When he didn't, he was in trouble. I always seek God in situations. My life has fewer complications.

Science is trying their research on you. Technology and exploration are advancing fast to take people's eyes away from the Lord. You will not find a solution from technology but in the Lord. Hip and knee replacement is getting so common, especially among Christians. Organ transplants and sickness cures are being done. What happened to God's people?

Can we seek the Lord for our sicknesses and trial for cancer? Seek God for our troublesome children. Facing marital problems or all kinds of issues ends up in messy divorces. Is there anyone who is proclaiming fasting and prayer to seek the Lord?

Isaiah 55:6 Seek ye the Lord while he may be found, call ye upon him while he is near.

In the old time, the King and people of God fasted and prayed to find the answer from God. Modern Christianity has lost the old path.

King Jehoshaphat sought the Lord.

2 Chronicles 20:3 And Jehoshaphat feared, and set himself to seek the LORD, and proclaimed a fast throughout all Judah.

He had the victory in battle. Can our nation call for fasting and prayer? We also have trouble everywhere.

Ezra 8:21 Then I proclaimed a fast there, at the river of Ahava, that we might afflict (fast) ourselves before our God, to seek of him a right way for us, and our little ones, and all our substance.

We must find the right way. Seekers of God got success in their trials and trouble. Only God has a solution to your problems. Seek the Lord to wait on Him and see what He does for you.

Proverbs 3:5 - Trust in the LORD with all thine heart, and lean not unto thine own understanding.

LET US PRAY

Lord God gives us people who seek God and do not lean on their own understanding. We seek wrong solutions to the problem, but we have unbearable, unbelievable, and uncountable issues. The Lord gives us spiritual authority, like Moses, Joshua, Ezra, and Esther, for this modern time. Who can bring us out of all fear, killing, shooting, suicide, divorces, sicknesses, and many, many problems? Lord, we are losing a battle since we got rid of you from our school, home, depending on den called churches. We do not proclaim biblical fasting and prayer. We do not seek until we find an answer. Forgive us, Lord. We are the modern-day Sodomite. Oh, Lord, help us to turn to you. We tear our hearts and not clothes. We cry out, please save, deliver, and heal in Jesus's name. Amen! God Bless you!

MARCH 6

GOD BEAUTIFIES MEEK WITH SALVATION!

Everyone desires to appear beautiful. People get a stunning look when they get saved. I am a first-hand witness. I have seen for years when a person gets saved the dark shadow of sins disappears. When someone repents, is baptized in Jesus's name, and receives the Holy Spirit, they appear stunning. They do not change beauty products, but they use the touch of the Lord. God comes in the body which He has made for Him to stay. That temple gets defiled by committing all fleshly sins.

Fleshly Sins are in Galatians 5:19b fornication, uncleanness, lasciviousness, 20 idolatry, witchcraft, hatred, variance, emulations, wrath, strife, seditions, heresies, 21 Envyings, murders, drunkenness, revellings,

1 Samuel 16:7 But the Lord said unto Samuel, Look not on his countenance, or on the height of his stature; because I have refused him: for the Lord seeth not as man seeth; for man looketh on the outward appearance, but the Lord looketh on the heart.

All sins of the flesh will be apparent on your face and cannot be covered up. You do not have joy when you are not happy. The jealous person will have bone disease. They will die getting ugly and skinnier, and their skin tone will turn dark or pale. I have seen this kind of person whose beauty vanished away. Facial makeup and surgeries cannot conceal the visible signs of depression, worry, and hatred.

If you turn away from evil and embrace Jesus's name for washing sins, His Spirit will bring inner change.

I have a memory of a certain prophet. When he wasn't saved, he would sit on the curb, going in and out of jail, his appearance reflecting the ugliness of his sins. As he embraced the Lord, Jesus came to him and he had a radiant appearance. When the Lord comes to us, He renovates His dwelling place. Our body is His temple. The face shines, and features change.

Ladies who walk with the Lord have a beautiful glow on their faces. I visit the convalescent home where I meet many ladies. The Ladies who are Christian have beautiful shiny countenances. Once in India, a Hindu friend told me you know, in an enormous crowd, I can tell who Christian is. I want to know how she can identify something. Her response indicated a light shining on their face.

People care so much about the outer look. Growing up in India, I never had much knowledge about makeup. We just cleaned up our bodies and combed out our hair; that was all we did.

There are a few women who have recently converted to Christianity. Their coworker noticed they looked gorgeous after baptism. Gigi said everyone told me I look beautiful. See, God created all things beautiful.

ELIZABETH DAS

Ecclesiastes 3:11 He hath made everything beautiful in his time: Beauty comes from heaven. All of Job's daughters were beautiful.

Job 42:15a And in all the land were no women found so fair as the daughters of Job:

God has the power to turn ugliness into beauty. I learned a woman with anger, jealousy or pride has the harshest ugly look. The way you look is a reflection of your insight. Inner ugliness becomes visible on the face. Satan will not deceive people who know the truth.

A search from Google says in the year 2003, analysts at Goldman Sachs estimated that the global beauty industry—comprising skincare worth $24 billion; makeup, $18 billion; $38 billion of hair-care products; — is growing at up to 7% a year, more than twice the rate of the developed world's GDP.

Plastic surgery, cosmetics, and dermatologists make billions of dollars a year. A lost human does not know that the devil is playing with their mind. He is selling the beauty product, convincing them they will look beautiful. The devil also makes you feel ugly and worthless.

Friend, do not have faith in Satan. Who is the creator of your physical form? Jesus is your creator, while Satan is causing harm to your body. How long are you going to live on this earth? All these plastic surgeries and beauty products will harm you. Who cares for you? Only The Lord! Satan will point out your eyes, nose wrinkles, and little detail that no one cares about or notices. It would be best if you changed your thinking. You refocus your eyes on the things above. Come in His presence and worship the Lord. Read His Word in order to follow, pray, and fast. You will look beautiful. Inner beauty will shine through your face. Speaking for myself, I am beautiful!

Psalms 140:4 For the LORD taketh pleasure in his people: he will beautify the meek with salvation.

Jesus sees you as His bride and desires you to radiate beauty, not as the world defines it. Remember, God has made your body and every detail in the body. Satan is the ugliest creature and talks about beauty. He makes you feel what he is. All fallen angels are making this evil plan to make you feel ugly. I want you to know that you are beautiful, no doubt about it!

Proverbs 16:31 The hoary (grey) head is a crown of glory if it is found in the way of righteousness...

When the Lord comes within to deliver you from drugs, alcohol, jealousy, envy, pride, anger, lies, and deceit, you will look beautiful. The responsibility belongs to the Lord alone, not anyone else. After spending a significant amount on plastic and cosmetic surgery, how long will your beauty endure? Some are not happy with eye color, skin tone, or whatever. You need to come to the great beautician Lord Jesus.
Come in His presence as Moses did.

Exodus 34:30 And when Aaron and all the children of Israel saw Moses, behold, the skin of his face shone, and they were afraid to come to nigh him. 35 And the children of Israel saw the face of Moses, that the skin of Moses' face shone: Moses put the veil upon his face again until he went in to speak with him.

The devil is deceiving you by introducing all these eye, face, and skin products. We have never utilized any of this before. Then why now? We distance ourselves from God's presence and fall for Satan's deceptive introduction. The devil deceivers aim to steal both you and your money from the Lord. God will try your faith on earth. You stand believing and doing what the Lord says. The devil will cower and flee from the radiant light emanating from you. Remember, the devil was the most beautiful creature of God. When he sinned, he became the ugliest creature. Look around his images or skeleton; homely scary, right? Yes, and guess what? The way he wants you to look is identical to one.

God made you beautiful in His image. You do not need help from Satan. Just say I look like my father Jesus; I am beautiful. I made it in His image. Jesus made me attractive. And I am beautiful inside and out.

2 Corinthians 4:16 For which cause we faint not; but though our outward man perishes, yet the inward man is renewed day by day.

Godly people look beautiful, even in old age.

Psalm 92:14 They shall still bring forth fruit in old age; they shall be fat and flourishing.

LET US PRAY

May the Lord of heaven give a heavenly touch to beautify you. You are the image of God, and the Lord knows how to make you beautiful. You are His future bride. Lord, help us keep self-spotless, without wrinkles and blemish for Him. No one but the Lord knows how to care for His temple, our body. Lord, we bring ourselves to your altar as a living sacrifice. I trust you. He made us in His beautiful image. Lord, we love you and bless you in Jesus's Name. Amen! God Bless you!

MARCH 7

JESUS LOVES ME!

Have you ever heard people say Jesus loves me, so I can do whatever? Well, Jesus is Love since Jesus is God and God is Love. People justify Jesus as God, and God is Love. There is no place for hate in God. God is Spirit and not Flesh. The flesh has all evil since our origin is sinful and not innocent. Adam's unholy blood runs in our bodies. Adam's sin has contaminated the flesh.

God's love is the reason He wants to save us at any and every opportunity. He loves to bless His creations. No matter what you do, if you get cleaned up by repenting and turn from evil and ask for help, without fail, Jesus will help you. He will rescue you. He condemns those who continue to embrace their wicked ways, promising no salvation. According to John 14:6, Jesus is the correct way of eternal life. Jesus shows us the right way. Many will try to pull you in the wrong ways. Jesus said I am the way. Jesus said, turn from your ways. No one but you have to face the outcome of your ways.

Like a naughty kid seeking the best treatment despite their actions. Breaking laws, you will be punished. Police will lock you up. Wickedness is dangerous to families and society.

When the speed limit is 50 miles, but you decide to drive 60 or 70, the police will give you a ticket. Police do not hate you. Police do not whip you. The authority advises careful driving in order to grant access. If you get caught doing something wrong, the police will fine you or put you behind bars. No one hates you. They will press charges for breaking the law, and you will suffer consequences, fines, and punishments.

Jesus is Love, and in Him, there is no hate. He loves you, whether he's sending you to heaven or hell. God's virtue does not change when He punishes you. Like the way you use discipline to correct your children. Parents punish children, judge fine, and send you behind bars for your wrongdoing. The laws of God are eternal and do not undergo any changes. God is steadfast; that is why He said to repent and turn from your wicked ways. Cleanse your sins by immersing yourself in water in the name of Jesus. His blood is available under the name of Jesus. Clean up your act.

God's goodness is beyond measure. That is why He gave a book called the Bible. It took 1500 years to write. For all dispensation, God has shown the way of return to Him. Isn't that great? Our God is Love. Our wickedness is the root of the problem. Even though we break the laws of God, we still seek benefits.

In our current time, we tend to do what feels good. This generation copies everything that Hollywood or Bollywood does. We just accept the evil ways of the world and jump in. Do not follow blind people; the blind cannot lead. You get right with God and move by His Spirit. Be a light in the darkness. Understand? Ignorance does not count.

MARCH 7

What happens if you touch fire, or jump from a tree, or enter an ocean? Can you say I did not know? Be careful; ignorance is not an excuse. Do you know many go to hell and take many as well? Israel did evil enough to be removed from their land. People of other nationalities occupied the land. They brought their gods and worshiped them. So God punished them. People fear God but still do what they like.

2 King 17:26c therefore he hath sent lions among them, and, behold, they slay them, because they know not the manner of the God of the land. 27 Then the king of Assyria commanded, saying, Carry thither one of the priests whom ye brought from thence; and let them go and dwell there, and let him teach them the manner of the God of the land. 41 So these nations feared the LORD, and served their graven images, both their children, and their children's children: as did their fathers, so do they unto this day. Fear God only,

Joshua 24:14 Now therefore fear the LORD, and serve him in sincerity and in truth: and put away the gods which your fathers served on the other side of the flood, and in Egypt, and serve ye the LORD.

God's love for you is evident through the gift of true prophets and teachers filled with the Holy Spirit.

1 Samuel 7:3 And Samuel spake unto all the house of Israel, saying, If ye do return unto the LORD with all your hearts, then put away the strange gods and Ashtaroth from among you, and prepare your hearts unto the LORD, and serve him only: and he will deliver you out of the hand of the Philistines.

God can rescue us from sickness, diseases, substance abuse, marital breakdown, violence, and gun violence.

Deuteronomy 13:4 Ye shall walk after the LORD your God, and fear him, and keep his commandments, and obey his voice, and ye shall serve him, and cleave unto him.

Everyone wants blessings, benefits, and desires to inherit heaven.

But what God says in Jeremiah 7:23 But this thing commanded I them, saying, Obey my voice, and I will be your God, and ye shall be my people: and walk ye in all the ways that I have commanded you, that it may be well unto you.

God is Love. He sends the Prophet like Jeremiah, Isaiah, John the Baptists, who laid their lives speaking the truth. Lord Jesus does not have to die if He did not care.

Jeremiah 7:13 And now, because ye have done all these works, saith the LORD, and I spake unto you, rising early and speaking, but ye heard not, and I called you, but ye answered not;

Always remember that you are loved by God. He went above and beyond, and now it's your turn to give a response. Do not make the word of God non-effect.

Mark 7:13 Making the word of God of none effect through your tradition, which ye have delivered: and many such like things do ye.

Do not add or subtract to His given the word. Teach your children the word and not the World. Teach your child right and not wrong. Be a good example for your children and not bad. Keep your life in order, intact with the word. Obey the word to be blessed and the generation after you. You can inherit the earth with your children, with doing and not. Why? Because God is Love. He cared enough to die on the cross. Rich God becomes poor just to show you the way of heaven. What is our problem? We need God's righteousness and not ours.

Isaiah 64:6 But we are all as an unclean thing, and all our righteousness are as filthy rags, and we all do fade as a leaf; and our iniquities, like the wind, have taken us away.

Remember, God loves you more than a mother.

Isaiah 49:15 Can a woman forget her sucking child, that she should not have compassion on the son of her womb? Yea, they may forget, yet will I not forget thee.

God's love surpasses human comprehension.

John 15:13 - Greater Love hath no man than this, that a man lay down his life for his friends.

Back when I started learning about the Bible, my dress line didn't meet the standard set by it. One day, I was at work and felt I was in the presence of God. I could not look up. That very moment Jesus wrote on every cell of my body, "I love you sincerely." I know we hear with the ear, but all my cells of body listened to His voice that I love you sincerely, not for a day but days. I came home and cleaned up my closet. I couldn't turn His Love down. God loves you. Do you care? Can you clean up your life and be sincere in obeying His commandment? Love Him; it's worth living for Jesus as He instructed in the word. Action always proves empty words mean nothing. Look to Jesus, look at the cross, look at His stripes. Now, do you believe Jesus loves you and He did it all? Do you love yourself? Love is action.

LET US PRAY

Lord, help us show our Love by our actions. Lord, you never change. Your Love is the same yesterday, today, and forever. Help us love ourselves. Help us keep our life in order with the word of God. Precious Word you have given to follow, not just to read, argue, or debate. Your word is life-giving and good. Help us have Love where people see Jesus through us. We cannot do what you have done, but we give our life for your service in Jesus 'name. Amen! God Bless you!

MARCH 8

I PRAY YOUR FAITH FAILS NOT!

Luke 22:31 And the Lord said, Simon, Simon, behold, Satan hath desired to have you, that he may sift you as wheat: 32 But I have prayed for thee, that thy faith fails not: and when thou art converted, strengthen thy brethren.

If you have Faith, you can have Hope for the results.

Hebrews 11:1 Now Faith is the substance of things hoped for, the evidence of things not seen.

Peter claimed to have great Faith, and the next moment, the devil shifted him. His Faith was on the test. Jesus prayed. How much should we pray for each other? Knowing that Faith is targeted, I always pray for the countries and people, not just me, my family, and my situation. I believe God of heaven takes care of one; then He can take care of all.

God's chosen minister encounters Satan's opposition. The Faith of believers is targeted by Satan. Faith is the most needed virtue to stand. Without Faith in God, you cannot please Him. Demonstrate to others and yourself the existence and power of God. Act according to your Faith. By utilizing the authority given to us in the name of Jesus, we too can carry out healing, miracles, and deliverance, just as He did. We have power in Jesus's name.

The reality of the Lord Jesus cannot be denied. He hears all your prayers. I've seen incredible miracles occur when praying for sick individuals. The devil wants to wipe out people, but a prayer of Faith destroys the enemy's plan. Prayer snatches matter out of the hand of Satan, who only knows to kill, steal and destroy. When you pray, God releases the ministering Angels to fight against Satan and his Angel.

I am sharing this testimony, so you understand how prayer destroys Satan's work. By praying, Jesus, who was God incarnate, exhibited the result. If individuals understand the strength of prayer, they will prioritize it and pray continuously.

I love to pray. I make sure to pray whenever I have a bit of free time. Prayer is everything to me. Once, I said Lord; I would like you to do some crazy miracle. So I figured out how and what I wanted to see or hear. I expressed my desire for a healing miracle to occur while the doctor assesses the MRI films. The Bible says if you have Faith in the mustard seed, you ask, and you will receive.

ELIZABETH DAS

I was in one meeting, and a visitor preacher came from another state and preached. According to his testimony, a pastor had cancer. The treating doctor of this pastor was an atheist.

He did not believe in God, so how could he believe in miracles? His certainty grew after reviewing the MRI results, leading him to conclude that there was no God. If there is, then this pastor should not get cancer. During the examination of the cancer on the MRI screen, the tumor started to fade away. The doctor checked all all-areas where cancer started vanishing away from the film. The doctor could not believe what was happening right before his eyes. He immediately called the pastor, asked about his health, and showed him what he saw. He ordered a new MRI. Guess what? The new one was clean. No signs of cancer. The Visiting Preacher testified to the pastor that he was a man of Faith. He did not doubt his healing. The miracle I had prayed for was witnessed by none other than the Atheist Doctor.

Your prayer is much needed to rescue the ministry and people of God from the hand of Satan.
Our Faith has the test. Prayer of Faith can go miles away. Lord Jesus prayed for Peter as a chosen vessel. Peter's Faith fails not so he can continue the mission of Lord Jesus. Fear was over and around the disciples when Roman and religious Jews killed Jesus. It was the time anyone's Faith could fail. Someone has to pray for you, so your Faith fails not. God will try your Faith. The devil has to get out if you keep the Faith. Satan's fiery dart will be quenched if you keep the Faith.

Satan targets your leader, teacher, school, country, and home. That is why the devil got rid of prayer. What happens when you pray? See the example of Jesus praying for Peter. If you pray, then what can happen? All the surrounding chaos will disappear. Just like Peter came out of Satan's hand, so are the others if you pray. The pastor got healed, and an Atheist Doctor was a first-hand witness.

1 Timothy 2: I exhort therefore, that, first of all, supplications, prayers, intercessions, and giving of thanks, be made for all men; 2 For kings, and for all that are in authority; that we may lead a quiet and peaceable life in all godliness and honesty. 3 For this is good and acceptable in the sight of God our Savior;

See what the devil does all day and night.

Job 2:2 And the Lord said unto Satan, From whence comest thou? And Satan answered the Lord, and said, From going to and fro in the earth, and from walking up and down in it. 8 And the Lord said unto Satan, Hast thou considered my servant Job, that there is none like him in the earth, a perfect and an upright man, one that feareth God, and escheweth evil?

Satan's targets include the righteous and their Faith. Satan targets the followers of God. Watch how much he dares. Satan knows we are mortal; his destructive plan can destroy ignorant creation. With God on our side, we can have both an Angel and a protective hedge.

Maintain your faith and cling to God when your children, marriage, finances, or health are under attack. Start praying and fasting so Satan's destructive plans get cursed and destroyed.

When I returned from India in 2015, my Pastor said the Devil wanted to destroy my ministry. I already knew in the Spirit. The people of the devil followed me to India. I know prayer and fasting have destroyed their plan. We all have the measure of Faith and act according to our Faith. Some are doing minor and some a more incredible job in the kingdom! The devil comes against all work and workers to destroy. He thinks since Eve and Adam handed the earth to him so he can do all the killing, stealing, misleading, and destroying ministry. Satan believes he can destroy whoever stands on the Faith. But if you know our Faith is a powerful weapon against the enemy. Weapons of Faith will crush Satan's agenda, making his agent homeless and hopeless. So carry on the mission on your knees by praying and fasting. It will take you to your destiny. Faith will rise as you see victory, healing, prosperity, and deliverance.

Remember, Jesus has given you the example of Daniel. He came out of the Lion's Den. The fire couldn't burn Faith. Your trust in the power of God is worth keeping it.

Hebrews 10:38 Now the just shall live by Faith: but if any man draws back, my soul shall have no pleasure in him.

LET US PRAY

May the Lord of heaven shield your Faith; your Faith fails not. Your Faith rises above and beyond measure. May your life be like the people of Faith. Your testimony gives God glory. Your faith test provides the devil with a black eye. Through your faith testimony, people shout with joy, Hallelujah! May the Lord of Heaven grant all that you hope so the Lord gets all glory, honor, and praise in Jesus's name. Amen! God Bless you!

MARCH 9

A LITTLE HELP CAN REVIVE AND RESTORE!

A man passing by Jericho picked up a wounded man and helped. This man was robbed, stripped, and targeted for murder by the devil. But a good passer-by saw and walked to him. I took care of the wound, picked him up, and brought him to a safe place. Satan's agenda was to destroy, but the good Samaritan helped the wounded man so the wounded man revived, and survived. It's operational in aiding others. If we follow the way Jesus instructed, someone will be revived and survive, and Satan's work will be demolished.

To revive meant resuscitate, to bring around, bring back to consciousness. The Bible's definition is to return to life, to recover life. I work as a missionary, talking to people internationally. It may look like a little complicated and inconvenient job. But I never look for the microphone, millions in the audience, and the pulpit for my show. I need people who are hurting, sick, possessed, and depressed to give the message of hope. I do it heartily. I talk to the new converts, pastors, and also new disciples. I do not know why, but some pastors are thieves. All that they do is sing beautiful songs, pray, and ask for money.

Giving must be the lifestyle of Christians. Giving is necessary for receiving blessings. Our job is to work. We labor to receive wages from God. Jesus did not have time to eat or drink. His laboring brought revival, healing, deliverance, and comfort to many. The same missions belong to you and me. Don't expect the usual prosperity teaching and preaching that you hear and see today. A small act of assistance can bring someone back from the brink of failure. Offer assistance and prayers to individuals experiencing depression. If you see poor people, then stop and buy something. All money goes to eating out, a new dress, new shoes, nails, hair, and after an expensive lifestyle. But if you stop at a restaurant, buy food and give it to the hungry. God will bless you beyond measure.

You are the divine extension of God's power. Your hand's work for the kingdom will lead to restoration and revival by someone. My purpose is to pray over individuals at the convalescent, hospital, and home. I see people depressed, discouraged and hurt. Our duty as ministers includes praying for the sick. Provide them with a Bible, holy oil for anointing their home, and a prayer cloth to place inside the house. As all yoke and chain destroy, they revive. Despite pastors trying to hinder me, I persist in my work and witness major upheaval in the devil's realm.

Keep in mind that Christianity is not a lucrative enterprise. Please run from them if you see just the word and no sign following. Jesus gave an example right before your eyes. Watch the life of Jesus and see what He did. If you do not see the similarity of His work from religious authorities, then you are with the counterfeit. I visit different convalescent homes.

MARCH 9

I met a 93-year-old lady in a convalescent home; she lost her only son when he was 30. Now she has no one to care for her. I found out she was cold, had no blanket, and not enough warm cloth, so I went shopping and gave her all she needed. I saw her revived. I saw joy and happiness. Her countenance changed. If you give someone who has everything, they will not care for the gifts. Do not please those who have a lot. Just give someone who does not. You will make a big difference in their life. The Lord will bless you.

Proverbs 19:17 He that hath pity upon the poor lendeth unto the LORD; and that which he hath given will he pay him again.

Every Christmas, I spend money on converted Christians. As they turn to Christianity, no one nurtures them. I bought some sewing machines, clothes to wear, and a lovely luncheon to enjoy Christmas and New Year. They are excited to know that Christianity is caring, sharing, and loving. Their family rejects them as they turn to Jesus. They are my family now. I love them like my own. Guess what? They started doing the same as I do. They learn verses and teach others. I pray for them, and they pray for others. They get stuck, then immediately call for help, and I help. I do not care what time of the day. I will get up and pray. Many will survive if we take the time to minister.

See what Jesus says in His word.

Luke 10:30 And Jesus answering said, A certain man went down from Jerusalem to Jericho, and fell among thieves, which stripped him of his raiment, and wounded him, and departed, leaving him half dead. 31 And by chance there came down a certain priest that way: and when he saw him, he passed by on the other side. 32 And likewise a Levite, when he was at the place, came and looked on him, and passed by on the other side. 33 But a certain Samaritan, as he journeyed, came where he was: and when he saw him, he had compassion on him, 34 And went to him, and bound up his wounds, pouring in oil and wine, and set him on his own beast, and brought him to an inn, and took care of him. 35 And on the morrow when he departed, he took out two pence, and gave them to the host, and said unto him, Take care of him; and whatsoever thou spendest more, when I come again, I will repay thee. 36 Which now of these three, thinkest thou, was neighbor unto him that fell among the thieves? 37 And he said, He that shewed mercy on him. Then said Jesus unto him, Go, and do thou likewise.

What Lord is saying, many can revive if you stand and help. Be cautious not to act like a priest or Levite who is merely a so-called Christian in this time period. They saw a wounded man, crossed the road, and ran away. That is why many are sick, hurting, suicide, depressed, dying of cancer, and in prison and jail. Satan called a thief, stripped of the man.

John 10:10 The thief cometh not, but for stealing, and to kill, and to destroy: I am come that they might have life, and that they might have it more abundantly.

What a beautiful scripture! Lord Jesus will not strip, rob, or kill, but will bless, nurture, and help you. The Lord will provide healing deliverance and heal your broken heart. Jesus revives people if you are His hand and mouth. Satan is doing a marvelous job. If no one visits the sick, hurting, poor, widow, or orphan, they will not survive, revive, or restore. They will be killed by the thief Satan, stripped by Satan, and wounded by the devil. God hides your blessings under minor acts of mercy and kindness. Work for King Jesus. People are dying, killed, and injured by the enemy Satan. Our job is not to run from them but to run to them and do the necessary.

Being in the medical field, my parents brought sick people home and took care of them. They got the brokenhearted, rejected people and helped them to settle down. Help to finish their schooling, and we babysit their children. My home was a sanctuary for all those who were abused, wounded, and in need. My parents only rejected our evil company if they perceived it. I never had a problem accepting their wisdom.

As you know, they were more experienced than me. My parents were not wealthy but shared from the little. You need not have much to share; you just need a little help.

There is a special woman I know who has a strong relationship with the Lord. Due to her health issues, she frequently reaches out to me for prayers. Whenever I pray for her, she improves without fail. In the past, her daughter rescued a child from drug-addicted parents residing in the garage. The grandmother doesn't have many means to support her grandchildren. She welcomed this young child into her household. The family came together to purchase items for the young girl. As of 2019, she is now two years old. The little girl was brought back to life and made it. She said she went to a church building, according to the elderly lady. (since you represent the church). It was no secret that she was sick, extremely poor, and had many grandchildren. There was no help provided to her or her grandchildren. Nobody sought divine intervention for her sickness. People walked around her. No interest in asking or visiting. On a certain day, she crossed paths with me, and I successfully ended the curse of poverty, causing it to break. Now she has been my prayer partner. Happy all the time! We fill our lives with busyness by going to tea parties, engaging in church activities, practicing choir, and attending conferences. We allocate a significant amount of money towards shopping. The only action we take for the kingdom of God is going to a program that is nothing more than a gathering of thieves on Sundays. Take the time to visit hurting orphans, widows, and the sick in the hospital. Keep in mind that there is a way to be revived and restored by someone if you perform a specific act.

LET US PRAY

The Lord grants us a heart that is filled with compassion. Let us serve as the Lord's hands and feet. May the Lord use us, so someone revives and survives. May our life be like the life of Jesus! Lord, bless us with a nature that is both sharing and caring. the Lord, Let us take your mission back from Satan's hand. Help us so we help many in Jesus's name. Amen! God Bless You!

MARCH 10

LEARN TO CRY OUT!

Jesus, reveal to us the way to request help. God, please soften our hearts with your grace. Lord, we seek your reminder that you are the sole provider of our help. We are reminded by our Lord that a God in heaven hears our cries.

The power of crying is immense. It captures the attention of God. You are His creation; it is His responsibility if you call and cry out to God for help.

Nowadays, individuals are pleading for aid from those who lack the ability to help. When confronted with bloodshed, pain, suffering, and hopelessness, they express their emotions through tears and complaints.

When they seek help, all they find is confusion, discouragement, and fear. People are in tears everywhere, whether you're following the news on TV, YouTube, or any media source. People's eyes are fixated on those in power. People have abandoned God, the one they should seek solace and guidance from. In the land, if you are a slave, who would be there to hear you? Where should you direct your complaint? Thankfully, God in heaven is able to rescue those who are oppressed, possessed, sick, and suffering.

To gain knowledge and offer assistance, it's crucial to know who and where to reach out.

Exodus 3:7 And the LORD said, I have surely seen the affliction of my people which are in Egypt, and have heard their cry by reason of their taskmasters; for I know their sorrows; 8 And I am come down to deliver them out of the hand of the Egyptians, and to bring them up out of that land unto a good land and a large, unto a land flowing with milk and honey; unto the place of the Canaanites, and the Hittites, and the Amorites, and the Perizzites, and the Hivites, and the Jebusites. 9 Now therefore, behold, the cry of the children of Israel comes unto me: and I have also seen the oppression wherewith the Egyptians oppress them.

If you have knowledge of the Lord and His ability to set free, you will cry out to HIM. The government is not the answer. Joseph avoided looking at the government. He directed his eyes towards the Lord God. Peter did not look to the government; he cried out to the Lord.

Esther learned the slaughter was days apart for her people; she cried out. The Lord, not man, is the one who delivers, as Jesus said. People who require assistance are reaching out to others via phone calls, written messages, and text messages, even when help is not accessible. Do you know what you are doing to yourself?

The Bible says.

Jeremiah 17:5 Thus saith the LORD; Cursed be the man that trusteth in man, and maketh flesh his arm, and whose heart departeth from the LORD.

By relying on your money, job, government, king, or anyone else, you are inviting trouble upon yourself. Trusting in the Lord, as the Bible instructs, results in receiving help and being blessed.

Jeremiah 17:7 Blessed is the man that trusteth in the LORD, and whose hope the LORD is.

Trusting in the Lord allows anyone to benefit from the promises and teachings in the Bible. Through Jesus' blood, gentiles can also partake in Jehovah God's blessings. Gentiles, like us, are part of the chosen generation. Through the blood of Jesus, we are granted free access to the throne room of God. I can be in the throne room of God because of His cleansing blood, without relying on a priest or high priest. Knowing what resources are at your disposal will prevent you from relying on doctors, the government, money, medical insurance, and other deceptive methods of Satan. Fix your eyes on God, who should not be mistaken for an idol. God is Spirit. If you call out to Him, he will assist you. Hannah was tired of her husband's 2nd wife's torture. Hannah was without children. She went to where she could find help to open the womb.

1 Samuel 1:10 Deeply hurt, Hannah prayed to the LORD and wept with many tears.12 And it came to pass, as she continued praying before the LORD, that Eli marked her mouth

She was noticed praying by the high priest. Eli said to her.

1 Samuel 1:17 Then Eli answered and said, Go in peace: and the God of Israel grant thee thy petition that thou hast asked of him.

Not Eli or her husband, but the God of Israel grants your petition.

Do you understand why we have so much chaos? Why so many divorces? There are churches everywhere without true preachers, prophets, teachers, and pastors. Our failure to cry out to the Lord resulted from false teaching and prophets. Your problem cannot be resolved in any way. Taking all kinds of medicine, you are sick all the time. You are raising beautiful children and losing them in prison, jail, and the world. You imparted education to them, yet failed to instruct them on where to seek support.

Rachel, who didn't have any kids, expressed her pain through complaints and tears. Listen carefully to the answer.

Genesis 30:1 And when Rachel saw that she bare Jacob no children, Rachel envied her sister; and said unto Jacob, Give me children, or else I die.2 And Jacob's anger was kindled against Rachel: and he said, Am I in God's stead, who hath withheld from thee the fruit of the womb?

She went to the wrong person for help. Where did her help come from? If she had known, she wouldn't have sought her husband's help but would have gone straight to the Lord. She found out about the God of Jacob. That is why she prayed to the gods of Abraham, Isaac, and Jacob.

Genesis 30:22 And God remembered Rachel, and God hearkened to her and opened her womb.23 And she conceived, and bare a son; and said, God hath taken away my reproach:

Only Jehovah God can help.

Genesis 30:24 And she called his name Joseph; and said, The Lord shall add to me another son.

Jehovah God granted her the gift of another Son, Benjamin.

Blindly following blind leaders leads us astray. Leaders like Moses and Joseph would tell you to cry to the Lord Jesus. Seek someone who can lead you towards the correct path. Aren't you tired of seeing drugs, bloodshed, chaos, and false promises? My purpose here is to encourage you to shift your focus from false hope to the Lord.

Power is not in the King and authority. If it is, then King David wouldn't cry out to the Lord.

Psalms 18:6 In my distress I called upon the LORD, and cried unto my God: he heard my voice out of his temple, and my cry came before him, even into his ears.

The Lord delivered King David. We pray that our King and Authority learn how to cry out to the Lord. We need spiritual and secular leaders to learn how to cry out to the Lord.

Psalms 118:5 I called upon the LORD in distress: the LORD answered me and set me in a large place.

If you are sick, where do you go?

Psalms 30:2 O LORD my God, I cried unto thee, and thou hast healed me.

Remember, you need to learn to cry out for people. Satan took cities and countries because you were not crying out to God for help. Teachers, moms, dads, family, pastors, preachers, prophets, and Christians learn how to cry out to God. Help comes faster than lightning. There is God in heaven who has an ear and an army of angels to minister. The Lord of the host is a way-maker, pathfinder, helper, and deliverer. Lord Jehovah makes impossible things possible. Shout out to this generation, county, young people, marriages, and authority in position. Cry out, so God sends deliverance from the demon of cancer, drug, alcohol, and mental illnesses. God can break the chains and yokes that the devil has put on them. Cry out for help. Would you let God be God?

LET US PRAY

Our Almighty God touches and cures us of all infirmities which medical science has labeled. The Lord who has created our body is our physician and surgeon. Lord Jesus is our spiritual, physical, and emotional help and health. May His hand touch the sick and afflicted! May the Lord touch your emotional, mental, spiritual, and physical health! Let Jehovah Rapha give you divine health, in Jesus's name. Amen! God Bless You!

MARCH 11

TAKE COUNSEL FROM GOD!

The Bible says that God is a counselor.

Isaiah 9:6 For unto us a child is born, unto us a Son, is given: and the government shall be uponhis shoulder: and his name shall be called Wonderful, Counsellor, The mighty God, The everlasting Father, The Prince of Peace.

The definition of counselor meant an adviser who consulted to gather. A guide or mentor counselor will instruct you.

Proverb 12:1 Whoso loveth instruction loveth knowledge: but he that hateth reproof is brutish.

Get wise and hear the counsel of the Lord. If not, you will get destroyed.

Proverbs 1:5 A wise man will hear, and will increase learning, and a man of understanding shall attain unto wise counsels:

King Josiah was the best King who followed the Lord wholeheartedly *2 Kings 22:2 And he did that which was right in the sight of the Lord, and walked in all the way of David his father, and turned not aside to the right hand or to the left.*

King Josiah Removed all witchcraft, familiar spirits, and wizards. Removed all idols from the Land of Judah. He idol worshipper priest. He cleaned up Judah from the pollution of the Idols. God was pleased with King's actions.

2 Kings 23:25 And like unto him was there no king before him, that turned to the Lord with all his heart, and with all his soul, and with all his might, according to all the law of Moses; neither after him arose there any like him.

But when Pharaoh-Necho, King of Egypt, went against Assyrians on the command of Jehovah God. King Josiah came against Pharoh Necho without taking counsel from God. Like King Josiah, we can become prideful after successes and ignoring God's counsel. We need someone to help us think straight.

2 Chronicles 35:20 After all this, when Josiah had prepared the temple, Necho king of Egypt came up to fight against Carchemish by the Euphrates: and Josiah went out against him. 21 But he sent ambassadors to him, saying, What have I to do with thee, thou King of Judah? I come not against thee this day, but against the house wherewith I have war: God commanded me to make haste: forbear thee from meddling with God, who is with me, that he destroy thee not. 22 Nevertheless Josiah would not turn his face from him, but disguised himself, that he might fight with him, and hearkened not unto the words of Necho from the mouth of God, and came to fight in the valley of Megiddo. 23 And the archers shot at king Josiah; and the King said to his servants, Have me away; for I am sore wounded.

A good and righteous king Josiah missed taking the counsel of God from the mouth of Phero and got killed. God Loved this man; he was the wise King. Even Jeremiah lamented over King Josiah.

Proverb 11:14 Where no counsel is, the people fall: but in the multitude of counsellers there is safety.

Proverb 24:6 For by wise counsel thou shalt make thy war: and in multitude of counsellors there is safety.

The righteous parents, elder brothers, sisters, pastors, prophets, teachers, and loyal friends are good counselors.

I receive many calls for counseling since I have the Spirit of God. When people choose their path, they do not call me. I know they want to hear their flesh. Flesh and Spirit are contrary to each other. Why do we have chaos, teen pregnancy, gangs, suicide, and problems beyond us? Because We do not have a good godly counselor.

Please listen to the experienced, righteous grey hair wise man and woman. In Israel, the King always had a counselor. And the King took counsel from them. The counsel of the wise counselor established the great Kingdom.

Chronicles 27:33a And Ahithophel was the King's counselor:

Samuel 16:23 And the counsel of Ahithophel, which he counseled in those days, was as if a man had inquired at the oracle of God: so was all the counsel of Ahithophel both with David and with Absalom.

I admire the counselors. I use the Holy Ghost and wise people as my counselors. We all need a good counselor to protect us from harm and danger. Always keep a godly, wise counselor. Also, be careful about taking advice from misguiders—especially your young friends and people who might have the wrong motive. King Solomon's son King Rehoboam was an example of taking counsel from bad people.

1 King 12:8 But he forsook the counsel of the old men, which they had given him, and consulted with the young men that were grown up with him, and which stood before him:

Listening to the wrong counseling, King Rehoboam lost ten tribes. Evil counsel will divide the kingdom, separate families and friends, divorce, and cause harm.

1 King 12:16 So when all Israel saw that the King hearkened not unto them, the people answered the King, saying, What portion have we in David? Neither have we inheritance in the son of Jesse: to your tents, O Israel: now see to thine own house, David. So Israel departed unto their tents.

Wrong counseling caused a division of the kingdom into two, northern and southern. King Rehoboam ruled in the South, which had two tribes.

I see children or grown-ups also a victim of bad advice. Only good advice will save, spare, and guide you in the right direction. I do not know what I would do without good people's counseling. The Holy Spirit is also your counselor. Wise counseling will establish you. Always pray for every major or minor matter of life. If I do not get the answer, I go to a counselor. I only take counsel from Spiritual people or prophets. Life will go on a higher level. If you are a hearer and have a wise heart, then life could be smooth and successful.

My mom was a godly, righteous, unselfish lady. I share many of my problems with her. I took her advice since she had a great perception and discernment. Very bold to speak the truth. I have different friends to guide me on the right path. They are bold and not afraid to tell me the truth. It is like the Prophet Nathan, John the Baptist, and many who are not afraid. They will spare your life. We need a counselor on earth, not in heaven.

Rebellious children are the mouths of selfish parents. Wicked parents like to use children for their evil agenda. Please do not misguide your children. Many parents teach wrong to their children; they do not speak but use their children's mouths. You might see them as family, mom, dad, brother, sister, spouse, or friends, but they can be dangerous. Remember, the one who speaks to your ear is very close to you. Maybe your wicked friend, family, spouse, spiritual authority, or any authority over you. Run away from them. They aim to come to your house to curse you and separate you from God, family, and friends. Unless you tell the truth to bless you, no one is your family or friend.

Read Psalms chapter 1.

God's interest is to bless you and spare your life. Pray, and ask God to give you a good counselor, and He will.

LET US PRAY

In the name of Jesus, Lord, give us an ear to hear. Help O Lord to take good counsel through your spirit. People who are sitting in darkness send them the best counselor, friend, elder, or teacher to guide them. You are our counselor. Counsel us through your precious words. Make us godly counselors to others. Lord, give us a generation of wise people in Jesus's name. Amen! God Bless you!

MARCH 12

THE DOCTRINE OF GOD VS. THE DOCTRINE OF MAN!

The Bible talks about the doctrines. Different Churches and organizations, denominational or nondenominational teachers, also have different philosophies. As we know, someone joining any denomination must follow its Doctrine. Baptist, Pentecostal, Methodist, Mormon, and Jehovah's Witnesses teach their doctrines. Hindus, Muslims, and other religions have their Doctrine as well. The Bible says Jesus, the one God who came in the flesh, has the true Doctrine. So what is Doctrine? Doctrine means instruction applies to life, the teaching of a particular religion, or something taught. In short, it is teaching. There is a specific instruction in the Bible that talks about how to Establish Doctrine. To establish a Biblical Doctrine, you need two or more scriptures to develop a particular doctrine. You cannot establish a doctrine by finding one scripture for the subject.

2 Corinthians 13:1 In the mouth of two or three witnesses shall every word be established.

Deuteronomy 19:15 at the mouth of two witnesses, or at the mouth of three witnesses, shall the matter be established.

John 8:17 It is also written in your law, that the testimony of two men is true.

The Bible says you need to look for apostles 'and prophets 'teaching to establish Doctrine on any subject or matter since in

Ephesians 2:20a And are built upon the foundation of the apostles and prophets.

The Book of Acts did not continue since man started a false doctrine called teaching. False teaching can nullify the power of God in His word.

Mark 7:13 Making the word of God of none effect through your tradition, which ye have delivered: and many such like things do ye.

Matthew 16: 6 Then Jesus said unto them, Take heed and beware of the leaven of the Pharisees and of the Sadducees 11 How is it that ye do not understand that I spake it not to you concerning bread, that ye should beware of the leaven of the Pharisees and of the Sadducees? 12 Then understood they how that he bade them not beware of the leaven of bread but of the Doctrine of the Pharisees and of the Sadducees.

What is leaven? Leaven is a sin. The Bible says little leaven, a sin, can contaminate the whole lump. The false Doctrine or teaching can bring evil. Remember, tradition is not Doctrine. Tradition is man-made teaching to control people and to make God's Word non-effect.

Matthew 15:1 Then came to Jesus scribes and Pharisees, which were of Jerusalem, saying, 2b Why do thy disciples transgress the tradition of the elders? 3 But he answered and said unto them, Why do ye also transgress the commandment of God by your tradition?

The Bible mentions the Doctrine.

Hebrews 6:2 Of the Doctrine of baptisms, and of laying on of hands, and of the resurrection of the dead, and of eternal judgment.

To establish the Doctrine of Baptism, One God, laying on hand, needs two or more scriptures for witness or support. The Bible needs two or more scriptural evidence, not traditions. Be careful.

Let us examine the tradition of man on baptism.

Matthew 28:19 Go ye, therefore, and teach all nations, baptizing them in the name of the Father, and of the Son, and the Holy Ghost:

You will not find this scripture anywhere except once. But while baptizing, mentioning the name of Jesus is everywhere in the history of the ancient church since it focuses on the name of the title.

Acts 2:38a Then Peter said unto them, Repent, and be baptized every one of you in the name of Jesus Christ for the remission of sins,

Acts 8:16 (For as yet he was fallen upon none of them: only they were baptized in the name of the Lord Jesus.)

Acts 10:48 And he commanded them to be baptized in the name of the Lord.

I want you to study baptism in the book of Acts, the history of an ancient church. Find out if you are following Jesus's instruction or Man-made tradition. Be careful of the following false doctrines established by false teachers and prophets. The Bible says the word will be effective if you stay in Jesus's Doctrine. How to know that this is the correct Doctrine? If the following event occurs, you are in Jesus's Doctrine. If not, then you are following tradition.

Mark 16:17 And these signs shall follow them that believe; In my name shall they cast out devils; they shall speak with new tongues;18 They shall take up serpents; and if they drink any deadly thing, it shall not hurt them; they shall lay hands on the sick, and they shall recover.

If you follow the man-made tradition or false Doctrine, Jesus will not work with you. You are making the word of God ineffectual. If you are following the instruction of Jesus, then Jesus will do all that He has said.

Mark 16:20 And they went forth, and preached everywhere, the Lord working with them, and confirming the word with signs following. Amen!

Years ago, when I started learning the Book of Acts and read the truth, I learned how false teachers and prophets had misled the people. Not having a revelation of Jesus, they started their brand churches and organization and not Jesus's brand. They traditionally baptized me in India. I saw Jesus's name baptism, but having a scale in my eyes, I could not see. God spoke, saying go baptize. But the demon of tradition was so strong that I had difficulty following the truth. It was a marvelous experience to hear God's voice to be baptized, which I did. It overpowered me with the demon of religion. I started studying the scripture, considering Jesus's Doctrine. It took time to be delivered from false teaching and tradition. Seek the truth and continue to be free. Nowadays, many false teachers and prophets don't know who Jesus is. Without revelation, they have started different churches. It is apparent man made Doctrine will not be effective. Miracle healing and deliverance are the only evidence of having the truth. Now you understand why we have many buildings or dens called a church?

2 Timothy 3:5 Having a form of godliness, but denying the power thereof: from such turn away. Paul says to run from false Doctrine and man-made tradition. 2 Timothy 4:3 For the time will come when they will not endure sound Doctrine; but after their lusts shall they heap to themselves teachers, having itching ears;

The advisory devil works nonstop by teaching wrong.

1 Timothy 4:1 Now the Spirit speaketh expressly, thatin the latter times some shall depart from the faith, giving heed to seducing spirits, and doctrines of devils;

Do you ever question why we do not see signs and wonders? Why can we not open blind eyes, demons come out, deaf hear, and lame walk? Why did we see so many hospitals? Even though God has given the power to heal the sick. What is the difference between the disciples and us? The Lord Himself said you could do greater. The answer is simple: you are following the Doctrine of the devil or men and not God.

LET US PRAY

May the Lord of heaven bless us with His Doctrine. The Lord teaches the way of God. Lord delivers us from the false teachers, prophets, tradition, and Satan's doctrines. Lord, show us the way, the truth in your word. Please give us the courage to do what is right in your sight. Lord, give us the true teachers and prophets of God. Lord, give us the true Doctrine to experience the power of God in operation in Jesus 'name. Amen! God Bless you!

MARCH 13

LET LOST FIND THE WAY OUT!

The relationship between the creator and His creation is authentically portrayed in the Bible. Here's the narrative of a father and his son who went astray. The story of a lost sheep. The story of the woman who lost the coin. She found it when she looked for it. The Pharisees and scribes had a tendency to judge others and believe they were superior to everyone else. The self-righteous offer no assistance to sinners. The Bible talks about Pharisees, the group of strict sects of Israel. Their knowledge was limited to God's laws, without truly knowing the God behind those laws. The self-righteous fail to perceive the Lord's plan for his arrival on earth. Our self-righteousness does not determine our entry into heaven. Have compassion for lost sheep. Pray fast for the one lost in the building called church, in your home, and around you. Make time to call and look for those who are out there lost.

Jesus came on earth to find His lost creation. Finding the person who is lost is our top priority. Sick needs a physician. It is necessary for the dead to be resurrected.

Our job is to find sinners, help them, and not criticize them. A genuine shepherd shows care and compassion, seeking out the lost sheep. Lost sheep are defenseless and targeted by the wolf. Sheep are known for being followers. Before anyone can harm them, a true shepherd finds the sheep and protects them. We must focus on the lost and lead them towards the right path.

The Bible says in Luke 15:7 I say unto you, that likewise joy shall be in heaven over one sinner that repenteth, more than over ninety and nine just persons, which need no repentance.

Luke chapter 15 exemplifies God's extreme love and compassion toward His lost creation. His desire and hope for them to return safe and sound. Father rejoices over the safe return of the sinner. Father is waiting to receive the lost son and throw a grand party when he repents. God considers the prodigal son a dead soul.

The Bible says it doesn't matter what he did,

Luke 15:20 And he arose, and came to his father. But when he was yet a great way off, his father saw him, and had compassion, and ran, and fell on his neck, and kissed him.22 But the father said to his servants, Bring forth the best robe, and put it on him; and put a ring on his hand, and shoes on his feet:23 And bring hither the fatted calf, and kill it; and let us eat, and be merry:

God teaches from the example there is no fun out there in the world. There is hardship, starvation, and devourer out there. You only have privileges if you are under God's umbrella of grace and mercy. God has provided you all. Even if you made wrong choices, God cares. It is true that when people stop serving God, their situation gets unfortunate and bad.

There is another example of a sheep.

Luke 15:4 What man of you, having a hundred sheep, if he loses one of them, doth not leave the ninety and nine in the wilderness, and go after that which is lost, until he find it? 5 And when he hath found it, he layeth it on his shoulders, rejoicing. 6 And when he cometh home, he calleth together his friends and neighbors, saying unto them, Rejoice with me; for I have found my sheep which was lost. 7 I say unto you, that likewise, joy shall be in heaven over one sinner that repenteth, more than over ninety and nine just persons, which need no repentance.

God is urging us to find the one who has gone astray. When they come back, please receive them, take care of them, celebrate, carry them on your shoulders, and throw a party. People leave God complete and come back empty. They return naked, hungry, hurt, and experiencing the illusion given by the Devil. It is Satan's lie to tempt you.

A lady had ten pieces and lost one. For one, she took time and diligently searched for it. When she findeth, she rejoiced with friends and neighbor

Luke 15:10 Likewise, I say unto you, there is joy in the presence of the angels of God over one sinner that repenteth. 32 It was meet that we should make merry, and be glad: for this, thy brother was dead, and is alive again, and was lost, and is found.

The Bible is the story of the loving father who did everything for you and me. Father put on flesh and died instead of us.

He wants to take away our sorrow.

Isaiah 61:3 To appoint unto them that mourn in Zion, to give unto them beauty for ashes, the oil of joy for mourning, the garment of praise for the spirit of heaviness; that they might be called trees of righteousness, the planting of the LORD, that he might be glorified. 9 And their seed shall be known among the Gentiles, and their offspring among the people: all that see them shall acknowledge them, that they are the seed which the LORD hath blessed. 10 I will greatly rejoice in the LORD, my soul shall be joyful in my God; for he hath clothed me with the garments of salvation, he hath covered me with the robe of righteousness, as a bridegroom decketh himself with ornaments, and as a bride adorneth herself with her jewels. 11 For as the earth bringeth forth her bud, and as the garden causeth the things that are sown in it to spring forth; so the Lord GOD will cause righteousness and praise to spring forth before all the nations.

There is no sin so great, the problem so complex, and the mountains are so high for the Lord. No matter what type of sin you have committed, return home. Your heavenly Father is waiting with open arms to receive and bless you. Angels are there to dance and rejoice with you.

LET US PRAY

Our heavenly Father, please send laborers to look for the lost. Lord, we ask for sinners to receive a spirit of repentance through our prayers. May the Lord send them His light to find their way home. Help us fast and pray for the lost, rebellious, and sinners to return home. Lord Jesus put love and compassion for the one who needs compassion. Lord Jesus, give us mercy and kindness. Oh, Lord God, direct the way of sinners toward you in Jesus's name. Amen! God Bless you!

MARCH 14

WAITING IS THE KEY TO RECEIVING PROMISES!

To wait means to stay in a place until an anticipated event happens, hold on, or be patient.

Waiting brings maturity. If you are patient, you will witness the beauty of full bloom. Your 18th birthday doesn't happen the day after you're born. You have to reach a certain age to obtain a driver's license. Do not open the bud; wait until it opens up itself.

Ecclesiastes 3:11 He hath made everything beautiful in his time:

Preparation and maturity are the essence of the waiting period. The Bible says,

Psalms 27:14 Wait on the Lord: be of good courage, and he shall strengthen thine heart: wait, I say, on the Lord.

It takes courage and patience to endure waiting. Throughout this waiting period, God is responsible for managing all forces, temptations, and situations. You'll face a constant offensive of internal and external pressure, pushing, and questioning. Knowing the Lord will make you willing to wait. You won't know when God will arrive, but rest assured, He will be punctual. Don't forget, God is in control and knows what He's doing. You do not have to worry; God never forgets His promises.

King Saul was waiting for priest Samuel. Samuel was coming at the appointed time by God. King Saul became tired of waiting and broke the rules.

1 Samuel 13:7 And some of the Hebrews went over Jordan to the land of Gad and Gilead. As for Saul, he was yet in Gilgal, and all the people followed him trembling. 8 And he tarried seven days, according to the set time that Samuel had appointed: but Samuel came not to Gilgal; and the people were scattered from him. 9 And Saul said, Bring hither a burnt offering to me, and peace offerings. And he offered the burnt offering. 10 And it came to pass, that as soon as he had made an end of offering the burnt offering, behold, Samuel came; and Saul went out to meet him, that he might salute him. 11 And Samuel said, What hast thou done? And Saul said, Because I saw that the people were scattered from me, and that thou camest not within the days appointed, Anticipating God's divine approval to come.

God calls with promises but throws time in the middle. In between times, He monitors how you are handling the situation. What is your reaction to testing and trying time? Are you faithfully following His ways or going against the given instructions?

What God promised, He can give to you. If you don't succeed, God will assign someone else who can wait and carry out His instructions. Keep in mind, you're being interviewed by God.

13 And Samuel said to Saul, Thou hast done foolishly: thou hast not kept the commandment of the Lord thy God, which he commanded thee: for now would the Lord have established thy kingdom upon Israel forever. 14 But now thy kingdom shall not continue: the Lord hath sought him a man after his own heart, and the Lord hath commanded him to be captain over his people because thou hast not kept that which the Lord commanded thee.

God appointed Saul as King over God's people Israel. King Saul feared people but not the Lord. He saw people scattering. He did what He shouldn't. Despite ruling for 40 years, God deposed King Saul. After turning him, God dismissed his family. Do you understand? Don't let the situation, fear, worry, or surroundings control you. God's plan requires someone who both listens and obeys. Never forget that God calls you with a purpose in mind. So get rid of your agenda.

We have the true story of Abraham. God promised him a son. He waited long where situations with their age made him not believe. His wife aged where she couldn't conceive. He listens to his wife and has a son from an Egyptian maid named Hagar. Abraham did not wait on the Lord's promise. Abraham cannot say, my wife. All Excuses are lies. It is all your fault and not part.

Ishmael was not the promised one. Not waiting for the time, He had Ishmael. Abraham brought trouble for the future. Remember, God does not need your help to fulfill His promise.

Genesis 17:6 And I will make thee exceeding fruitful, and I will make nations of thee, and kings shall come out of thee.19 And God said, Sarah, thy wife shall bear thee a son indeed; and thou shalt call his name Isaac: and I will establish my covenant with him for an everlasting covenant, and with his seed after him.

Genesis 22:17 That in blessing I will bless thee, and in multiplying I will multiply thy seed as the stars of the heaven, and as the sand which is upon the sea shore; and thy seed shall possess the gate of his enemies;

God is not man, so He forgets. God again reminded me of His promises.

Genesis 17:21 But my covenant will I establish with Isaac, which Sarah shall bear unto thee at this set time in the next year.

Genesis 21:2 For Sarah conceived, and bare Abraham a son in his old age, at the set time of which God had spoken to him. 3 And Abraham called the name of his son that was born unto him, whom Sarah bare to him, Isaac.

Ishmael was a mistake by Abraham for not waiting on promises. In our time and age where people do what feels good and not what is right. We see young people doing what they are not supposed to. Even little children are misguided by their surroundings and parents. Do not keep up with the Joneses. It is a game of the enemy. Wait till you receive yours. Do not get in a hurry. Wait for the right time to drive, marry, and work.

Isaiah 40:31 But they that wait upon the Lord shall renew their strength; they shall mount up with wings as eagles; they shall run, not be weary, and they shall walk, and not faint.

We have promises given by God for life to be more abundant. No matter how long it takes, just wait. Life span on earth is too little compared to eternity. We are here for a bit of time. Wait, He has the plan to bless and prosper you.

As Eve and Adam were misguided, so we are. Satan's agenda is to throw you out of God's beautiful plan.

I meet many nationalities and cultures of people. They have the same rushing spirit. Rushing and going before God produces havoc, uproar, and lawlessness. We see divorces, children in prison, shootings, killing, and depression as the output of not waiting. Wait on God for all petitions you have filed.

LET US PRAY

May the Lord give you all that you desire. May God provide you with faith and trust to wait! Lord, you have the best plan and not us. Lord, Help us stay in the direction you are taking us. The Lord gives us courage and boldness in the plan of God, no matter what happens around us. Help us, Lord, to be one accord with you. There is a time to fulfill what God has promised. May God make you mature while waiting. I pray whatever has been pushed back by the devil will be free. You find the patience to reach the destiny prepared for you in Jesus's name. Amen! God Bless you!

MARCH 15

FIVE FOOL, FIVE WISE!

The Parable in Matthew 25:1-13 talks about ten virgins. Five fools and five wises.

Before discussing this parable, let's take a look at some definitions. Five were foolish, thoughtless, brainless, unintelligent, and careless, and five were wise [far-sighted, practical, knowledgeable, or enlightened, having the power of discerning and judging correctly.].

The bride is patiently waiting for Jesus Christ, who is the groom. When talking about a virgin or woman, the Church uses the term "bride". There will be a day when we will meet as the bride-to-groom, Jesus.

Although these church-goers know of Jesus, Jesus does not know them because they are foolish virgins. Is it possible? There are those who believe that attending Church makes them suitable. The duty of attending Church does not make them wise. It's possible that they are choir members, standing on the pulpit or holding a microphone. Is this the reason God called you to the kingdom? The power of prayer in the Kingdom of God allows you to connect with your groom. There has to be an act of casting out a demon, healing the sick, raising the dead, opening blind eyes, and breaking chains and yokes as King Jesus has commanded us to further His kingdom. First, we should know the Word of God. The Lord enlightened me with the understanding that "The Word is God and God is the Word. By knowing the Word, you come to know God." Lord Use the Word of God as a light to travel your life. Good will come from words empowered by the Holy Spirit.

Are you familiar with what Jesus said during his time on the mountain? Blessed are those who have a hunger for righteousness, mourn, visit widows, go to prison, preach the gospel, and pray for others. Remember all that Jesus and His disciple did, do it today. There are those who believe that dumping in water, getting church building membership, and sitting in the pew is all that is necessary. Continuously funding the religious industry to sustain its existence. I've completed my job.

Do you know the five fools? The fool becomes entangled in a sinister system, goes blind, and uses up their oil reserves. In the religious world system, their oil was completely burned up. They overlook the fact that one day they will encounter Jesus and realize they are running out of oil for their lamp. Not keeping sufficient oil is called a fool. To keep your lamp full of oil, pray, fast, and seek God.

Matthew 25:1 Then shall the kingdom of heaven be likened unto ten virgins, which took their lamps, and went forth to meet the bridegroom. 2 And five of them were wise, and five were foolish. 3 They that were foolish took their lamps, and took no oil with them: 4 But the wise took oil in their vessels with their lamps. 5 While the bridegroom tarried, they all slumbered and slept. 6 And at midnight there was a cry made, Behold, the

MARCH 15

bridegroom cometh; go ye out to meet him. 7 Then all those virgins arose and trimmed their lamps. 8 And the foolish said unto the wise, Give us of your oil; for our lamps are gone out. 9 But the wise answered, saying, Not so; lest there be not enough for us and you: but go ye rather to them that sell, and buy for yourselves. 10 And while they went to buy, the bridegroom came; and they that were ready went in with him to the marriage: and the door was shut. 11 Afterward came also the other virgins, saying, Lord, Lord, open to us. 12 But he answered and said, Verily I say unto you, I know you not. 13 Watch therefore, for ye know neither the day nor the hour wherein the Son of man cometh.

Five wise knows the groom and the groom knows them. Wise is in a relationship with Lord Jesus, the groom. Motivated by the plan of Jesus Christ, they possess knowledge and understanding. They are aware that they are the temple, not the building or den. Those who are wise always have a purpose and goal in life. By keeping His Word, the wise virgins exemplify their true commitment to following Christ.

1 Thessalonians 5:4 But ye, brethren, are not in darkness, that that day should overtake you as a thief. 5 Ye are all the children of light, and the children of the day: we are not of the night, nor of darkness.

Foolish virgins exhibit specific characteristics.

Lot's wife is an excellent example of a fool. Angels rescued her, but her heart was in her wealth. She turned back to see where her riches were and transformed into a pillar of salt.

God saved you from the World, but the World is not out of you. You bring all the systems of the World to entertain the flesh. Those who still carry the World within them are not beneficial to the kingdom and King Jesus.

Many false teachers and prophets operate within the established church system. Some are falling asleep. There are those who identify as Christian but don't exhibit any change in their attitude and lifestyle. They think that their secret is unknown to anyone. The assumption is that God's interest lies only in your presence at the Church. I advocate for Jesus as a pure virgin, not for all the agendas and activities of organizations and churches.

2 Corinthians 11:2 For I am jealous over you with godly jealousy: for I have espoused you to one husband, that I may present you as a chaste virgin to Christ.

Stay loyal to each other, not to institutions like churches, organizations, and denominations. So be careful about all that you have entangled yourself with. Avoid deception. Prepare yourself, pray, study, and follow God's Word.

Luke 21:34 And take heed to yourselves, lest at any time your hearts be overcharged with surfeiting, and drunkenness, and cares of this life, and so that day come upon you unawares.

Currently, a religious system has taken the place of Jesus Christ and declared themselves the rulers. Watch out! See what the Bible says; check what they are doing. Jesus Christ does not enforce the necessity of attending Church on Sundays or mid-week. Did Jesus follow this kind of agenda? He was praying in the night, fasting, and teaching the Word.

His heart was compassionate toward the broken-hearted. He healed their broken hearts. Do not slumber and sleep. Wake up. It is time to fast and pray. Time to be light in the dark World. The end time is a time of persecution. Many persecuted Christians need prayer and intercede for them. Look around; how many are awake? Do you see the trouble? I see nothing but trouble. The bride has fallen asleep. The five fools do not know their responsibility. They have no or very little oil in their lamps.

Never think God is coming for a fool who is enjoying life, eating, having pleasure in the World, heartless, without self-control.

Getting ready and preparing yourself is a process. It is not about music, hair, clothes, or shoes. It is about your soul, attitude toward Jesus, and lifestyle. In the end, we have the test, persecution, and trial.

We must be full of His Spirit, which is oil. His Word must work through us. We are the light in the darkest time we are facing. That is why there are many warnings in the Bible about getting ready, watching, and praying so you can escape. We found Jesus praying before facing Crucifixion.

It is the bride who has to prepare, not Jesus the Groom. He is waiting for us and warning us. Keep sending the prophet and preacher to warn us. Be ready; keep your lamp full of oil. Let it overflow and run over. In a time like such, the Lord has a plan for the wise virgin.

LET US PRAY

Oh Lord, we do not know when the groom will come but help us be ready. Help us watch our time in prayer. We must get prepared and help others to be ready as well. It is our job to be an authentic light-giving lamp so others can see and find the way. Lord, as you said, you are coming, and no one knows when. Could you help us be ready all the time? Let us be that knowledgeable and perceiving virgin to wake others to be prepared. In Jesus 'name. Amen! God Bless you!

MARCH 16

THE RIGHTEOUS SHALL NOT BE MOVED!

The Bible guarantees over 5000 promises, but only for the righteous. God bestowed countless promises upon the righteous. Backing up their actions is essential for righteous individuals to receive God's promises.

Psalms 112:6 Surely, he shall not be moved forever: the righteous shall be in everlasting remembrance.

Earth is the temporary abode. Since wickedness has increased, people end their life at an early age. They live with many illnesses and sorrows. Some individuals have so much money that they disregard their spirituality, family, and behave inappropriately. They make it known that they possess wealth and don't need others. Don't forget, money flies away quickly. The only thing that will be established is righteousness. The protection of money lies in its purity. Our God became human and demonstrated a tremendous act of love towards us.

2 Corinthians 5:21 For he hath made him to be sin for us, who knew no sin; that we might be made the righteousness of God in him.

Proverbs 10:30 The righteous shall never be removed: but the wicked shall not inhabit the earth.

What is the definition of righteous? Righteous means principled, blameless, moral, and saintly. Those who are righteous are both confident and brave. The just take up the cross to witness the Lord's actions and receive divine favor.

Our God is righteous. If we follow His ways, then we become righteous. Our enemies 'evil scheme will be defeated. What you sow so you will reap. Righteousness brings the covering of grace and mercy over the next generations. Food stamps from God will be passed down to your children for eternity. What a wonderful opportunity if we have righteousness.

The Hindu faith teaches the concept of Karma, which signifies performing positive actions. There is no bias or discrimination in the way our God treats everyone equally. Why? His role as a creator is what defines Him as a father. I remember one of my Hindu friends always telling me; I taught my son to do right. This led him to be kind and helpful to others from a young age. She expressed how she never had enough money, but her son, being compassionate, dedicated his time to aiding elderly individuals. People would give money that has always helped with his school tuition. I sent her clothes when I could, and it was perfect for his school uniform. I did not know the size or color of the uniform. See how good God is. Just because someone is not saved doesn't mean they won't be rewarded by God if they are righteous.

Psalms 37:25 I have been young, and now am old; yet have I not seen the righteous forsaken, nor his seed begging bread.

Our God is righteous; he sees people not based on the person's skin, color, look, language, wealth, or religion. If you are righteous, blessings may come your way.

God instructed you to teach your children. Teach them what thus saith the Lord. In this world, people's true colors are exposed when they acquire wealth. Their actions are all evil, and they actively encourage their children to be deceptive and two-faced. Can you tell me what they are doing? They are preparing the next generation of a wiper, the snake. Those children will be a snare to their parents. They will not be continued on earth. They are on their way to receive curses. Please teach what is right in the sight of God. With His grace, they have the freedom to explore any corner of the world, knowing that His mercy will be with them.

If you think your children are educated enough, they won't need anyone's help. If you instruct them to act wickedly towards your in-laws or people you despise, you have done them a great disservice. God utilized three of Jochebed's children to rescue the Hebrews. People could argue that Moses passed up a tremendous chance to become the future ruler of Egypt. No, he knew what was right in the eyes of God to be established. Refuse to make compromises when it comes to earthly opportunities. The earth belongs to the Lord! Our righteousness is upheld when we allow the teachings of the Spirit of God.

Isaiah 64:6 But we are all as an unclean thing, and all our righteousnesses are as filthy rags, and we all do fade as a leaf; and our iniquities, like the wind, have taken us away.

Seek God's guidance in a difficult time. Find God's leading and teaching. You will come out blameless and be blessed. Someone at work told me that the unrighteous have no trouble but a good time. I do not believe so. Wait and see the end.

King Saul wanted his children to get to the throne. Saul tried to kill David, but he could not. It was God's Angels who protected David. A mighty warrior would have wiped out King Saul in a second. The Lord was faithful since David was righteous. He remained honest, refusing to harm the anointed one of God. He came out untainted and rose to power as the King of Israel.

2 Samuel 7:16 And thine house and thy kingdom shall be established forever before thee: thy throne shall be established forever.

The Messiah is descended from the bloodline of David. Jesus is the king forever. David brought eternal blessings to His generation.

Through the righteousness of Abraham, Isaac, and Israel, immense blessings were bestowed and a virtuous nation of God's people was born. He inherited the best nations, and many great kings came out of them. As you enter the throne room and acknowledge the God of Abraham, Isaac, and Israel, you are welcomed into their covenant and bestowed with the blessings of their righteousness.

There were individuals who stood on the pulpit and expressed their desire for peace in their homes. Why? There is a lack of peace within the house. Would you believe that a pastor can overlook the importance of righteousness? Why? Because they are self-righteous.

James 3:18 And the fruit of righteousness is sown in peace of them that make peace.

Everyone is subject to God's laws and judgments. God's righteousness is a requirement for your title as well. Holding the title in churches meant nothing. You do not have the authority to nullify God's righteousness. In the New Testament, you are the Church, the body and Temple of the living God, bought with His own blood.

(Acts 20:28 Take heed therefore unto yourselves, and to all the flock, over the which the Holy Ghost hath made you overseers, to feed the church of God, which he hath purchased with his own blood.)

My mom was an example of a righteous woman. She was a bold woman. She always treated the servants who worked under her with kindness and fairness. She displayed no fear towards higher authority due to her righteousness. I actually said she's righteous, not a churchgoer, because I've never witnessed her going to church. Not only will she fight for herself, but also for those who are unable to defend themselves. I have a strong belief that my parents have brought us wonderful blessings. Many people have received blessings through her as well. The act of seeking vengeance belongs to the Lord. My mom never harmed those who harmed her but did well for them in return. Her testimony claimed that those who wronged her died unjustly. Wicked gone in a few days. Being Christian, she believed revenge was the Lord's. When you act in righteousness, God will grant you wisdom and favor. The righteous are used by God. Those who are unrighteous are used by Satan. Not only does the Word of God teach righteousness, but it also has the capacity to transform anyone.

Gospel will talk to your heart.

Roman 1:16 For I am not ashamed of the gospel of Christ: for it is the power of God unto salvation to everyone that believeth; to the Jew first, and also to the Greek. 17 For therein is the righteousness of God revealed from faith to faith: as it is written, The just shall live by faith. History shows that the most successful individuals were righteous, not necessarily intelligent, talented, or wealthy. Don't forget to live righteously and pass on the teachings to your children and grandchildren. God will bless you and your offspring on earth.

LET US PRAY

May our Lord, who is just and righteous, guide and bless us with His righteousness. Let our actions in distress and disaster be right. Lord, bless us with wisdom to navigate the path of opportunity with discernment. Help us not to be deceived by what seems to be a success. Our success is only through God's righteousness. So help the Lord be a wonderful teacher to our children and theirs. May Lord give us healthy fear in our hearts to stay on the right track in Jesus's name. Amen! God Bless you!

MARCH 17

DO YOU KNOW WHAT'S AVAILABLE?

As Christians, God is the one who provides for us. It could be helpful for you to learn about the many promises that are available. Everything you want, need, trust, and request, knock, and seek is right there. Your father in heaven owns the cattle on thousands of hills. Go shopping and cash all promises in Jesus's name.

Psalms 50:10 For every beast of the forest is mine and the cattle upon a thousand hills.

The Bible does not talk about poverty but about riches. Your God is rich.

Psalms 104:24 O LORD, how manifold are thy works! In wisdom hast thou made them all: the earth is full of thy riches.

To locate this treasure, the people of God require a map. The secrets lie hidden in the vast collection of books known as the KJV Bible. We look everywhere for riches. Money drives us to do anything and everything. People can kill their families or relatives for money. Your relatives are the ones you should be careful of if you want to protect yourself. It is a fact that some people kill their family members for money. Your every evil deed is a wicked scheme by Satan to bring curses upon you. Have you ever witnessed the devil arriving with his horn to cause harm? No, he does not have to; he got you as long as you have the lust of eyes, lust of flesh, and pride of life. Fleshly desire will make you a slave of the devil. You can be a slave of the devil or a free child of King Jesus. What would you prefer? The choices are yours. Do you have any recollection of a lady named Eve? Despite our opinions, we are all affected by our human nature.

Sin is activated by the flesh. Safeguard yourself against the urge to look, eat, and desire. God can give you all that you want, desire, and crave without you having to put in any effort. When I need something, I pray and ask God to give it to me. It will come when the timing and season are right. Your father in heaven knows what you need.

Matthew 6:8 for your father knoweth what things ye have need of before ye ask Him.

God has a vineyard to provide, He says,

Matthew 6:33 But seek ye first the kingdom of God, and his righteousness; and all these things shall be added unto you.

Do you get it? It is all free. Open your Bible and start working on His vineyard. Everywhere and all the time, work in the field of the Lord. Be a Laborer on the vineyard of God and work joyfully and gladly. Do not get jealous when God's worker receives the best. If you want it all, leave your agenda and start working on the vineyard. Seek His righteousness. Do you see the sign + it adds, and the opposite is subtractions?

You can experience peace, protection, provision, and a multitude of privileges.

He has created Angels for our help.

Hebrews 1:13 But to which of the angels said he at any time, Sit on my right hand, until I make thine enemies thy footstool? 14 Are they not all ministering spirits, sent forth to minister for them who shall be heirs of salvation?

Exodus 23:20 Behold, I send an Angel before thee, to keep thee in the way, and to bring thee into the place which I have prepared.

Once I read a book called "*A Deliverance from the Darkness*" By Emmanuel Eni
http://www. divinerevelations.info/dreams_and_visions/delivered_from_the_powers_of_darkness.pdf

After finishing this book, I felt fearless, as if no devil in hell could ever intimidate me. That night I went to sleep feeling victorious. A few minutes before midnight, my bedroom was entered by something, causing me to wake up. The scariest howling reached my ears from my back and side yard. These two noises were completely unfamiliar to me; beyond anything I could have imagined. But I had peace beyond explanation; I was calm and fearless. Then I went back to sleep. Once again, I was awakened by something else and heard eerie cries coming from the side yard. My God has given me peace and protection beyond measure.

That scream and noise have the potential to give anyone a heart attack.

Through that book, I encountered the power and anointing firsthand. By following the KJV Bible, KJV is the accurate version, unlike the majority which are distorted. you are immune to the influence of hell. I spend hours in this book, and I pray for many hours. I realize what we are looking for is all available without toiling. So many things you own have never been used. When you die, can you take it? Remember to focus on what is best for you and your soul. Ask, seek, and knock with great wisdom. You do not want something that can scare you and your children. Wisdom is available; ask for it.

James 1:5 If any of you lack wisdom, let him ask of God, that giveth to all men liberally, and upbraideth not; and it shall be given him.

Intelligence, judgment, and prudence are the foundations of wisdom. Ask God to give you wisdom for all matters and see what happens. You will be amazed. I always ask for wisdom and guidance for everything. Guidance for big or little matters. His Spirit is to guide, teach and empower for the matter concerning you. Can you imagine water from the rock? Highway in the red sea? Yes, it is available. Think about something and believe in it. Not understanding but called blockage or a blinder of the mind. Read the Bible and pray for yourself. It is a direction to enter the supernatural. All supernatural things that happened in the past are available today.

In Sunday school, little children learn the following scriptures.

Mark 11:23 For verily I say unto you, That whosoever shall say unto this mountain, Be thou removed, and be thou cast into the sea; and shall not doubt in his heart, but shall believe that those things which he saith shall come to pass; he shall have whatsoever he saith.

I heard this true story about an enormous mountain in front of their house. Children came out and spoke to the mountain to move in Jesus' name. One morning, a child woke up and saw big trucks and workers working to remove the mountain. They practically came out and spoke to the mountain by believing in words. Why are we so grown up? I only believe in the Lord and no one. There is so much available that I cannot imagine. Guess what people should ask? I think contentment since people have over too much. They do not enjoy what they have, but they look for more.

1 Timothy 6:6 But godliness with contentment is significant gain.

Parents can provide only what they can. But if parents teach children that God can give anything they like if they pray to believe in their heart.

The following scriptures are my favorite since it gives the excess to the wealth of the heavenly father.

Revelation 5:12 Saying with a loud voice, Worthy is the Lamb that was slain to receive power, and riches, and wisdom, and strength, and honor, and glory, and blessing.

We can receive from Jesus by believing and following Him. He got all; no need to roam from country to country for prosperity. Just believe in Jesus.

LET US PRAY

Our Lord and Savior Jesus, Bless your people with esoteric knowledge and wisdom. We know it is available to us. We need the heart to believe and the power to conquer. Give us wisdom, so we teach our children the map of God's wealth, wisdom, and power. We teach alive and resurrected Jesus. It is our duty. Could you help us be accurate in knowing the Word? Only truth will remain forever. We have so much available, so allow us to open the Bible and seek and claim it in Jesus 'name. Amen! God Bless you!

MARCH 18

RECONNECT WITH GOD!

God, assist us in reestablishing our connection with you and severing ties with wrongdoing. Allow the revival of your connection with the Lord. Having a strong connection is crucial. Your problem can be resolved by connecting with God. When Adam and Eve connected with God, they were in a state of safety, security, and blessings.

The devil knows what God is and can do for His creation, so he tries to disconnect us from God. Satan can successfully carry out his agenda of stealing, killing, and destroying by disconnecting us from God. As we recall, the woman who had the blood problem,

Matthew 9:21 For she said within herself, If I may but touch his garment, I shall be whole.

She wanted to be whole, not just healed. Whole means body, spirit, and soul complete, unbroken, and uninjured. So she got connected with God, and the issue of blood stopped.

Mark 5:29 And straightway the fountain of her blood was dried up, and she felt in her body that she was healed of that plague.

John Baptist came to connect us with God. He gave the baptism of repentance. After repenting, they reconnected with God. We must connect with God. In the Old Testament, prophets and priests were connected to God. First, get associated with God, then help others.

The connection is very important. Connecting with the wrong company will contaminate you. Psalms chapter 1 discusses connecting with the ungodly, sinner, and scornfully will infect you.

The evil spirit will reveal itself through their wicked actions. Alcohol demons are interested in connecting with men who drinks. Cigarette demons are drawn to cigarette smokers. The death spirit enables a connection with sick bodies. If you encounter the cancer demon, you would develop cancer. All attachments will show what type and kind of connection you have. If a home has a termite infestation, it will eventually be destroyed. Connecting with a malicious company will lead to your downfall. The devil seeks to disconnect us from God by connecting us to the internet, movies, and the world. Your behavior will show a manifestation of a connection. The connections you make will be evident in your behavior.

Because of his transgression, King Saul became disconnected from God.

ELIZABETH DAS

What is transgression? Transgression means you are knowingly stepping over the laws of God. It is called crime or rebellion. King Saul, in his distress, sought to. connect with God, but God completely disconnected him.

1 Samuel 28:5 And when Saul saw the host of the Philistines, he was afraid, and his heart greatly trembled. 6 And when Saul inquired of the LORD, the LORD answered him not, neither by dreams, by Urim, or by prophets.

Let us reconnect with God, where wealth, treasure, knowledge, wisdom, and power flow.

Ephesians 2:13 But now in Christ Jesus ye who sometimes were far off are made nigh by the blood of Christ.

We are grateful that God has reconnected us to His throne of mercy and grace through His precious blood. The Ouija board, Witches, warlocks, astrologers, psychics, and magicians all establish a connection with the evil spirit world. Your connection should not be with the wrong spirit. The Holy Spirit is the only true spirit, all others are counterfeit. It will connect you to all truth.

How to connect with God? Very simple, first repent your sins, then baptize in Jesus's name to wash away your sins. Praying and talking to the Lord is a way to connect with God. Our God, Jesus, has the ear to hear, eyes to see, and power to help. Your phone can connect with anyone who has a phone. If you have the internet, you get connected anywhere in the world. Not like TV, but now you are in control of the world.

Sin severs our connection with God and links us to punishment and curses.

Cain killed his brother. This is the reason why God linked him to punishment and curses.

Genesis 4:11 And now art thou cursed from the earth, which hath opened her mouth to receive thy brother's blood from thy hand; 12 When thou tillest the ground, it shall not henceforth yield unto thee her strength; a fugitive and a vagabond shalt thou be in the earth. 13 And Cain said unto the LORD, My punishment is greater than I can bear.

Always remember, the earth belongs to the Lord. When you connect with the owner of the earth, you gain access to treasure, blessings, power, wealth, and health. All will be yours. The Lord seeks a relationship with you. He sends His word; He sends prophets, preachers, pastors, and missionaries, and finally, he comes Himself. Gave His Blood. God's desire is solely to be connected with us.

Sending out 12 and later 70 disciples was His way of connecting with us. He desired for you to recognize that your sickness, broken heart, lostness, possession, oppression, and darkness are all consequences of your lack of connection with God.

Do you know how terrible it is to lose internet connection? The world's collapse could lead to business failure and bank closures. The world's collapse was a result of disconnecting from God, leading to incurable diseases and mental-physical suffering.

His last message after the resurrection is simple; go preach to reconnect my creation with me.

Mark 16:15 And he said unto them, Go ye into all the world, and preach the gospel to every creature. 16 He that believeth and is baptized shall be saved; but he that believeth not shall be damned. 17 And these signs shall follow them that believe; In my name shall they cast out devils; they shall speak with new tongues; 18 They shall take up serpents; and if they drink any deadly thing, it shall not hurt them; they shall lay hands on the sick, and they shall recover. 20 And they went forth, and preached everywhere, the Lord working with them, and confirming the word with signs following. Amen!

Are you willing to preach the gospel in order to unite people with the creator? People should recognize the creators instead of just labeling the building as a church. He wants to share Jesus 'reconnection plan with the world. Give all that Jesus has provided us free to give free. He will manage the remaining tasks. You need not worry; He is in charge. Please reconnect with God!

LET US PRAY

Lord Almighty God, help us reconnect with you. Please provide the right pastors and prophets to connect us with our creator. We do not need an internet connection but infinite connections. May we be granted the ability to see and understand Satan's plan to separate us from God. May Lord help us disconnect from Satan and the world. Lord, help us find a connection through the Precious blood of Jesus. The heavenly Father is patiently waiting for you to reconnect and embrace the abundance He has in store for you, in Jesus's name. Amen! God Bless You!

MARCH 19

GOOD SEED VS TARE!

In Matthew chapter 13, the focus is on the parable of the Kingdom of God.

Matthew 13:24 Another parable put he forth unto them, saying, The Kingdom of heaven is likened unto a man which sowed good seed in his field: 25 But while men slept, his enemy came and sowed tares among the wheat, and went his way. 26 But when the blade was sprung up, and brought forth fruit, then appeared the tares also. 27 So the servants of the householder came and said unto him, Sir, didst not thou sow good seed in thy field? From whence then hath it tares? 28 He said unto them, An enemy hath done this. The servants said unto him, Wilt thou then that we go and gather them up? 29 But he said, Nay; lest while ye gather up the tares, ye root up also the wheat with them. 30 Let both grow together until the harvest: and in the time of harvest, I will say to the reapers, Gather ye together first the tares, and bind them in bundles to burn them: but gather the wheat into my barn.

The disciples received an explanation of the wheat and tare parable from Lord Jesus.

Matthew 13:37 He answered and said unto them, He that soweth the good seed is the Son of man; 38 The field is the world; the good seed are the children of the Kingdom; but the tares are the children of the wicked one; 39 The enemy that sowed them is the devil; the harvest is the end of the world; and the reapers are the angels. 40 As therefore the tares are gathered and burned in the fire; so shall it be in the end of this world. 41 The Son of man shall send forth his angels, and they shall gather out of his Kingdom all things that offend, and them which do iniquity; 42 And shall cast them into a furnace of fire: there shall be wailing and gnashing of teeth. 43 Then shall the righteous shine forth as the sun in the Kingdom of their Father. Who hath ears to hear, let him hear.

Have you ever wondered why there are so many organizations, non-denominations, denominations, and churches? Is everything owned by Jesus? Just good seeds, nothing else. Children of the Kingdom are Good Seeds. God is a king of kings. King has a kingdom. Satan wants to overthrow King Jesus; his agenda is to divide the Kingdom by bringing false teachers and prophets. Many are the followers of false teachers, known as tares.

The offspring of God are represented by good seeds, while Satan's children are symbolized by tare. When confronted with various denominations, the children of Satan distort the Word of God through twisting, changing, adding, and subtracting.

MARCH 19

Tare has excellent communication skills and behaves in a fair manner. You may wonder what the difference is. Their teachings are not in line with what the Word of God says. According to Jesus, these are the attributes of the wheat, representing God's offspring.

They cast the demon out in Jesus's name. This is the first character as being a child of God. Tare's statement is that there are no demons within Christians. Really? Tare will not tell the truth. There are some who claim that demons are not real. Some tares will say when you become Christian; you have the Holy Spirit. Tares are associated with organizations or churches founded by Satan, whose purpose is to harm God's obedient children. Following organizations, denominations, and non-denominations causes tares to become blind and deaf. You are supposed to act as spectators, focusing solely on them and refraining from crossing any limits.

2 Corinthians 7:1 Bible says clean yourself from all filthiness of the flesh and spirit, perfecting holiness in the fear of God.

We must cleanse ourselves of any spiritual or fleshly sin that has clung to us. Our actions of fasting, praying, and obeying God's Word allow Lord Jesus to work through us. Hallelujah! Unclean individuals are not used by God.

Tares are skeptical about the notion that a demon resides within them, the house, the office, or even exists at all. If they don't believe it, how do they manage to drive them out? The demon cannot cast out a demon. Those working as tares are actually children of Satan. I encounter numerous tares while growing and working alongside good wheat seeds. The world has been blessed with good seeds planted by God. God's favor is not limited to the Hebrews; anyone who believes in Him is granted privilege.

Speaking in a new language, similar to the events of Pentecost, is a second sign of a good seed. The church of new testament disciples spoke in the heavenly language. But tares will not believe in speaking tongue. Why? It's confusing for Satan. The children of God speak in a way that Satan cannot comprehend.

Third, no hurt or harm to the king's children. Tares will constantly be experiencing sickness. The immune system can cause problems such as reactions, cancer, heart attacks, and others. They are unable to acknowledge their status as tares because of their false teaching. Tare are good deceivers as their king Satan is.

According to the Bible, nothing can harm the good seeds. Their belief is that stripes have the ability to bring about healing. They anoint the sick with oil, and they recover. Tares attend church, where nothing occurs. The devil possesses the knowledge to provide medicine when they are sick. Can you spot two snake symbols on a medical sign? They won't be able to receive healing because Satan prevents them from being anointed with oil. Tare will eat food without faith. The wicked seed would trust in the perniciousness of a lethal object or the harm caused by a serpent, even the goodness of food will cause harm to unwanted plants! Tare and good seed have conflicting beliefs.

I do not take medicine, but I always carry oil, anoint the sick and pray over them. Tare uses the Bible to go to church, but their false teacher, prophet, and pastors follow the teachings of Satan. The Lord Jesus's teachings are manipulated by them through twisting, adding, and subtracting. I have noticed that tares are strong in arguments, too good for their hurt. The antichrist doctrine began during the time disciple John was alive, which is quite sad. He warned us in the 1st, 2nd, and 3rd epistles of John. Tares don't accept the idea that Jesus was God in human flesh. One Spirit God walked in the flesh to shed blood. Sin causes sickness. The reality of generational curses cannot be denied. The power of Jesus's name can drive away sickness. By misleading, the devil will maintain his children in a state of sickness, possession, and oppression. The majority of tares have a liking for the church. Satan has made Broadway sayings come as it is. You do not have to repent. Feel free to live as you please, without the need to renounce sin or embrace God's teachings. He is dedicatedly working on the creation and study of medicine to challenge God's plan of salvation. Due to their constant sickness, Tares, a follower of Satan, loses all their money, good times, and joy. Satan cannot heal, deliver, or set free.

I encountered a man's testimony while reading. As he traverses a narrow mountain road, he notices a snake, prepared to attack. The man started speaking in the Holy Ghost's tongue, and that snake went crazy.

Tares will not believe in speaking in tongues also testimony like this. Accepting Jesus is when Tares will believe you have the Holy Spirit. No, you don't. The Holy Spirit will come to you with the ability to speak in tongues as evidence. Tares are skeptical. That was the reason the Lord spoke in parables. Their sight and hearing are present, but they remain oblivious.

Matthew 13:10 And the disciples came, and said unto him, Why speakest thou unto them in parables? 11 He answered and said unto them, Because it is given unto you to know the mysteries of the Kingdom of heaven, but to them, it is not given. 12 For whosoever hath, to him shall be given, and he shall have more abundance: but whosoever hath not, from him shall be taken away even that he hath. 13 Therefore speak I to them in parables: because they seeing see not; and hearing they hear not, neither do they understand.

God assures the growth of these churches, but ultimately, He will bring judgment and gather His righteous children, referred to as wheat, in His Kingdom.

The good seeds include wheat, spreading the truth, driving out demons, and dismantling Satan's Kingdom with the Holy Spirit's power. Please have patience till the end. Recognize the tares by their unbelief and having no fruits of the Holy Spirit. Have faith in the lesson of the parable before you go. Jesus came to destroy the work of Satan by setting the oppressed and possessed free. Casting out the demon, healing the sick, opening blind eyes, the lame walk, raising the dead, healing the broken heart, doing a great job. The followers carried out God's work after receiving divine power. It hurts me to witness Tare's continuous illness. According to Jesus, they are unable to see, hear, or understand, despite reading the Bible. That's the explanation for why they can't go against Satan. And so, how can they cast out the demon? Satan's love for sin prevents tares from repenting and purifying themselves from their fleshly desires. Keep in mind that in this context, wheat symbolizes the followers of Jesus.

LET US PRAY

In the name of Jesus, Lord put the drop of your blood mixed with the Holy Spirit in our eyes and ear. Let the Lord make us wheat and not tares. The world recognizes the tares and sticks them around the grain. The Lord keeps the wheat from harm and danger. Lord, make us good seeds and multiply. Let your divine protection be on the field. Lord let your eyes watch over the wheat and keep it from harm in Jesus's name. Amen! God Bless you!

MARCH 20

WE WORK IN ADVERSITY!

Christians promise victory, which means we will have a battle. Those who believe in God persevere in difficult circumstances. Jealous, envious, prideful liars and the forces of the enemy are present in the work of Christians. We are part of God's military force. Allow the Lord to fight for us. Daniel encountered many enemies, but the Lord had a way of changing the situation in his favor. Jesus is capable of shielding and preserving His loved ones.

The devil singles out important people as his targets. He cunningly devised plans to harm them. The devil closely watches the actions of the righteous. Faith and knowledge of God result in the devil's defeat. The devil schemes destruction, but God counters with a plan for your victory when you call out to Him. Satan's worker plots the best plan to get rid of the righteous. But God says I know how to overthrow and turn the table against. God allows the same plan against the enemy. So the enemy dies without remedy. Isn't that wonderful? We cry out, wondering where God is in the face of adversity. He is engaged in watching and coordinating a rescue operation, commanding His Angels to deliver us. The Lord is busy shutting the mouth of the lion. God is very busy attending to our cry. It is not visible, but you will know when you see deliverance. Once God's plan takes effect, you'll receive a promotion while the enemy is permanently destroyed.

We work in adversity.

Daniel 6:5 Then said to these men, we shall not find any occasion against this Daniel, except we find it against him concerning the law of his God.

So they plan to destroy Daniel.

Daniel 6:7 All the presidents of the kingdom, the governors, and the princes, the counsellors, and the captains, have consulted together to establish a royal statute, and to make a firm decree, that whosoever shall ask a petition of any God or man for thirty days, save of thee, O king, he shall be cast into the den of lions.8 Now, O king, establish the decree, and sign the writing, that it be not changed, according to the law of the Medes and Persians, which altereth not.11 Then these men assembled, and found Daniel praying and making supplication before his God.

Wow! Their plan succeeds. But the Lord of heaven honors those who honor His laws. We do not live for God when it is convenient. We live for God in adversities.

15 Then these men assembled unto the king, and said unto the king, Know, O king, that the law of the Medes and Persians is, That no decree nor statute which the king establisheth may be changed. 16 Then the king commanded, and they brought Daniel and cast him into the den of lions. Now the king spake and said unto Daniel, Thy God whom thou servest continually, he will deliver thee.

God responds to the way you speak, act, and carry yourself. He has no adversities but blessings prepared for those who stand tall, immovable, and steadfast in the word of God. We work in trouble for God. God rescued Daniel by the hand of His Angels.

Daniel 6:21 Then said Daniel unto the king, O king, live forever. 22 My God hath sent his angel, and hath shut the lions' mouths, that they have not hurt me: forasmuch as before him innocency was found in me; and also before thee, O king, have I done no hurt.

God turned the table against the adversary. His word has been established for eternity. Knowing this, Daniel did what was right. God's commandments are universally good for everyone, regardless of nation or situation. He faithfully followed God's commandment. God reversed the situation against the enemy.

Daniel 6:24 And the king commanded, and they brought those men which had accused Daniel, and they cast them into the den of lions, them, their children, and their wives; and the lions had the mastery of them, and brake all their bones in pieces or ever they came at the bottom of the den.

King commanded his kingdom and dominion to fear the God of Daniel, but not only that, *28 So this Daniel prospered in the reign of Darius, and in the reign of Cyrus the Persian.*

Those in power might attempt to work against you. Let God handle matters of justice; avoid taking matters into your own hands. God says to take revenge is mine. He knows how to deliver the righteous. He ensures his deliveries are fair. Regardless of whether He does or not, we must remain loyal to His laws and commandments. God is good!

Earth needs faithful people to prove God's wonderful work. The people in Babylon always saw the lion-eating man in the den. Yet, the sight they beheld that evening was unlike anything they had ever seen before. Daniel was not there for a few hours but all night. God's power was revealed to the King in Babylon. King said,

27 He delivereth and rescueth, and he worketh signs and wonders in heaven and in earth, who hath delivered Daniel from the power of the lions.

Jesus worked in adversity. Jesus finished His mission and what he came for. Satan is plotting to dismantle everything you represent. Devil plans to stress you out and see what your reaction is. Do you give up, give in, or try to compromise in any way? Due to Adam and Eve's carelessness, Earth is now under Satan's dominion. He planned to crucify Jesus. Jesus turned the table against the devil! He shed His blood to cleanse humanity's sins. Blood has life; it is for your and mine life. Our healing was secured through his endurance of 39 stripes. He gave the Holy Spirit so that we can cast the devil out. We can lay our hands to heal the sick in Jesus's name. Satan desires to eliminate all individuals who stand up for Jesus. We all who stand for Jesus will work in adversity.

Christians do not have a rosy road, but if we stand on the Word of God, we get the victory. Those who are godly experience deliverance, healing, and witness the resurrection of the dead. Don't assume there are no battles on earth just because you follow Jesus. Earth is the place where you have an adversary devil with a plan to bring calamity, difficulty, suffering, and afflictions. Discover the strength of relying on God's word for deliverance and victory.

We need a single mind and heart to focus on the Word of God and not on the problem. When God affirms that He is my provider, I should not dwell on what I lack but boldly declare that I receive His provision. Do not worry about what kind of sickness, but focus His stripes heal me. When Jesus was crucified, all storms, illnesses, oppression, and possession were also crucified. No weapons of an adversary have power over you if you trust in the Lord. A prison door will be open if you stay focused on your mission. We always will work in adversity. Remember, the devil, the adversary, has an agenda.

1 Peter 5:8 Be sober, be vigilant; because your adversary the devil, as a roaring lion, walketh about, seeking whom he may devour:

As an adversary, the devil obstructs and hinders. Under Satan's command, there exists an army of fallen angels and demons, working on a destructive plan. The devil is constantly pursuing and opposing you, regardless of your location or actions. Pray and fast as Daniel, and our Lord Jesus did.

Daniel 10:13 But the prince of the kingdom of Persia withstood me one and twenty days: but, lo, Michael, one of the chief princes, came to help me; and I remained there with the kings of Persia.

Revelation 12:7 And there was war in heaven: Michael and his angels fought against the dragon; and the dragon fought and his angels, 8 And prevailed not; neither was their place found anymore in heaven. 9 And the great dragon was cast out, that old serpent, called the devil, and Satan, which deceiveth the whole world: he was cast out into the earth, and his angels were cast out with him.

We have the key to overcoming the devil.

Revelation 12:11 And they overcame him by the blood of the Lamb, and by the word of their testimony, and they loved not their lives unto the death.

LET US PRAY

Lord Jesus, help us overcome the adversary. The finished work of the Messiah is symbolized by the cross. Lord, grant your people the faith and steadfastness of Daniel, David, and other believers in the Word of God. We all have testimony and testimonies written in the word of God. By relying on that evidence, we confidently proclaim that no weapon can intimidate us through an adversary's scheme, but we thwart the adversary's plan and its influence in the name of Jesus. Amen! God Bless you!

MARCH 21

GET VIOLENT. TAKE IT BY FORCE!

Matthew 11:12 And from the days of John the Baptist until now the kingdom of heaven suffereth violence, and the violent take it by force.

God is entrusting you with the key to the kingdom. But you have to use the force of prayer, the force of fasting, and swing the sword of the Word of God. In this world, we see that marriage is insecure, children are being misled, drinking, drugging, killing, shooting, jails-prisons are full, etc. God said I give you the key to use the power of prayer and fasting to whip Satan out. If you use it correctly, the devil will be cut off. As Jesus went to set the man free, the devil brought the storm. Jesus quiets down a storm, reaches the legion-possessed man, and liberates him. Jesus said you also can do what I am doing. I give you the key; it is the word by obeying. I give you the power over a serpent and scorpion.

Luke 10:19 Behold, I give unto you power to tread on serpents and scorpions, and over all the power of the enemy: and nothing shall by any means hurt you.

God has allowed you to do the work by using the authorities in His name, Jesus. By receiving the Holy Spirit, God comes on you to empower you. It is Jesus who will do work by using our bodies. Yield to His Spirit. Learn to operate by listening to the Holy Spirit's guidance through the Word of God. Knowledge is power, the key is knowledge. If you know what you have or are available to you, then you will pray, fast, and destroy Satan and its agenda to kill, steal, and destroy.

If your family is the victim of drugs, alcohol, oppression, possession, mental illnesses, cancer, aids, and all kinds of problems, then the key is to put on the armor of God not only by saying but also by doing. Fasting, praying, and practicing the Word as the armor works, not just reading. It is the breastplate of righteousness. If someone is sick, anoint with Holy Oil and pray. I always see a victory by anointing the sick with oil. Anointing places, trees, and homes destroy Satan's work. Peter was in prison, and Satan's agenda was to kill him. But some people wore armor and went non-stop, praying to destroy the plan. God sent the angel and rescued Peter. The opposing devil sets its sights on Christians; it is essential to engage in aggressive prayer to eliminate Satan's plan. Make the devil's idea non-effect. This is the armor of righteousness.

Acts 12:5 Peter therefore was kept in prison: but prayer was made without ceasing of the church unto God for him.

We must do the same. Do not talk about the situation, but pray against the situation.

MARCH 21

Acts 12:7 And, behold, the angel of the Lord came upon him, and a light shined in the prison: and he smote Peter on the side, and raised him up, saying, Arise up quickly. And his chains fell off from his hands. 8 And the angel said unto him, Gird thyself, and bind on thy sandals. And so he did. And he saith unto him, Cast thy garment about thee, and follow me. 9 And he went out, and followed him;

There was a violent encounter with Satan that resulted in Peter being freed from jail. Pray with aggression and passion. Cry out, travail. Do you cry and labor in silence? Have you ever observed a woman silently delivering a baby? Can you tell her to shush, please?

The devil wants you to shout while entertaining flesh. Keep quiet in church, please. Who told you to be quiet? Satan is cunning and tricks those who enjoy being deceived. I have no interest in being deceived or visiting places with dead people on the pews. Wherever I go, I cast the devil out, heal the sick and pray aloud. I am not dead. A disciple shouted when they received the Holy Spirit. Power lies in the hands of the living, not the dead. Was Jesus the one who told them to stay silent? No, He opened His mouth and spoke. Obviously, individuals who are spiritually lifeless cannot shout. You understand, right?

Jesus said, Luke 22:31 And the Lord said, Simon, Simon, behold, Satan hath desired to have you, that he may sift you as wheat: 32 But I have prayed for thee, that thy faith fails not: and when thou art converted, strengthen thy brethren.

Is prayer something you turn to when Satan is sifting through someone?

I entered into prayer when Satan sought to kill one of the family members, aiming to keep her safe. I took her out of the mouth of Satan.

There was a time when I saw a witch in a vision. She was trying to connect with the demon with the purpose of destroying my family. I witnessed it in a vision and then ordered it to go back to her. All demons went into her body. Do not mess with godly, righteous saints. In the spiritual realm, they are skilled at employing violence against Satan and his army. Being vigilant and praying involves recognizing the spiritual realm and ordering the devil to back off. In Jesus's name, I bind you and destroy your influence.

I experienced the terrifying sound of a hell scream as I successfully bound a spirit, causing it to collapse at my feet and lose its power. Jesus instructed to bind the strongman, who represents Satan, in order to overcome and defeat him. I first bind Satan and then ruin his plan of stealing and killing. Release the Holy Spirit and Angels.

Jesus went to deliver the man who had a legion in his body. The devil is the prince of the air who brought the storm to block. Jesus calms the storm by speaking to it. Command the storm and raging water of trouble and trials. Speak to the mountain of trouble; get out. Fight aggressively to eliminate the dark forces of the spirit world. Jesus took it by force. Lord Jesus delivered the man. Pray until you perceive the result.

There was a time when the children of a close family were in trouble. It appeared that their mother's overwhelming care for her family could have put them in a vulnerable position. Her plan was to use her money to support her parents and siblings by sending children to her mother's side family. But children were the victims of Satan's agenda. I was concerned for the children. God said in the night; you pray till the sun comes out. I did. The Lord intervened and rescued children from Satan's plan. The mother cast a spell on her daughter, causing her to send the children to their grandmother's place. Charming the family members is to take advantage for a selfish reason.

Romans 14:17 For the kingdom of God is not meat and drink, but righteousness, and peace, and joy in the Holy Ghost.

Have you heard some churches talk about the food, and program and not healing and deliverance? It is foreign to some religious churches to fast and pray. Instead, they praise the lovely lunch or chicken. Well, kingdom work is to destroy Satan and rescue the victim. Have you seen Churches crying out and sweating blood like Jesus? An Angel will come down if we carry out this action.

Luke 22:43 And there appeared an angel unto him from heaven, strengthening him.

The new converts received training from the Lord and His disciples. They won by the key called the truth. Truth is the key to deliverance.

The devil stole the key called truth. Please look for the key called truth and get violent against the drug demon, shooting and killing the demon, cancer demon, depression demon, snitch people out of its hand. Pray using tongues, pray using God's word, pray while fasting. Join the army and do as Word says.

Matthew 6:33 But seek ye first the kingdom of God, and his righteousness; and all these things shall be added unto you.

Is seeking the kingdom of God something you prioritize first, last, or whenever you have time? Do tears come when your children are incarcerated? Do you cry when they are addicted to drugs, mentally ill, and sick? Keep the enemy out by watching in prayer. Job's regular prayers and sacrifices to God were offered on behalf of his children's sins. Upon their departure, he enveloped them in prayer. Prayer will secure your children.

Choose fellowship where they acknowledge Satan as Jesus did. They can expel demons, cure the ill, and revive the deceased. Do not Preach love only. Do not listen to Satan's deceptive programs.

What has happened today? No one knows the devil and his army. Learn to invade and destroy before Satan destroys you. Throughout the day, countless people are being incarcerated, beheaded, and murdered. Get violent and get Satan's hand off of God's people. Take them out by force.

LET US PRAY

In Jesus's name, give us holy boldness. Please give us the key to your truth. Give us the sword to chop off the head of the devil since he is chopping many heads off. Lord, Help us fast and pray as your word says. We want to escape from evil, watch and pray. Lord, you prayed before going on the cross, and the angel gave you strength. Please help us pray until the prison door opens, drugs are out, and cancer disappears. We break the back of Satan in Jesus's name. Amen! God Bless you!

MARCH 22

DO NOT RUIN MY REPUTATION!

Proverbs 23:7a For as he thinketh in his heart, so is he: Eat and drink, saith he to thee; but his heart is not with thee.

The saying "*like father, like son*" is indeed true. The history of an individual can be traced through their father's last name. Parents advise children to protect the integrity of their names. Please do not ruin the reputation of my country. We are so careful about our importance; so is God. We can give Lord Jesus credit as God or ruin His credibility on earth.

The Bible says in Proverb 23:7a the man who thinks exactly what he is.

If you are bad, it means you have evil thoughts. No one believes the thinker is crazy. We, Christians, know our God; we represent Jesus Christ. It depends on the person's understanding of God and how he describes Him. You either publish His name like a lady who had an issue for 12 years. Lord who has the power to cleanse lepers, open blind eyes. You can simply say that you are unfamiliar with the Lord. You have the option to complain, murmur, or withhold what is owed to the Lord.

The Egyptians were filled with fear of the God of Hebrews after witnessing a powerful miracle. Hebrew gave God glory seeing the ruin of Egypt. The Hebrews experienced God's miracles and received favors, but later voiced their complaints and murmurs.

Numbers 14:2 And all the children of Israel murmured against Moses and against Aaron: and the whole congregation said unto them, Would God that we had died in the land of Egypt! or would God we had died in this wilderness!

God is the provider; He was giving them manna. People got the Angels 'food instead of being thankful and hearing what they said.

Exodus 16:3 And the children of Israel said unto them, Would to God we had died by the hand of the LORD in the land of Egypt, when we sat by the flesh pots, and when we did eat bread to the full; for ye have brought us forth into this wilderness, to kill this whole assembly with hunger.

God's reputation can be damaged by complaining and murmuring. God's blessings are attracted by your righteous behavior.

A man with the legion gave God credit and honor for doing the mighty work. He was free from cutting, screaming, and torment by Satan. How sad and horrifying to see the situation.

As Jesus delivered the man,

Luke 8:39b And he went his way and published throughout the entire city how great things Jesus had done unto him.

Give credit to which credit is due. The entire village was eager to receive Jesus.

Luke 8:40 And it came to pass, that, when Jesus was returned, the people gladly received him: for they were all waiting for him.

Hebrews 13:8 Jesus Christ the same yesterday, and today, and forever.

If Jesus is the same, then what and where the problem lies? We are the problem. Do not want to align with His commandment. We refuse to revere His Holy name by believing and trusting in everything. You can ruin or raise His word higher than heaven. What are you doing? When you receive your miracle, testify, give God glory, and lift Him High.

Psalms 78:56 Yet they tempted and provoked the highest God, and kept not his testimonies:

I wrote a book named "I did it His Way" to give Him glory. Every testimony in the book gives God glory. No one but the Lord! The disciple went out and testified about the name of Jesus, but it upset priests and the High Priest.

Acts 4:18 And they called them and commanded them not to speak at all nor teach in the name of Jesus.

The greatness of a miracle performed in the name of Jesus was extraordinary. People started placing their faith in Jesus. Yet, according to Israeli leaders, Jesus was labeled as a thief, deceiver, and the son of Joseph and Mary. Jesus' followers were committed to safeguarding His reputation. They were aware that Jesus was the chosen Messiah.

Acts 5:28 Says, Did not we straitly command you that ye should not teach in this name? And, behold, ye have filled Jerusalem with your doctrine, and intend to bring this man's blood upon us.

Acts 3:14 But ye denied the Holy One and the Just, and desired a murderer to be granted unto you;

Lord Jesus was denied and then murdered. If you identify as a Christian, then strive to lead a holy and pure life. Don't forget to be righteous in your private life as well. Think Holy in the chamber of your mind. The devil wouldn't even think about defiling the name of Jesus. The demon spoke to Jesus.

Mark 1:24 Says, Let us alone; what have we to do with thee, thou Jesus of Nazareth? art thou come to destroy us? I know thee who thou art, the Holy One of God.

Listen to two witnesses; they gave God glory.

Luke 24:19 And he said unto them, What things? And they said unto him, Concerning Jesus of Nazareth, which was a prophet mighty in deed and word before God and all the people:

What is your testimony about Jesus? Are you complaining or witnessing that He raised me from my sickbed? Are you stating that Jesus cannot do it, or acknowledging that touching His garment will bring healing? Are you letting people know I am healed by the shadow of Peter, Jesus, or Paul? Jesus is reflected in your life, not just in the words you speak. The reputation of the Lord Jesus can be impacted positively or negatively by how you live your life. Your faith can either support or challenge your belief in Jesus. A tongue can say well, but life can say much more. 12 disciples and then 70 not talked but showed the name of Jesus. They said, in thy name, demons were under subjection. Can you say in thy name Lord Jesus demons are under domination or label them schizophrenia, bipolar, ADD, ADHD, or PTSD? Do not ruin the name of Jesus.

The man's faith impressed Jesus, who exclaimed that he had never seen anything like it in Israel. What about you? Are you convinced, or is it a secret that Jesus can make the impossible possible? Jesus's reputation was destroyed by his own village. Lord Jesus's credibility was destroyed by Faithless.

Matthew 13:58 And he did not do many mighty works there because of their unbelief.

Does God see your faith in Jesus as something to marvel at? Has the Bible lost its credibility, or is it still considered reliable? Has anyone ever knocked on your door to learn about healer Jesus, about your deliverer? Or watch and affirm that I have no desire to be like her.

My phone rings. My phone is constantly buzzing with prayer request texts around the clock. They request my prayers for their situation and guidance in learning about Jesus. He wanted me to pray for others. It's a busy life, but worth it, to raise Jesus's name higher. I desire for His name to receive blessings, be raised higher than the heavens, and bring Him glory. God depends on me since He said to go into this world and preach the gospel by casting out the demons and healing the sick. When the Word of God is combined with faith, it brings praise and reverence to God and establishes Jesus 'kingdom. Preaching the gospel without faith and signs undermines the reputation of Jesus. There is no power, taste, or credibility to it. Abide by the Lord's commands and trust in Him alone.

LET US PRAY

In the name of Jesus, please help us give you all glory by doing the sign and wonder among the sick in the dark world. Many have ruined your name by not showing the truth. Lord, we will give you all the credit and keep our faith in you alone during this time. God has all power, so let us be the broadcaster and proclaim by healing and setting captives free. May your name never bring harm to our lives through false beliefs. You said and meant it, so let us be the receiver of blessings. Your name is blessed by healing the sick and delivering the oppressed and possessed. In Jesus 'name. Amen! God Bless you!

MARCH 23

YOU CAN DO NOTHING WITHOUT ANOINTING!

Can you provide a definition for anointing? The action of applying oil or perfume by rubbing or smearing.

Before assuming the throne, Saul, David, and Solomon were anointed. The priest anoints them at God's command. It is when the Holy Spirit descends upon them to fulfill the purpose. They are empowered by the Spirit of God to fulfill their assigned role.

1 Samuel 16:13a Then Samuel took the horn of oil, and anointed him in the midst of his brethren: and the Spirit of the Lord came upon David from that day forward.

Powerlessness resides in the flesh without the spirit. The Holy Spirit within you can make a powerful impact. The presence of God's Spirit is invoked through the act of anointing with oil.

Zechariah 4:6b says, Not by might, nor by power, but by my spirit, saith the Lord of hosts.

The Lord Jesus was anointed by God.

Acts 10:38 How God anointed Jesus of Nazareth with the Holy Ghost and with power: who went about doing good, and healing all that were oppressed of the devil; for God was with him.

Is 61:1 The Spirit of the Lord God is upon me; because the Lord hath anointed me to preach good tidings unto the meek; he hath sent me to bind up the brokenhearted, to proclaim liberty to the captives, and the opening of the prison to them that are bound; Each day, I anoint myself as a personal practice. As soon as I start casting out demons, they break immediately.

Why do we use Blessed oil to anoint the sick? When oil is used for anointing, it represents the Holy Spirit. The act of anointing releases the Spirit of God, who destroys the yoke and chain of Satan. Whenever someone is sick, use blessed holy oil and pray over them. The demon responsible for fever and illness will be unleashed. The power of anointing allows one to do God's work. The anointing has the power to shatter the yoke.

Do you know the meaning of the word "yoke"? A yoke is bondage or burdens the devil puts on any living thing. For example, all kinds of sicknesses, depression, ADD, ADHD, PTSD, cancer, Schizophrenia, Bipolar, and other diseases are put on us by the devil called a yoke. When you see ungodly behavior, then recognize that something is not right.

MARCH 23

God put on flesh and came down to set the captive free. The freedom that was taken away in the Garden of Eden has been brought back by God. The devil isn't the issue; disobedience and rebelliousness are. Satan gains a legal right when you choose to disobey God. Satan takes you away from Jesus Christ and destroys you in hell. The breaking of God's commandments, laws, and statutes causes us to fall into the bondage, burden, and chains of darkness. We are now under Satan's control.

His voice is heard through God's written Word.

It was God who said I granted you a simple way to get out. Will you trust it and act upon it? I would. It's simple, just believe and take action. The Bible says:

Is: 10:27 And it shall come to pass in that day, That his burden shall be taken away from off thy shoulder, And his yoke from off thy neck, And the yoke shall be destroyed because of the anointing.

Anointing has the power to break the yoke. What does it mean? Once it's in pieces, it's impossible to reassemble. Amen!

It is very simple; anoint yourself regularly with blessed olive oil. The devil persistently employs different tactics in an attempt to destroy us, and I am well aware of it.

How can you anoint and with what? With blessed olive oil. Anoint yourself, your house, clothes, and shoes. Use anointing oil on your work, office, children, and the areas in your house. Make your way to the city for the purpose of anointing. Anoint trees, water, roads, and markets. The difference will become apparent to you. All demons will run, and their works will be destroyed. By going out and anointing the sick, they will be healed.

Mark 6:13 And they cast out many devils, and anointed with oil many that were sick, and healed them.

Experience miracles by faithfully practicing the Word of God. Look to the Bible alone to seek a connection with God. Seek Him. I'd like to tell you about what happened when I received the anointing with blessed oil. God instructed me to anoint the public schools, and I carried out that instruction. At one school, I saw the fruit on the school grounds. So I poured anointing oil over it, and fire came out of the little fruit, which scared me. That caught me by surprise. Individuals can engage in Woodoo, witchcraft, black magic, and leave objects behind. But if we anoint, we will see God's power working against the power of darkness. Remember, this is a battle. View God's direction as firm instructions, not optional suggestions. There is no doubt that God speaks with complete knowledge.

Once Lady asked me to pray and anoint her house. Ever since her husband returned from complaining about his depression. I couldn't pray over him since he was not present. She remembered to anoint him when he was asleep. While anointing him with oil, she noticed strange behavior. She said after pouring oil on his head, he sat on the bed, started barking, and went back to sleep. It terrified her. Since it was nighttime, she had no one to reach out to for help. In the morning, she told her husband what he did in the night when she anointed him. According to him, he had no idea. Of course not. It was the demon that made its presence known. After anointing, the depressed demon left him. Would you bless your family while they are asleep? Watch what happens.

James 5:14 Is any sick among you? Let him call for the elders of the church; and let them pray over him, anointing him with oil in the name of the Lord: 15 And the prayer of faith shall save the sick, and the Lord shall raise him up; and if he has committed sins, they shall be forgiven him.

Hallelujah! Double for the trouble.

Psalm 45:7 Thou lovest righteousness, and hatest wickedness: therefore God, thy God, hath anointed thee with the oil of gladness above thy fellows.

The anointing will block the devil's door and break its power. I make it a priority to practice the principles of the Bible. I teach whom God gives me the opportunity. I teach them to anoint and always give them blessed oil. I hear about the amazing healing and deliverance as they anoint sick, possessed, and oppressed individuals.

Practice the Word. It is simple. Don't complicate matters by including your personal input. Believe and obey. Continue doing it. Actions required for God's work. I anoint paper works and what concerns me. I even anointed the car, photos of the people, and kidnapped children.

Pass on the practice of truth to the next and upcoming generations. Religion has not affected us, but the truth will set us free.

Psalm 92:10 But my horn shalt thou exalt like the horn of a unicorn: I shall be anointed with fresh oil.

Please anoint yourself with Blessed olive oil everyday.

John 8:31 Then said Jesus to those Jews which believed on him, If ye continue in my word, then are ye my disciples indeed; 32 And ye shall know the truth, and the truth shall make you free.

Freedom is in the truth and not in religion. Please anoint self, family and practice the truth with Holy Blessed Oil.

LET US PRAY

Lord Jesus, we come before your altar, the altar of mercy. Please forgive all our sins. Let our sin be under the precious cleansing blood of Jesus Christ.

We asked you to break the chain, bondages, and yoke Satan has put over our children and us. Bondage of illnesses, mental illness, demonic oppression possession, high and low B. P, diabetes, fever, all cancer, and nightmares, we come against them in the name of Jesus Christ; we command them to get out and break us loose. Lord, anoint us with your blood and Holy Spirit in the name of Jesus Christ. Amen! God Bless You!

MARCH 24

YOU CAN MAKE GOD MOVE!

If you know how, you have the ability to move God. God is real, and we can change His mind. We have the power to prevent Him from taking action, or we can choose not to. Learn how to move God in your situation. You can change God's mind from judgment if you change your action by repenting of your sins.

God sent Jonah to a city called Nineveh, which was due for punishment.

Jonah 1:2 Arise, go to Nineveh, that great city, and cry against it; for their wickedness is come up before me.

Instead of going there, Jonah chooses to flee in another direction. Once he faced punishment from the storm for his disobedience, he repented and successfully survived inside the belly of the fish. Jonah entered the city of Nineveh and started preaching.

mightily unto God: yea, let them turn every one from his evil way, and from the violence that is in their hands. Who can tell if God will turn and repent and turn away from his fierce anger that we perish not? 10 And God saw their works that they turned from their evil way; and God repented of

Jonah 3:4 And Jonah began to enter into the city a day's journey, and he cried, and said, Yet forty days and Nineveh shall be overthrown. 5 So the people of Nineveh believed God, and proclaimed a fast, and put on sackcloth, from the greatest of them even to the least of them. 6 For word came unto the king of Nineveh, and he arose from his throne, and he laid his robe from him, and covered him with sackcloth, and sat in ashes. 7 And he caused it to be proclaimed and published through Nineveh by the decree of the king and his nobles, saying, Let neither man nor beast, herd nor flock, taste anything: let them not feed, nor drink water: 8 But let man and beast be covered with sackcloth, and cry mightily unto God: yea, let them turn every one from his evil way, and from the violence that is in their hands. 10 And God saw their works, that they turned from their evil way; and God repented of the evil, that he had said that he would do unto them; and he did it not.

Your actions have the power to influence God's actions. Start your spiritual journey by following the commandments in the Bible. Follow His Word and don't deviate from His instructions. There is a sin factor in our flesh that can bring calamities. Many sorrows, punishments, and sicknesses are a consequence of our wrong actions towards each other or against God. All judgment starts by not listening to God. On the other hand, if you choose to humble yourself and repent, replacing your sinful actions with righteous ones, God's judgment will be lifted.

ELIZABETH DAS

2 Chronicles 7:14 If my people, which are called by my name, shall humble themselves, and pray, and seek my face, and turn from their wicked ways; then will I hear from heaven, and will forgive their sin, and will heal their land.

Our wrong action brings problems to the land. Change your action for the land to be healed. No need for police, guns, or prisons. One day, while citing

2 Chronicles 7:14, I realized I am His people called by His name. So I question God, which is my wicked way. Lord answered that what you do without my approval is your wicked ways. We are very much responsible for all moves without getting God's approval. Actions taken without God's counsel are known as wicked ways. To receive God's blessings, submit to God's will and way with a humble heart. Let your action and priority be pleasing to God. God can either bless you or curse you, depending on your actions. The ability to make God move is within your grasp. The decision is up to you.

Believing and trusting in God allows Him to work in your life. Having faith in God turns the impossible into possible. God claims that He can accomplish anything.

Luke 1:37 For with God nothing shall be impossible. Keep in mind that God is sovereign. That is Supreme,

God is limitless, unbounded, absolute, and infinite. The problem we encounter is our minds, which are limited, finite, and restricted. Our disbelief prevents us from acknowledging what God is capable of.

My journey of discovering the miracles of God began when I started going to the Pentecostal church. Moreover, engaging with other believers helped me gain a deeper understanding of faith. It was beautiful! It's always been God that I've sought after, and that hasn't changed, not even today. I am seeking God through His Word to receive His hidden treasure. You can find no other place but in the Bible; riches and treasure are hidden there. What people seek is in the 66 books called the Bible. If you believe, you can have easy, more significant, and cheap everything you want and desire.

Once I had a stuffy nose with a sinus problem and couldn't breathe. One night I could not sleep because I could not breathe. I participated in morning worship, where the elders prayed over me. I danced when God spoke to me during praise and worship. And I started dancing. Guess what? The sinus stuffiness loosened and cleaned up. Ever since, I have had no trouble with the sinus, praise God! You can obey and receive a tremendous blessing.

Do you remember ten lepers in the Bible? When they saw Jesus, they knew Jesus could not touch lepers, but still, they cried out and asked for His mercy.

Luke 17:13 And they lifted up their voices, and said, Jesus, Master, have mercy on us. 14 And when he saw them, he said unto them, Go shew yourselves unto the priests. And it came to pass, that, as they went, they were cleansed. 15 And one of them, when he saw that he was healed, turned back, and with a loud voice glorified God, 16 And fell down on his face at his feet, giving him thanks: and he was a Samaritan. 17 And Jesus answering said, Were there not ten cleansed? but where are the nine? 18 There are not found that returned to give glory to God, save this stranger. 19 And he said unto him, Arise, go thy way: thy faith hath made thee whole.

Thanksgiving heart can move God to make you whole. Whole Means your body, soul, and spirit are complete and unbroken, like Adam and Eve before the sin. How wonderful! Learn how to make God move. Learn to

MARCH 24

be thankful to God. Thanksgiving words to God give heavenly access, what you desire, and much more. God does not give little, but it is in your hand to receive beyond.

That is why He said in.
Jeremiah 33:3 Call unto me, and I will answer thee, and show thee great and mighty things, which thou knowest not.

I am sure if we call Him by faith, He will. I am not attracted to anything in this world. Cars, houses, machinery, and all amazement you see on earth are an illusion of Satan. You can move God to do miracles, healing, and greater work. God can do what your mind cannot comprehend. If God of heaven can send manna, he can send honey from the rock. Do not bind His hand. Do not esteem God a little. Please read the Bible to see how you can move God beyond. Your believing in Him will do mighty. Hanna was barren and prayed for a male child. She offers her child to the Lord.

1 Samuel 1:20 Wherefore it came to pass, when the time was come about after Hannah had conceived, that she bare a son, and called his name Samuel, saying, Because I have asked him of the Lord.

As she gave her son for the service of God, she got more. You can move God to give you more.

1 Samuel 2:21 And the Lord visited Hannah, so that she conceived, and bare three sons and two daughters. And the child Samuel grew before the Lord.

Let go and surrender your heart to God. Know that it is in your hands to make God move. Modify your actions, reactions, thinking, and life. He'll go after you and shower you with blessings.

LET US PRAY

In the name of Jesus, Lord, please help us guard our lips, actions, and reactions. Lord, help us believe in the impossible. We seek your help in offering thanks and praise in your royal court. Keep our lips from any negative word that can stop God's move. May we find faith, like Hannah, Daniel, and others who witnessed God's power through prayer. Let our hearts believe and trust. We need a change of thinking and not Jesus. You were the same yesterday, today, and forever. Lord, help us in Jesus's name. Amen! God Bless you!

MARCH 25

LET GOD DO HIS WORK!

We will see God move if we leave the matter in His hand. His level of knowledge and wisdom goes beyond what is important to our situation. The spirit of God has unlimited power, knowledge, and wisdom. Keep this in your mind.

Romans 11:34 For who hath known the mind of the Lord? or who hath been his counselor? 35 Or who hath first given to him, and it shall be recompensed unto him again? 36 For of him, and through him, and to him, are all things: to whom be glory forever. Amen

It secures a mortal man under God's protection, direction, and guidance. Man's responsibility is to carry out God's plan.

Isaiah 43:7 Even everyone that is called by my name: for I have created him for my glory, I have formed him; yea, I have made him.

God created with His plan and purpose:

Isaiah 55:8 For my thoughts are not your thoughts, neither are your ways my ways, saith the LORD. 9 For as the heavens are higher than the earth, so are my ways higher than your ways, and my thoughts than your thoughts.

First, God created the garden of Eden, and then he made man to look after it. Don't these plans seem great? No sweating, no laboring! The ability to control animals and have total dominion over the planet. We need to engage in self-reflection and educate children about God, His plans, and the provisions He provides. Surrendering to Him is the key to a life of abundance.

Humanity that is lost requires assistance, safeguarding, and direction. By listening and obeying, we can make it possible.

Revelation 4:11 Thou art worthy, O Lord, to receive glory and honor and power: for thou hast created all things, and for thy pleasure, they are and were created.

God made me as His masterpiece for His own enjoyment. I must listen exclusively to God in order to carry out His plan for my life.

MARCH 25

Many, including Abraham, Isaac, Jacob, David, Moses, and more, are embracing God's plan and achieving great things. They were just like any other human being. Their impressive achievements were a result of following God's plan. Letting Jesus take the wheel as the helmsman, pilot, or wheelman in the boat. Keep your hands off the steering wheel. You will invite trouble. The men who were the most successful were the ones who heard and obeyed God without questioning. Can you beat God?

Jeremiah 29:11 For I know the thoughts that I think toward you, saith the Lord, thoughts of peace, and not of evil, to give you an expected end.

The key to your boat reaching its destiny is surrendering to God's plan. Predestine means prefixed destiny. It's as if you're currently on a plane headed to New York. It was predestined. Stay calm and rest until you reach your destination.

The mind belongs to God, and we need His mind to have the same thoughts. Remove yourself and engage in prayer. Agree to follow Him. Understanding the mind of God comes from obeying Him and learning His ways.

1 Corinthians 2:16 For who hath known the mind of the Lord, that he may instruct him? But we have the mind of Christ.

There are instances when we invalidate promises by doubting or speaking contrary to them. Do not be in a hurry. He mentioned that things will take place in his own time. The time factor matters.

Eccles 3:11 He hath made everything beautiful in his time: also he hath set the world in their heart so that no man can find out the work that God maketh from the beginning to the end.

Moses witnessed God's deliverance by patiently waiting. His understanding came from faithfully following God's guidance. I have always gained knowledge by listening and following His guidance. He is an on-time God. He is aware of the plan's result. Wait to see what He is doing till it is over.

Abraham saw the son Isaac in God's time. David was crowned King according to God's timing. At the designated time, Jesus made his arrival. So do not rush your life into a storm or accident. It won't benefit you in any way.

By not waiting and listening, you will continue to make the same mistakes. To Listen and obey is the key to seeing His handy work.

I can still remember the voice assuring me, "I will provide healing for you." Lost my memory and job and was about to lose my car and house. Nevertheless, I held onto promises. Every situation appeared unfavorable, but God worked His supernatural power and turned them into blessings. God did a miracle in His time, and I came out of the wheelchair. Later, God moved me to Dallas, and everything turned around.

Joseph, the dreamer, encountered hardships in every aspect. The road chosen for him by God seemed illogical. But later, it did. All of us engage in complaining, questioning, arguing, and reasoning. Stop! Wait! And see the result. You will say.

Psalm 118:23 This is the LORD'S doing; it is marvelous in our eyes.

Remember, do not think; rather, submit. Do not worry; rather, trust and take a deep breath and live. All is well! When you see the ocean, it will dry up if you let God. Let God do His Work! Your enemy is pursuing, but you will see them no more. When you are sick and afflicted, look at the cross. See the healing and deliverance of the Lord!

God says in His Word.

Zechariah 8:6 Thus saith the LORD of hosts; If it is marvelous in the eyes of the remnant of these people in these days, should it also be marvelous in mine eyes? saith the LORD of hosts.

Jeremiah 32:27 Behold, I am the LORD, the God of all flesh: is there anything too hard for me?

You can ask Sarah, Abraham, Mary, the mother of Jesus, Daniel, Shadrach, Meshach, and Abednego. Once you understand God in the same way they did, you will trust Him to fulfill His purpose.

Surrender yourself to the guidance of God. Your faith and trust are like a vehicle for God. Just hold on. Displaying humility similar to that of a donkey. Promises only can be fulfilled if you let Him ride and you be the vehicle.

Hebrew 10:35 Cast not away, therefore, your confidence, which hath great recompense of reward. 36 For ye have need of patience, that, after ye have done the will of God, ye might receive the promise. 37 For a little while, and he that shall come will come, and will not tarry.

Look at the butterfly. Looking at a beautiful butterfly is a lengthy process. It's certain to happen. The process is universally unpopular. Trust in God's ability to handle things!

LET US PRAY

Lord Jesus, we hold deep admiration for your greatness and goodness. Teach us thy way, O LORD; we will walk in thy truth: unite our heart to fear thy name. Help us obey the commandment so we receive blessings. Let God grant us the wise heart to learn the truth of the Lord. Keep us in the plan of God to see the expected end. We know, Lord, you plan to bless us, so help us and our children fear and obey God. We want to be called blessed on earth. Lord, do your work for us, In Jesus 'name. Amen! God Bless you!

MARCH 26

AUTHORITY APPOINTED BY JESUS CHRIST!

The Lord is both excellent and compassionate towards His creations. With our children, our main concern is their welfare and making sure they receive the best care possible. Parents and God both want to protect children from harm. God created Adam and Eve in the Garden of Eden to care for His creation. Our rights and blessings are lost due to our poor choices.

Despite the people of Israel's desire for a king to distance themselves from God, God still provided priests and prophets. Asking for a King, who is flesh, will misuse power no matter what. Humans lack the ability to care for us as a divine father would. He gave the Torah and Bible to teach and guide.

God, known as Jehovah, manifested in human form to act as our shepherd and provide salvation, deliverance, and healing. Exemplary parents are protective, defensive, and preventive of their children's welfare. They give birth and also watch over us with love.

None of this is from us, but rather from the heavenly father. The Lord has blessed parents with His love and care in their hearts.

When our heavenly father assigns different authorities, it is with the same purpose in mind. The concept of God is to provide guidance. He communicates with us through the assigned authority and directs us by the Holy Spirit.

Humans are hard of hearing. They don't care what happens to them and others.

Make sure you don't miss out on God's assignment. It is very important. Every assignment holds equal importance, regardless of size. How you carry out your job is important. A sweeper, servant, king, rich, poor, or slave has their part in the performance. Do it as pleasing to the Lord. There will be a day it will promote you.

Colossians 3:23 And whatsoever ye do, do it heartily, as to the Lord, and not unto men; 24 Knowing that of the Lord ye shall receive the reward of the inheritance: for ye serve the Lord Christ.

The purpose of humans created by God is eternal, not temporary. There is a soul in a fleshly tabernacle that has an eternal destiny. The destiny of the Lord is to bless and prosper us. The future of Satan is to destroy us. So warnings from God and commandments of God are not to control or dictate to us. It is like a relationship with your children. You desire to love, protect, and provide for your children.

Israel rejected God by asking for a king.

1 Samuel 8:7 And the LORD said unto Samuel, Hearken unto the voice of the people in all that they say unto thee: for they have not rejected thee, but they have rejected me, that I should not reign over them.

Accept God. The flesh yields the spirit of Satan and not the Spirit of God. Two different purposes, Satan's purpose is to destroy, and God's eternal purpose is to Bless you. God came down to defeat Satan and buy back what we lost in the garden of Eden by putting on flesh.

Is 35:3 Strengthen ye the weak hands, and confirm the feeble knees. 4 Say to them that are of a fearful heart, Be strong, fear not: behold, your God will come with vengeance, even God with a recompense; he will come and save you. 5 Then the eyes of the blind shall be opened, and the ears of the deaf shall be unstopped. 6 Then shall the lame man leap as a hart, and the tongue of the dumb sing: for in the wilderness shall waters break out, and streams in the desert.

God came in the flesh and took revenge by healing, delivering, and setting captives free. The Lord shed His blood for His creation.

All He did was buy back what we lost. He lost His bride created for Him. Now, after Shedding His blood, we have access to the throne room. He gave a helper called the Holy Spirit.

He trained and sent His disciples and gave all authority. After His own blood covenant, He gave some.

Ephesians 4:11 And he gave some, apostles; and some, prophets; and some, evangelists; and some, pastors and teachers; 12 For the perfecting of the saints, for the work of the ministry, for the edifying of the body of Christ: 13 Till we all come in the unity of the faith, and of the knowledge of the Son of God, unto a perfect man, unto the measure of the stature of the fulness of Christ: 14 That we henceforth be no more children, tossed to and fro, and carried about with every wind of doctrine, by the sleight of men, and cunning craftiness, whereby they lie in wait to deceive;

Word Apostle means *"one who is sent out."* The apostle holds a unique position." An apostle performs the sign and wonders. They are the messenger of the Gospel of Christ. They introduce a fresh work where people have never heard of the Lord Jesus. They lay a foundation for the truth.

Ephesians 2:20 And are built upon the foundation of the apostles and prophets, Jesus Christ himself being the chief corner stone;

Let us see what this authority does:

The apostles: The foundation laid by 12 disciples, later called apostles in the book of Acts. Do not follow the tare planted in Nicaea 325 by dividing one God into three. Those who had a revelation of Jesus laid the foundation already. Remember to follow the book of Acts. Be on the path of Peter and Paul, who had the revelation of Jesus and had given the key to the Kingdom. Devil's doctrine is called tare, wait until the end to see their judgment. The devil destroyed the first commandment; One God became three. Prophet: the prophet is a spokesperson of God. He brings the Word directly from God to the People. Their job is to direct, admonish, encourage, counsel, and take you to a higher level of prosperity.

MARCH 26

Evangelist: Evangelist means the person who evangelizes. Evangelists go around inspiring and proclaim the Gospel to revive the new converts. As they go from place to place, they encourage and bring the ministry of saints to a higher level; they revive people.

Teacher: Teachers called by God have the revelation of Jesus's identity. In the first century, the time of disciple John, the false teachers and prophet started their antichrist mission. They are called false teachers and prophets. Go back to the book of Acts and epistles to find the teaching of genuine teachers and prophets. One church will continue if we build the work founded by apostles, prophets, and teachers in the book of Acts. Follow the true doctrine to see the change in life. Blood is under the name of Jesus. False teachers and prophets removed the name in baptism, so the blood of Jesus was removed by removing the name of Jesus. Only the blood of Jesus has the power to take away our sins. The Prophet and Apostle John warned us to avoid false teachers and prophets.

The antichrist removed the name of Jesus, where the blood is hidden.

1 John 5:6 This is he that came by water and blood, even Jesus Christ; not by water only, but by water and blood. And it is the spirit that beareth witness, because the spirit is truth.8 And there are three that bear witness in earth, the spirit, and the water, and the blood: and these three agree in one.

In order to have your sins washed away, go into the water invoking the name of Jesus. Blood is hidden under the name of Jesus. Sin will be forgiven and sickness will be gone. Try it.

2 John verse 7: For many deceivers are entered into the world, who confess not that Jesus Christ is come in the flesh. This is a deceiver and an antichrist.

I have a memory of participating in an organization that practiced baptism using Jesus 'name. I had never heard of it before. I read the Bible so many times, but the false teacher blocked the truth by forcing false doctrine. Those doctrines started after 325 AD, divided one God into three, then removed the name Jesus by titles. Can you fathom the level of deceitfulness Satan possesses? Speaking the name of Jesus in baptism is something Antichrists strongly dislike. This explains why we lack the experience of blood's power.

Hebrew 9:22 And almost all things are by the law purged with blood; and without shedding of blood is no remission.

Through water baptism, we establish a blood covenant using the name. Purge means rinse, refine, purify, clear from accusation, and wash away.

Remember, the name Jesus is out by the antichrist of whom John warned in His three epistles.

My mother and I had a wonderful experience going under the water, in Jesus's name. It cleansed us of our sins and I felt a weight lifted off me. Upon being baptized in Jesus's name, my mom claimed to have been sick and then miraculously healed.

LET US PRAY

In Jesus's name, Lord, please send us the true teachers and prophets. Give us a revelation of you. We desire the truth, since only the truth will set us free. Please, Lord, give us love for truth. Let people be free from the rare, false teachers, prophets, and pastors. True to your warning, we observe the corruption present in

Churchianity. Through Christianity, biblical truth, and the power of the Holy Spirit, we aim to demonstrate that God continues to heal, deliver, and set captives free in the name of Jesus. Amen! God Bless you!

MARCH 27

HUNT FOR THE HIGHEST BLESSINGS!

There are diverse types of blessings. Certain blessings can grant you access to the highest levels of favor, prosperity, knowledge, and wisdom.

Of course, it comes from the Lord alone. You can buy the best gift and education and leave an inheritance of millions. Nevertheless, the blessing of God surpasses everything. When you are blessed, you will always be taken care of.

The King of Moab wanted to curse Israel. They found an enchanter Balaam to condemn Israel. Excellent protection accompanies God's blessings. No weapon can prosper against us, so no chanting, curses, spell, or witchcraft can work against God's people.

Numbers 23:23 Surely there is no enchantment against Jacob, neither is there any divination against Israel: according to this time it shall be said of Jacob and of Israel, What hath God wrought!

Numbers 24:2 And Balaam lifted up his eyes, and he saw Israel abiding in his tents according to their tribes, and the spirit of God came upon him. Balaam went into a trance and, with eyes open, Spoke 5 How goodly are thy tents, O Jacob, and thy tabernacles, O Israel! 6 As the valleys are they spread forth, as gardens by the river's side, as the trees of lign aloes which the Lord hath planted, and as cedar trees beside the waters. 7 He shall pour the water out of his buckets, and his seed shall be in many waters, and his king shall be higher than Agag, and his kingdom shall be exalted. 8 God brought him forth out of Egypt; he hath as it were the strength of a unicorn: he shall eat up the nations his enemies, and shall break their bones, and pierce them through with his arrows. 9 He couched, he lay down as a lion, and as a great lion: who shall stir him up? Blessed is he that blesseth thee, and cursed is he that curseth thee.

No force can prevail against those whom God blesses. Hunt for the blessings. Jacob and Esau were different from each other. Unlike his twin older brother Esau, Jacob was not an excellent hunter, but rather skilled in hunting blessings. Notice how individuals like Jacob have the power to alter the course of their future generations.

During his journey back home, Jacob had an encounter with a man who was acknowledged to be an Angel. Jacob wrestles and prevails. Find out what Jacob asked the angle before releasing him.

Genesis 32:26 And he said, Let me go, for the day breaketh. And he said, I will not let thee go, except thou bless me. 28 And he said, Thy name shall be called no more Jacob, but Israel: for as a prince hast thou power with God and with men, and hast prevailed.

Obeying God's voice brings blessings. The Blessings are truly amazing!

Deuteronomy 28:1 And it shall come to pass, if thou shalt hearken diligently unto the voice of the Lord thy God, to observe and to do all his commandments which I command thee this day, that the Lord thy God will set thee on high above all nations of the earth: 2 And all these blessings shall come on thee, and overtake thee, if thou shalt hearken unto the voice of the Lord thy God.

James 1:12 Blessed is the man that endureth temptation: for when he is tried, he shall receive the crown of life, which the Lord hath promised to them that love him.

In chapter 5 of Matthew, Jesus bestows blessings upon people. If you possess a humble spirit, mourn, show gentleness, hunger and thirst for righteousness, show mercy, have a pure heart, work towards peace, are persecuted for righteousness, and endure insults for righteousness, then you are blessed. The blessings can last for thousands of generations. When God grants blessings, he goes all out.

Deuteronomy 7:9 Know therefore that the LORD thy God, he is God, the faithful God, which keepeth covenant and mercy with them that love him and keep his commandments to a thousand generations;

God, or the one appointed to pronounce a blessing on us. God's blessings enable you to bless others. Nevertheless, you need to have it in your possession.

1 Chronicle 4:10 And Jabez called on the God of Israel, saying, Oh that thou wouldest bless me indeed, and enlarge my coast, and that thine hand might be with me, and that thou wouldest keep me from evil, that it may not grieve me! And God granted him that which he requested.

Jacob blessed the Pharaoh since God blessed him.

Genesis 47:10a And Jacob blessed Pharaoh,

Matthew 5:44c bless them that curse you,

Ways to offer blessings to your enemies. May God bless them with repentance and forgive their sins, protecting them from death and illness.

There is a blessing called the Aaronic blessing.

Numbers 6:24 The Lord bless thee, and keep thee: 25 The Lord make his face shine upon thee, and be gracious unto thee: 26 The Lord lift up his countenance upon thee and give thee peace.

There was a time when my mother had a hard time moving due to her poor health. Going to the bathroom was not possible for her. I did not know what to do. I was searching everywhere for something to assist my mom. I helped mom in bed to take care of her business. I had an encounter where the Holy Spirit spoke to me. If she blesses you today, then you will be blessed. I sat next to her and in a few minutes, my mom said God will bless you and she blessed me herself. Yes, hunt for blessings. The righteousness of God yields abundant blessings through right actions.

During visits to convalescent homes, I often interact with older individuals who occasionally engage in prayer and offer their blessings.

I feel grateful to have their blessings in my life. While some value money, houses, and education as blessings, I consider God's Blessing to be the greatest. People seek after goals, financial gain, and accomplishments. Every champion and gold medalist has made sacrifices to reach their goals.

Lord Jesus says that, but out of all.

Mark 10:29 And Jesus answered and said, Verily I say unto you, There is no man that has left the house, or brothers, or sisters, or father, or mother, or wife, or children, or lands, for my sake, and the gospel's, 30 But he shall receive a hundredfold now in this time, houses, and brothers, and sisters, and mothers, and children, and lands, with persecutions; and in the world to come eternal life.

Instead of ignoring the poor, extend your blessings to them.

Psalm 41:1 Blessed is he that considereth the poor: the Lord will deliver him in time of trouble.

Receiving blessings is unlocked by the Bible. There is no greater accomplishment in the world than receiving a blessing. Make sure to put in your effort to receive the blessings.

Jeremiah 17:7 Blessed is the man that trusteth in the Lord, and whose hope the Lord is.8 For he shall be as a tree planted by the waters, and that spreadeth out her roots by the river, and shall not see when heat cometh, but her leaf shall be green; and shall not be careful in the year of drought, neither shall cease from yielding fruit.

Don't forget, Jacob risked his life to snatch God's blessing away from his reckless brother, Esau. He instructed us on the importance of seeking God's blessing, which is the ultimate and eternal.

LET US PRAY

In the name of Jesus Lord, give us a seeking heart to seek through the pages of the Bible. Assist us in obtaining eternal blessings for ourselves, our children, and future generations. Bring us the God-fearing people in our life. We believe in blessing and not cursing. Help us pronounce blessings over our enemy and the people of God. Joseph brought the blessing of Jehovah God in the house of Potiphar and to the land of Egypt, being righteous. Let us also bring blessings wherever we go, in Jesus's name. Amen! God Bless you!

MARCH 28

GIFTS OF THE SPIRIT ARE AVAILABLE!

The Bible is a rich book, a powerhouse, and full of wealth. Seek knowledge and wisdom through the volume of the book called the Bible. God has given His word to everything He has created. There is a truth in the Bible for your life to stay wise, healthy, wealthy, knowledgeable, and free from Satan's tactics.

It is a powerhouse if you believe and obey.

Obedience is the Key to this book. Despite not knowing everything, have faith, follow, and witness a miraculous result. No question asked, hear the voice of God, which is in the Word of God, and obey. The Bible is an instruction book for those who want to have success. Throughout the ages, God desired to keep us on top. His goal is to leave behind an extraordinary legacy for us.

Today, I urge you to dig into this book, flip every page, and eat the word to digest. Make it the number one priority. Study day and night. The word of God has the power to transform you into present-day versions of Daniel, Esther, Moses, David, or Paul. You can do as Jesus said.

John 14:12 Verily, verily, I say unto you, He that believeth on me, the works that I do shall he do also; and greater works than these shall he do;

Bible says in Revelation 5:12, Saying with a loud voice, Worthy is the Lamb that was slain to receive power, and riches, and wisdom, and strength, and honor, and glory, and blessing.

If you obey God and fear no one, everything can be yours. In short, do not follow the lost denominational, organization, or religious authority who do not believe in God's simple instruction. Israelites have the High IQ and wealth since they have the blessings of God Jehovah. The blessing of God has made them rich, powerful, and intelligent. By believing and obeying God, Abraham left a legacy for future generations.

By obeying and keeping His commandments, we receive everything that God possesses. How Daniel and all His Jewish fellows found ten times better,

Daniel 1:17 As for these four children, God gave them knowledge and skill in all learning and wisdom: and Daniel had understanding in all visions and dreams.20 And in all matters of wisdom and understanding, that the king inquired of them, he found them ten times better than all the magicians and astrologers that were in all his realm.

MARCH 28

King Solomon asked for wisdom to rule over God's people Israel,

1 King 3:12 Behold, I have done according to thy words: lo, I have given thee a wise and an understanding heart; so that there was none like thee before thee, neither after thee shall any arise like unto thee.13 And I have also given thee that which thou hast not asked, both riches, and honor: so that there shall not be any among the kings like unto thee all thy days. 14 And if thou wilt walks in my ways, to keep my statutes and my commandments, as thy father David did walk, then I will lengthen thy days.

When Lord Jehovah took on human form, He became our High Priest. He gave us spiritual gifts. The Gifts are available for you to receive.

1 Corinthians 12:7 But the manifestation of the spirit is given to every man to profit withal. 8 For to one is given by the spirit the word of wisdom; to another the word of knowledge by the same spirit; 9 To another faith by the same spirit; to another the gifts of healing by the same spirit; 10 To another the working of miracles; to another prophecy; to another discerning of spirits; to another divers kinds of tongues; to another the interpretation of tongues: 11 But all these worketh that one and the selfsame spirit, dividing to every man severally as he will.

What is the reason behind people seeking out psychics, witch doctors, tarot card readers, Ouija boards, palm readers, horoscopes, magicians, astrologers, spiritual healers, familiar spirits, or soothsayers? Christians, be careful and do not make mistakes going to this kind of medium, which provides information from the false familiar evil spirit and not from the Holy Spirit. People will come to us if we have God's 9 spiritual gifts promised in the New Testament. Spirit gifts, words of knowledge, and wisdom work to gather. If you have this Gifts of Spirit, then you can tell the name, address, phone or house number. The solution to the problem lies in the spirit of wisdom. Learn from King Saul's experience and avoid unnecessary complications by going to the familiar spirit and invite trouble. I came across Hindu individuals and religious Christians who rely on familiar spirits for guidance. With the gift of faith, miracle, and healing, the spirit of faith can amplify your ability to perform miracles and heal.

Acts 19: 11 And God wrought special miracles by the hands of Paul:12 So that from his body were brought unto the sick handkerchiefs or aprons, and the diseases departed from them, and the evil spirits went out of them.

Matthew 10:1 And when he had called unto him his twelve disciples, he gave them power against unclean spirits, to cast them out, and to heal all manner of sickness and all manner of disease.17 And the seventy returned again with joy, saying, Lord, even the devils are subject unto us through thy name.

We are currently residing in the most powerful period. All you have to do is to believe and ask. Coveting these powerful gifts of the spirit would be beneficial. When going out, lay hands on and cast out the demon. The disciples had access to power and authority which they utilized. You will witness the Lord's work, just as His disciples did. The credit for the supernatural work goes to the Lord. Your vessels must be sanctified and you must obey His voice. According to the Lord, nothing is beyond His ability.

Vocal gifts include spiritual gifts of speaking in tongues and interpreting tongues. It assists in delivering a divine message. You can receive a tongue; it means language. I have seen people showing messages in different languages they do not know. Discerning the spirit will help you understand what kind of spirit is in operation. Through the gift of Prophecy, we can understand the divine will and purpose of God. The nine gifts excel tenfold over evil mediums, simply to welcome the Spirit of God. It is available to anyone who desires it.

1 Corinthians 12:31a But covet earnestly the best gifts You can receive spiritual gifts by laying the hand of one who has these gifts.

1 Timothy 4:14 Neglect not the gift that is in thee, which was given thee by prophecy, with the laying on of the hands of the presbytery.

The 9 gifts of the Spirit need to operate through us, as we are the church, not the building. Suppose we obey the truth of God; the promise of 9 gifts is for us if we desire. He will come to us and do this special spiritual work through us.

Peter did many miracles and gave God glory.

The Bible says in Acts 3:6 Then Peter said, Silver and gold have I none; but such as I have give I thee: In the name of Jesus Christ of Nazareth rise up and walk.8 And he leaping up stood, and walked, and entered with them into the temple, walking, and leaping, and praising God.

Can you imagine what can happen if we work through the nine spiritual gifts? The entire world will believe in Jesus. Jesus is more than a sermon or lecture; he is a manifestation of miraculous power. People used to approach me for prayer while I was working at the Post Office. They still asked me to pray for them even after I quit my job at the Post Office. I believe in casting the demon out, healing the sick, and prophecy. There was a lady who joined me while I was working in a department. Lord said testify to her, so I did. She said I am a backslider. I ask the Lord to give me the discerning spirit to feel how they feel. To experience Jesus's healing and curing power, we need to place our hands on them and pray. We have to surrender and yield to the spirit of God. You are just a vessel; make yourself available to God. Amazing knowledge of the word God gave it to them. If you yield His Spirit, He will do Supernatural through us.

LET US PRAY

Lord, we covet all spiritual gifts, so you're one church may edify. May the people of this world know that you have the Spirit of God who heals, delivers, and sets captives free! We desire that our clothing, shadow, and hand heal and deliver the sick. We are more than just a church building; we are followers of Jesus Christ who perform miracles, heal the deaf, make the lame walk, and restore sight to the blind. Offer everything possible to bring you glory, honor, and praise. Let all nations know Jesus is the savior of the World and the only true God in Jesus's name. Amen! God Bless you!

MARCH 29

DO NOT LIVE UNDER THE PRIVILEGES!

You may have been rejected, sold to be a slave, or maliciously accused by people like Joseph, but keep pressing through.

Joseph's brother saw him coming.

Genesis 37:19 And they said one to another, Behold, this dreamer cometh. 20 Come now therefore and let us slay him, and cast him into some pit, and we will say, Some evil beast hath devoured him: and we shall see what will become of his dreams.

God possesses the ability to both bless and curse. Joseph remained true to his principles. He followed God's commandment.

Proverb 2:22 But the wicked shall be cut off from the earth, and the transgressors shall be rooted out of it.

Potiphar's wife tried to push him into trouble. In all hardships with opposition, Joseph never doubted the plan of God. Simply enter and continue moving forward. Push through to receive what is rightfully yours.

Genesis 39:9 There is none greater in this house than I; neither hath he kept back anything from me but thee, because thou art his wife: how then can I do this great wickedness and sin against God?

Joseph faced accusations and was imprisoned. Joseph refused to give up as he pushed his way through. One-day God allowed him to interpret the dream for Pharaoh.

Genesis 41:39 And Pharaoh said unto Joseph, Forasmuch as God hath shewed thee all this, there is none so discreet and wise as thou art: 43 And he made him to ride in the second chariot which he had; and they cried before him, Bow the knee: and he made him ruler over all the land of Egypt.

Joseph said I refused to be called a slave in Egypt, I refuse to stay behind the bar. I refuse oppression and misusing by men or women. I fear God.

Proverb 22:29 Seest thou a man diligent in his business? he shall stand before kings; he shall not stand before mean men.

Do not live under your privileges!

David was not troubled by what took place in his father's house. David took the victual to his brother on the battlefield. And his brother scolded him.

1 Samuel 17:28 And Eliab, his eldest brother, heard when he spake unto the men; and Eliab's anger was kindled against David, and he said, Why camest thou down hither? and with whom hast thou left those few sheep in the wilderness? I know thy pride and the naughtiness of thine heart; for thou art come down that thou mightest see the battle. 29 And David said, What have I now done? Is there not a cause?

David did not mind being disapproved and rejected by others and even by his own family. David chose not to let it affect him. He kept pressing through until he reached the highest position.

2 Samuel 5:3 So all the elders of Israel came to the king to Hebron, and king David made a league with them in Hebron before the Lord: and they anointed David king over Israel.

Every person who desired to kill David was eradicated.

Proverbs 2:22 But the wicked shall be cut off from the earth, and the transgressors shall be rooted out of it.

Israel was ruled by King David for a span of forty years. May your battle bring victory; your sickness brings healing! I pray you receive a promotion from heaven! The Lord opens all doors, and blessings come like a flood! Lord Jesus, send His Angels to open every prison door and bring the captive out! May the Lord visit you on your sickbed, in afflictions, and give you hope! There are over 5000 promises in the Bible; claim them and make them personal. Do not live under your privileges. People can label and put you down, but press on and claim everything you can receive. You will reach the top, blessed and favored. We all have someone like King Saul trying to kill. Potiphar's wicked wife tried to destroy the reputation of the God-fearing man. Jealous, prideful, and envious brothers and sisters want to destroy you, but don't worry, keep on going, keep on claiming your promises, and you will see success and triumph.

Aim high and never settle for anything less than the best.

Say, I am designated to receive 100-fold blessings if I stay focused on the path of God. Say I will prosper as my soul prospers. It is time not to allow anyone to preach or misguide you, to settle for less. God calls you to do greater and exploit. It is time to believe in the impossible, miracle, sign, and wonder. Let the sky be the limit.

It is time to do an exploit. No one can beat you if you pursue and overtake.

Don't be swayed by the false prophets and teachers 'agenda. Please don't allow Jezebel's plan to succeed in churches. Don't allow the devil's lie in your city or country.

Psalms 146:8 The LORD openeth the eyes of the blind: the LORD raiseth them that are bowed down: the LORD loveth the righteous:

Keep on trying, and keep on believing. One day you will see the miracle of the dead body coming out of the grave after four days. He's going to elevate you. He is a promise keeper. The Bible says is there anything too hard for the Lord?

MARCH 29

I experienced a lot of pain due to my Tonsils. I could not sleep at night. Due to my blood condition, surgery was not possible for the doctor. I continuously asked the church to keep praying without ceasing. One day a visitor preacher stood on a pulpit, and instead of greeting, he asked if anyone was sick. I said I am; he asked me to come up, so I did. After receiving his prayer, I made my way back to my seat. The devil spoke, you will not be healed. I said I am, too, and instant healing came. I was healed completely. But the liar devil brought the cloud of unbelief. The devil lied to my ear; you were not sick. In my response to the devil, I was suffering and in pain, and God made sure that pain was experienced on both sides consecutively. I gave the devil a black eye saying see, I was sick. The pain vanished as I confronted the devil with its lie and spoke the truth, thanks to God. I thank God for healing. On that day, I gave testimony about my journey to recovery. I know I have to take it by force from the devil.

The doctor's inability doesn't imply that it's impossible for God, does it? We are the living testimony of Jesus Christ only if we claim what is available to us. Don't allow the devil to deceive you into thinking it's unattainable. By trusting and believing in what it promised to you, you can give the devil a black eye. Have fearless trust. It's important for us to be steadfast in what we believe. It will be yours; just say I refuse to live under my privileges.

I had cancer; I said no to cancer; I was freed from the cancer demon by shedding tears and praying. I was in a wheelchair, but I refused to be in a wheelchair. I am walking miraculously. No Devil, no! I refuse to stay down; I am coming against you in the name of Jesus. Say to Pharaoh, let my people go. Let the blind see, let the lame walk, and set the captive free. Our children have the privilege of being at the top, leading, being first, surpassing, and being blessed. We are responsible for teaching them about the powerful God, so they can receive blessings instead of curses. Just as Jochebed taught Moses, Aaron, and Mariam, we parents teach our children the laws, commandments, and precepts of God. We don't put our trust in Sunday school teachers for teaching. If you love your children and want them to continue in blessings, then take your time to prepare the truth of the Bible. You will live overflowing. Amen!

LET US PRAY

In the name of Jesus, let your sorrow turn into joy. May the Lord release you from the enslavement of drugs, alcohol, smoking, and other forms of addiction. May the Lord grant you the power, bravery, and audacity to exalt and honor His name! I pray you are the present-day David, Daniel, and Joseph. You are the Esther who delivers His people from the devil's plan. It is a privilege for us that the devil's plan is defeated and you are able to get away. Grace and mercy are the umbrella under which you live in Jesus's name. Amen! God Bless you!

MARCH 30

ONE ACCORD AND ONE MIND!

The unbreakable, unchangeable, and unshakable force lies in the harmony of one accord and one mind.

The Bible affirms that determination cannot be stopped by anyone. The devil divides one accord and one mind, then destroys the work. The devil knows the power of harmony and unity of one mind. The principle has been applied by the all-knowing God. Jehovah God destroys the unity and agreement among people in order to put an end to their evil plan.

When God himself said in the Book of Genesis, *Genesis 11:1 And the whole earth was of one language, and one speech. 4 And they said, Go to, let us build us a city and a tower, whose top may reach unto heaven; and let us make us a name, lest we be scattered abroad upon the face of the whole earth. 5 And the LORD came down to see the city and the tower, which the children of men builded. 6 And the LORD said, Behold, the people is one, and they have all one language; and this they begin to do: and now nothing will be restrained from them, which they have imagined to do. 7 Go to, let us go down, and there confound their language, that they may not understand one another's speech. 8 So the LORD scattered them abroad from thence upon the face of all the earth: and they left off to build the city. 9 Therefore is the name of it called Babel; because the LORD did there confound the language of all the earth: and from thence did the LORD scatter them abroad upon the face of all the earth.*

God created humanity to fill the earth. But people wanted to stay in one place. God himself admits that nothing can impede them if they are united in their plan. When all have the same belief, language, thinking, and custom, then there is nothing that can stop them. The very act of changing the languages will separate people and will shatter their plans. The same principle is used by Satan, just in reverse. As the Bible says, there is one God, and the devil says no, there are three. Divide and rule.
If you have faith in this fundamental commandment of God, you possess His earthly kingdom.

Deuteronomy 6:4 Hear, O Israel: The LORD our God is one LORD: The truth of the Bible is revealed through the understanding of ONE GOD, not three.

If you are one accord with the Spirit of God, then you are working with God. Those who believe in a false doctrine of three gods are in alliance with the devil and will never discover the truth. Identifying Jehovah revealed in Jesus 'human form is the key to understanding truth in the New Testament. The spirit of God reveals that the Spirit of God manifested in the flesh. Jesus Christ's true identity cannot be revealed through physical means.

MARCH 30

Revelation is only possible through the Spirit of God. People who didn't walk in the spirit were exploited by the devil.

The scribes put Lord Jesus to the test to evaluate His understanding of God. Jesus was challenged by the Scribe and Pharisee, who were unaware of His true identity, to demonstrate His understanding of the foundational principles of the Bible. Does Jesus have knowledge of the fact that there is only one God?

Mark 12:28 And one of the scribes came and having heard them reasoning together, and perceiving that he had answered them well, asked him, Which is the first commandment of all? 29 And Jesus answered him, The first of all the commandments is, Hear, O Israel; The Lord our God is one Lord: 32 And the scribe said unto him, Well, Master, thou hast said the truth: for there is one God;

The truth is, there is one God and not millions. The belief in numerous gods and goddesses leads to confusion, not a resolution. Once you grasp the revelation of Jesus 'true nature, there will be a unified church continuing the mission of Peter and the 12 disciples. No gates of hell can prevail against the church. With one accord and one mind, the disciples of Lord Jesus revolutionized the world.

Acts 17:6b These that have turned the world upside down are come hither also;

The disciples, with one mind and one accord, transformed the world by following Jesus in their understanding, actions, and work.

Acts 1:14 These all continued with one accord in prayer and supplication, with the women, and Mary the mother of Jesus, and with his brethren.

Acts 2:1 And when the day of Pentecost was fully come, they were all with one accord in one place. 2 And suddenly there came a sound from heaven as of a rushing mighty wind, and it filled all the house where they were sitting. 3 And there appeared unto them cloven tongues like as of fire, and it sat upon each of them. 4 And they were all filled with the Holy Ghost and began to speak with other tongues, as the spirit gave them utterance.

The devil does not like us to follow God. When we join forces with God, we can accomplish great things. Acts provides a historical record of the early days of Christianity. The church would have continued its course.

Philippians 2:2 Fulfil ye my joy, that ye be likeminded, having the same love, being of one accord, of one mind.

Roman 15:6a That ye may with one mind and one mouth glorify

Matthew 16:18 And I say also unto thee, That thou art Peter, and upon this rock, I will build my church; and the gates of hell shall not prevail against it.

How to destroy the work of God? The devil acknowledges that our body serves as the Holy Spirit's temple. Without the revelation of Jesus as God Jehovah incarnate, we cannot know this truth. The devil plotted the scheme against this truth by using false teachers and prophets. Let's make sure we pay attention to what Paul and Peter are doing as they receive a revelation of Jesus. The revelation of One God manifested in the flesh doing the mighty work. Then our church building would have no problem with baptism in Jesus's name. The fact is Jesus, their God Messiah, is walking in the flesh.

Satan realized his kingdom was in jeopardy. How to come against God's kingdom? The devil said I have to divide and separate. Using one scripture, Mathew 28:19, and never let them have the revelation of Jesus. The devil did a remarkable job by removing the name Jesus, which is above all previous names of Jehovah God used in the Old Testament. Satan introduced false doctrine in 325 AD at the Nicea conference, so people never found the truth. Through the act of altering the Bible, he caused destruction by removing the truth. The devil started theological colleges introducing three gods called the trinity. The identity of Jesus comes from the revelation; the devil introduced false doctrine and started teaching by his false teacher and prophets.

Christianity is so divided that there is no one agreeing. The church has become a den of thieves where there is no power to shake hell, but hell is shaking us. No devil is being cast out, but people are full of demons. The truth comes from revelation alone. One lady stated that God would make His identity known through the use of a single scripture. I patiently awaited the revelation of Jesus. One-day God used one scripture to reveal the savior as servant Jesus by seeing Jehovah in Him.

Is 43:10 Ye are my witnesses, saith the Lord, and my servant whom I have chosen: that ye may know and believe me, and understand that I am he: before me, there was no God formed, either shall there be after me. 11 I, even I, am the Lord; and beside me, there is no savior.

I knew that Philippians 2:6 Who, being in the form of God, thought it not robbery to be equal with God: 7 But made himself of no reputation, and took upon him the form of a servant, and was made in the likeness of men:

Wow! God is so amazing! No one but God's word, which is spirit, to reveal the truth.

God prevented me from pursuing my education at theological college. I delved into the teachings of different religions, including Jehovah's Witnesses, Seventh-day Adventists, and dabbled in Mormonism. The truth is unstoppable, even against the Gates of Hell. Make sure we are one accord and one mind with truth. Confusion will disappear.

LET US PRAY

Lord, we have confusion, not having the truth. Lord, reveal the truth to us. We haven't sought you, so we haven't witnessed demons being cast out or healing the sick and broken-hearted. Please help us find the truth and let us be one accord one mind. Our mission, Lord, is to turn the world upside down by spreading the truth. Only truth sets the captive free. Don't hold back, give us the truth. We want to cast out the demon, heal the sick, and heal the broken-hearted. Lord, give us revelation of truth and help us be one mind, one spirit to do your mission, where people see and know the power of the truth and power in uniting with you. In Jesus' name. Amen! God Bless you!

MARCH 31

TAKE IT BACK FROM SATAN!

What is mine is mine, and there is also an abundance beyond that. We need to be aware of our possessions and reclaim them.

Take control of what is hidden, stolen, and destroyed. Health, wealth, prosperity, victory, knowledge, wisdom, and earth belong to us. If your father God is Jesus, then you are an owner of all He created.

I can still recall the time I met an elderly lady; whenever I visited her, she complained about having nothing to eat. Maybe some food, bread, beans or rice. I do my best to offer assistance, but there are limitations to what I can accomplish. She had many little grandchildren. Jesus stated that He became poor in order for me to become rich. She is a good Christian lady. She deserves to have an abundance of everything. So, while praying, I broke the spirit of poverty. Ever since, she has had all that she needed. The children now have a new car, a large house, and plenty of food. Hallelujah! Dare to destroy the stealer and killer the devil. Take it back by force.

John 10:10b I am come that they might have life and have it more abundantly.

Devil, the thief, takes it away and keeps it hidden from us.

John 10:10a: The thief cometh not, but for to steal, and to kill, and to destroy:

Our blessings, money, possessions, children, and all that God has given us are the devil's main focus. History demonstrates that impoverished nations find wealth through their adoption of Christianity. Our God blesses our basket, land, health, crops, animals, and land. As we turn to Jesus, we finance with the Blesser.

2 Corinthians 9:8 And God is able to make all grace abound toward you; that ye, always having all sufficiency in all things, may abound to every good work:

To stop Satan from stealing, extend your hand in every direction and declare in the name of Jesus that Satan must release everything that belongs to you. Bind the devil, its cohorts, and demons and destroy them. In the name of Jesus, you have been granted power and authority by God.

Proverbs 10:22 The blessing of the Lord, it maketh rich, and he addeth no sorrow with it.

The assurance comes from your God's promise.

Deuteronomy 15:6 For the Lord thy God blesseth thee, as he promised thee: and thou shalt lend unto many nations, but thou shalt not borrow, and thou shalt reign over many nations, but they shall not reign over thee.

It's amazing to see how nations become wealthy when they turn to Jesus. As Christians allow other deities in their land, the once wealthy nation becomes poor and experiences homelessness. Only the True God possesses the power to bless. The United States is prosperous because their ancestors dedicated themselves to serving God wholeheartedly. Take a moment to observe America. Witnessing our departure from God, we can see the blessings slipping away.

Psalms 33:12 Blessed is the nation whose God is the Lord; and the people whom he hath chosen for his own inheritance.

I heard the testimony of an atheist who is also my brother in Christ. He commented that during my stay in Korea, the country did not believe in Jesus and was in a state of extreme poverty. We have one meal a day, where we cook a handful of rice in a big pot of water and add plenty of salt. Just to feed all my brothers, parents, and grandparents. Since Jesus came into our nation, we have become wealthy. Only Jesus can bless so turn to Jesus. By wholeheartedly dedicating yourself to serving Him, you'll observe the contrast between you and your nation. Satan has an army of fallen angels with demons. Demons are a lost soul that works under Satan. We do not see the spiritual world with our physical eyes. We are completely unaware and have no idea how to safeguard ourselves.

Malachi 3:11 And I will rebuke the devourer for your sakes, and he shall not destroy the fruits of your ground; neither shall your vine cast her fruit before the time in the field, saith the Lord of hosts.

Devourers are Satan, fallen angels, and demons who work in Satan's army. Sickness, diseases, locusts, cankerworms, caterpillars, and palmer worms are all tools Satan uses to destroy us. Also, to destroy your harvest. The devil devours to whom he can.

Live with the knowledge of the adversary's devil. He exists and works as a prince in the air. Learn how to receive blessings by giving as God has commanded. Support those who labor in God's work of preaching, teaching, casting out demons, and healing the sick in God's field. Also, please give to the poor, hungry, orphaned, and naked since, in this dispensation, our body is the temple, not buildings. If you find yourself caught up in a building called a church, a thief in the den can steal your money and prosper.

1 Peter 5:8 Be sober, be vigilant; because your adversary the devil, as a roaring lion, walketh about, seeking whom he may devour:

Devil's vocabulary is deceptive, with hidden plans to destroy. Beware, the devil can snatch your prayer away. Stay humble and persistently seek, ask, and knock until you are liberated from the grasp of Satan.

Daniel 10:12 Then said he unto me, Fear not, Daniel: for from the first day that thou didst set thine heart to understand and to chasten thyself before thy God, thy words were heard, and I am come for thy words.13 But the prince of the kingdom of Persia withstood me one and twenty days: but, lo, Michael, one of the chief princes, came to help me; and I remained there with the kings of Persia.

The prince of your region, known as the devil, and his fallen angels often hinder our prayer requests. You may think it is not God's will to get the answer. No, Satan is holding and hiding it. Go into warfare, take it from his hand. Order him to leave, say I rebuke you, Satan, in Jesus's name. Say I command you, devil, to get out of my case in Jesus's Name. Call on God, and say, Lord, I need special help for my situation and case.

There's this friend I remembered who turned really mean towards me. I am unable to grasp what led to her becoming this way. I wondered why she was snapping at me when she had so much. I asked Jesus what had caused her to become this way. Through a dream, Jesus provided the answer. Two women appeared in my dream, and to my surprise, one of them was this friend. God stated that both possess jealousy, envy, and pride towards you. Their personalities often gave me the impression that they were like twins. It's important to understand that there are instances where your family member and friend could be connected to Satan's army. Pray for protection from those people and their harmful intentions. In the flesh we are weak and we need help. Angels were created by God for that reason.

Luke 22:43 And there appeared an angel unto him from heaven, strengthening him.

Psalm 34: 7 The angel of the Lord encampeth round about them that fear him, and delivereth them.

If we all call on Jesus for help, then our home, city, county, and nation will be free from drugs, divorces, jails, prisons, hospitals, sickness, kidnappers, guns, and war. Can you spend time in prayer? Call on God, not 911. Call on Jesus and not the police. You have the power to declare war on the true origin, Satan, and tell the devil, "Enough is enough." I am coming against you in the name of Jesus. I am not made for cancer, stroke, sicknesses, or mental and physical illnesses. I will not be poor. I refuse to be poor. What belongs to me comes back in double. Knowledge is the key.

Discover the key to reclaiming your stolen health, wealth, children, marriage, success, and prosperity. Use it and take it back from the enemy.

Hosea 4:6a; My people are destroyed for lack of knowledge:

I am convinced that the Word of God is more effective than medicine in all seasons and situations. My atheist friend had cancer. I witnessed her for ten years. When faced with immense challenges, she turned to Jesus for support. She realized I had a deep understanding of the Lord. She asked me to come over to her house for prayer. During my prayer for her, I witnessed a bright light entering, followed by Jesus entering her room. That night, my friend experienced healing for numerous conditions. She remains alive, but a majority of the women in her cancer support groups have lost their lives. My friend now adores Jesus and has been baptized in His name. Jesus can destroy the destroyer. By invoking the name of Jesus, Lord liberated her from Satan's control over her life. I delivered the truth to her, and now it's your chance to rescue others from the devil's clutches by teaching them the truth.

LET US PRAY

Lord, we are thankful for your blood. You paid the price for all sins and redeemed our souls from eternal death. Please give us the knowledge of your word to receive the fullness of heritage. We have abundance but are stolen by the enemy. In the name of Jesus, we ask to liberate the individual entangled in drugs, alcohol, cigarettes, and sinful behavior. Devil, we command the devil to get out of our family. Let us come against the devil. We bind and send you devil, to the pit of hell where you belong. Let your trap catch you in Jesus's name. Let all that belongs to us come back in abundance, in Jesus's name. Amen! God bless you!

APRIL

APRIL 1

YOU CAN RESURRECT!

Jesus was resurrected on the 3rd day. According to Jewish belief, the dead body starts decaying after three days.

God shows us He can break every natural law; He is the God who makes the dead alive. You were dead since the key to death is in the hand of Satan. Jesus, following His resurrection, presented His blood on the Holy altar in heaven as a sacrifice for the sins of the world. Anyone can be resurrected from sin, since it is available for those who desire it.

Revelation 1:18 I am he that liveth, and was dead; and, behold, I am alive for evermore, Amen; and have the keys of hell and of death.

Now death has no power since Jesus gave us life; life is in the blood. Blood does not die. Jesus resurrected Himself and all who died in the Lord without blood.

Ephesians 4:8 Wherefore he saith, When he ascended up on high, he led captivity captive, and gave gifts unto men. 9 (Now that he ascended, what is it but that he also descended first into the lower parts of the earth? 10 He that descended is the same also that ascended up far above all heavens, that he might fill all things.)

Jesus sacrificed Himself on the altar, shedding His blood to save the righteous who died in the Old Testament. Once they offer Jesus 'blood, they no longer bear Adam and Eve's curse. Abraham, Moses, and all the righteous were taken up with Him. God's purpose in becoming human and sacrificing himself was to redeem all those held captive by Satan. Furthermore, its purpose was to set others free from Satan's plan of stealing, killing, and destroying. In God's plan, we need Satan's villain role to fulfill and establish a blueprint of God. Satan thought he destroyed Jesus by killing him. Satan thought the plan successfully destroyed the Kingdom of God, but it backfired on Satan.

Lord Jesus demonstrated that the miracle of fish is evidence of boundless regeneration. He provided evidence that dead fish can reproduce.

I remember in my yard; the tree kept dying. I talked to a friend, and she said, "I can pray over it; they will come alive." So she did and it came alive.

I remember I prayed over many dead or near-dying patients in the ICU and they came alive. Jesus said you could raise dead in my name; I am giving you power over death. I took the key from Satan; now killer Satan is out of business. Don't lose the key; it is in the word of God called the Bible.

How many believe this? Satan utilizes diverse tactics to manipulate us into thinking we cannot bring the dead back to life. Satan makes us think that demons like alcohol, drugs, cancer, or heart attacks cannot be healed or set free. All demons are working day and night to destroy. Here's some good news for you: there's a chance for you to be renewed and reconciled.

2 Corinthians 5:17 Therefore, if any man is in Christ, he is a new creature: old things are passed away; behold, all things have become new. 18 And all things are of God, who hath reconciled us to himself by Jesus Christ, and hath given to us the ministry of reconciliation; 19 To wit, that God was in Christ, reconciling the world unto himself, not imputing their trespasses unto them; and hath committed unto us the word of reconciliation.

Just the key to knowledge is what you require. The only thing that can hurt us is our lack of knowledge. By resurrecting yourself from sins, you condemn yourself to eternal death in hell.

Galatians 5:19 Now the works of the flesh are manifest, which are these; Adultery, fornication, uncleanness, lasciviousness, 20 Idolatry, witchcraft, hatred, variance, emulations, wrath, strife, seditions, heresies, 21 Envyings, murders, drunkenness, revellings, and such like: of the which I tell you before, as I have also told you in time past, that they which do such things shall not inherit the kingdom of God.

The blood of Jesus, symbolized by the lamb, has the ability to forgive sins and give us a clear conscience. Pure consciousness does not negatively impact your heart and life. The power of sins is erased, removing the memory of sin from life. How wonderful is this?

Romans 6:1 What shall we say then? Shall we continue in sin, that grace may abound? 2 God forbid. How shall we, that are dead to sin, live any longer therein? 3 Know ye not that so many of us as were baptized into Jesus Christ were baptized into his death? 4 Therefore we are buried with him by baptism into death: that like as Christ was raised from the dead by the glory of the Father, even so, we also should walk in newness of life. 5 For if we have been planted together in the likeness of his death, we shall also be in the likeness of his resurrection: 6 Knowing this, that our old man is crucified with him, that the body of sin might be destroyed, that henceforth we should not serve sin. 7 For he that is dead is freed from sin.

Jesus brought many people back to life to demonstrate His power of resurrection. Through His Spirit, he can change us completely. When you receive the Holy Spirit, Jesus Himself comes within you. His work now includes not just the external, but also involves working through you as the Holy Spirit. You are His creation. Trusting Him allows us to live forever, just as He does. The resurrecting power in us has life-giving power. Don't let the devil deceive you into settling for less than you deserve. You need to be aware that you have the power to bring the dead back to life. The attack of Satan is to kill. The devil wants you to believe he still possesses the key to death, but he doesn't. Each sin causes 39 categories of sickness that can cause death. Jesus paid by taking 39 stripes where blood gushed out. Everything has been accomplished by God. Do not think death; think resurrection. Reach out and bring hope to those sitting in darkness, whether in a hospital, bar, drug den, prison, or jail. The death demon was ordered by God to leave. Release them from Satan's clutches, proclaiming the Devil's defeat in Jesus' resurrection.

Do you know what belongs to you? The Church built on Rock holds the key. Rock signifies the unveiling of Jesus Christ's identity. Knowing who Jesus is makes the gates of hell powerless. Jesus is Jehovah's savior in the flesh, and you are the Church with authority and power.

The only thing Satan wants you to believe is that you are powerless. All we have to do is tell him that the devil is powerless against the blood of Jesus. I cover the city, home, people, and everything with the blood of Jesus. Bring them back to life. The power of Satan and death are destroyed when everything is covered with the blood of Jesus. Blood has life.

Isaiah 33:6 And wisdom and knowledge shall be the stability of thy times, and strength of salvation: the fear of the Lord is his treasure.

Remember, you can resurrect and regenerate in Jesus's name.

LET US PRAY

In Jesus' name, we recognize that this is not a holiday focused on egg hunts or bunnies. The devil is a liar. Give us the wisdom, knowledge, and understanding of your resurrection. You have conquered death and now live in triumph. Corruptible will put on incorruptible, and the mortal shall put on immortality. Believing it in our hearts gives us the power of resurrection in our words. Satan has been defeated by the living God Jesus within us. Thank you for giving us the key to your kingdom. We are victorious by your truth and power in the Holy Spirit. Not by might, nor by power, but by the Holy Spirit. In the name of Jesus, we bring back to life all that is dead around us. Amen! God bless you!

APRIL 2

ACTIVATE YOUR FAITH!

Your faith will materialize. The unseen will become visible if we hold onto our faith. Faith is something what you hope for. Faith is the most powerful if you know how to activate it. Faith makes a mountain to move, a lame to walk, and blind to see. If you know how to maintain it, faith can accomplish a great deal. If you keep faith in your money, family, degree, health, children, or any gods or goddesses, then it will not work. Regretfully, it won't come to pass and you'll feel sorry.

I often hear my heathen friends expressing frustration when they pray to multiple gods-goddesses and see no results. However, when I pray to Jesus, they are the ones who receive the blessings. I politely ask them to express gratitude by saying thank you, Jesus. Only he has the power to move mountains, heal the sick, remove obstacles to your blessings, perform miracles, and defeat the destroyer.

Learn how to activate your faith; that is the key to receiving what you desire, and you will receive it.

The primary introduction we make is Jesus: the embodiment of Jehovah God, able to fulfill all your wishes. Lord Jesus, as the true God, can bless you in contrast to the numerous powerless false gods and goddesses created by man.

Hebrews 11:6 But without faith, it is impossible to please him: for he that cometh to God must believe that he is and that he is a rewarder of them that diligently seek him.

By believing in Jesus as God, you can receive all the rewards you desire and request. Present your petitions, then seek and pray.

If you're unfamiliar with Jesus, I recommend getting the KJV Bible, an uncorrupted translation from the original Hebrew and Greek texts. That is the Word of God, so make sure to read it. Allow the Word of God to touch your heart and bring about a powerful transformation.

I encountered a Bangladeshi who converted from Buddhism to Christianity. He said, "I did not like to go to sanctuary because they have too much love. Second, I would not read the Bible". Yet he said the day he opened his Bible; he could not put it down till he finished.

A preacher distributed Bibles to people on the street. A man said, "I will use Bible pages for tobacco and smoke it." Preacher said, "You may, but before burning, would you read that page and then smoke"? The man agreed and continued for a few pages, but he couldn't go on when he reached the book of John. He fell on his face and surrendered to God. The Word of God has the power to change lives.

APRIL 2

Seek to find God. It will change your life as well. It will save you. Second, you will,

James 2:14 What doth it profit, my brethren, though a man say he hath faith, and have not works? Can faith save him? 17 Even so, faith, if it hath not works, is dead, being alone.

Faith is activated through work, action, and obedience to the word.

Activate your faith with your action today. If your goal is to become a teacher or preacher, then start teaching and preaching. Abraham earned the title of father of faith. Abraham acted without seeing the promised nation birthing before his eyes. Despite his wife's inability to conceive due to old age, Abraham's faith led him to receive a son. With faith, he brought his son Isaac to Mt. Moriah to be sacrificed. Faith demands obedience without questioning or reasoning. It demands a faith that can make oceans into dry roads and rocks produce water. By sending the Word of God to different places, we can actively express our faith.

The miracle was impossible for Jesus to perform in His own town. Why?

Matthew 13:54 And when he was come into his own country, he taught them in their synagogue, insomuch that they were astonished, and said, Whence hath this man this wisdom, and these mighty works 58 And he did not many mighty works there because of their unbelief.

Their negative faith allowed them to destroy and aboard what it entitled them to. I uphold my faith while engaging in activities like shopping, traveling, or working. Having faith in God means believing He will give me what I need. I go shopping with Jesus. I always find what I'm looking for at an affordable price.

During my trip to India, the prophet foretold that you would serve as a minister to all Hindus. He also prophesied that someone will cover the cost of my flight to India. Someone provided me with enough money to support my missionary trip. On the last day of leaving India and Dubai, I noticed that I ministered to Hindus or converted Christians. I choose not to speculate about what the future has in store since I have faith in the one who determines my destiny.

On numerous occasions, I plead with Hindus to believe in Jesus. The Hindu person will agree. Hindus have no problem believing in Jesus as they believe in multiple gods and goddesses. Jesus is simply one more. Among the multitude, Jesus is the one and only true God.

Abraham did not belong to that group. By placing his trust in the living God, he followed God's lead and departed from his country. Abraham's obedience is the reason why the nation of Israel exists today. Jehovah God promised Abraham and gave him this land.

The Bible teaches that knowledge is the key to achieving success.

Hosea 4:6a My people are destroyed for lack of knowledge: because thou hast rejected knowledge, I will also reject thee,

Your situation can change if you manage to find the key to your problems. What steps should be taken to gain the knowledge needed for restoration, building, and preservation?

Romans 10:17 So then faith cometh by hearing and hearing by the word of God.

Listen to Jehovah God, the author of the Bible. What are His capabilities, who is He, and where does He live? How much does he love you? Etc.

My friend mentioned that they always find me reading the Bible, no matter when they come. Continuing her questioning, she asked if you read your study books. I was in a science college, majoring in math and physics. The question arose in her mind: what am I doing and how? I was hungry for the Word of God. One of my friends advised me to read the Bible when I get old. Make the most of the present moment and enjoy your life. Her suggestion was to read the Bible in old age, but for now, enjoy life while you're young. Simply attending church is sufficient.

I began reading the Bible when I was young, and it sparked numerous questions. I started seeking God early in the morning and late at night. It brought blessings into my life. I came out of the wheelchair since I knew healing was available. I had faith in receiving healing for various eye problems, cancer, and all sickness. I don't need to take any medication.

The Bible provides knowledge and protects us from destruction.

When I read the testimony in the Word of God, I talk to God; I claim this since I am also eligible. I stand on the word, and I say; you do this for me since your word says. Lord, I desire these things as I trust in your promises. I hear testimony that increases my faith. I pleaded, "Lord, just as you did it for others, please do it for me." Just like how a child says, what about me? I want it". If God did it for others, He can do it for me as well. It brings me joy that we can believe and obey to claim His word. By laying my hands and praying, I have seen the sick regain their health. It's amazing to see people being baptized in Jesus's name and coming out of the water completely cleansed of sins and sicknesses, looking absolutely beautiful. I have personally observed the breaking of demonic yokes and bondages.

Start exploring the Scriptures for lessons on becoming wealthy. The measure you give is the measure you will receive. Greater faith releases greater results. All is in your hands if you believe, obey, and take action for Amen! What do you have to do? Lose what you are holding, two fishes, step in the water to see a dry road, and go in the water in Jesus's name for the remission of sins. Actions speak louder Than Words...Keep faith in the WORD only.

LET US PRAY

Lord Jesus, we seek the courage to act upon our faith, as it holds great value. Faith is abundant among those in poverty. Jesus blesses us with a faith that holds fast, just like the poor. We put forth efforts to activate our faith, Lord. Lord, grant us the faith to believe. God, we receive by faith all that is available to us. May we be filled with unwavering faith in Jesus's name, O Lord. Amen! God bless you!

APRIL 3

AN ACTIVE CHRISTIAN FULFILLS GOD'S PLAN!

The general belief is that being Christian involves attending church on Sundays and, in some cases, mid-week services. What actions do active Christians take to further God's work? To continue in Christianity is like joining the army. Satan has an army as well. Satan and your flesh are similar in their strength and their efforts to break you down. Satan is aware of the Bible. There are workers in his army. They are also called pastors, preachers, prophets, teachers, fallen angels, and demons to mislead people. The devil works to destroy the work of God.

To begin with, Jesus prayed throughout the night to choose His disciples, and then the Lord provided them with training. They were all taught and trained by Him, first the 12 and then the 70, to follow Him.

Jesus dispatched them to teach, preach, and walk in His footsteps. Before calling, God examines our hearts. Jesus qualifies the one whom he calls. All training will be like Joseph, Moses, Daniel, Joshua, Paul, Peter, and others.

Virtuous people will have the same integrity, purity, and righteousness. The Lord will put you through trials in every aspect to see you come out as gold. The test will get you ready for the training period for your testimonies. Both Moses and Paul underwent wilderness training. The cave and wilderness served as David's training ground. All whom the Lord tried came out intense, clean, and faithful. God is looking for the faithful, not behind the door drinking, drugging, stealing, gambling, lying, and standing on Sunday on a pulpit. Paul was imprisoned for preaching the gospel. Once they have endured trials and challenges, followers take on the roles assigned to them by the Lord. The Lord controls the direction of your life, and if you can swing in His direction, then you are qualified.

I remembered my situation. One day while working in the Postoffice, walking out of there, I heard the voice, "you will never come back to this place." I had a severe back injury and could not walk during that time. I chose not to look behind where I worked 19 years, as I left the building thinking about what will happen next. God gave me a little piece of the puzzle, but I knew the voice I heard was of the Lord. Subsequent to that, I never went back, and the battle began. The uncertainty of my life, finances, and future made everything seem unpredictable. Flow is your state within God's plan. You need not know or understand. You will never see the shore. The fire is hot, but He is in control. Lions are ready to tear you down, but He has the power to stop.

The Lord spoke to the sister in the faith about my trial. According to her, the Lord appeared and mentioned that Sister Das was facing a fiery trial. Lord said it is a long trial, and she will come out as gold.

ELIZABETH DAS

Job 23:10 But he knoweth the way that I take: when he hath tried me, I shall come forth as gold.

Leaving my job required me to handle all the legal matters, leaving me with no choice. Despite the circumstances, I was unsure about my healing, but I held onto a promise. Do you have a promise? Stand on it, it will happen.

Proverb 4:12 When thou goest, thy steps shall not be straitened; and when thou runnest, thou shalt not stumble.

I always believed that one day I would be able to walk.

I was faced with the choice of disability retirement or continuing with the compensation program. I was told by God to take disability retirement, even though it wasn't much. I'm grateful that God sent me a prophet who confirmed my decision to retire. In my calculation, it was impossible to survive through a little check. But again, I heard the voice saying, "I will take care of you." During that time, the Lord prepared me for training. To fulfill your calling, you must complete the trials and tests of God's school.

Wait for God alone when you receive a calling from Him. There's a multitude of misleading and confusing counterfeit workers of the enemy. Surprisingly, there are those who, like their father's devil, stand on the pulpit and lead people as demons of religion. Simply using or holding the Bible doesn't make you a true believer. Check their fruits. Search for the one who matches the characteristics the Lord has described. Only obey the individual chosen by the Lord.

Mark 16: 17 And these signs shall follow them that believe; In my name shall they cast out devils; they shall speak with new tongues; 18 They shall take up serpents; and if they drink any deadly thing, it shall not hurt them; they shall lay hands on the sick, and they shall recover. 20 And they went forth and preached everywhere, the Lord working with them, and confirming the word with signs following. Amen.

Acknowledge that it's a battle between the devil and God. You must know how to cast the devil out. If not, then you have called yourself and not God. If I can't cast out the demon there, what course of action should I take? People need deliverance from sickness, demons of alcohol, lies, drugs, cancer, diseases, gambling, adultery, and all kinds of evil spirits. Nowadays, numerous pulpit standings require deliverance. If you see a person casting out demons, it is sent by God and not by Church or organization.

Moreover, they speak in a fresh and unknown tongue. "Glossa" in Greek refers to a language you haven't learned in school. Just like on the day of Pentecost, they received the Holy Ghost and spoke languages they did not know. This saying is from Jesus, not from me. Those who don't speak in tongues are not true followers of Jesus, but rather counterfeit antichrists. Be careful going to churches because Jesus is real, and so is the devil. Eternal rest is necessary for your soul. Love your soul. Jesus gave a direct explanation on who to have faith in and who to avoid.

Third, I will protect them from deadly drinks and serpents.

Fourth, they will heal the sick. For what purpose do you go to Church? I look to God for healing and will attend services where people speak in tongues, demonstrating the presence of God's spirit. The Spirit of God can heal, so they also have the ability to heal. Save your time and skip visiting any churches. Quality and demonstration are both expected by the Lord.

When someone is contacted by churches, organizations, or themselves, they pursue their own interests.

Upon assuming the throne following King Solomon's demise, Jeroboam disregarded God's plan and implemented his own agenda.

1 King 12:31 And he made a house of high places and made priests of the lowest of the people, which were not of the sons of Levi.

1 Kings 13:33 After this thing, Jeroboam returned not from his evil way but made again of the lowest of the people priests of the high places: whosoever would, he consecrated him, and he became one of the priests of the high places.

In this scenario, you'll witness various name-brand churches, organizations, and denominations utilizing the same Bible to advance their agenda.

In God's plan, the importance of our soul cannot be lessened.

Just like what Jesus did in *Matthew 4:23 And Jesus went about all Galilee, teaching in their synagogues, preaching the gospel of the kingdom, and healing all manner of sickness and all manner of disease among the people.*

The Church in Acts did the identical thing. Jesus gave the power which is through the Holy Ghost.

Acts 5:16 There came also a multitude out of the cities round about unto Jerusalem, bringing sick folks, and them which were vexed with unclean spirits: and they were healed every one.

If you are following the teaching of the Lord, then you will not compromise. Disciple John warns us in an epistle of.

1 John 4:1 Beloved, believe not every spirit, but try the spirits whether they are of God: because many false prophets are gone out into the world.

Beware Satan's antichrist spirit working hard today. At a fellowship meeting, they go into great detail about a person, as if they have complete understanding of them. Pastor is allowing the Holy Spirit to minister to people. Break cures, heal, cast out the demon, and send them back whole. Original Church in operation! I have no time to waste. I am looking for the original and real Amen!

LET US PRAY

Oh Lord, we search, inquire, and seek to uncover the truth. We want the salvation of God by following the truth taught by true teachers and prophets. Lead us by your spirit so we do not follow the antichrist's spirit. The Lord gives us spiritual perception and discernment. The Holy Spirit leads, guides, and teaches us. We know many are false teachers and prophets in the world but keep your sheep from a wolf. Help us keep your word as a guideline in Jesus's name. Amen! God bless you!

APRIL 4.

UNDERSTAND THE SPIRIT OPERATION!

The enforcement of our world is truly controlled by the spirit world. You can find a solution if you have the knowledge of the spirit world and an understanding of its power. The devil tries to prevent belief in the existence of the spirit. I was the victim of the false teachings of religious churches. Since my brother's situation, I drew myself to find help and the truth. The truth is, the spirit operation is the invisible force that governs everything. It is functioning correctly but encourages you to turn a blind eye and a deaf ear to it.

We watch the operation of the killing, stealing, and destructive power of Satan. We label it as cancer, heart attack, stroke, TB, or any disease, but never the devil. Let the devil know that it's reign of stealing, killing, and destroying is finished.

Knowing and believing the truth is necessary to receive deliverance. There are deceiving teachers and prophets among us. They do not see the spirit's power to perform miracles. They are professional nonbelievers and protesters of the truth. The labels of illnesses such as diabetes, blood pressure, and different names. People accept physical conditions as false teachers, and prophets train and teach them. In order to get assistance, they have to rely on pharmaceutical medications. Make sure to read the label and see what side effects the devil has included. Still, trust and believe medicine rather than relying His stripe. Believe and say I am healed. Instead of repenting of every sin, baptize in Jesus's name to wash away all sins they choose to suffer. The purpose of baptism is not to join a church, but to seek forgiveness for sins. Satan is working hard by planting tare. Tares are false pastor-preacher teachers. It is a great idea for the devil to destroy the work of God by training them to misguide God's creation. John advises against obeying all spirits. Workers like pastors, preachers, and evangelists have also been recruited by the devil. Churches and organizations are being influenced by a deceptive form of an antichrist spirit. These seeds are said to be bitter, like Satan.

Acts 1:8a But ye shall receive power, after that the Holy Ghost comes upon you:

The power bestowed upon Samson came from Jehovah: God's Spirit.

Judges 14:6a And the Spirit of the LORD came mightily upon him, and he rent him as he would have rent a kid, and he had nothing in his hand: By the power of God's Spirit, Othniel, an average man, achieved victory in the battle.

Judges 3:10 And the Spirit of the LORD came upon him, and he judged Israel and went out to war: and the LORD delivered Chushanrishathaim king of Mesopotamia into his hand, and his hand prevailed against Chushanrishathaim.

APRIL 4

1 Samuel 16:13 Then Samuel took the horn of oil, and anointed him in the midst of his brethren: and the Spirit of the LORD came upon David from that day forward.

David, not relying on his own strength, killed the bear and lion with the power of God.

1 Samuel 17:36 Thy servant slew both the lion and the bear: and this uncircumcised Philistine shall be as one of them, seeing he hath defied the armies of the living God.

Through the Spirit of God, the ordinary man can accomplish extraordinary tasks. Similarly, an evil spirit is capable of performing destructive tasks.

Physical might and power may enable individuals to perform incredible acts, but the Holy Spirit surpasses them all. Don't forget, the man was possessed by countless demons.

Mark 5:2 And when he was come out of the ship, immediately there met him out of the tombs a man with an unclean spirit, 3 Who had his dwelling among the tombs. No man could bind him, no, not with chains: 4 Because that he had been often bound with fetters and chains, and the chains had been plucked asunder by him, and the fetters broken in pieces: neither could any man tame him.

It wasn't the man who broke the chains, but rather the demons. The demons entered the pigs and caused their destruction. Evil spirits like Satan, fallen angels, and demons exist in the form of spirits. They do destructive works of killing, stealing, and destruction.

Mark 5:12 And all the devils besought him, saying, Send us into the swine, that we may enter into them. 13 And forthwith Jesus gave them leave. And the unclean spirits went out, and entered into the swine: and the herd ran violently down a steep place into the sea (They were about two thousand;) and were choked in the sea.

While the spirit world holds power, God's Spirit surpasses all others in strength and potency. That is why God gave the Holy Spirit on the day of Pentecost. Wonderworking power of spirit to deliver, heal, prophecy, and do miracles. Spiritual nine gifts, like words of knowledge and wisdom, are in the spirit of God.

Zechariah 4:6 Not by might, nor by power, but by my spirit, saith the Lord of hosts.

God says by Zechariah that if the prophet leans on my spirit, it will get phenomenal results.

Acts 19:2 He said unto them, Have ye received the Holy Ghost since ye believed? And they said unto him, We have not so much as heard whether there be any Holy Ghost.

Nowadays, people are familiar with the Holy Spirit but mistakenly assume they already received it. If you have the Holy Spirit, then speaking in tongues is the evidence. You can do healing and deliverance through the Holy Spirit.

The early church knew how to receive the Spirit of God:

Acts 19:6 And when Paul had laid his hands upon them, the Holy Ghost came on them; and they spake with tongues, and prophesied.

Historic congregations were established by the disciples of Jesus, demonstrating the works of the Holy Spirit. Receiving the Spirit of God was always accompanied by a pattern, indicating the ability to speak in tongues. They never believed another way. Can you explain why you're believing like this? In our churches today, we witness either the presence of the Holy Spirit or a lack of power. You could be employed by a church or organization, but the Spirit of God is not operating through you.

Acts 8:14 Now when the apostles which were at Jerusalem heard that Samaria had received the word of God, they sent unto them Peter and John: 15 Who, when they came down, prayed for them, that they might receive the Holy Ghost: 16 (For as yet he was fallen upon none of them: only they were baptized in the name of the Lord Jesus.) 17 Then laid they their hands on them, and they received the Holy Ghost.

Peter and John came and laid a hand. Paul placed his hand on others to receive the Holy Spirit. During baptism in Jesus's name, the Holy Spirit frequently comes upon people, but if not, it can also happen through the laying on of hands. The evidence is you will speak in your tongue.

1 Corinthians:12 talks about nine gifts of the spirit. The same Spirit God, the same Lord, operates through you.

These gifts are given individually for the advancement of the one church of the Lord Jesus: word of knowledge, wisdom, healing, faith, miracle, tongue, interpretation of tongue, discerning the spirit, and spirit of prophecy. The church consists of those who repented, were baptized in Jesus's name, and received the Holy Spirit by speaking in tongues, not the building.

1 Corinthian 12:31 But covet earnestly the best gifts: The Spirit gift.

The ancient church saw a significant increase in followers due to their yielding vessels. Open yourself up to the Holy Spirit of God and let it guide you. There's no need for people to seek out psychics, tarot card readers, palm readers, magicians, astrologers, witches, or ouija boards.

The needs we have are looked after by God's spirit. We need to get ready for the spiritual gifts we have. The purpose of their teaching is to make you doubt and reject the spirit of God. Have you seen the current situation? The country has suffered from curses due to sick churches. Remember, they do not allow Holy Spirit operation. Being in control is something that false teachers and prophets enjoy. Allow the Spirit of God to solve and resolve all problems. If the Spirit of God is at work, we have the power to completely transform the world. We welcome you, Holy Spirit.

LET US PRAY

Lord, we acknowledge that God is a spiritual being, and we desire to worship you sincerely and truthfully. The power of truth lies in its ability to set us free. The Spirit of God can truly lead, teach, and guide us. We can operate powerfully on earth if we yield to your spirit. We welcome Spirit God to come and do mighty like Samson, David, Paul, Peter, and all Spirit-filled operating vessels in time past and many now as well. Could you give us your spirit? We can heal, be victorious and have salvation if we have the Spirit of God. We want more of your Spirit in Jesus's name. Amen! God bless you!

APRIL 5

VISION WITH REVELATION!

Christians who are not fully committed don't realize that we can experience the Heavenly vision just like watching television. TV is broadcast on earth, but God broadcasts His vision from heaven.

During my vacation, I stayed in different places and shared bedrooms with a friend. In the middle of the night, a noise woke me up. Since the motel was located by the lake, I looked towards the source of the noise. I saw a bunch of ladies with many hands coming out of her heads. I looked at her, but she was sound asleep and snoring. Beside her head, a group of women were causing a commotion, their hands moving in a circular motion from their shoulders.

While distributing Bible tracts at the DMV, I had the opportunity to meet a Hindu woman. Because she was experiencing a demonic attack, she started coming to my house. She was sharing what and how she was tormented. I also was new to a spiritual walk. As you know at the beginning of my search I was still just a religious Christian seeking God.

When I saw the ladies with many hands, it reminded me of idols of women I saw in India. These were not idols but actual demons. I told her in the morning what I saw in the night by her head. I could tell that Satan was causing her distress as she tried to explain her feelings. As soon as I saw those demonic forms, I was certain that the devil was seriously causing her confusion. I started giving her Bible study, and she was baptized in Jesus' name. She stopped worshiping idols. I learned she was exposed to Christianity even before I met her.

I shared with her the vision I experienced in the hotel room. I specifically asked her not to invite demons through worship. She understood and said, "I am not." She said demons attacked me since she worshiped those idols in the past. As I started casting the demon out, she felt released. Teach people how to come against demons. Training is important for the new convert.

2 Corinthians 12:1 It is not expedient for me doubtless to glory. I will come to visions and revelations of the Lord.

Paul founded numerous churches in various regions worldwide. Paul was being visited by visions and revelations from God. Without receiving information from the Lord, preaching and teaching are impossible. Access knowledge from the divine realm.

When I travel to unfamiliar places, I rely on vision and revelation due to my lack of knowledge about the people and culture. A doctor needs an X-ray, MRI, or diagnostic film to diagnose the problem, so how much do we do? We must screen heavenly vision with an understanding of how to be treated.

I have had numerous visions while engaged in prayer, whether it's during phone conversations or when I'm alone. The provided information was beneficial for my assignment. Oftentimes, individuals learn to accept their circumstances, but God provides solutions through visions or spoken guidance. Instead of exercising like medical doctors, our God focuses on curing, healing, delivering, and forgiving.

Acts 18:9 Then spake the Lord to Paul in the night by a vision, Be not afraid, but speak, and hold not thy peace:10 For I am with thee, and no man shall set on thee to hurt thee: for I have many people in this city.

Having vision is essential when working for God. The existence of Jesus, your God, is real. He is alive, and He talks. His interest in taking care of His creation is proven by his actions. Listen to Him, in tune with Him. Lord, I am earnestly seeking your presence. The Lord talks to me through visions. Please give me a revelation of it. Yet, the problem is we are in a hurry, no time to talk to God. Can we slow down and take our time, please? Make it a habit to pray and fast with God, incorporating it into your everyday life. Our actions can be the key to saving ourselves, our families, and those around us.

Peter saw the vision in Acts chapter 10. It enabled him to serve gentiles in his ministry. God commanded Peter to have no fear in meeting Cornelius, even though he is a gentile. The Angels gave Cornelius directions, which included the address. Angels are given to us to serve as ministers. You will receive insights about different places through the guidance of God's Spirit.

Due to Paul's actions of killing Christians, nobody wanted to be near him.

Acts 9:10 And there was a certain disciple at Damascus, named Ananias; and to him said the Lord in a vision, Ananias. And he said, Behold, I am here, Lord. 11 And the Lord said unto him, Arise, and go into the street which is called Straight, and inquire in the house of Judas for one called Saul, of Tarsus: for, behold, he prayeth ,On the other hand, Paul received a vision from God of Ananias approaching him. 12 And hath seen in a vision a man named Ananias coming in, and putting his hand on him that he might receive his sight.

God addressed the concerns of both sides. Paul was prepared, but Anania feared him because he persecuted Christians. Do you agree that you would be afraid as well? When I am sent to nations by God, I carry divine information. Let me tell you; God provides information, which I love it. By using vision and revelation, we can uncover the underlying causes of problems. You'll receive information before being sent anywhere. Would you send someone without the address or facts?

Acts 16:9 And a vision appeared to Paul in the night; a man of Macedonia stood, and prayed him, saying, Come over into Macedonia, and help us.

They will receive you with open arms when you go with the information. A vision from God provides information.

Genesis 15:1 After these things, the word of the LORD came unto Abram in a vision, saying, Fear not, Abram: I am thy shield, and thy exceeding great reward.

Abraham journeyed from one kingdom to another. There were places where his life was in danger. Because of a beautiful wife, his life was in danger.

The Lord brought him out of his country and kindred and shielded him. God is real. I received a map from him to facilitate my movement between places. God provided extra angels and visions to continue his journey.

If the Lord is in control, your journey will be protected. He never sends you without a plan, regardless of where or what you need to do. He will lead and guide you, but are you ready to follow? Are you ready to submit? Are you ready to accept the task? Do not be afraid when God calls. Through his vision, he offers protection, instruction, warning, and information. Just listen and trust.

Without complete information, vision, and revelation, the task will become challenging. I cannot work without information from God. King Jehovah is accurate and precise. You need to remove all fear and doubt.

God gave the dream and vision to Daniel.

Daniel 7:1 In the first year of Belshazzar, King of Babylon, Daniel had a dream and visions of his head upon his bed:

Sometimes people get visions but do not have revelation or understanding. The facts are disclosed through revelation. Discover individuals gifted by God for interpreting dreams or visions. Please do not go to any medium.

Even ancient pagan rulers employed individuals with access to supernatural knowledge. Many kept astrologers, magicians, and soothsayers, but we keep the one who has wisdom from Jesus. Only Jesus has the correct information. Seek God and desire vision with revelation from heaven above.

LET US PRAY

Lord, you are a true and real God. Teach us how to walk through your vision by giving us revelation. We know all the information you give is true. Lord, please teach us to use these authorities we have. We do not want to be addicted to worldly television but desire and seek a heavenly vision. We need knowledge by visions of assignment to take care of the situation. Thank you to godly people through whom you provide information. Give us an understanding of visions and dreams since they are available in Jesus's name. Amen! God bless you!

APRIL 6

HOW TO MAKE ONE FALL!

What causes the downfall of a nation, family, or individual? Simply by taking the truth out, making one forget God's ways, laws, and commandments.

In short, misguide people from the truth and fall will come swiftly. Evil companies or friendships have the power to corrupt individuals. I understand this as I am getting older. My parents were aware of this, and they oversaw our friendship. Our parents, siblings, teachers, and elders always watched our association since they knew how deadly it was. Ask God to give you perception, discernment, wisdom with boldness, and courage to guide and protect. Always listen to the righteous parents. Be cautious of a sibling who may have negative or immoral intentions. You can also be harmed by them. Pay attention and be cautious. Satan directs his attention towards individuals, families, and nations.

America, being a Christian country, is blessed. Why? Because they followed the laws, commandments, and statutes of God. If anyone, whether it be family or nation, obeys Jesus 'laws and commandments, their life story will be completely transformed. An individual or family will be head, incredibly favored, first, and blessed. God will give riches, knowledge, wisdom, and understanding to them. No weapons of an enemy can prosper, and every tongue rise in judgment will condemn. This is the heritage of the Lord. I inherited this by being born again. I love to follow the laws and commandments of God. I am blessed and exceptionally favored. Did Joseph's brother show an extreme favoritism towards him? Joseph's brother planned to destroy him. A lustful adulteress woman tried to sleep with Joseph and lied. The laws of God should not be on your lips but in your heart. The heart is where life begins. A pure heart brings forth a life filled with blessings and success. Sin goes against God because He gave us laws and commandments to obey, not disobey. You wouldn't sin against your spouse when they are around. Whether they are present or not, you live a righteous life by following God's commandments.

A man named Saul became king. At first, he was a sincere and humble ruler. Their downfall was caused by his actions, bringing destruction to himself and his family. King Saul expressed his fear of people. Remember to fear God, not people. The truth sets us free, not fear. Stand on the word of God.

Joshua faithfully followed God by observing His laws and commandments. That is why God used him to establish the nation of Israel.

Joshua 24:15: And if it seems evil unto you to serve the LORD, choose you this day whom ye will serve; whether the gods which your fathers served that were on the other side of the flood or the gods of the Amorites, in whose land ye dwell: but as for me and my house, we will serve the LORD.

APRIL 6

When King Jeroboam took charge of Israel, he corrupted the northern kingdom by altering the laws of the living God. Jeroboam became king and corrupted the people of God by changing the laws of God and teaching idol worship. False priests, teachers, and prophets can easily misguide and bring down nations and that is exactly what we see today.

The land of northern Israel was taken away by the Lord in 722 BC, and subsequently occupied by other ethnic groups. Disregarding the law will bring about your downfall. Have you made any changes to it, either by replacing or removing? Check how far you have gone from the LORD.

Don't forget, God is present when you need Him the most. When you receive blessings from God, remember Him on the mountain, even when your belly is full and your houses are beautiful, and your children have everything. Even if it's not required, make a commitment to live for God. Observe the law. Remember your adversary Satan has many plans to kill, steal, and destroy you. The devil showed the glory of the kingdom and said, "All this glory of the nations I give if you fall down and worship me." Jesus rejected all. Remember, the devil owns nothing. Don't let yourself be shaped by the world's expectations. It doesn't matter what you possess. No matter if you reside in a prosperous country, stay focused on Jesus. The devil is using marketing tactics to promote hell. The devil has a destructive plan to kill you, your family, and your nation.

King David saw a beautiful lady from the top and brought her in. When you reach height, pride will come. Satan's deceitful lies will try to lure you. He will say no one will know or see; how sad. God sees everything you do, at all times. David's evil deed led him to bring the sword into his house and face judgment. Remember, people who sin in secret do not know God.

Teach to observe.

Matthew 28:20 Teaching them to observe all things whatsoever I have commanded you: and, lo, I am with you always, even unto the end of the world. Amen.

As pastor-teachers, siblings, or spouses, you are under the control of an evil authority, yet you still maintain integrity. Remember, God's word does not change. Watch and abide by God's teachings. Do not be afraid of anyone but God. Don't make a fool out of yourself.

Mathew 23:3 All therefore whatsoever they bid you observe, that observe and do; but do not ye after their works: for they say, and do not.

The moment you take your eyes off God, your kingdom and prosperity cease to exist. When you shift your focus from God to humans, they take on the role of idols.

What happened to the United States of America? By removing prayer and Bible reading, the US started its decline in 1963. The country reached its peak and then was brought down by its rulers. Rulers removed the light, the truth, and the word of God. Departing from the truth has brought calamity as the nation declined. Always stay connected to God. Your victory, blessings, healing, prosperity, and protection are in the book called the Bible. To achieve success, ensure you teach the Word of God to your nation, family, and yourself.

Joshua 1:8 This book of the law shall not depart out of thy mouth; but thou shalt meditate therein day and night, that thou mayest observe to do according to all that is written therein: for then thou shalt make thy way prosperous, and then thou shalt have good success.

The fall of an individual, family, and nation starts by rejecting His commandments.

1 Samuel 2:27a And there came a man of God unto Eli, and said unto him, Thus saith the Lord, 29 Wherefore kick ye at my sacrifice and at mine offering, which I have commanded in my habitation; and honourest thy sons above me, to make yourselves fat with the chiefest of all the offerings of Israel my people? 30 Wherefore the Lord God of Israel saith, I said indeed that thy house, and the house of thy father, should walk before me forever: but now the Lord saith, Be it far from me; for them that honor me I will honor, and they that despise me shall be lightly esteemed. 31 Behold, the days come, that I will cut off thine arm, and the arm of thy father's house, that there shall not be an old man in thine house. 33 And the man of thine, whom I shall not cut off from mine altar, shall be to consume thine eyes, and to grieve thine heart: and all the increase of thine house shall die in the flower of their age. 36 And it shall come to pass, that every one that is left in thine house shall come and crouch to him for a piece of silver and a morsel of bread, and shall say, Put me, I pray thee, into one of the priests' offices, that I may eat a piece of bread.

Don't forget to abide by God's laws. Follow His commandments and precepts. May you, your family, and your nation be blessed.

I came to the USA with the sole intention of seeking His face, not for financial gain or education. I know the source of my help, health, protection, blessings, and prosperity with peace. It is from the Lord, the creator of heaven and earth.

Observe the laws of God or you are inviting a fall and calamities.

LET US PRAY

Lord, unite our hearts to observe your laws. Give us true prophets and teachers to teach the righteous laws of God. Keep our hearts from evil. Teach our hearts to hide the flaws and commandments of God in our hearts. Keep us from sins and temptation. All we need is your word to receive your blessings. Give us a hungry heart to learn to seek your kingdom and righteousness. Our blessing is in the book called the Bible by observing it. We thank you for giving us the Word of God in Jesus's name. Amen! God Bless you!

APRIL 7

HOW DOES THE KINGDOM WORK?

The intention of God, who is the King, is to establish His Kingdom on earth. Since the time of Adam and Eve, God has desired to rule over us in order to bless us. The righteous and Holy God will make the best head. He desires obedience to His command. The continuation is possible in any kingdom if you abide by the ruler. The ruler knows what and how He wants His Kingdom. God wants His Kingdom on earth as wonderful as it is in heaven. In your mind, how do you imagine heaven to be like? Imagine a world free from sickness, imprisonment, corruption, and bondage—a place of pure beauty and tranquility. Of course, no shooting, killing, or kidnapping. Yes, and He wants to provide the same security on Earth.

When people become disorderly or smarter than their heads, that creates a problem. Just think of your five-year- old children leading you. How do you feel about children taking on the role of parents? What is the problem if you become ruler instead of God, even if you say it's not allowed? Why not heed God's commands and listen to Him?

There is a definite way to bring the Kingdom of God onto the earth. First, He needs a worker who listens and obeys. Just like your home or company, or the country needs good workers. If no one follows the rules or regulations, then your prison and jail will be full of rebellion.

Raised as a prince, Moses developed a sense of obedience. He possessed the knowledge to serve as a military commander and chief. Moses had no difficulty obeying the command of the chief God for this reason.

Delivering the commandment to Moses is not a challenge for God. All laws, precepts, and statutes were given to Moses. Why did God choose to keep communicating with Moses? Since Moses listened and obeyed. If you listen and obey, God has the power to do the same. David obeyed God's command, but when he made a mistake, God corrected him through the prophet. Have you discovered David's response? Repentance! Repenting and facing the punishment from God. God granted forgiveness and remains connected with Him. This is something that pertains to everyone. If you want to continue your relationship, repent of all sins and reestablish a relationship with God.

Have you noticed discipline and indiscipline families? Those who are disciplined easily follow the rulers, while the undisciplined face challenges.

To correct children is a headache; it is a tough job. Parents raise well-behaved children through training. Keeping them under control is a challenging task. Raising children becomes challenging when parents are not in harmony. We are a bride of Christ. Let us have the mind of God. In order to avoid divorce, it's important to stay connected and obedient, as Jesus desires to stay united with His bride. Working together is advantageous for everyone.

Jeremiah 42:6 Whether it be good, or whether it be evil, we will obey the voice of the LORD our God, to whom we send thee; that it may be well with us when we obey the voice of the LORD our God.
When you choose to serve God, He will not let you wonder but keep you by His truth.

Acts 7:36 He brought them out, after that he had shewed wonders and signs in the land of Egypt, and in the Red sea, and in the wilderness forty years.

Do not wander away from the Lord; it will not be well for you and your children. Although the devil has a beautiful screen, there's a burning hell waiting behind it. Resist the devil's temptation.

Let the Lord lead you beside still water. He will anoint your head with oil and will give overflowing Joy. Keep yourself in His presence and be watched over by His Angels. He alone knows what is ahead as you do not. Despite my ignorance, I trust in divine protection as I walk. Even though the situation and financing conditions may not appear favorable, rest assured, He is a timely God. He performs miracles. He is preparing a table which you do not know. By believing in the King and accepting HIM as your ruler, the God Kingdom can manifest. The Lord desires for you to spread His Kingdom to the ends of the earth. He will go alongside you, using his power to perform mighty signs and wonders. Before you, He will march alongside His army of angels. Jesus won't send you alone. Trust me, I've experienced the slums of Bombay, places I never thought possible. I firmly believe that my God shielded me from all attacks, whether spiritual or physical. God performs supernatural acts. You need to trust and believe. Share the teachings of the Kingdom. Just as a successful company needs an intelligent manager, CEO, and skilled employee, so does our God.

Receiving training from the Lord is a must. Paul got training in Arabia, Moses retreated to the wilderness, and the LORD Jesus provided guidance to the disciple. Nowadays, the Holy Spirit desires to educate us. Listen to that small voice, do as it says. Do not see the circumstances. Your mind cannot comprehend like God's. Let Him think for you. God can use signs and wonders to spread the message of the Kingdom. People of the country will say we have never seen this.

Mark 2:12 And immediately he arose, took up the bed, and went forth before them all; insomuch that they were all amazed, and glorified God, saying, We never saw it on this fashion.

Be the one who believes and obeys. Do not tolerate those who obstruct the Kingdom and lack faith.

John 20:29 Jesus saith unto him, Thomas, because thou hast seen me, thou hast believed: blessed are they that have not seen, and yet have believed.

Saying "Lord, thy kingdom come on earth as it is in heaven" requires understanding its implications, not merely reciting the words. Let us Desire to be one who goes and works to bring the Kingdom of heaven down. Put your prayers into action instead of just praying.

Luke 10:1 After these things the Lord appointed other seventy also, and sent them two and two before his face into every city and place, whither he himself would come. 2 Therefore said he unto them, The harvest truly is great, but the laborers are few: pray ye, therefore, the Lord of the harvest, that he would send forth laborers into his harvest.

APRIL 7

Surrender with your will and life to the one you choose to be King of you.

Remember to seek the Kingdom of God and HIS righteousness first. To do this, you must have knowledge of the Old Testament and then continue with the New Testament. It is important to have knowledge of Jesus during this transition. The New Testament of Jesus is the Old Testament of Jehovah. In Jesus, the Spirit God from the Old Testament takes on human form. The baptism of the Holy Ghost is necessary for saints to be born again.

What is the reason for the existence of numerous churches, organizations, denominations, and non-denominations? Someone chose not to listen. Humanity is facing a challenge concerning its relationship with God. This problem is from the beginning. To save mankind, He paid the ultimate price, with His life contained in His blood.

Living in a free country is dangerous. We hope someone loves us enough to correct and discipline us. I've observed mothers and fathers going their separate ways. Children are on their own. It's extremely difficult to be in this jungle full of giants. Many are in prison, on drugs, dying with illnesses, or killing some. Whose actions are to blame for these losses? It's our fault. A great ruler makes a good kingdom. Wise rulers are responsible for maintaining peace. An effective leader pays attention to their superior. David, Jehoshaphat, Hezekiah, and Asa were obedient Kings since they followed the head. The head was Jehovah God. The Kingdom prospered not because they were wise but because they obeyed God. Obey the voice of God which is the Word of God.

LET US PRAY

Lord Jesus, grant us the ability to listen and the willingness to follow your commands. Your kingdom, my Lord, is what we desire to see on earth. We desire for you to serve as our Lord, Ruler, King, and God. We want the world to know that you are real. It is I who has to preach this kingdom. Lord, anoint me, Help me, so your kingdom comes. I am looking in the mirror; change me. I look at you in the mirror of God. Transform me. The weight of responsibility for your kingdom on earth rests solely on my shoulders. Make and model me to be your laborer. Thank you, love you in Jesus's name. Amen! God bless you!

APRIL 8

SEND THE WORD!

It is important for individuals to understand their authority and power through the teachings of God. In every era, God has provided us with distinct laws to follow. During the era of innocence, humans had no knowledge of sin. How nice! The knowledge of good and evil came from disobeying and eating the forbidden fruit.

Then God ruled by the laws and commandments, with prophets and kings.

The current time period is referred to as God's dispensation. The current era is unmatched in its power. The Holy Spirit is Jesus manifested as the Word, dwelling within us. The Holy Spirit has all the authority to do as you speak. Speaking in Jesus's name gives your word authority.

Only if you know what we can achieve and establish by believing and sending the Word of God work. Control of this world is on the tip of your tongue. Use your words to bring it to life. Send the word mixed with faith!

A man recognizes the word of command.

Luke 7:8 For I also am a man set under authority, having under me soldiers, and I say unto one, Go, and he goeth; and to another, Come, and he cometh; and to my servant, Do this, and he doeth it.

God's assurance is found in His Word. Learn to pray by claiming His Word. Pronounce His Word by believing in it. We can establish mighty works by sending His Word.

God's word is rain check, will never come back void.

Isaiah 55:11 So shall my word be that goeth forth out of my mouth: it shall not return unto me void, but it shall accomplish that which I please, and it shall prosper in the thing whereto I sent it.

With 5467 promises, a word becomes a sword, light, and nourishment. You can have all of them. Give life to your claims through your words. Look for the verses on healing. Start sending it to all the sick, and to the hospitals.

Psalm 107:20 He sent his word, healed them, and delivered them from their destructions.

Order the devil to leave your circumstances. Send the Word. According to the scriptures, if you remain silent, the rock will proclaim. Wow! I started praying, requesting that the Lord allow this stone idol to tell the truth. I was told about a Hindu man who prayed to idols for healing, and I heard his testimony. An idol spoke, I cannot heal, go to Jesus; he can heal you. I was grateful to God! I said, Yes, Lord, do it again and again and again.

Direct your attention to the incredible creation. According to the Bible, God's spoken Word brought creation into being.

Psalm 33:6 By the word of the LORD were the heavens made, and all the host of them by the breath of his mouth.

A great prophet of God, Samuel obeyed the voice of God. Two kings of Israel were also anointed by him. The prophet Samuel is highly praised in the Bible. God established what came out of the mouth of Samuel.

1 Samuel 3:16 And Samuel grew, and the LORD was with him and did let none of his words fall to the ground.

Why the Word of God?

Hebrews 4:12 For the word of God is quick, and powerful, and sharper than any two-edged sword, piercing even to the dividing asunder of soul and spirit, and of the joints and marrow, and is a discerner of the thoughts and intents of the heart.

Use the Word of God as a powerful tool to oppose the enemy's work. Experiment with sending the word and witness its creative power. Positive or negative words have power. Positive words have the power to create, while negative words have the power to destroy. I love the Word of God. When I pray, I use the Scriptures. I say I dwell in the secret place of the most high God. Elizabeth was healed 2000 years ago by His stripes. Jesus took stripes, so I am healed. I stand on His word for my success, healing, deliverance, protection, peace, provisions, comfort, or anything I need.

I deploy the Angels to ensure the safety of small children. I send the Holy Spirit to comfort the broken heart. Just like the centurion, send the word of God to fulfill your desires.

I Send the anointing over the city, state, county, and country by speaking the word. Through my words, I send the covering of blood over sinners. How lovely and easy it is, right? You have the power to build so much just by speaking. You don't have to leave your house.

I pray with words of God over the individual, overall prayer request. I've witnessed transformation, triumph, recovery, and powerful outcomes. Cover your children with prayers using the Word of God. Say that God has given me wise, godly truthful children. Speak the Word and pray for the future of the children. Your prayer will remain even after you're gone. My mom prayed all the time. I see the results of it. When people have no prayer life, I can tell they do not know the power in it. The children remain in the mouth of Satan because no one is sending them the word of deliverance. Do not be too busy. Remember to prioritize the safety and protection of your children and take your time doing so.

You have the ability to ask God to speed up the fulfillment of your desires and promises.

Ezekiel 12:28 Therefore say unto them, Thus saith the Lord God; There shall be none of my words be prolonged any more, but the word which I have spoken shall be done, saith the Lord God.

I request that you send the word. Choose the correct scripture that fits the situation. Study Word! Target person, city, and country, and send the word over to them.

While people are praying to a false God, send the word of God. Make idols speak for you by sending them words. By speaking with authority and believing, you can turn your words into prophecy.

The prophet's mouth carried the Godsend word, disclosing the location of His ministry. When Satan tempted Jesus on the mountain, He used the word. The devil used the Word of God in an attempt to tempt. Discover how to effectively use the right Word to confront the devil's deceit. A net has been created by the devil to catch us. At the time of temptation, your victory is in the word of God you speak. The power of words is known even by the devil. This is the reason why translations like NKJV, NIV, and others have altered the word. The devil knows the word is alive and powerful to destroy his plan and tactic. The devil has changed the word by removing truth, altering words, and adding and subtracting the word.

Satan is going to hell, but he wants you as well. Love your soul and love yourself. Use the true word of God. Say God has a plan for me to prosper. Angels have been stationed around me by God. I hide in His blood and wings. Lord is my shield and buckler. I prospered by walking in His plan, which is higher than mine. The enemy's weapons are ineffective against me, but they rebound back to him. The Lord is my Shepherd. I stand on His Word; I am highly favored, healed, and prospering as my soul prospers.

I always send the word of deliverance, truth, healing, and salvation in prison and jail. I send the word, visions, and dreams to palaces, government offices, the UN, Israel, and all Prime Ministers, presidents, and rulers of each nation. Send the Word of God and discover how it can bring about change in the situation. In Jesus's name, death will be transformed into life, sickness into healing, mourning into dancing, poverty into prosperity, darkness into light, and so much more.

LET US PRAY

Lord, your word holds an incredible hidden power. Teach us how and when to use the power of the word in the situation. We know you came against the devil by using the Word since Psalms 138:2 says thou hast magnified thy word above all thy name. The words we speak in faith can cure and heal. Send your worries and problems into the ocean, let them be washed away. We send the word as lightning to devour the enemy. We express gratitude for granting us permission to speak in Jesus's name. Amen! God bless you!

APRIL 9

INCLINE TO GOD!

The term "incline" refers to giving attention, heeding, listening, and paying attention. When God becomes your focus, life shifts into a different mode. Life without your attention to His voice is like a ship without a shipmaster. A sheep wandering aimlessly, without a shepherd, and children without any parents. To lead a successful life, you need someone to drive you in the right direction.

Without listening to the true God, Christian's life is in chaos. I wonder what happened to Christianity. Some wander away from the Lord. Walk-in guideline of the word of God. Turn to Him and pay attention. Things will fall in line if you do. Pay attention to God because He knows the way out, distinguishing right from wrong. He has the ability to protect you from evil and lead you away from trouble. If you incline your ear, a hopeful and bright future awaits. Aren't you tired of repeating the same mistakes, wandering without direction?

What is causing it to happen repeatedly? Because we do not incline our ears to the Lord. Pay attention to those who care about your well-being. God makes all things new every day if you surrender! Tilt your ear towards Him and understand the significance in your temporary life. A purpose to establish on earth. Take caution not to follow in the footsteps of Eve-Adam, King Solomon, and others who made a mess of their lives. Solomon, the wisest king, fell when he neglected to listen to God's voice. He found many outlandish women and started inclining his ear to them and bringing calamity to self and the kingdom. I am not talking about routine life; I am talking about hearing and deciding. David discovered his life's purpose by listening to his God.

Paul, a scholar who had a deep understanding of the Torah, turned into a killer as he followed his understanding of God. While traveling on the road to Damascus, God struck him and he came face-to-face with someone he thought he knew. Saul became Paul, a total transformation, and he started listening to Jesus. A man who thought to be right and found out he was wrong. I think you finally grasp my point.

Many times, you prioritize others over listening to God. I recently encountered a retired pastor couple. He knew what religion talks about. During the meeting, the prophet told him that he knows about God, but doesn't truly know God.

I once found myself in a similar situation. I started listening; I inclined my ear. My life story has undergone a transformation. What I considered to be correct ended up being incorrect. Be careful! Give full attention, listen attentively, and achieve prosperity.

Psalms 119:36 Incline my heart unto thy testimonies, and not to covetousness. 112: I have inclined mine heart to perform thy statutes always, even unto the end.

Do not believe anyone, since no one knows all about God. Without God's guidance, your journey will become more complex. Many afflictions, trials, tests, and situations are on a life journey. Incline your ear; God is in charge. Do not get stagnate, stuck, and confused. Study the life of Jesus by opening the Bible and following Him. Avoid obeying to the doctrine created by man or Satan. Churches and organizations all have their doctrine, and they'll encourage you to abide by it. Do not follow their confusion. Let me tell you, Open the Bible and study the life of Jesus. Follow Him and Him alone by taking His example. Incline your ear to hear the Holy Spirit; you will sail to your shore. You will be the sheep of His pastures. You will have a father.

Joshua 24:23: Now, therefore, put away, said he, the strange gods which are among you, and incline your heart unto the LORD God of Israel.

The priest and high priest, having lost their connection with God, became overly concerned with doctrine and ended up crucifying Him. Do not neglect the one who provides the laws, commandments, and precepts. You become nothing but dangerous to yourself, people, and God.

Learn to pay attention, open the Bible, and let the Spirit speak. Do you want the Spirit to strike you in the way, like Paul, Jonah, Like King Solomon, and many who refused to incline to God?

Man-made doctrines are the cause of confusion, not God. Truth is found through the spirit, not through the appointed man like the priest or high priest. Do not let anyone manipulate you. Do not let anyone confuse you, or do not let anyone say you have to believe and obey them. They can listen until they are receptive to God's voice, just like Moses, Aaron, and Joshua. Is it clear to you? Don't be fooled by someone's position or job title, it can be deceiving.

1 Kings 8:58 That he may incline our hearts unto him, to walk in all his ways, and to keep his commandments, and his statutes, and his judgments, which he commanded our fathers.

Psalms 78:1 Give ear, O my people, to my law: incline your ears to the words of my mouth.

King Solomon, an exceptional monarch, demonstrated his devotion to God by actively listening to Him. In the end, he missed out. So stay in tune with God till the end. Listen to God's voice and avoid getting caught up in denominational or non-denominational and organizational matters. Abide by the teachings of the Apostles and prophets, which were already established. You do not need to follow false prophets, teachers, pastors, evangelists, and apostles.

Nehemiah 13:26 Did not Solomon, king of Israel, sin by these things? Yet among many nations was there no king like him, who was beloved of his God, and God made him king over all Israel: nevertheless, even him did outlandish women cause to sin.

Is 55:3 Incline your ear, and come unto me: hear, and your soul shall live; and I will make an everlasting covenant with you, even the sure mercies of David.

I always say I am passing by on earth. I only incline my ear to God. He knows the way, and I don't. Can God misguide you? No, He will not. He will send the help of true prophets, teachers, or whatever is needed in your direction.

Jeremiah 7:24 But they hearkened not, nor inclined their ear, but walked in the counsels and the imagination of their evil heart, and went backward, not forward.

Jeremiah 17:23 But they obeyed not, neither inclined their ear, but made their neck stiff, that they might not hear, nor receive instruction Daniel and others like him are not afraid of standing alone. Deciding to listen is a personal choice. You will witness the result as expected.

Daniel 9:18 O my God, incline Thine ear, and hear; open thine eyes, and behold our desolations, and the city which is called by thy name: for we do not present our supplications before thee for our righteousnesses, but for thy great mercies.

Encourage your children to listen to God's voice. They will be blessed. Dive into His Word and gain knowledge. It's a guaranteed success.

Proverbs 4:20 My son, attend to my words; incline thine ear unto my sayings.

LET US PRAY

We are blessed by our Lord with attentive ears and devoted hearts to heed your instructions. Lord, put the blood of Jesus mingle with your spirit drops in our ears, eyes, nostrils, tongue, lips, and mouth. Let God attend to our prayer when we call on your name. Let His directive hand show us the way to salvation. Word of God, commandments, statutes of God is your voice, Lord. Give us an attentive ear. Your words should be taken more seriously than those of any individual, religious organization, or system of belief. We believe your word is the highest authority. We want to follow as it is written in Jesus's name. Amen! God bless you!

APRIL 10

REBUKE THE STOPPER AND BLOCKER!

Can you identify the stoppers and blockers? It is the Devil!

You might be curious about why your prayer remains unanswered. It's possible that you're curious as to why my life situation keeps repeating. What is the reason for no progress? Be aware that there exists a realm of Satan, his fallen angels, and demons, all conspiring against you, your prayers, and your promises.

In the Garden of Eden, the devil observed the beautiful and bright future of Adam and Eve. The devil started thinking about how and what to do to destroy God's plan. Satan believed his dark kingdom would be endangered if he didn't cease.

Satan knows humanity has limited eyesight and has never seen heaven. So the devil planned to make them do the opposite of what God wanted them to do. He has expertise in identifying the appropriate method and location for targeting. The truth is what he aims for. Satan believed that once he succeeded, he would obtain them for the kingdom of darkness.

They will become disconnected from God's almighty power. Well, he did it successfully. The same planning continues by the devil. His target is the almighty's instructions on what is acceptable and what is not.

You will wonder why when you pray and do not receive the answer. Keep doing as the bible says: knock, knock, knock, ask, ask, ask, and seek, seek, seek until you receive. In short, no matter how long it takes, continue what you are doing.

Why? The unseen world has not just God and Good Angels to minister to us but opposers Satan, fallen angels, and demons who block and stop what belongs to you.

While God gives promises, Satan tries to hinder them, just as he stole blessings from Adam and Eve. Stay on guard.

Revelation 12:12 Therefore rejoice, ye heavens, and ye that dwell in them. Woe to the inhabiters of the earth and the sea! for the devil is come down unto you, having great wrath, because he knoweth that he hath but a short time.

70 Disciples returned rejoicing and told Jesus; even the devils are subject unto us. Jesus disclosed that the devil is among us, ready to obstruct and deprive you of what you deserve. The power of the Holy Spirit will be hindered by the devil, preventing healing and deliverance. He will steal, kill and destroy the truth, which

APRIL 10

is the only weapon to free you. The devil will twist, add and subtract to the word of God as he did in the Garden of Eden.

Luke 10:18 And he said unto them, I beheld Satan as lightning fall from heaven.

Be vigilant and follow Jesus's example by praying, fasting, preaching, teaching, baptizing, casting out demons, and healing the sick.

During my visit to India a few years back, I recall… Evangelists from the USA visited India during that time. He organized a group of prayer warriors who would go to each city early in the morning and pray on street corners, specifically asking to bind and destroy their power in Jesus's name. In his meeting, much healing and deliverance took place. The evangelist knew how to eliminate the blocker and stopper devil. He brought defeat to the kingdom of darkness. Do not enter any territory without binding and destroying with fasting and prayer. Without doing so, winning is impossible.

Prior to my departure for mission work abroad, I make it a point to pray and fast. Not obeying will result in Satan's plan to destroy me. Whenever you go out, pray and tell the demon to leave, whether it's for work, shopping, or anywhere else. You may wonder why it keeps happening. It's an ongoing occurrence that goes against you.

Put on the armor of God and come against the assignment of the devil and his army. Command the devil to get out and break his army and agenda in the name of Jesus.

Satan withholds Angel, not to reach Daniel.

Daniel 10:13 But the prince of the kingdom of Persia (that is fallen Angel) withstood me one and twenty days: but, lo, Michael, one of the chief princes, came to help me; and I remained there with the kings of Persia.

Peter escaped from the plan of Satan.

Acts 12:5 Peter, therefore, was kept in prison: but prayer was made without ceasing the church unto God for him.

Peter was rescued by an angel from Satan's plot to kill him the next morning. The devil is a blocker and stopper. Peter, appointed by God to care for sheep, would've perished if not for prayer. Your prayer has the power to deliver not just you, but also children and even nations.

Keep in mind, this is more than just having faith - it involves warfare and prayer. The concept of simple faith originates from hell. People who are lazy have a tendency to have a doctrine of simple faith. Remember, faith without work is dead. Do as scripture and the Holy Spirit are asking you to do. Get violent and take it from Satan by force. Any doctrinal organization influenced by Satan would refuse to baptize you in Jesus's name and wouldn't allow you to receive the Holy Ghost. All activities that take place in churches, including post-church meals, tea parties, birthday celebrations, Christmas banquets, singing, running, and dancing, as well as elaborate hairstyles and fashionable clothing, are considered evil. After being born again, you enroll in the army of God, fast, pray, and get some spiritual muscles to fight against the enemy. What were Jesus's followers doing? Follow Jesus.

1 Peter 5:8 Be sober, be vigilant; because your adversary the devil, as a roaring lion, walketh about, seeking whom he may devour:

The devil, our enemy, wants to consume and engulf you. He rules in high places, organizations, churches, and high government posts. The devil seeks to influence all rulers.

Revelation 12:9 And the great dragon was cast out, that old serpent, called the devil, and Satan, which deceiveth the whole world: he was cast out into the earth, and his angels were cast out with him.

A tactic is used in a different nation, city, or same home. Lie and deceptions are his weapons of the enemy. He blocks your progress by introducing religions, customs, and cultures. Fit in the word of God, and get transformed.

I recall arriving home late from work and spending ninety minutes in prayer. One night, leaning on the couch, prying, I fell asleep. As I opened my eyes, I witnessed an overweight older man dressed in a suit walking. I got up and walked by shouting; he disappeared. He made me fall asleep. I am grateful that God woke me up to witness this.

The devil knows how to make you tired, hungry, sick, oppressed, possessed, and much more. He uses his weapons to stop you from praying, fasting, reading or teaching the Bible. He blocks the ministry.

Corinthians 15:32 If after the manner of men I have fought with beasts at Ephesus,

Timothy 4:7 I have fought a good fight, I have finished

Throughout my journey, I have remained faithful.

If the mother is wicked, the daughter will follow in her footsteps. One member passes away due to cancer, while the other becomes infected with the same deadly illness. As soon as one person consumed alcohol, all children were possessed by the same demon. Pray to God for protection from the devil. Anoint your surroundings with oil, including your clothes, and pray to break chains and bondages. By praying over clothes or pillows, I aim to bestow the anointing upon them and give them to individuals for their deliverance.

LET US PRAY

The Lord gives us the power of the Holy Ghost to fight against the adversary devil to defeat His agenda. Lord, give us the weapons of our warfare to the pulling down of strongholds of an enemy. We use the word of God as a sword to defeat Satan and his army. We pray for the blessing and freedom of our county, state, and city, and for protection against any hindrance to progress caused by Satan. Let your people wake up and pray to destroy the devil and his agenda in Jesus's name. Amen! God bless you!

APRIL 11

BLESSING OF GOD ADDS NO SORROW TO IT!

How beautiful! Let God be your source, resource, provisions, and what you desire. The blessing of God that makes us rich. The Lord has an act of multiplications and additions. God has the power to rebuke the devourer. God can rebuke anyone who tries to steal, kill, and destroy us. Jehovah God has an unbreakable hedge of protection that the devil cannot penetrate.

God's blessing carries the name brand; it is original and doesn't compare. God says nothing is impossible. The owner of the universe has power overall. He will promise to give us all if we choose to listen.
When King Josiah followed God's commandment, God gave him faithful people. He broke down all images and altars of other gods and goddesses. His action brought the blessings of God. Hilkiah, the priest, found a book given by Moses.

2 Chronicles 34:14b Hilkiah the priest found a book of the law of the Lord given by Moses.12a And the men did the work faithfully: 18 Then Shaphan the scribe told the king, saying, Hilkiah the priest hath given me a book. And Shaphan read it before the king. 19 And it came to pass when the king had heard the words of the law, that he rent his clothes. King Josiah repented of wrong practicing. The priest read the law from the Torah in the ear of all the people, and they changed their wrong actions. God also removed judgment from them. God made Josiah a king and gave no sorrow to him and his kingdom. Do the right to earn what you desire. Do not play a dirty game, get bribes, or kill to go higher. If you do not want curses attached to your life, then read the word and put it into action. Remember, there will be a day you will receive the summons or subpoena from God, and that is the end of you.

2 Chronicles 34:27 Because thine heart was tender, and thou didst humble thyself before God, when thou heardest his words against this place, and against the inhabitants thereof, and humbled thyself before me, and didst rend thy clothes and weep before me; I have even heard thee also, saith the Lord. 28 Behold, I will gather thee to thy fathers, and thou shalt be gathered to thy grave in peace, neither shall thine eyes see all the evil that I will bring upon this place, and upon the inhabitants of the same. So they got the king's word again.

God gave King Josiah peace, protection, and blessing during his reign.

I remember a police inspector having a position that did much damage to people. As I recall, the man did nothing but torment and misuse the power. All the money he collected was drunk by his children with alcoholism. In old age, his children were beating him up. He also buried many of his children and daughter-in-law! When he died, there were no tears but hatefulness toward him. Practicing the Christian religion has no power, but practicing God's laws, commandments, and precepts does.

Don't covet someone's wealth. Plan not to steal or take advantage of single, widowed orphans. Do not rob them. You will be cursed, and the end will be sad. When I see this kind of person, my heart goes to the children and grandchildren. I say, Lord, punish the unrighteous, but not to the children and grandchildren of a jealous man.

Proverbs 10:21 The lips of the righteous feed many: but fools die for want of wisdom.11 The mouth of a righteous man is a well of life: but violence covereth the mouth of the wicked.

The Word of God works as it says. There is nothing better than obeying the word.

Deuteronomy 8:18 But thou shalt remember the LORD thy God: for it is he that giveth thee power to get wealth, that he may establish his covenant which he sware unto thy fathers, as it is this day.

Living in 21 century, many try to compromise and adopt the ways of the World. We reap what we sow. I said we experience sorrow and still refuse to turn to God.

Do not believe in yourself; believe in God. I know some corrupted people have no fear of God. The judgment of God does not shake them. How sad; reading the Bible will bring more punishment if you do not obey.

Genesis 26:12 Then Isaac sowed in that land, and received in the same year a hundredfold: and the LORD blessed him. 13 And the man waxed great, and went forward, and grew until he became very great:

Wealth will not disappear when you get old if it is from God.

Genesis 24:1 And Abraham was old, and well stricken in age: and the LORD had blessed Abraham in all things.

When God gives, He will not take away. It is yours. The devil tried in Job's case. Job lost all. He knew it was from God, so he was fine with it. He said naked; I came, naked I will go.

Job 42:12 So the LORD blessed the latter end of Job more than his beginning: for he had fourteen thousand sheep, and six thousand camels, and a thousand yoke of oxen, and a thousand she asses.

Job 8:7 Though thy beginning was small, yet thy latter end should greatly increase.

In the New Testament, He showed the miracles of two fishes. Fish were multiplied and leftover. He showed the supernatural power to perform miracles. No wonder whose trust is in the Lord and not in someone's wealth to get rich will bless.

King Solomon got his riches from the Lord.

1 King 3:13 And I have also given thee that which thou hast not asked, both riches, and honor: so that there shall not be any among the kings like unto thee all thy days.

APRIL 11

Eccles 5:19 Every man also to whom God hath given riches and wealth, and hath given him the power to eat thereof, and to take his portion, and to rejoice in his labor; this is the gift of God.

Obtaining wealth in an unrighteous way brings with it sickness, disease, curses, and sorrow.

Proverb 23:4 labor not to be rich: cease from thine own wisdom. 5 Wilt thou set thine eyes upon that which is not? for riches certainly make themselves wings; they fly away as an eagle toward heaven.

Learn God knows how to transfer the wealth of the unrighteous to the righteous.

Proverb 13:22 A good man leaveth an inheritance to his children's children: and the wealth of the sinner is laid up for the just.

By believing in and obeying the Lord, you can receive all that you want and desire through His blessings.

Sadly, I witness many parents experiencing the pain of burying their children and grandchildren. How sad! Be careful! Many children are in prison and jail, on-street, and mentally ill. Why? The blessings of God were not passed down by the parents. Our main duty is to impart knowledge about God's laws, commandments, and ways. Your children will be able to enjoy the wealth and treasure bestowed upon them by God. A young man died and left wealth. He could not use it. Money and gold are sometimes buried with individuals in a casket. I can't find any reason for it. There are no blessings, only sorrow, in that kind of wealth. Let us be blessed with wealth that is accompanied by God's grace. To obey is to receive God's blessings.

LET US PRAY

May contentment be bestowed upon us in the name of Jesus, a great reward. Give us the power to be wealthy. Many received the blessing by doing as you asked them. We desire the same. Our wealth brings peace and provision for many. We can receive blessings if we care for the poor, orphans, and widows. We desire blessings of addition and multiplication with peace attached to our wealth. Thank you that our God is rich and knows how to bless us with His riches. Thank you, Lord; let the Lord bless with no sorrow attached in Jesus's name. Amen! God bless you!

APRIL 12

GOD PICKS THE LOWLY!

What is Lowly? Lowly meant humble or submissive. It is the opposite of pride, arrogance, and self-exaltation. God picks the meek because He has a mission and only needs a worker to complete it. He chooses the humble to follow His instructions. When you let God use you, He will exhilarate you as well. It is only to let others know that the working power behind laborers is God and not them. His wages are an abundance of blessings. Which will last for eternity. Depending on your profession as a doctor, lawyer, engineer, or teacher, your wages will vary.

1 Peter 5:6 Humble yourselves therefore under the mighty hand of God, that he may exalt you in due time.

Knowing their corrupt hearts, God requested the Israelites to eliminate the surrounding nations.

Numbers 33:35 But if ye will not drive out the inhabitants of the land from before you; then it shall come to pass, that those which ye let remain of them shall be pricks in your eyes, and thorns in your sides, and shall vex you in the land wherein ye dwell.

It was clear to God that the people of the land were both powerful and threatening. God said, wipe them out, or you will suffer the consequences. In order to follow God's instruction, it is necessary to have obedient individuals who are lowly. Don't try to reason with God, just listen. Did Israel obey God's commands?

Joshua 23:13 Know for a certainty that the LORD your God will no more drive out any of these nations from before you; but they shall be snares and traps unto you, and scourges in your sides, and thorns in your eyes, until ye perish from off this good land which the LORD your God hath given you.

Heaven is where God resides. Our needs are taken care of by Angels under His command. While God is sovereign, we are in need of help. We need direction; we need protection. God, in His mercy, gave all the information. Despite this, people refused to listen. Other nations will eventually capture and take them as captives. To receive blessings, we must practice humility and obedience. Only the humble and lowly are obedient and submissive. The humble do not prioritize themselves. Teach your children the importance of being submissive from a young age. Because babies are in their early stages of development, they can be trained. Training is necessary for all of us. How? Listen to God; He has the best interest in our welfare. Moses was the most humble man.

Numbers 12:3 (Now Moses was very meek, above all the men who were upon the face of the earth.)

APRIL 12

Moses, in his humble manner, permitted God to take charge. Avoid seeking loopholes through the exploration of religions. Allow God to be the one who leads you. Are you not fed up with the way you do things? I show my devotion to God by obeying His scriptures. You only need to heed God's words, and ignore everyone else. Mary, Esther, Paul, and many others were bold and humble, not afraid of death. Blessings come to those who read and submit to the Word of God in the Bible. God can and will use you if you obey. If not, seek out your religion and the sorrowful tale will never conclude.

Exodus 10:15 And the LORD gave the people favor in the sight of the Egyptians. Moreover, the man Moses was great in the land of Egypt, in the sight of Pharaoh's servants, and in the people's sight.

If you follow the Lord's commands and obey His voice, you will succeed. You'll experience His favor. The heart can be touched and transformed by God's power.

Practice humility and pay attention to God. All trouble, trials, sicknesses, and diseases because of our hard hearts and disobedience. Your enemy is the hard heart. Fall on the floor, cry out to God. Confess to the Lord. Lord, guide me as I acknowledge my failure to be humble. Look for someone who can be honest with you and won't just tell you what you want to hear. The first step is repentance. You will receive help from God.

Exodus 3:21 And I will give this people favor in the sight of the Egyptians: and it shall come to pass, that, when ye go, ye shall not go empty:

Submitting to the Lord God and His Word is all that matters, not to everyone else. In the same way as Daniel, he exemplified humility. Shadrach, Meshach, and Abed-Nego stood firm in their refusal to worship idols, dedicating themselves solely to God. Their actions were characterized by submission to God. Being humble doesn't mean you are a yes person. God is the highest authority, and you must know that.
If you obey God's words, He will take control. If you don't, your life will be chaotic, confused, and tumultuous.

C. S. Lewis "True humility is not thinking less of yourself; it is thinking of yourself less."

Andrew Murray "The only humility that is ours is not that which we try to show before God in prayer, but that which we carry with us in our daily conduct."

Jesus, being Lowly, played the role of a human. God manifested in the flesh to give an example and pay the price for our sins. How wonderful! Lowly will obey but not proud. God remained alive even though the flesh died.

Philippians 2:6 Who, being in the form of God, thought it not robbery to be equal with God:7 But made himself of no reputation, and took upon him the form of a servant, and was made in the likeness of men:8 And being found in fashion as a man, he humbled himself, and became obedient unto death, even the death of the cross.

The New Testament Jesus, also known as Jehovah Savior, is the same as the Old Testament Jehovah God. In a temporary role, Jehovah God became flesh as a lamb to shed blood. Blood has life, and Jesus gave His life through the blood for you and me. Can you explain how it happened? Lord Jesus humbled Himself and submitted.

One must be humble to fulfill God's plan. Since we are unaware of God's plan, it's best to simply trust. In Hebrews chapter 11, the faith chapter, we read about ordinary individuals who surrender to God's will. Anyone who submits and surrenders can be used by God. Humble in heart will do the will of God; our understanding stays silent.

No questions asked. Request strength through prayer, be receptive to hearing, and surrender. That's the only thing you need to do.

When Paul met the disciple of John the Baptist, He asked about the Holy Spirit. Since they had never heard, they further inquired about baptism. John the Baptist baptized them, but they had to be baptized again in the name of Jesus after His blood was shed. Why? They fell in two dispensations that had different approaches to sin remission. John Baptist's disciples did not argue over baptism. Proud will say if Jesus was baptized by John the Baptist, so did I, then why again? Humble people obey, not argue.

Acts 19:2 He said unto them, Have ye received the Holy Ghost since ye believed? And they said unto him, We have not so much as heard whether there be any Holy Ghost. 3 And he said unto them, Unto what then were ye baptized? And they said, Unto John's baptism. 4 Then said Paul, John verily baptized with the baptism of repentance, saying unto the people, that they should believe on him which should come after him, that is, on Christ Jesus. 5 When they heard this, they were baptized in the name of the Lord Jesus.

Lowliness is an attitude or quality of mind

[Acts 20:19 Serving the Lord with all humility of mind].

We recognize the importance of God and acknowledge our limited understanding as humans. A humble man acknowledges his limitations and relies on God's strength. Being humble leads to receiving blessings.

LET US PRAY

Lord, we are your creation. We need a creator to carry us on for our benefit. We have spiritual, physical, financial, and emotional needs. Please help us. Grant us a heart that is both wise and pure, so that we may recognize and follow you in all that we do. According to the Lord, our righteousness is comparable to filthy rags, so we ask for your guidance in obedience. We thank you, Jesus, for being merciful and kind. Let your mercy and grace never depart from us. God, you know the best. Please take over the reign of our life. Lead us beside still water, bless us and grant us your mercy and grace in Jesus's name. Amen! God Bless you!

APRIL 13

REPENTANCE IS A FOUNDATION!

The foundation is the first thing to dig before constructing the house. As long as the foundation is correctly established, the house will remain intact even when subjected to external or internal pressure. Remove every last bit of rubbish, debris, and trash before initiating the building process. The term "foundation" refers to the establishment or settlement of something. If your foundation is solid, deep, and wide, your house will be able to withstand anything.

A well-established foundation determines the beauty of one's life. The foundation of Life must be based on the Word of God. Your life will end in any storm without a solid foundation. You wouldn't be able to resist the tricks of the enemy. The devil is known for being deceitful in various ways. Wiles meant tricks, schemes, and craftiness to disconnect you from God to destroy you.

Ephesians 6:11 Put on the whole armor of God that ye may be able to stand against the wiles of the devil.

Eve fell victim to the devil's cunning wiles. The devil played on the lust of the flesh, lust of eyes, and pride of life.

That is why the bible says.

Colossians 3:5 Mortify therefore your members upon the earth; fornication, uncleanness, inordinate affection, evil concupiscence, and covetousness, which is idolatry: 8, But now ye also put off all these; anger, wrath, malice, blasphemy, filthy communication out of your mouth. 6 For which things 'sake the wrath of God cometh on the children of disobedience:

Baptizing in the name of Jesus is the second step to wash away sins. The Lord will give you the powerful gift of the Holy Spirit to start your new life. Through his false teachers and prophets, Satan utilizes the pulpit, TV, and radio to spread deceitful messages and discourage the expression of honest message. The Bible is an accurate guide for those seeking a fulfilling life. The Bible does not mislead, but instead provides guidance to those who are lost. Witness how the ancient prophets connected humanity with the Creator God.

John Baptist was restoring the damaged relationship caused in the garden of Eden. Baptizing them of repentance in water for the remission of sins built the bridge between God and us.

He said.

Mark 1:3 The voice of one crying in the wilderness, Prepare ye the way of the Lord, make his paths straight. 4 John did baptize in the wilderness and preached the baptism of repentance for the remission of sins.

Many sought out John the Baptist and experienced a complete life transformation.

Matthew 3:7 But when he saw many of the Pharisees and Sadducees come to his baptism, he said unto them, O generation of vipers, who hath warned you to flee from the wrath to come?

Repentance is the starting point for turning to the Lord. Without repentance, there is no connection with God. Sin has disconnected us from the Garden of Eden. Turn away from Satan's deceitful teachings, repent, and renounce sin. Repentance means to feel pain, sorrow, or regret for something done or spoken.
The first message of Jesus,

Matthew 4:17 From that time, Jesus began to preach, and to say, Repent: for the kingdom of heaven is at hand.

The first step is repentance. Repentance comes when you view yourself as the Lord does. Changing your life is the result of having conviction in your heart.

Twelve disciples went out and preached repentance.

Mark 6:12 And they went out and preached that men should repent. Jesus preached repentance after being resurrected.

Luke 24:47 And that repentance and remission of sins should be preached in his name among all nations, beginning at Jerusalem.

Repent and cleanse yourself by baptizing in the name of Jesus to wash away sin's impurity. Sin has a stein. Water baptism in Jesus' name has the power to cleanse dirty sins, spots, and scars. Satan consumes sin like food. If wiped out, Satan would refuse to come back.

Peter addressed the first message to Jews. It was said that Peter held the key to the kingdom of heaven.

Acts 2:38a Then Peter said unto them, Repent, and be baptized every one of you in the name of Jesus Christ for the remission of sins.

The early church had a foundation laid by the Apostles and Prophets. That is why the Lord was working through them with signs and wonders. Again, Satan started working in churches by putting his crew of false teachers and prophets on the pulpit. Jesus instructed us to follow him, not the misleading teachings of a building named after them.

2 Corinthians 11:14 And no marvel; for Satan himself is transformed into an angel of light.

The devil has a deep understanding of God's word. His disciples usually disguise themselves as the angel of light. The devil's strategy involves destroying the foundation to ensure the destruction of the house. You represent the House of God.

Psalms 11:3 If the foundations are destroyed, what can the righteous do?

APRIL 13

The Bible is strictly against sin. It short-circuits your relationship with God.

John 8:11b go, and sin no more.

Jesus told the man sin no more. Illnesses are caused by sin, so repent and abandon your sinful lifestyle.

John 5:14 Afterward Jesus findeth him in the temple, and said unto him, Behold, thou art made whole: sin no more, lest a worse thing come unto thee.

Roman 6:1 What shall we say then? Shall we continue in sin, that grace may abound? 2 God forbid. How shall we, that are dead to sin, live any longer therein?

Separate yourself from sin and those who engage in it.

Roman 6:6 Knowing this, that our old man is crucified with him, that the body of sin might be destroyed, that henceforth we should not serve sin.

Jesus is the sinless Rock. Jesus, the embodiment of Jehovah, is the rock foundation upon which we have built.

Isaiah 28:16 Therefore thus saith the Lord GOD, Behold, I lay in Zion for a foundation a stone, a tried stone, a precious cornerstone, a sure foundation: he that believeth shall not make haste.

Refrain from seeking out obvious messages labeled as simple faith. This is the battle over your soul. The devil is fighting to take it to hell. Seek truth to win. From 2006 to 2012, 30,000 churches closed down. Why? People are not interested in music, go to church sick, and come out sick. People burdened by emotional trauma with no hope of finding deliverance. Why bother attending a church that doesn't uphold truth in words or actions? No experience of the new birth. Study the Bible, search for the truth, and the truth will set you free. Don't be deceived by an adversary who makes false promises to misguide you.

Hear the Lord thy God:

Matthew 7:24 Therefore whosoever heareth these sayings of mine, and doeth them, I will liken him unto a wise man, which built his house upon a rock:

The foundation begins with repentance as its initial step. Repent of every sin, not just a few. Start afresh with Jesus, as if you were born again. May your new life bring you joy and fulfillment!

LET US PRAY

In the name of Jesus, Lord, grant us the spirit of repentance. According to the word, repentance is brought about by godly sorrow. We ask for forgiveness for our sins. We bow at your altar of mercy. Please forgive all our sins. We ask for forgiveness for sins that we have committed knowingly or unknowingly. Grant us a new life. Forgive all our and our ancestor's sins. Thank you for your blood. Purify us from our sins through your precious blood. Your blood speaks the righteousness of God. Thank you for forgiving our sins and healing us from all diseases, in Jesus's name. Amen! God bless you!

APRIL 14

SATAN'S VERSION BIBLE!

While the Bible is considered the written word of God, Satan introduces numerous false versions of it.

When I spoke to my brother, he mentioned that reading the King James Version of the Bible creates a connection with the Spirit of God. God spoke to me that the Word of the Bible is God and God is Word of the Bible. Through my involvement in translation and teaching, I have compared different versions of the Bible. I found out the devil has planted some tares in the Bible. It is not the Bible, but the Bible version of the devil. I am careful when I engage with the Bible. It is my light, lamp, food, sword, hammer, and the truth to set me free. The Word of God says not to add or subtract. So who can dare? If I follow the words, this is the story that defines my life.

It is my life, Manuel. I don't want to be deceived like the devil deceived Eve and Adam. I give heed to the Lord's words, for they can liberate the captive. The beautiful Word of God is to make my path successful. Let's examine the alterations made by the devil to the Word of God.

My interest and journey to find the truth started when I found out the missing verses while giving Bible study to a group of different languages. I noticed an error in the Bible readings when different individuals read from it. Unexpectedly, the KJV stood out as the precise translation from the original Hebrew and Greek. The KJV Bible translation in 1611 was done by Hebrew and Greek Scholar theologians. The translation of the 66 books of the Bible from early original scrolls is being carried out by a group of fifty-four distinguished scholars. It's no surprise that the Spirit of God communicates through reading the KJV Bible. Let me share some versions which can shatter the first commandment.

Deuteronomy 6:4 Hear, O Israel: The Lord our God is one Lord:

By altering just one word, Satan deceives you into believing in the existence of the trinity.

1 Timothy 3:16, "God was manifest in the flesh" (KJV)

The devil typically substitutes "he" for "God" in other versions. Who is "he" in this context? This can provide evidence for the belief in three gods. The first commandment of the Bible was transformed into three gods when the word God was removed. That leads to polytheism.

Satan's Verson's of the Bible reads: "He appeared in a body" (Many Bibles translated from the corrupted manuscript of Alexandrian have this lie. Roman Catholic Vulgate, Gujarati Bible, the NIV Bible, Spanish, NKJV, and other modern versions of the Bible.

APRIL 14

{ΘC=God} in Greek language but by removing the little line from ΘC, "God" changes {OC = "who" or "he"} to who, which has a different meaning in the Greek language. The distinction lies in the fact that 'he ' can be anyone, whereas 'God 'specifically refers to Jesus Christ incarnate.

Modifications aimed at challenging the One God Doctrine. Satan has changed or removed Scripture about ONE GOD.

1 John 5:7 eliminated. This verse proves that there is but one God. Do not expect there are three in heaven. By removing this verse, you will never find the truth.

1 John 5:7 KJV For there are three that bear record in heaven, the Father, the word, and the Holy Ghost: and these three are one.

Revelation 1:8 KJV: I am Alpha and Omega, the beginning and the ending, saith the Lord, which is, and which was, and which is to come, the Almighty

NIV translation: Revelation 1:8 "I am the Alpha and the Omega," says the Lord God, "who is, and who was, and who is to come, the Almighty."

(Gujarati Bible, NIV, NKJV, and other translations have removed "Beginning and the ending")

Revelation 1:11 KJV: Saying, I am Alpha and Omega, the first and the last: and, What thou seest, write in a book, and send it unto the seven churches which are in Asia; unto Ephesus, and Smyrna, and unto Pergamos, and unto Thyatira, and unto Sardis, and unto Philadelphia, and unto Laodicea

NIV: Revelation 1:11 "Write on a scroll what you see and send it to the seven churches: to Ephesus, Smyrna, Pergamum, Thyatira, Sardis, Philadelphia, and Laodicea."

(Modern versions of the Bible, Gujarati, NIV Bible, and all other versions have removed "I am Alpha and Omega, the first and the last") I couldn't provide evidence for the existence of 'One God 'while teaching from their Bible.

My teaching was taking along. To my great disappointment, using the devil's version of the Bible, I couldn't prove that there is One God. This has motivated me to study extensively.

Acts 20:29 I remember Paul said: For I know this, that after my departing shall grievous wolves enter in among you, not sparing the flock.

I would like to share the fact by searching for the truth of the corrupted 'Word of God. 'The Alexandrian manuscript was a corrupted version of the original true manuscript of the Bible. They removed many words like Sodomite, hell, and blood, created by Jesus Christ, Lord Jesus, Christ, Alleluia, and Jehovah, along with many other words and verses from the original manuscript.

In Alexandria, Egypt, scribes were the antichrist. They did not have a revelation of the one true God. That is why the Bible changed from the original manuscript to their version of belief. Corruption originated in the first century.

At first, Greek and Hebrew Bibles were written on Papyrus scrolls, which were perishable. So they would handwrite 50 copies in different countries every 200 years to preserve them for another 200 years. Our forefathers, who had an accurate copy of the original manuscript, practiced this. The Alexandrians applied the same method to protect the corrupted manuscript.

This corruption started when Paul and John were still alive. The Alexandrians ignored the word of God. In the Nicaea conference in the year of 325 AD, they established the doctrine of the Trinity. Many of the attendees at this conference were previously polytheistic heathens. Nicaea is a modern-day Turkey, known as Pergamum in the Bible, where Satan's seat is.

Revelation 2:12-13 And to the angel of the church in Pergamum write; These things saith he which hath the sharp sword with two edges; I know thy works, and where thou dwellest, even where Satan's seat is: Nicaea (is the same as Pergamum or Pergamon or Pergamos in the Bible)

Satan removed the Oneness of God and added the trinity in 325 AD at the council of Nicaea. Instead of accepting the revelation of Jesus through His Spirit, they want you to join their organized lie known as churches. One God has been divided into three by false prophets and teachers of Satan. They removed the name "Jesus" from the baptism formula by adding the Father, Son, and Holy Ghost.

John 10:10 The thief cometh not, but for to steal, and to kill, and to destroy: I have come that they might have life and that they might have it more abundantly.

Pergamum (later called Nicaea and now called Turkey) is a city built 1000 'above sea level. This place is home to the worship of four distinct gods. Asclepius, the main deity, had a serpent as his symbol.

Revelation says: 12:9 And the great dragon was cast out, that old serpent, called the devil, and Satan, which deceiveth the whole world: he was cast out into the earth, and his angels were cast out with him.

Revelation 20:2 And he laid hold on the dragon, that old serpent, which is the devil, and Satan, and bound him a thousand years,

Within this temple, there were countless massive snakes. Moreover, these areas were surrounded by thousands of snakes. The Pergamum temple attracted people who sought healing. Asclepius was known as the chief god among the four gods, and he was worshipped as the god of healing. In this location, he was known as the deity of healing. He introduced a variety of herbs and medicines to help with the healing process. Asclepius intends to eliminate the stripes and Jesus' name in order to facilitate healing. His plan is to replace Jesus and eliminate Christ as the Savior. Asclepius also professed himself to be a savior. The serpent symbol used in modern medical science was derived from Asclepius.

So be careful of the Bible version you read. May Lord Bless you with truth and truth only. In my book "I did it His Way," I provide detailed information on this subject. The book is available in audiobook, ebook, and paperback formats, and is translated into several languages. Allow the truth to be your guide to freedom.

LET US PRAY

Lord, in your glorious name, give us a revelation of your word. Give us revelation of who Jesus is.

We are aware that Satan seeks to seize your seat. He intends to sow confusion, but God, you are not a supporter of confusion. Lord, give us your revelation. Let your Spirit of Truth teach, lead, and guide. Lord, your word is true and has the power to deliver, heal, and set the captive free, so give us the truth and nothing but the truth. We have faith in the concept of One God, who revealed Himself in the physical body of Jesus Christ for our salvation. We thank you for the Bible, our life manual. Teach us, Lord, in Jesus's name. Amen! God bless you!

APRIL 15

CHANGE YOUR LIFE STORY!

Many of us long to be someone else instead of being ourselves. They desire to become a different person. Yes, you can. The life story of an alcoholic can be transformed. A murderer can rewrite their life story. Regardless of your background as a slave, poor, druggy, adulterer, or liar, your life story has the potential to be rewritten through the faith element. It needs the courage to let yourself, your idea, situation, disability, surroundings, and feelings go.

When God directs your life, He will rewrite your story. There was a time when I was **murderer**, but now I am saved. Once I was a fisherman but now an apostle. I used to lie, but now I serve truthfully. Once a tax collector, I am now a devoted disciple of God. By being baptized in the name of Jesus and serving the kingdom, I am cleansed by His blood. Paul claimed I was a **murderer**, but God rewrote my life's narrative. I spoke in favor of what I was previously against. A prostitute found redemption in God and transformed her wicked lifestyle. The kingdom now considers her its most valuable asset. Life takes a complete turnaround when God's superpower strikes. This is the Lord's doing. We have been granted the power by God to accomplish what the average person cannot. You possess the power to fix what is impossible for humans to fix. A surprise, surprise!

Luke 7:39 Now when the Pharisee which had bidden him saw it, he spake within himself, saying, This man, if he were a prophet, would have known who and what manner of woman this is that toucheth him: for she is a sinner.

Jesus was making it clear to the Pharisees that her life story was about to take a dramatic turn.

Luke 7:47 Wherefore I say unto thee, Her sins, which are many, are forgiven; for she loved much: but to whom little is forgiven, the same loveth little. 48 And he said unto her, Thy sins are forgiven. 50 And he said to the woman, Thy faith hath saved thee; go in peace.

The life story of an adulteress woman or a prostitute was transformed at that moment. She was profitable to the kingdom of God from there.

Matthew 17:15 Lord, have mercy on my son: for he is lunatick, and sore vexed: for ofttimes he falleth into the fire, and oft into the water. 18 And Jesus rebuked the devil, and he departed out of him: and the child was cured from that very hour.

APRIL 15

A lunatic was freed from the devil and was cured. When you meet the Lord, a new chapter in your life begins. Instead of relying on the church, doctor, or other resources, what you truly need is the Lord. Encounter Jesus and experience a life transformation.

A blind person meets the light of this world and receives light in their eyes. When the blind regain their vision, their entire world is transformed.

John 9:1 And as Jesus passed by, he saw a man which was blind from his birth. 6 When he had thus spoken, he spat on the ground, and made clay of the spittle, and he anointed the eyes of the blind man with the clay, 7 And said unto him, Go, wash in the pool of Siloam, (which is by interpretation, Sent.) He went his way, therefore, and washed and came seeing.

Blind followed Jesus' instructions precisely. Obedience unlocks the door to receiving promises. Do not say why, what, when, and how. Take action and do it. It demands intense action, but the outcome justifies it.

The multiplication of blessings is linked to the act of giving. Who and where do you consider important? If it is given to the prophets and laborers of the Lord, you will have an unlimited blessing. Multiplication will be attached to your giving. You can become a billionaire, so you feed many.

John 6:9 There is a lad here, which hath five barley loaves, and two small fishes:

It fed almost five thousand. Your life story of starvation, hungr, and wanting to be filled and leftover. The story changes when you invest in the kingdom.

John 6:13 Therefore, they gathered them together and filled twelve baskets with the fragments of the five barley loaves, which remained over and above them that had eaten.

Obedience is essential for transforming your life. Lord said He would change your branch; trust and do as He asked, and your story will be rewritten.

Those afflicted with leprosy are required to keep their distance from others and reside in designated areas. People might not be touched by them. The story of this man's life is incredibly sorrowful and the worst. A nightmare!

Luke 17:1 And as he entered into a particular village, there met him ten men that were lepers, which stood afar off: 3 And they lifted up their voices, and said, Jesus, Master, have mercy on us. 14 And when he saw them, he said unto them, Go shew yourselves unto the priests. And it came to pass that, as they went, they were cleansed. 15 And one of them, when he saw that he was healed, turned back, and with a loud voice glorified God, 16 And fell down on his face at his feet, giving him thanks: and he was a Samaritan. 17 And Jesus answering said, Were there not ten cleansed? But where are the nine?

It completely changed the life stories of everyone in the group of ten. However, a particularly notable miracle took place when expressing gratitude to Jesus. He experienced benefits from receiving wholeness. His life story changed beyond what he expected. His body, soul, and spirit became complete and perfect. In just a moment, he found himself bestowed with the world's most exceptional blessing of total wholeness.

I remembered, at work; I was witnessing this alcoholic man. Once, during a drive over the freeway in Los Angeles. Gazing downwards, he revealed to me, Sister Elizabeth, I had visited all these churches in Los

Angeles. He mentioned that there has been no progress up until now. My life is still a mess, despite my drug and alcohol use. I told him, but if you uphold the truth of the Lord, you'll experience the transformation. Afterward, he received a baptism in the name of Jesus and was entirely freed from drugs, alcohol, and any complications. He married his girlfriend and became a preacher.

The moment he met Jesus, the truth set him free. You do not need false doctrine. Since then, his life story has been extraordinary.

No one remains unchanged after encountering Jesus. Everyone has undergone transformation, healing, deliverance, and change. Your life story depends on your obedience to the Word of God. Attending the church, enrolling in an organization, or changing religion will never change your life story. But the day you meet the Lord, He will place you in his book as a free man, delivered, and set free. One was lame, now walking, was poor, now rich, and much much more. You must encounter the creator and giver of everything you want. It's marvelous! Many pastors, church attendees, preachers, bishops, theologians, and scholars need to meet Jesus. Their life report will transform and inspire others through their testimony. Surrender and follow Jesus. Your life story is about to be transformed.

LET US PRAY

In the name of Jesus, we need a divine encounter with the Lord. I know life has many trials and troubles, but if I find the key to open the wealth, healing, direction, and all that I need, my life story can also be changed. If I listen and obey God's voice, He will take action. So Lord, help me, encourage me to stand boldly to change my story. I long for a fresh start in life. It is you, Lord; I have to come in contact with. Lord, empower me to reach the level where I can receive divine healing, deliverance, and salvation. I desire my life story to be changed in Jesus's name. Amen! God bless you!

APRIL 16

SYSTEM OF THE KINGDOM!

The Kingdom of Heaven has a system to rule on earth. This is the distinct method that God follows to carry out work on earth. Our abilities are insufficient, but God's design empowers us. Every church organization operates with its systems. Governments across nations, states, counties, and cities have come up with their operational plans. Success is achieved when both the system and the ruler are exceptional. If both your system and its workforce are corrupt, it will result in failure and catastrophic consequences.

God has a plan in place that He must follow for His Kingdom. God's command is clear: one must be born again to serve him. The initial step involves being born again, which means being born from above. In the word Born again, Again means anōthen, meaning from above. So the first step is to be born from above. Jesus said to Nicodemus, a teacher of the Jew, that you could only enter the Kingdom of God if you are born from above. Jesus explained to Nicodemus that being born again involves being born of water and the spirit.

Peter, whom the Lord gave a key to open the Kingdom,

Said Acts 2:38, Then Peter said unto them, Repent, and baptized (born of water.) Every one of you, in the name of Jesus Christ, for the remission of sins, and ye shall receive the gift of the Holy Ghost. (born of the spirit.)

By following Jesus 'teachings like Peter and the other disciples did, you can be born again in God's kingdom. If you maintain a life of prayer, fasting, and righteousness, you can heal the sick and expel demons.

Furthermore, God has assured us of nine gifts from the spirit. God's spirit will perform a one-of-a-kind work through you. You are simply a container for oil, or flour, or rice. The vessel is a container to store.

Your body becomes a container or vessel for all or some of the nine spiritual gifts. You are just a container or vessel to store God's spirit. Your body, where the Spirit of God lives, performs accordingly.

It is stated in the Bible that you can covet these gifts.

1 Corinthians 12:31 But covet earnestly the best gifts:

These nine gifts are the word of knowledge, wisdom, faith, miracle, healing, discerning the spirit, prophecy, tongue, and interpretation of the tongue. Anyone possessing any of these nine gifts can utilize them for the special office. If you possess these gifts, you can both work for the Kingdom and glorify God. The gift from God was specifically meant for you, the born-again church. The utilization of spiritual gifts will lead people to have faith in and turn to the One true God, who is their creator and father. Numerous individuals falsely claim to possess gifts they do not have. Seek the person who possesses the spiritual gifts to comprehend the distinction.

Only God empowered us to do the mighty great supernatural operation of the Gifts of the Spirit. Remember, it is the Spirit of God that works, not the individual. We cannot; Lord Jesus's Spirit in individuals will do supernatural only if they have the gifts which are called charisma.

The system of Satan's kingdom is identical. The Devil has granted some people with special abilities. Satan has trained warlocks, magicians, wizards, soothsayers, palm readers, or astrologers to bewitch. Not everyone is a magician, wizard, warlock, or psychic. God operates under the same system if the Spirit of God is active.

Avoid attending every church. Make sure they are born again according to the teaching of the Book of Acts and continue the acts with the Spirit of God. You must be receiving training for the army of God. Must-haves include prayer, fasting, and the teaching of the word.

This subject has been the source of confusion due to false doctrine. If you need rice, do you open any containers? Common sense says no. You only open the one which is filled with rice. When you need the word for direction, find the one with the gift of the prophecy.

Word of Knowledge and Word of Wisdom work together. This gift from the Spirit of God gives information about the name, birthdate, address, and problems with a solution. If you need a miracle, go to one who has this gift from God.

I had a spine problem; I looked for a person with the gifts of miracles and healing. For gas, we go to the gas station; for money, we go to the bank; for groceries, we go to the market. I search for the prophet who is not defined by their thoughts or emotions. Not everyone who claims to have gifts is believable, except for the ones who can demonstrate it. Instead of water, they could potentially give me poison. Make sure you go to the one who has gifts of Spirit from Jesus Christ.

The Bible says, Only 12, then 70, received the power;

Luke 9:1 Then he called his twelve disciples together, and gave them power and authority over all devils, and to cure diseases.

Luke 10:1a After these things, the Lord appointed other seventy also.

Not everyone's shadow can work, but the one who has an anointing of the spirit. Instead of going to anyone who believes they can, seek out those who have the Spiritual gifts. God gives the gift of spirit to whom He calls and if they desire.

Have they deceived many into going to churches? Do they refuse to permit the utilization of the gifts of the spirit? Many argue over receiving the Holy Ghost exactly the way the Bible says.

Hosea 4:6a, My people, are destroyed for lack of knowledge: because thou hast rejected knowledge, I will also reject thee,

Job 36:12 But if they obey not, they shall perish by the sword, and they shall die without knowledge.

APRIL 16

Proverbs 5:23 He shall die without instruction, and in the greatness of his folly, he shall go astray.

Don't let the title deceive you. Many antichrists are working in the World. Always watch for their fruits, work, and spiritual gifts in operation. If not, then get out of there. Never look at the operation of gifts in the box of organizations, denominations, and churches. Since God has not established organization, denominations of churches are not looking for the gift of the Spirit. He gave those who covet the Spiritual gifts to edify the Kingdom. Gifts will prove that God is doing miracles, healing, prophecy, etc.

Acts 19:11-12 And God wrought special miracles by the hands of Paul: So that from his body were brought unto the sick handkerchiefs or aprons, and the diseases departed from them, and the evil spirits went out of them.

God performed a miracle, utilizing Paul's calling as a preacher of the Gospel.

To address heart, eye, blood, or bone issues, seek out a doctor who specializes in these areas. You do not go to art college to be a doctor; you go to a medical college to be a doctor. The antichrist, false teachers, and prophets misguide people. I go to the one who operates by the Spirit of God.

I have been baptized and filled with the Holy Spirit, speaking in tongues as a sign of my new birth. God has given me some gifts of the spirit, like healing, prophecy, faith, tongue, interpretation of tongue, and discerning the spirit. These offices are suitable for me, or we can say I am ready to be used by God in this faculty. Many people reach out to me for help with healing and deliverance from demonic oppression. When I pray for them, they get healed and set free.

Request that God utilize you as a laborer for His Kingdom. Initially, he had 12 disciples, then he added 70 more, and finally increased the group to 120. He did not fill the whole of Jerusalem with the Holy Spirit, but 120 and whosoever coveted.

To sum up, the Kingdom System follows a specific structure.

If you follow the instructions written in the Bible, you won't make any mistakes.

LET US PRAY

In the name of Jesus, Lord, we need the knowledge of your Kingdom. Do not let us deceive the wolf who has transformed to be the Angel of Light. Protect us from antichrist teachers and prophets. Lead us to the genuine prophets, teachers, and the one who has the Gifts of spirits. We thank you for giving uncommon gifts to the spirit to edify One Church. We covet these gifts of the spirit to glorify your magnificent name and Kingdom in Jesus's name. Amen! God bless you!

APRIL 17

TRUTH VERSUS FALSE!

Jesus versus Devil! Jesus does not view the devil as a a competitor.

Jesus is the supreme party, not the devil. In many games, we see the two opposite players playing the game and trying to block one another, or one is stopping to get the point. Same way, in the life game, one is trying to do right, and another is enticing them to do wrong.

Paul wrote the letter to Rome.

Roman 7:21 I find then a law, that, when I would do good, evil is present with me.23 But I see another law in my members, warring against the law of my mind, and bringing me into captivity to the law of sin which is in my members.

Understand the conflict that exists within us. Two conflicting ideas are at play within us, each favoring a different foreign leader. The ultimate winner will be the champion, regardless of the heavenly or hellish trophy you obtain or the team you play for.

Satan has a trophy in hell for the heads of Jesus, Paul, Peter, and many others. Hundred percent dedicated to the party, don't care for the life or head. Losing life is gaining life.

Paul said in Philippians 1:21 For to me to live is Christ, and to die is gain.

When you firmly believe in the truth, life and death become insignificant. It is all about the one you serve until death. The mindset of Christ is all that matters, so it doesn't make a difference. Having a determined mindset is crucial for achieving success in the role you are playing.

Galatians 2:20 I am crucified with Christ: nevertheless, I live; yet not I, but Christ liveth in me: and the life which I now live in the flesh I live by the faith of the Son of God, who loved me and gave himself for me.

Paul says that once you enroll for the party, keep faith in Jesus. Many workers of Satan have the same mindset to play for the devil. Complete dedication is what matters, regardless of the outcome. Those who work for the devil on earth are offered enticing rewards. These bad, unrighteous people will be the subject of many complaints and scrutiny.

Do Christians question why we experience so many troubles?

APRIL 17

Well! Are you working against the Devil or Jesus? Choosing is yours? Having a thinking correction would be helpful. Your thought process requires assistance.

The devil plays with your mind, while Jesus touches your heart. Your heart is where the truth begins. The game of the mind deceives the flesh, and it's false. The Master and father of the lie is Satan. The deceiver will find every tactic, scheme, and game to defeat the opponent.

His accomplishments, including victories, medals, and trophies, are only temporary and won't have lasting value. The devil's soul-winning game is worthless. We are promised eternal assurance and a priceless crown through Jesus. Just be faithful until the game finishes. The devil doesn't possess anything, but he tempts with forbidden things just like he did to Eve. The glory of this world belongs to Jesus. He shows different things and plays on the lust of the mind, the lust of the flesh, and the pride of life. He wants you to sacrifice your talent, money, and strength. Jesus doesn't enroll the skilled ones, but He qualifies them to whom He calls. Choose the right party to play. Think of your life as a game. The party you choose is the one you will serve for eternity. In the end, hell or heaven is the place you go to.

There was a war game going on between the Philistines and the Israelites. Philistines had a giant on their side. The Israelites were frightened by the sight of giant. God hid the truth from the Israelites because of the wrong leader. But David had the fact and played for the Israelites. It does not matter how strong, tall or skilled. Once you are playing on behalf of truth, you will win.

1 Samuel 17:45 Then said David to the Philistine, Thou comest to me with a sword, and with a spear, and with a shield: but I come to thee in the name of the LORD of hosts, the God of the armies of Israel, whom thou hast defied. 49 And David put his hand in his bag, and took thence a stone, and slang it, and smote the Philistine in his forehead, that the stone sunk into his forehead; and he fell upon his face to the earth.

David played for the party where the truth prevailed. It's worth playing a game on the right side. The devil's big mouth and false promises aim to destroy you in a burning hell. He has no protection or victory. When you work for Jesus, you work for truth; when you work for the devil, you work for lies. Working for Jesus guarantees a beautiful heaven, while working for the devil leads to an intensely painful and terrifying place.

Make a wise decision about which side to choose. The player has to be confident about the one they are playing for. Confidence in the devil is shared by many. The devil offers gold, fame, money, position, and power, which ends as you leave the earth.

Jesus' promises are not tangible but can become tangible if you have faith. As you go, Jesus accompanies you to fulfill His role. He never leaves you or forsakes you. He is there to protect you. You believe in His truth.

2 Chronicles 32:8a with him is an arm of flesh; but with us is the LORD our God to help us, and to fight our battles.

Jesus trains as we play in war. The devil instructs us to get killed and destroyed.

2 Samuel 22:35 He teacheth my hands to war; so that a bow of steel is broken by mine arms.

David played on the truth of God, and He won the Kingship of Israel. You can also do your best if you allow Jesus. War will be a victory if you are playing on the right side.

Psalms 144:1 A Psalm of David. Blessed be the LORD my strength, which teacheth my hands to war, and my fingers to fight:

Select the winning side and truth will triumph over falsehood. The devil, who will burn in hell forever, is the source of falsehood. The destiny of Satan is set. Lake of fire is created by God for the devil and his angels. The devil plays on lies and deception. The devil offers promises that are not true. Nothing works. His party suffers violence, darkness, fear, worry, sickness, oppression, possession, and hunger, but he promises the big crown.

In a close game, it may seem like truth is losing, but don't forget that falsehood will ultimately fail if you maintain your faith. Play with all your heart, trusting God. The end will be a war to victory, beauty for ashes, peace, calm assurance, and much much more.

Daniel played for truth. The game ended with a great surprise.

Daniel 6:2 And over these three presidents; of whom Daniel was first: that the princes might give accounts unto them, and the king should have no damage.

Play the role of the truth side. You will be the top, first, and above. It will favor you overall.

Real life games exist. Don't ever believe that the party of falsehood is prevailing. Standing with truth leads to a path of success. The truth will ultimately succeed.

Proverb 12:19 The lip of truth shall be established forever: a lying tongue is but for a moment.

Choosing the party is choosing the destination. So be wise. Choose the truth and not the false. In the false party, the devil is the leader. Select the game with Jesus as the leader, and you will be the winner.

LET US PRAY

Lord, we thank you; you are true, and your promises are true. We ask you to give us your wisdom to choose what is genuine and not what looks right. We walk by faith and not by sight. The site may look horrible. We see lions, fire, and death at hand, but if we choose and play the role of the party called truth, whose leader is Jesus, we will end up winning. No matter what, we will have victory. We will receive the crown of righteousness. We will be the top, head, above, and highly favored in Jesus' name. Amen! God bless you!

APRIL 18

TAKE THE LAMP AND LIGHT!

The Bible says in Psalm 119:105 Thy word is a lamp unto my feet and a light unto my path.130 The entrance of thy words giveth light; it giveth understanding unto the simple.

Darkness is the absence of light. We become light in the dark world when we follow God and obey His Word. When there is no light, we need to have some. In the darkness of night, you can't predict what obstacles you may encounter. The Lady lived in the same house for years, tried to get up to go in the dark, stumbled, and broke her hip. Despite her years in the house, the absence of light left her perplexed. Similarly, if you allow the Word of God in your life, you will not stumble into a trap or obstacle of Satan. The ditch of the devil is to destroy you. Once you fall into it, you cannot come out.

This is when we must acknowledge the presence of darkness. Once you live in darkness long enough, it becomes custom. Do not let it become custom. Look for the lamp and light since the Bible is still available. The elderly couple witnessed us having nonstop Bible reading. There was a time for Bible reading for 24 hours or until they completed the Bible. She said she used to, which meant it was no more. Churches have ceased reading the Bible because they have been bewitched. What happened? When they were asleep, the devil took the word out. People find such comfort in darkness that they actually enjoy living in it.

I was advised by a pastor to begin the church. To obtain a permit, one must complete reading the Bible once. It shocked me. I prefer a pastor who has a deeper understanding of the Bible than just reading it once. Satan, fallen angels, and demons are present in the natural world. They love ignorant preachers and teachers on the pulpit. Without the Word of God as my light and lamp, I risk stumbling, falling, and perishing. Do you want blind leaders? I do not.

See what happens when you attempt to drive in darkness.

I recall reading about a real event that took place in a different country. People rely on the open Bible to let light pass through. Now, who limits this unlimited God? Who interprets this God according to their own level of perception? You disallow God to shine through in the family. We see the darkness brings divorces, drugs, alcohol, suicide, killing, and so on. Without the Word of God, there is no Light! The Light represents our divine God. Throughout their lifetime, people acquire 85% of their knowledge through learning. Properly chosen words can bring light.

Isaiah 60:19-20 The sun shall be no more thy light by day; neither for brightness shall the moon give light unto thee: but the LORD shall be unto thee an everlasting light, and thy God thy glory. Thy sun shall no more go down; neither shall thy moon withdraw itself: for the LORD shall be thine everlasting light, and the days of thy mourning shall be ended.

Wow! No wonder God is a word, and the written word of God is in the Bible. Darkness is where the devil operates, but the Bible, as the Word of God, is light. Therefore, removing the Bible would eliminate the light. The Bible is the light of your life. You work to provide for your beautiful family. You desire all good things. Work, Work, and Work and keep self-busy is not good. What happens in the end? There is no light or word of God that Satan sees. The Bible is collecting the dust. Wow! Satan comes and destroys. Mom and dad separated, drinking, adultery, alcohol, depression, lies, and stealing. Parents, you are opening prison and jail doors for your children. The lawyer receives the money when burying the family. Without the Word of God, life is like navigating a car in the pitch dark. You are driving your life in the pitch dark; your passengers are your family. You make significant accidents and then get killed, stolen, and destroyed.

The school's light was taken away by the leader of the US. No Bible reading in the school! Good job, devil! I wondered, are Daniel, David, Shadrach, Meshach, and Abednego in the country? What happened?

They were instructed by false teachers to obey them instead of God as their ultimate authority. Did you realize that you have been bewitched? Don't trust any authority that tells you to follow the government and disregard God's authority. False teachers and prophets will manipulate you using the Word of God. Only the Holy Spirit and His Word are permitted to lead, guide, and educate you. Teaching you correctly is guaranteed if they follow God's Word. As long as the government doesn't interfere with you or your faith in God, you obey them.

See what Jesus said.

John 8:12 Then spake Jesus again unto them, saying, I am the light of the world: he that followeth me shall not walk in darkness, but shall have the light of life.

Instead of false churches, organizations, pastors, teachers, or prophets, choose to follow Jesus.

In the absence of Bible reading, people lost their way and wandered into darkness. The religious authority left a sour taste in people's mouths with their tests about God. Now people are drifting in the darkness, questioning what, why, and how to get out. The individual in charge, referred to as a priest or pastor, as well as high priests, bishops, or superintendents, are prepared to cause harm to Jesus. Those who follow them are misled by them.

Take a moment to reconsider attending churches just because they have a good choir, a cross on the building, Hebrew scholars, and leaders with a one-page theology degree. Jesus light is nowhere to be found. It is completely overrun by darkness.

Start reading the word of God all day and night. Words will manifest in your life if you believe and obey. Witness the healing of passers-by, the restoration of sight for the blind, and the healing of broken hearts. Protect yourself from others who might try to misguide your life. False teachers and prophets can lead you to deeper darkness. Open the Bible and start letting the Word of God illuminate your life.

I love this scripture and have memorized it.

APRIL 18

John 3:20 For every one that doeth evil hateth the light, neither cometh to the light, lest his deeds should be reproved.21 But he that doeth truth cometh to the light, that his deeds may be made manifest, that they are wrought in God.

The mere mention of this scripture brings forth light and causes the devil to leave. It's as if the sun is beaming in that location. Try it; Devil will flee from you. The devil will suffer from headaches, migraines, and confusion. Satan will attempt to persuade you that you're insane, but don't believe him.

Keep in mind that the Word of God serves as a sword, light, and lamp. Light meant Bright; clear; not dark or obscure; as the morning is light;

Proverbs 6:23 For the commandment is a lamp, and the law is light, and reproofs of instruction are the way of life:

Eliminate the laws and commandments of God and witness what is broadcasted on TV. No one seems to have the answer. All have gone astray in darkness, Right? The media and TV spread negative news, while leaders lack honesty, resulting in increased chaos and darkness. You and your nation are drifting deeper into darkness.

Life is like painting your life picture. Paint little by little every day. Use the Word of God as a paintbrush to color your life. It will shine through. Your life portraits will bring light to this world. What kind of portraits do you intend to paint, ones without words or with the word's radiance? The painting will enlighten on pieces of every part.

Psalms 97:11a light is sown for the righteous.

In the darkness, God will guide you as a light. In the most challenging trials, He will be there to carry you.

Recall that God created two lights in the beginning of creation.

Genesis 1:16 And God made two great lights; the greater light to rule the day and the lesser light to rule the night: he made the stars also.

Two lights were the initial creation of God.

Genesis 1:2 And the earth was without form, and void and darkness were upon the face of the deep. And the Spirit of God moved upon the face of the waters.3 And God said, Let there be light: and there was light.4 And God saw the light that it was good: and God divided the light from the darkness.5 And God called the light day, and the darkness he called night. And the evening and the morning were the first days.

LET US PRAY

Lord, give hunger and thirst for your word. Your word is also food, sword, light, and lamp. Without it, we can stumble into hell. Lord, illuminate our minds with the light of your word. You are the Light of the Word. Help us follow you passionately to reach the place where you live. We want our eternity to be spent in heaven, where Jesus is the light. Lord, we are guided by your teachings. We want to be light for many, so bless us with the word to live respectively in Jesus 'name. Amen! God bless you!

APRIL 19

RELIGION IS CONFUSING!

When you modify the original by adding or subtracting, it becomes impure and is referred to as adultery. That's why Jesus told people to come with him. You can attend a meeting or fellowship with others, but the bottom line is you must seek God and make sure you align with His word.

Being Christian is not determined by the presence of crosses on buildings or people carrying the Bible. The interpretation of the Bible by various religions causes confusion. Instead of solving it, you're making the problem worse. Your thinking will be transformed by understanding the purpose of Jesus coming to earth.

God has instructed me to attend the church via the internet. If the Holy Spirit is conducting the service, then distance should not be the problem.

Several months back, I expressed my desire to attend church to the Lord. I asked for a church that is genuinely guided by the spirit. That night, God gave me a dream.

God gave me the dream of a church building, and I was inside. Upon relocating to Texas, I experienced a profound spiritual presence in the building I attended. However, the spirit was different.

After someone recommended taking this as a service, I started searching for things. I came to the realization that my purse was missing. I had thought that I would discover my purse since I was still in that building. The service would commence in a mere second within the dream, then vanish instantly. It lasted throughout the entire evening. The purse is still nowhere to be found. Later, I inquired if a lady could give me a ride to my house in Wylie. She looked at me and didn't care to answer. I couldn't determine if she lacked language proficiency or didn't grasp my words. Individuals of all nationalities and colors would come to the building for a short service, and then suddenly disappear in the blink of an eye throughout the day. I realized I couldn't go home since I did not have a car or house key to open the house. My dream had come to an end.

I was pondering to understand the meaning of the dream. Throughout that week, I made an effort to comprehend the significance of that dream. I received a divine revelation that my purse represents my identity. I risk losing my sense of self if I enter the modern church building. I understood I would become Catholic, Baptist, Jehovah's Witnesses, Mormon, Pentecostal, or whatever organization I choose to attend but not the Christian. Christians follow Jesus.

God declared that you will recognize your identity as my follower through casting out demons, healing the sick, and preaching the Gospel. The broken heart is healed, blind eyes see, the lame can walk, and the deaf can hear. Attending the church building puts your identity in danger.

APRIL 19

Many churches would like to control you and never allow the Holy Spirit to complete its work. And some places, they stopped me from doing what God asked me to do. The pastor expected us to believe day was night. Going to present-day churches would result in the loss of your identity, as God has stated. This is not about structures or individuals on the podium.

It's important that you follow through with the online services I asked you to attend. I was awakened by God one morning, and He played a church sermon on my phone. He repeated it on two occasions. The Lord woke me up at 2 am and asked me to join this online church. Guided by the Spirit of God, the pastor has been ministering to me remotely. The spirit is not bound by distance and is omniscient.

I came to the realization that God is deeply concerned about the Soul's well-being.

Now I know how people have lost their identity by attending different name-brand churches established by the false doctrine. So far, all talk about Jesus, but their teaching disagrees with Jesus's. Using the same Bible, add and subtract the part that they like or dislike. Religion has so much confusion that nowadays, more crimes happen in the religious world by religious leaders.

It's important to remember that the religious authorities Jesus confronted were criminals. They trained people to destroy the God of heaven. God has to come out of the temple by dividing the curtain. It is risky to trust both church authorities and those who claim to be saints. Walk in the footsteps of the Lord Jesus!

The absence of His presence in churches will cause confusion among people. Humans will lose hope and faith in the Lord. The church causes more harm to people than the secular world. People are expelled from their faith in Jesus by religious groups, denominations, and so-called Christian organizations.

God said we shouldn't get fooled by present-day Satan's formula of being saved. What they offer are empty promises. If you attend the building called the church, you have no choice but to follow them, or they will gang up against you. The instruction from the Lord was to obey his words. Follow my lead. People will know you are my follower by your identity given in the Bible.

Mark 16:17 And these signs shall follow them that believe; In my name shall they cast out devils; they shall speak with new tongues; 18 They shall take up serpents; and if they drink any deadly thing, it shall not hurt them; they shall lay hands on the sick, and they shall recover. 20 And they went forth and preached everywhere, the Lord working with them, and confirming the word with signs following. Amen.

Luke 10:9 And heal the sick that are therein, and say unto them, The kingdom of God comes nigh unto you. 16 He that heareth you heareth me; and he that despiseth you despiseth me; and he that despiseth me despiseth him that sent me.19 Behold, I give unto you power to tread on serpents and scorpions, and over all the power of the enemy: and nothing shall by any means hurt you.17 And the seventy returned again with joy, saying, Lord, even the devils are subject unto us through thy name.

God wanted me to stay focused and not look for the building where nothing was happening. Miracles, healing, and deliverance happen outside of the building. We must reach the sick, possessed, broken-hearted, orphans, poor, widows, and needy. It is guaranteed that they will receive the Gospel. Attending the building, which Lord Jesus said den, you will lose the disciple's identity.

I am happy that God imparted knowledge to me in the dream. Christian should make a noticeable impression.

The fact that Peter and John healed the lame was a clear demonstration of a miracle. The priest and the high priest did not want them to speak the name of Jesus.
People were able to identify Jesus's disciples.

Acts 4:13 Now when they saw the boldness of Peter and John and perceived that they were unlearned and ignorant men, they marveled; and they took knowledge of them, that they had been with Jesus.

The work we do supernaturally shapes our identity. The devil has formed different well-known churches, denominations, and organizations to steal our identity. Their job is to control you and me. They go fishing for us and keep us in their barns with their brand name.

Be aware of thieves. I sometimes watch court cases and witness how religious leaders maintain control over individuals with a spirit of perversion. The prosperity doctrine is held by a few preachers. This is the worst of them all. It is the leaders, not the spectators/members, who have gained wealth by preaching prosperity. They are acting like a king and queen.

Roman 16:18 For they that are such serve not our Lord Jesus Christ, but their own belly; and by good words and fair speeches deceive the hearts of the simple.

All around us, people are depressed, alcoholic, possessed, confused. Hospitals are full of sick children, killing parents, parents molesting children, killing wives and children, and being oppressed. Why? Attending religious churches made them busy. People work for the church agenda to fill up their pew and not the kingdom of God. God's Spirit is active within us, advancing the Kingdom of God. There are nine gifts included.

These extraordinary spiritual gifts, often termed "charismatic gifts," are the word of wisdom, word of knowledge, advanced faith, gifts of healing, gift of miracles, prophecy, the discernment of spirits, diverse kinds of tongues, and interpretation of tongues. (wikipedia.org)

1 Corinthians 14:12 Even so ye, forasmuch as ye are zealous of spiritual gifts, seek that ye may excel to the edifying of the church.

The Word has been given by God through His Spirit. The purpose is not to satisfy our hunger or make money. His thoughts were focused on the sick, hurting, poor, afflicted, and needy. The children were dearly loved by their father. Let's continue the work assigned to us, just as He did. Please do not follow confused so-called name-brand churches, organizations, and denominations. Read the Bible. In this dispensation, you and I have to give to the poor, widow, naked, and orphan and take care of the laborers doing what the Lord did. Your blessing will release as you take care of these people and do not make thieves millionaires by attending different dens. Please also train people to Follow Jesus! God Bless you!

LET US PRAY

Lord, you have chosen us to work for you. We desire to continue your work in the world. Many are lost and going to hell. Give us many laborers to do your will. Help us carry your burden. Help us, so we go places to preach the Gospel and empty hell. It is an assignment from you, Lord. Give us boldness, courage, and an obedient heart to carry on your work. Lord, let religious confusion disappear in Jesus's name. Amen! God bless you!

APRIL 20

THE WINDOW OF HEAVEN!

There is a window in heaven. Many places in the Bible talk about the window of heaven. God opens the window to send us something. Windows serve as openings in walls for light and access in homes or buildings.

Let us see some examples of the window of heaven.

Genesis 7:11 In the six hundredth year of Noah's life, in the second month, the seventeenth day of the month, the same day were all the fountains of the great deep broken up, and the windows of heaven were opened.

By closing the window, God stopped the rain. See in.

Genesis 8:2 The fountains also of the deep and the windows of heaven were stopped, and the rain from heaven was restrained;

Rain poured for days as God opened the windows. God does mighty, supernatural work by opening the window of heaven. When the earth was corrupted by sin, God sent nonstop rain and destroyed the earth and everything in it. It is now clear to you that the rain was a supernatural manifestation of God's power. You have never seen and would not see the Flood of Noah again.

God opens the window to do some action on earth.

2 Kings 7:2 Then a lord on whose hand the king leaned answered the man of God, and said, Behold, if the LORD would make windows in heaven, might this thing be? And he said, Behold, thou shalt see it with thine eyes, but shalt not eat thereof.

According to the Bible, the prophet or seer sees and relays the message of God. A prophet is a man selected by God to serve as a mediator between humans and God. God reveals His plan to a prophet, who then shares it with us. How great! According to the prophet, the man was crushed underfoot for his lack of faith in the prophet. How Sad! He would have prospered by believing in the prophet.

The Lord's command opens up a window in heaven for blessings to come your way.

Malachi 3:10 Bring ye all the tithes into the storehouse, that there may be meat in mine house, and prove me now herewith, saith the LORD of hosts, if I will not open you the windows of heaven, and pour you out a blessing, that there shall not be room enough to receive it.

By obeying, the window becomes the pathway for God's blessings. The key to open the window is in your hand. Many think, why give money to the laborers of God? In this dispensation, we offer support to the laborer who follows Lord Jesus. Do not give to the thieves who in return give you the receipt since you are supporting their business. Discover the blessings that come from keeping your actions secret between your left and right hand.

Allow me to explain why. Do you want to receive a blessing in abundance where leftovers are much more than what you gave? Would you like to see 10% receiving so much that there is no room to put it? You have the key to open the window by acting on the word of prophecy. You hold the key.

God not only protects your yard, bank, farm, children, and belongings from the destroyer but also,

3: 11 And I will rebuke the devourer for your sakes, and he shall not destroy the fruits of your ground; neither shall your vine cast her fruit before the time in the field, saith the Lord of hosts.12 And all nations shall call you blessed: for ye shall be a delightsome land, saith the Lord of hosts.

Do you mind free protection, or do you not care? To receive blessings, open the window of heaven through your actions. My desire is to always live in abundance and never experience lack. It is all about obeying and believing. Remember whose report you believe. You will have much more by following the Word.

Keep your window open, don't close it. I desire to see God demonstrate His supernatural abilities by keeping the window open. I like the window to stay open all the time. For forty days and nights, the Lord kept the window open, causing continuous rain. Through my prayers, God allows angels to exit through an open window and bring me blessings. Belief, obedience, and putting words into action define the way of living.

God's idea is not to keep the window shut, but it is ours. God showed us He has all you want, desire, and like, but you have the key. Use the key to open the window. Jesus can open the window and send the good news to you. Ask God to relay many visions and dreams. You hold the key to everything because God lives inside of you. Heaven on earth awaits those who obey.

James 1:17 Every good gift and every perfect gift is from above and cometh down from the Father of lights, with whom is no variableness, neither shadow of turning.

Are you interested in receiving abundant blessings?

James 1:22 But be ye doers of the word, and not hearers only, deceiving your own selves.23 For if any be a hearer of the word and not a doer, he is like unto a man beholding his natural face in a glass:24 For he beholdeth himself, and goeth his way, and straightway forgetteth what manner of man he was.

Embrace the role of a doer instead of a preacher or pastor. You are lying to yourself. God does not forget like Alzheimer's patients. He already knows who and what you are, but you don't.

When you lie or deceive, it only hurts yourself and no one else. God is a great God and sees, knows, and does all. A day will come when the window is opened, and judgment will follow, similar to the time of Noah. God opened the window during the day of judgment and sent rain to nurture those who deceive, lie, and act wickedly. The children were buried along with their parents under water. Who is responsible for the calamity? Nobody else but those who refuse to obey!

Before he opens the window, change your judgment into a blessing.

Prior to departing this earth, seek reconciliation by repenting and saying, "Lord, I want to make peace." If you have tried to pull another lady to squeeze in your arm, say sorry, Lord. No matter if nobody was looking in the car, the Lord was watching. Are you that blind? When your wife is traveling or not present, you seize the opportunity to exploit the woman living in the same house. Adulterer, make amends with God and seek His forgiveness. Stamping yourself as a Pastor won't be effective since those you deceive and lie to are just as dishonest as you. God cannot be deceived, although they can be. The Lord saw and still remembered. Hope before judgment catches you; you make right with God. When that day comes, don't be shocked if you have to face floods or fires. You will scream for help, but no remedy. Do not take shelter or hide under the title of pastor, ring on your finger, wife, the title of an evangelist, or saint. Acknowledge the truth and reconcile with the creator. There is no escape from the scorching heat of Hell. God, in His mercy, shed His blood and granted the Spirit of repentance.

God is granting blessings to believers and doers of the Word by opening the window of heaven. With the Lord, you have Angels and an ark to protect you from harm and danger. May righteousness save us from poverty, oppression, depression, and judgment as the Lord opens the window of heaven. God Bless you!

LET US PRAY

Lord from heaven above, please hear our prayer and make us a window opener for the Blessings. Thank you for entrusting us with the key to your Word. Your Word holds the power to release all promises. Please help us be the doer of the Word and not the hearer. So Lord, please open your window, see our situation, and send your supernatural help, healing, deliverance, and protection from above, in Jesus's name. Amen! God bless you!

APRIL 21

SIN NO MORE!

The consequences of sins are discussed in the Bible. Sin is our deadliest and most destructive adversary.

Jesus healed the man and said, sin no more or worst thing can come upon you. In the present day, individuals are unwilling to accept that their sins have led them to experience the most terrible consequences. It was incurable by medical sciences. According to Jesus, your sins are the cause of your illnesses. Jesus is your remedy; I can forgive if you confess and repent. I have my blood; it will wash away sins if you go in the water in my name.

I pray for many people. Some of them receive healing. There are people who are chronically ill and don't believe in repentance. They think they are saints just because they go to church. I have seen many people go under the water to be baptized in Jesus's name, are healed from sicknesses, and are delivered from drugs, alcohol, cigarettes, adultery, etc.

The Bible says in His Word,

John 8:11 She said, No man, Lord. And Jesus said unto her, Neither do I condemn thee: go, and sin no more.

Her opponents had plans to kill her, but God stepped in and rescued her. Jesus didn't judge her; he told her to stop sinning.

John 5:5 And a certain man was there, which had an infirmity thirty and eight years. 6 When Jesus saw him lie, and knew that he had been now a long time in that case, he saith unto him, Wilt thou be made whole? 7 The impotent man answered him, Sir, I have no man, when the water is troubled, to put me into the pool: but while I am coming, another steppeth down before me. 8 Jesus saith unto him, Rise, take up thy bed and walk. 9 And immediately the man was made whole, and took up his bed, and walked: on the same day was the sabbath.

After 38 years of sickness, a man was healed by the Lord. A warning was issued by Lord Jesus to him.

14 Afterward Jesus findeth him in the temple, and said unto him, Behold, thou art made whole: sin no more, lest a worse thing come unto thee.

Jesus is telling the man and us, " Don't sin, " since I made you whole. Jesus explains that the cause of sickness was a sin.

APRIL 21

Many Christian support medicine and praise the knowledge of doctors. It demonstrates the absence of truth. Is it hard to say, Lord, I am a liar, deceiver, cheater, and adulterer? In my company, everything just seems to fall apart, confess it. I am the great gossiper, wicked, alcoholic, self- righteous, prostitute, greedy, and name it. I ask for your forgiveness and assistance to set me free. I'm fed up with being sick all the time.

Luke 7:48 And he said unto her, Thy sins are forgiven. 50 And he said to the woman, Thy faith hath saved thee; go in peace.

Sin brought her distress, agony, and unrest, but the Lord forgave her and gave her peace. Don't forget, sin is connected to Satan. His role is to go against your soul, body, and spirit.

It's a blessing that we have the remedy for sins, thanks to God. There was no remedy for the deaths of Adam and Eve. God warned them that eating and disobeying would result in death. Their sins resulted in a punishment of eternal death in hell, despite their long lives on earth.

James 5:14 Is any sick among you? Let him call for the elders of the church; and let them pray over him, anointing him with oil in the name of the Lord: 15 And the prayer of faith shall save the sick, and the Lord shall raise him up; and if he have committed sins, they shall be forgiven him. 16 Confess your faults one to another, and pray one for another, that ye may be healed. The effectual fervent prayer of a righteous man availeth much.

God, who is full of mercy, understands the terribleness of sin. Sin is disgusting and terrible! Sinners do you a favor, repent and say, Lord, I am a sinner, forgive my sin. Your tongue can help you speak the truth. Put holy oil over your lying and deceitful tongue. In our discussion, he admitted that I was unable to battle against them. They are extremely bad. Their tongue is deceitful and quarrelsome. Liars, be careful; you are dangerous to yourself. No one but yourself! Sin will give you diabetes, high blood pressure, cancer, and many physical, mental, and emotional illnesses and diseases. Only a humble will repent and confess, not one filled with pride.

Psalms 25:18 Look upon mine affliction and my pain and forgive all my sins.

Certain people possess exceptional skills in lying and deceiving. They are always sick but go to church every Sunday. What happens if they get serious and say, Lord, please deliver me from my deceitfulness, lies, and sins? In addition, they have their own kind of fraudulent teacher and prophet who perpetuate the devil's agenda. I desire to be healthy and whole.

Jesus will grant you forgiveness and bring you peace if you repent. Make the choice to repent for your sins. Instead, you persist in being dishonest, covering up the truth, and embracing sinful behavior. There is no remedy for you. By attending church and holding a position, you are deceiving both yourself and those around you.

2 Peter 2:20 For if after they have escaped the pollutions of the world through the knowledge of the Lord and Saviour Jesus Christ, they are again entangled therein, and overcome, the latter end is worse with them than the beginning. 21 For it had been better for them not to have known the way of righteousness than, after they have known it, to turn from the holy commandment delivered unto them. 22 But it is happened unto them according to the true proverb, The dog is turned to his vomit again; and the sow that was washed to her wallowing in the mire.

Pay attention to God's message and seek forgiveness. Among his many promises, healing is included. Asking for forgiveness through kneeling is surprisingly effortless. As you receive forgiveness, you will feel lighter. Stand up and live in serenity. Let this be the end of your sinful ways!

Rather than opposing the truth, stand up for it. By doing so, you will lead numerous individuals to the cross and the altar of repentance. Witnessing your transformation will restore their faith in God. The person you have become will impress others with your strength, health, and change. Sin is becoming less and less emphasized in preaching, especially in these end times. All have sinned, repented, and been baptized to wash away their sins.

Psalm 107:20 He sent his word, and healed them, and delivered them from their destructions.

Sin no more! God has instructed dos and don'ts in His life manual called the Bible. Open it and read.

Psalms 103:3 Who forgiveth all thine iniquities; who healeth all thy diseases.

LET US PRAY

Lord, we thank you for being so wonderful. Knowing we are a sinner saved by your grace. You rescued us by shedding your blood, which has life, and giving yourself to us. It has washed away my sins in the water in the name of Jesus. I am always grateful for forgiving sins and healing illnesses caused by sins. Lord, it took so much to pay the price. You took 39 stripes for each sickness caused by sins. I am healed all the time when I confess my sins and repent. Lord, bless me to stay humble and repent in Jesus's name. Amen! God bless you!

APRIL 22

MINISTRY IS OUT THERE!

Ever since I received the Holy Ghost, my life has undergone significant transformations.

Acts 1:8 But ye shall receive power, after that the Holy Ghost is come upon you: and ye shall be witnesses unto me both in Jerusalem, and in Judaea, and Samaria, and unto the uttermost part of the earth.

I provided spiritual guidance to my colleagues at work. Once they received healing or deliverance, I would join in a conversation about the Gospel. The Gospel is the Death, Burial, and Resurrection of Jesus. Repenting of all sins is necessary to transform our thinking into action. In order to have our sins forgiven, we must proceed with the second step of water baptism in Jesus's name. Through the reception of His Spirit, we speak in new tongues as we come out of the water. It's commonly referred to as the Baptism of the Spirit or the Holy Ghost.

At work, I had a friend named Lena who was very dear to me. In the year 2000, I was very sick. I received a call from my friend one day, informing me that she was sick and had a surgery. In the beginning year of our friendship, she rejected the Gospel and told me, "I do not want your Bible or your prayers; I have my god." It didn't hurt me, but whenever she complained of sickness, I would offer to pray. She would always say, "No." Nevertheless, on a particular day, she felt unbearable pain in her back, which was soon accompanied by knee pain. The pain she experienced was worse than in her back. Upon hearing her complaints, I inquired if I could offer a prayer for her. She said, "Do whatever it takes." I took this opportunity to teach her how to rebuke this pain in the Name of the Lord Jesus. Her pain was unbearable, so she started rebuking the pain in the Name of Jesus. In a split second, the pain was gone. Nevertheless, her heart remained unchanged despite the healing. Affliction and problems are tools that God uses to make our hearts more tender. That's the rod of correction that He utilizes with His children.

There was a day in 2000 when Lena called me, sobbing, to inform me about a severe neck injury she had sustained. She begged me to pray. I was extremely pleased to offer prayers for my close friend. She continuously called me every hour seeking comfort and requested, "Can you come to my place and pray? She was informed of her thyroid cancer diagnosis through a phone call that afternoon. She cried intensely, and her mom collapsed upon hearing the news of her daughter's cancer. Lina was divorced and she had a son as well.

She urged me to come and pray on her behalf. Upon hearing this report, I experienced a sense of hurt as well. I searched for a person to give me a ride to her place so I could pray for her. Praise God, if there is a will, there is a way. My prayer partner came from work and took me to her home. Lena, her mother, and her son were sitting and crying. We prayed for all of them. The first time praying, I felt a little movement of the spirit; however, I believed God was going to do something. I volunteered to pray once more. She said, "Yes, pray all night; I will not mind." While praying for the second time, I saw a radiant light coming from the door, even though the door was closed and my eyes were closed. I caught sight of Jesus entering through the door, but the Lord advised me to continue my prayers.

As we finished praying, Lina was smiling. I couldn't figure out the cause of the change in her countenance. I asked her, "What happened?" She said, "Liz, Jesus is the true God." I said, "Yes, I have been telling you that for the past ten years, but I want to know what happened." She said, "My pain is completely gone. Please give me the church address. I want to be baptized." Lena agreed to do a Bible study with me. Later, she was baptized in the name of Jesus. Jesus used this affliction to get her attention.

God be praised! Please do not give up on your loved one. Keep praying day and night. One day, Jesus will answer if we faint not.

Galatians 6:9 And let us not be weary in well doing: for in due season we shall reap, if we faint not.

On her mother's deathbed, Lena called me one day, pleading for me to come to the hospital and see her mom. She pushed my wheelchair into her hospital room. During our ministry to her mom, she had a change of heart and cried out to the Lord Jesus, seeking forgiveness. By the following day, her voice had vanished entirely, and by the third day, she passed away. Now, my friend Lina is a good Christian. Praise the Lord!

Jenny, my co-worker from Vietnam, was a lovely woman. Her spirit was always so beautiful. On a day when she was sick, I inquired if I could pray on her behalf. She accepted my offer right away. I prayed, and she was healed. The next day, Jenny said, "If it is not too much trouble, pray for my dad." Her dad had constantly been sick for the past few months. I expressed my willingness to pray for her dad, assuring her that I was more than happy to do so. Jesus, in His mercy, touched and healed him.

After a few weeks, I bumped into Jenny and she was unwell. I offered to pray again. She said, "Do not take the trouble to pray for me"; however, her friend who works as a mechanic on another shift needs prayer. He couldn't sleep day or night; this disease is called Fatal Insomnia. She continued giving me information and was very concerned about this gentleman. The doctor had given him high doses of medicine, and nothing was helping. I said, "I am more than happy to pray."

Each evening following work, I devoted about 90 minutes to praying for the prayer requests and myself. As I pleaded on behalf of this man, I became aware that my sleep had been disturbed. I would be startled awake by a sudden clap or loud noise in my ear. Ever since I prayed for him, it's been happening almost every night. After a few days of fasting, I returned home from church and rested in my bed. Out of nowhere, much to my astonishment, something emerged from the wall above me and entered my room. Thank God for the Holy Ghost. Instantly the Holy Ghost spoke through my mouth, "I bind you in the name of Jesus." I knew in the spirit that I had bound something, and also broke its power in the name of Jesus.

Matthew 18:18 Verily I say unto you, Whatsoever ye shall bind on earth shall be bound in heaven: and whatsoever ye shall loose on earth shall be loosed in heaven.

Initially, I had no knowledge of what it was, but while working, the Holy Ghost started unveiling what had occurred. It became clear to me that the mechanic was being controlled by demons, which was why he couldn't sleep. I asked my friend to find out details about her friend's sleep condition. Later, Jenny brought the mechanic back to my work area. He told me he was sleeping well and wanted to thank me. I said, "Please thank Jesus. He is the one who delivered you." Later, I gave him a Chinese/English parallel Bible and asked him to read and pray daily.

Many people at my workplace, most of whom were atheists or from other religions, converted to Christianity. I had the opportunity to witness people from diverse nationalities, which was amazing.

Psalm 35:18 I will give thee thanks in the great congregation: I will praise thee among many people.

LET US PRAY

Heavenly father, our Lord, and savior, we come to you in prayer. Please anoint us with the Holy Spirit and Power. We want you to lead us to the needy, broken, sick, afflicted, and depressed people to help them. Let our plan be your plan to lead many to the cross. Our God is a true God and has much wonderful work, and we can, too, if we follow Him. You bless our work and use us to give you all glory and honor in Jesus's name. Amen! God bless you!

APRIL 23

SOUL TRAFFICKING!

What is trafficking? Trafficking means trade, deal, and trade between different countries or places.

Trafficking your soul is the devil's way of fulfilling his job to kill, steal, and destroy. Devil called a liar and the father of the lie. The lie had an impact on all of his products.

John 8:44 Ye are of your father the devil, and the lusts of your father ye will do. He was a murderer from the beginning and abode not in the truth because there is no truth in him. When he speaketh a lie, he speaketh of his own: for he is a liar and the father of it.

You must know and learn this devil; he is very ambitious. God's bride is a target of the devil's destruction. We repented, baptized in the water in the name of Jesus, and were filled with His Spirit. When we speak the name of Jesus during water baptism, it brings the lamb's blood to cleanse our sins. In the past, the devil resided in heaven. Heaven was Satan's previous address. But he corrupted himself with the lie. He was forcefully expelled by God. Up in heaven, the devil knows what is happening.

The Bible says.

James 2:19 Thou believest that there is one God; thou doest well: the devils also believe, and tremble.

The devil gets uncomfortable with the truth. Devil doesn't mind if you do all miracles, healing, and operations of gifts of the spirit, but don't talk about truth.

John 8:31 Then said Jesus to those Jews which believed on him, If ye continue in my word, then are ye my disciples indeed; 32 And ye shall know the truth, and the truth shall make you free.

The truth is being targeted by Satan's arrow. The truth is the Devil's target as he seeks to confuse people of God. Nevertheless, he engages in trafficking God's bride through deception and lies. Make sure to always depend on the Holy Spirit for guidance. Once you know the truth, don't let anyone tell you otherwise. Remember Jesus, John, the Baptist, Peter, and many others died for the truth. They would have been incredibly wealthy if they had chosen to compromise. Righteousness prevented the devil from trafficking the soul.

Satan was in heaven; he was an anointed cherub.

APRIL 23

Isaiah 14:12 How art thou fallen from heaven, O Lucifer, son of the morning! How art thou cut down to the ground, which didst weaken the nations! 13 For thou hast said in thine heart, I will ascend into heaven, I will exalt my throne above the stars of God: I will also sit upon the mount of the congregation, in the sides of the north: 14 I will ascend above the heights of the clouds; I will be like the most High. 15 Yet thou shalt be brought down to hell, to the sides of the pit.

According to the Bible, stars represent angels. The Devil has a desire to traffic your soul and kidnap you. He has been doing this job for a long time, making him an expert. Seek the truth for yourself. All words of God need revelation. You only get revelation by the Spirit of God and not flesh and blood. You do not need to be a theologian to know the truth, but allow the Spirit of God to teach you. The Holy Spirit wrote the Word of God. There is only one True spirit, and that spirit is God.

1 John 2:20 But ye have an unction from the Holy One, and ye know all things. 27 But the anointing which ye have received of him abideth in you, and ye need not that any man teach you: but as the same anointing teacheth you of all things, and is truth, and is no lie, and even as it hath taught you, ye shall abide in him.

While I was seriously ill, my only activities were fasting and praying. Once, as I walked in hell, the very ground shook beneath my feet. Satan fears the truth! The essential thing is to have knowledge of Jesus' identity. Hell is powerless against the revelation of Jehovah God in Jesus, causing the devil to tremble. Building your church on the Rock is possible if you have a revelation of Jesus. Rock is a revelation of Jesus's identity. I have that key. His idea worked against Adam and Eve and brought the curse to humankind. The devil has prevented blood access because it is the solution for sins. What was Satan's scheme to prevent the forgiveness of sins? The baptism in the name of Jesus was modified by the devil, replacing the title with Father, Son, and Holy Spirit. Blood hid under the name of Jesus. How deceptive is the devil? In his attempt to tempt Jesus, the devil used quotes from all the scriptures. The devil is an expert at distorting and perverting the word of God, which has the power to give us freedom.

1 John 4:1 Beloved, believe not every spirit, but try the spirits whether they are of God: because many false prophets are gone out into the world.

After Jesus's identity was unveiled, the Lord used Paul and Peter. Lack of knowledge about Jesus is acceptable for false teachers or prophets.

1 Peter 5:8 Be sober, be vigilant; because your adversary the devil, as a roaring lion, walketh about, seeking whom he may devour:

Satan is like a roaring lion, but Jesus is a Lion. Once, on Halloween day, I observed a big lion coming into my yard and sitting on the grass. Lord protected Daniel from lions, and He does the same even today. Remember, Jesus is the same yesterday, today, and forever. You will be worry-free if you stand on the truth. He is a mighty help in times of trouble; He will never leave you. Our bodies are the church around the clock and are a sacred creation of God.

Our disobedience to God resulted in the loss of our rights. Jehovah took on human form in Jesus and purchased our redemption by shedding His sinless blood. Don't think you are owned by the devil if you have been forgiven for your sins by being baptized in Jesus's name. Use aggression against Satan in order to reclaim your soul, children, city-county, and government. Reclaim all that he is taking, robbing, and wrecking.

Speak the truth, as there are numerous theological colleges where false teachers and prophets are trained by the devil. The devil is also preparing his army! I tried a few times to go to theological college, but each time Lord stopped me. Just open the Bible and study it. The Holy Spirit will teach you the truth. Seek out the key that is stolen by the false teachers and prophets.

I had the privilege of working with a powerful man of God. He performed a powerful miracle of healing and deliverance that I saw. He reminded me, sister, to always remember that there is one God, and knowledge can only be attained through revelation. I already had a revelation of Jehovah in Jesus. Flesh and blood or theological college cannot teach who Jesus is. Truth is not obvious but hidden. Find the truth to protect your soul from evil.

Matthew 25:41 Then shall he say also unto them on the left hand, depart from me, ye cursed, into everlasting fire, prepared for the devil and his angels:

Hell will be Satan's new residence. If you want to find this truth, seek, ask, knock, pray, and fast. Revelation can only be given by the spirit of God. There is one Spirit of God; allow the spirit of truth to teach and guide you.

I am interested in the truth, not in churches, positions, or degrees. I am passionate about the truth and have no interest in anything else. Jesus has entrusted me with the responsibility of healing the sick, driving out demons, and healing broken hearts.

Jesus will handle everything once I have the truth. Jesus will work miracles such as driving out demons, restoring mobility and vision, and perform an even greater miracle through you. The devil will play on your lust for eyes, flesh, and pride. With your consent, Satan will cast you out. He is highly skilled and has consistently performed exceptionally well for generations.

They admitted to singing in the choir while performing the demon expulsion. Check out the YouTube video called "23 Minutes in Hell." The devil mocks false teachers and prophets in hell. There are many crosses waiting to be hung for those who served as false teachers and prophets under the devil. The existence of hell is a reality. Only truth has the power to set you free. Keep going with the action represented in the Book of Acts, which is commonly referred to as the Acts of the Holy Spirit. Secure your place in heaven forever by embracing and spreading the truth through love, teaching, and preaching. Don't allow the devil's deceiver to corrupt your soul. By God's blood and the sealing of His Holy Spirit, you have become His bride. God Bless you!

LET US PRAY

Mighty God, the king of all Kings and Lord of all Lords, we thank you for your Word. We thank you for the help of your spirit. Help at these days and times. Make us vigilant and sober to escape the devil trafficking many souls. None of the devil's products are good. He steals, kills, and destroys what God has a plan for. Only the truth can set us free. Bless us with the truth. We are just passing by. Our temporary abode on the earth will soon burn, so give us wisdom, knowledge, and truth to protect our souls in Jesus's name. Amen! God bless you!

APRIL 24

NOT EXTERNAL, BUT THE INTERNAL ATTACK WILL DESTROY!

While you can escape external threats, those closest to you have the power to attack and bring you down.

Keep in mind, Judas was not an external figure. Judas was one of the disciples who received training from the Lord. He betrayed the Lord! Your body can fight the outer attack, but internal sickness can weaken you. The attack happening internally is deadly. If the family does not live in harmony and unity, it will be destroyed.

The devil distorts the Bible's teachings to spread corruption. In the Word, the devil both adds and subtracts. Be careful of false teachers and prophets and corrupted Bible versions. The devil is not to be underestimated. What was the reason behind Jesus praying? He gave us an example of how to overcome the flesh.

John 13:15 For I have given you an example, that ye should do as I have done to you.

1 Peter 2:21 For even hereunto were ye called: because Christ also suffered for us, leaving us an example, that ye should follow his steps:

God incarnated to provide a model for us to follow. How wonderful! We have an example to follow, so we overcome it. Do what the Lord said and stop following denomination and non-denomination.

The task of the Devil is to divide, steal, kill, and destroy the Lord's work. He stands against God and His purposes. The devil knows His time is close.

Revelation 12:12 Therefore rejoice, ye heavens, and ye that dwell in them. Woe to the inhabiters of the earth and the sea! for the devil is come down unto you, having great wrath, because he knoweth that he hath but a short time.

A group of 1/3 angels accompanied Satan when he descended. One-third of the angels serve under ArchAngel Gabriel, one-third under ArchAngel Michael, and the remaining one-third under Lucifer. When the devil fell into sin, he corrupted the angels working under him. We are grateful that God has the authority to expel the devil.

ELIZABETH DAS

Revelation 12:4a And his tail drew the third part of the stars (Star=Angels) of heaven, and did cast them to the earth: 9 And the great dragon was cast out, that old serpent, called the devil, and Satan, which deceiveth the whole world: he was cast out into the earth, and his angels were cast out with him.

A family can be torn apart by betrayal from within. If there is a sinner in the family, it can result in their destruction. If you have a family member like Eve who is foolish, it can ruin you. God's power and work can be destroyed by one of the members. Put your focus on following Jesus, not on following everyone. Having someone in your family, such as Mary or Elizabeth, who listened to and had faith in God would be fantastic. No longer interested in pursuing what seems appealing, tastes enjoyable, or fulfills worldly desires.

Eli was utterly destroyed by his pride. Discipline was a challenge for Priest Eli when it came to his children. The bloodline of Eli continued to face destruction. The devil now claims that sickness is hereditary. In Jesus' name, I declare that my bloodline is purified and cleansed. External change is a reflection of internal change. Healing comes through repenting and washing in the blood. The cycle of witchcraft, spells, curses, sin-induced illnesses, and bloodline problems will be broken. The most powerful thing is knowing the truth. Discover the root of all problems and pursue the devil to defeat him. Force him to go away. Seek forgiveness for the sins passed down through generations in your bloodline.

Internal issues can cause significant harm. Any Rebellious child or person in the family will destroy the family. We all know there is a black sheep in our family who makes wrong choices. If parents have been praying and caring, they will engage in a powerful battle against Satan and its tactics. If your spouse, friends, or connected family members become misguiders and play a dirty game, it will destroy you. Even your family, friends, and relatives will have a bad motive to bring you down. Many think family is family; all is well. Be careful of the wrong one! Stay tuned with the Lord. Do not be like Eli, King Saul, or Eve. Entering the earth is always risky due to Eve's careless actions.

Handing you over to Satan would be a dangerous act committed by a family member, ancestor, or friend. I will say run. God is truly incredible when you walk with Him. Learn to battle with the devil by the power given in the Holy Spirit and authority in Jesus' name. Refrain from using violence against someone practicing witchcraft within the family, but stand against Satan. That person is being used by Satan. Send the package back to the original sender.

The snake in the Garden of Eden became a vessel for the devil since there were no humans present. Numerous individuals are ready to use their bodies against their kin or friends. The pulpit, church, religious people, prophets, and teachers are considered the best places. Be careful, go only to places where God allows you to go. The presence of a cross or written church holds no meaning wherever you find it. Many churches were infiltrated by false teachers, theologians, Christian colleges, false prophets, and self-proclaimed saints brought by the devil. Many times someone says she is a pastor, pastor's wife, or Dickens; I get extra cautious. In the final days, our defeat will come at the hands of those we trust the most.

This one incident stands out in my memory. I saw the presence of various goddesses' spirits on the pulpit of the church I attended. I asked my friend if there were any Hindu communities nearby. She said, yes, it is all around this church. I didn't speak to this church again. The church followed the Pentecostal denomination. The name or title has nothing to do. Neither position nor title held any value.

The church attendee informed me that the pastor's wife, daughters, and mother-in-law are in charge of running the church. In the garage is where the pastor lives. By allowing this demon to work through them, those women transform into goddesses.

APRIL 24

If your family is under the wrong influence, keep your distance from those who misguide you. The mastermind behind them is not their family, but the devil. Rather than a snake, it's a devil pretending to be a family member. They possess excellent acting skills.

Eve and Adam had the privilege of walking and conversing with Jehovah God in a direct, face-to-face manner. Despite that, they successfully sabotaged God's beautiful plan. The attack that will destroy you is not external, but internal.

Handle the tasks related to God. Focus on yourself and don't worry about what others are doing. The love of money is the root of all evil. Judas couldn't spend his money; a prostitute could not use their money. Every temptation presented by the devil carries a hidden plan for devastation.

Who is easily deceived by it? People who have the lust for eyes, pride in life, and lust for the flesh. Seek out God and live by His commandment.

Jeroboam becomes king.

1 Kings 12:26 And Jeroboam said in his heart, Now shall the kingdom return to the house of David: 27 If these people go up to do sacrifice in the house of the Lord at Jerusalem, then shall the heart of this people turn again unto their Lord, even unto Rehoboam king of Judah, and they shall kill me, and go again to Rehoboam, king of Judah. 28 Whereupon the king took counsel and made two calves of gold, and said unto them, It is too much for you to go up to Jerusalem: behold thy gods, O Israel, which brought thee up out of the land of Egypt. 29 And he set the one in Bethel, and the other put he in Dan. 30, And this thing became a sin: for the people went to worship before the one, even unto Dan. 31 And he made a house of high places and made priests of the lowest of the people, which were not of the sons of Levi.

Lord wiped Israel out in the year 722 B.C. Northern Kings brought God and people down. Your growth will be nurtured by good individuals such as parents, spouses, siblings, and mentors.

God desires to bless and prosper you, but it is contingent upon your obedience to His instructions. Failure to do so will result in the weakening of both God and yourself. The self is at risk when one chooses to be disobedient. Follow the Lord's commands and receive blessings. You have the power to control both your destruction and construction.

LET US PRAY

Lord, we bring self as a living sacrifice. Let us sacrifice all which hinders our walk with Lord Jesus.

You have given the Word of God to read, so help us study and obey in the light of truth. We know many are bringing Christianity down, so help us, Lord. Lord, give us the love for ourselves and stick to you and your Word. Everything around us is changing, but you are the same for ages and ages. Your truth stands forever. Put your blood with the Holy Spirit drop in our eyes, ears, mouths, and nostrils to see and hear. Help us what you have planned us to be in Jesus's Name. Amen! God bless you!

APRIL 25

SEEK FOR THE GREATER!

The Bible talks about this dispensation as the greater, just like the Lord multiplying two fish into thousands. Peter fished abundantly in the direction given by God. He struggled to handle the overwhelming amount of fish he caught. God encouraged us to envision greater things. In the New Testament, the Lord seeks vengeance on the Enemy devil, who has committed lies, theft, murder, and destruction. Through the New Testament, we can see how God's abundance was restored to us.

A wonderful event could take place. It's right there on the tip of your tongue. No weapon can prosper. It is the power of the Holy Spirit. The power of God resides within ordinary individuals like us. That's amazing! According to him, he would reside in you and grant your every desire.

Our current era is known as Grace or God's dispensation. He came out of the man-made temple to live within us. God resides within us, making us His holy dwelling. God kicked corrupted temple authority out.

He desires to give us abundance, not scarcity. Knowledge holds the key. Peter's labor throughout the night was in vain. Following Jesus's instructions, he managed to gather the masses. Hallelujah!

Our mindset needs to be transformed. Ask God for guidance in overcoming lack, fear, worry, and doubt, which can interfere and consume us.

The greatness of our God is astounding, so why do we often settle for less? Expanding knowledge in computer technology can break through limited thinking. The limitations of our entrance can be overcome through reading the Word of God. The Bible reveals that God has an even more extraordinary message for you. You can surpass my accomplishments and achieve something more significant.

John 14:12a Verily, verily, I say unto you, He that believeth on me, the works that I do shall he do also; and greater works than these shall he do;

The battle was won by God, who reclaimed everything that was stolen in the garden of Eden. In addition, he empowered us to have control over the hidden forces of darkness. Only the ignorant can be ruled by the devil. He desires your ignorance, but I refuse to be ignorant. I have unwavering faith in the Lord's words. I believe in claiming and continuously receiving when I pray. Place your hand on what you want and pray. I witness powerful miracles, deliverance, and healing. I pray bold prayers, hoping to witness God's movement in that direction.

APRIL 25

Isaiah 35:1 The wilderness and the solitary place shall be glad for them, and the desert shall rejoice, and blossom as the rose. 2 It shall blossom abundantly, and rejoice even with joy and singing: the glory of Lebanon shall be given unto it, the excellency of Carmel and Sharon, they shall see the glory of the Lord, and the excellency of our God. 3 Strengthen ye the weak hands, and confirm the feeble knees. 4 Say to them that are of a fearful heart, Be strong, fear not: behold, your God will come with a vengeance, even God with a recompense; he will come and save you. 5 Then the eyes of the blind shall be opened, and the ears of the deaf shall be unstopped. 6 Then shall the lame man leap as a hart, and the tongue of the dumb sing: for in the wilderness shall waters break out, and streams in the desert.

Isaiah foretold the incarnation of Jehovah as Jesus. He reclaimed everything and brought us back. At the moment of conception, the devil is there, leading to possession, sickness, and other abnormalities in the baby. The devil's era is finished, as God declared after paying the price on the cross. Anticipate a victory that is not just small but significant. Have faith.

Mark 6:56 And whithersoever he entered, into villages, or cities, or country, they laid the sick in the streets and besought him that they might touch if it were, but the border of his garment: and as many as touched him were made whole.

They did not just receive physical restoration, but also the body, soul, and spirit became perfect. Don't compromise; strive for what you truly deserve. Seek out the extraordinary, the new and magnificent, the unheard of! Experience the amazement when people lay eyes on it. Amazing! Wonderful! It's incredible to see what cannot be achieved by man when encountering the supernatural. The doctor experiments with various medicines to find a cure. God has perfect knowledge of what we need to take care of, without any need for experimentation. The devil is occupied creating products, computers, technologies, and medical research to astonish humans.

But if you know of Zechariah 4:6 Not by might, nor by power, but by my spirit, saith the LORD of hosts.

If you have knowledge of the truth, sin, sickness, mental illness, depression, discouragement, and death in hell will become things of the past. The purpose of Jesus' arrival on earth was to restore our rights.

Isaiah 61:1 The Spirit of the Lord God is upon me; because the Lord hath anointed me to preach good tidings unto the meek; he hath sent me to bind up the brokenhearted, to proclaim liberty to the captives, and the opening of the prison to them that are bound; 2 To proclaim the acceptable year of the Lord, and the day of vengeance of our God; to comfort all that mourn;3 To appoint unto them that mourn in Zion, to give unto them beauty for ashes, the oil of joy for mourning, the garment of praise for the spirit of heaviness; that they might be called trees of righteousness, the planting of the Lord, that he might be glorified.

By healing the sick and setting captives free from illness, Lord Jesus proclaimed liberty during His time on earth. He cast the demons out and destroyed the work of an enemy. Around the clock, he dedicated himself to working and training disciples to do likewise.

Luke 9:1 Then he called his twelve disciples together, and gave them power and authority over all devils, and to cure diseases.

Luke 10:1 After these things the Lord appointed other seventy also, and sent them two and two before his face into every city and place, whither he would come.

Jesus instructed to stay in Jerusalem until you receive the Spirit of God.

Luke 24:49 And, behold, I send the promise of my Father upon you: but tarry ye in the city of Jerusalem, until ye be endued with power from on high.

The Holy Spirit empowers us to continue our work together. In the name of Jesus, we have the power to cast out demons, heal the sick, raise the dead, and do even greater things. Our problem is that we prioritize other things over making time for Jesus. Being a laborer requires time, effort, and commitment. Laborer needs total commitment. In order to be properly trained, we depend on true teachers and prophets.

The Gospel has the power to manifest the kingdom of God on earth when we live according to Jesus' teachings. The apostles and prophets acted precisely and obtained a noteworthy outcome.

I have personally witnessed numerous individuals performing extraordinary work. It's currently accessible. Observe the teachings of Jesus and abide by the ways of the Lord.

Jeremiah 33:3 Call unto me, and I will answer thee, and show thee great and mighty things, which thou knowest not.

Imagine the greatness and might that comes when we call upon God. He is determined to do it. Instead of getting wild on-screen or on the computer, let your imagination go wild in reality and Jesus will make it a reality for you.

LET US PRAY

My Lord, we know all these people walk without the limb; we call and ask, send the limb and make them whole. I commend the new mind to come so mental issues are resolved. We ask the mighty spirit of miracles to work on the sound of our voice. Sickly healed and whole. Unstop the deaf ear. Let the eyes of the blind be open in Jesus's name. Lord, cancel all immature death. Let God be our God. Let our relationship be like the relationship in the Garden of Eden. We want to talk and walk with you, oh Lord! May this relationship never break again, in Jesus's Name. Amen! God bless you!

APRIL 26

HOW CAN YOU GET DECEIVED AGAIN?

After paying the price for our sins, the Lord reclaimed all from the devil. The blood contains life, which he gave.

Leviticus 17:11 For the life of the flesh is in the blood: and I have given it to you upon the altar to make an atonement for your souls: for it is the blood that maketh an atonement for the soul.

Jehovah God put on flesh and shed the blood. By taking the stripes, he provided healing, freedom, and deliverance for us.

Jesus offered His blood within God's temple in heaven. He accomplished the job of bearing the cost for our transgressions. Subsequently, he descended to claim the deceased believer who died without shedding blood, and acquired the key to hell and death from Satan. How wonderful! Satan lost the key to hell and death; now Jesus has it.

Ephesians 4:8 Wherefore he saith, When he ascended up on high, he led captivity captive, and gave gifts unto men. 9 (Now that he ascended, what is it but that he also descended first into the lower parts of the earth? 10 He that descended is the same also that ascended up far above all heavens, that he might fill all things.) 11 And he gave some, apostles; and some, prophets; and some, evangelists; and some, pastors and teachers; 12 For the perfecting of the saints, for the work of the ministry, for the edifying of the body of Christ:

Hell is under the control of God, not Satan. The consequences went beyond eating the forbidden fruit in the Garden of Eden; they included losing eternal life and becoming enslaved by Satan. It's possible that you perceive your actions as a minor transgression. There is a larger mysterious plan that Sin has. All of Satan's ideas are malicious and designed to deceive. When the devil ensnares you in sin, he claims not only you but also your children, family, and descendants. You could call it a small pleasure, perhaps. Sin should not be a pleasure; only a fool does not know the reality. Those who are ignorant of sin do not have knowledge of the creator.

Revelation 1:18 I am he that liveth, and was dead; and, behold, I am alive for evermore, Amen; and have the keys of hell and of death.

Choose to devote your time to reading the Bible extensively and praying for God's revelation, rather than engaging in deceptive church activities. The most powerful weapon is prayer. The key to triumph lies in understanding God. Without a revelation of Jesus, people will perish. The Word of God reveals divine truths.

God's direction was evident in every step of the book of Acts. The first thing to do is to seek repentance. Absolutely no justification will be valid. Seek repentance for all sins including adultery, fornication, uncleanness, lasciviousness, idolatry, witchcraft, hatred, variance, emulations, wrath, strife, seditions, heresies, envying, murders, drunkenness, and revealings.

Then, purify yourself in the lamb's blood by immersing in the water using Jesus's name. You will receive remission of sins with a clean conscience. You'll be granted the power of the Holy Ghost for your work. The greatest truth leader, guide, and teacher is the Holy Spirit. I cannot live without the Holy Spirit; He is my guide. It can do a lot, including speaking, teaching, warning, reminding, empowering, and much more. I'm filled with gratitude for the package we received from the Lord.

Take forceful action against the devil to recover everything he has stolen, killed, and devastated. You have authority to get the devil out of others bodies, heal the sick and preach the Gospel with signs and wonders. The devil does not like you to know the truth, so he will misguide, lie, deceive and manipulate you. Let me tell you to use the Word of God to destroy this enemy from a long distance. What happened when Jesus prayed? An angel came and strengthened Him.

People of God, do not stay ignorant. There was a time when my stomach had a sudden attack. I experienced both an upset stomach and an unpleasant smell. It got worse. Because of that I came home from work one night feeling very sick and couldn't find the strength to pray. I lay down in bed and said Lord, I love you with all my heart, mind, soul, and strength. I experienced a miraculous recovery upon awakening. Lord said I fought your battle; you never have to suffer anymore. But the stubborn devil kept attacking me with the same illnesses. I know the Lord cannot lie. So I asked God why this was. The Lord said just worship me and praise me and so I did. It went away. Every now and then, I started experiencing the same problem. Worship praise was not working, so I started putting an open Bible on my stomach, and it worked. Hallelujah! Do you think the devil quits? Don't give up like the devil, learn from him instead. Find the right weapons that work, go after the devil, and whip him.

Peter would have been killed if the people had slept and said the Lord would take care. No, people know what it takes. See, knowledge is necessary for your help; they kept praying around the clock till help came from heaven.

Can you identify our problem? We become churchgoers, lost, misguided, misled, and ignorant people of God. To fight an enemy, one needs effort, dedication, determination, and knowledge of truth. The teachings of Jesus and His disciples were preserved in ancient churches. In our case, we find an organization where our flesh feels comfortable. We find the church does not care for your soul and does not know the truth. Their desire is to be in control. Going against their agenda will lead to being criticized and persecuted. Whispering and turning their followers against you is what happens when someone follows the truth. On the other hand, when they have needs, they'll contact you. It makes me wonder why they don't go to the individuals who misguide them. I guess they know they can't help.

The only help offered is fake sympathy. Gain knowledge of the correct way by familiarizing yourself with Jesus, Peter, Paul, and the history of the early church, and refrain from being misled by misguided leaders. Their lavish way of life is partially supported by you as well. Satan's operations, which include denominations, non-denominations, and organizations, are funded by your money. The devil put the cross on the building and convinced you that this is a church; pay your money. Don't forget, in this era, you represent the church. Blessings will come to you if you donate money to God's laborers, the poor, the widow, the naked, the hungry, and orphans.

APRIL 26

You can access healing, deliverance, salvation, peace, and joy. Just take a step of faith. Stand on truth by obeying and submitting. The truth remains constant, rooted in the teachings of God. I love the truth and nothing else. It is better than depression, discouragement, the money of this world, power, position, lust of eyes, pride of life, and the lust of the flesh. My goal is to use the powerful name of Jesus to command the devil to release blessings, promises, family, sicknesses, and mental and spiritual oppression. I have the power and authority; I know how to travail and get up early to meet God. I know how to destroy the devil and his strategy in the name of Jesus. I receive training and teachings from the Holy Spirit. With my spiritual eyes, I survey the world around me. Jesus' name is being used to command the devil to leave, be defeated, and go away. The devil must leave children alone. In Jesus' name, I rebuke any plans of accidents, premature death, heart attacks, strokes, shootings, killings, or attacks on my family. The devil has a plan against the Christians in many nations, and I come against it. The Lord was pleased to freeze and destroy the evil plan of the devil. Let them go backward, let them fall, and never rise. Every hospital receives the healing spirit from the Lord. A spirit of miracles for those who require one.

I pray that the Lord blesses those who are unaware of the creator with His visitation. Let the Lord remove the blinder of eyes and deafness of ear. Let the Lord give new courage and strength, and increase power daily.

Someone once brought their sister, who was possessed by a demon, to my house. The demon gave a warning, saying that she would take the lives of her children. Her eyes grew wide as I commenced the process of driving out the demon. Initially, her eyes were already huge, but they grew even larger. When I began to use Jesus's name to bind and break the power of a demon, she transformed into a powerless puppy. She began to beg and plead. In Jesus' name, I commanded the deceiving devil to leave. She was free in no time. Develop the ability to see through the devil's agenda and not be tricked. Careful of the operation of Satan through religious churches by his agent called whatever. You have the power to use it. Rejection shouldn't be a concern for you.

LET US PRAY

Lord, we come before your altar; we know you have done all and given all authority to tread upon the serpent and scorpion. Lord, help us to take over and get right with you. We believe and claim to do as it says. Religious churches and organizations have led us astray, causing us to lose our way. But today, we come before you to take what the devil stole from us. We rededicate our lives and start anew by following and obeying your Word of truth. We will recover what belongs to us and see glorious victory in the Name of Jesus. Amen! God bless you!

APRIL 27

WHAT IS MY JOB?

Is it my job to watch a movie, party, club, drink, gamble, attend church, or do what I think is important? As everyone claims, I will follow God's instructions if He tells me to do something. Your job description is outlined in the book known as the Bible. Let us read what it says; Jesus told in His parable, tell others, there is a room in my kingdom. Help out with the kingdom's workload. Do not get too busy when you have no time for God.

Luke 14:23 And the Lord said unto the servant, Go out into the highways and hedges, and compel them to come in, that my house may be filled.

Again, Jesus gave work instructions after His resurrection. Stay tuned, do not wander by false teachers and pastors, organizations and churches, and do not fail God. You are not called to support business under the name of the organization, church, denominations, or non-denominations. Follow Jesus as He gave an example through His life.

Mark 16:15 And he said unto them, Go ye into all the world, and preach the gospel to every creature.16 He that believeth and is baptized shall be saved, but he that believeth not shall be damned.

After being raised from the dead, He went up to heaven and presented His blood in the tabernacle's Holy of Holies as an offering for our sins. Upon his return, he started to teach. He prepared His disciple adequately for travel.

Acts 1:8 But ye shall receive power, after that the Holy Ghost is come upon you: and ye shall be witnesses unto me both in Jerusalem, and in all Judaea, and Samaria, and unto the uttermost part of the earth.

Have you read this? He said to stay in tune and harmony and agree with the Lord's teaching. Highlight your responsibility in your Bible. Prepare yourself by studying diligently.

1 Thessalonians 4:11 And that ye study to be quiet, and to do your own business, and to work with your own hands, as we commanded you;

The Bible holds a special place in my heart. His Word teaches me something new every single day. It is my instruction book. I don't want anyone to give me false information. There was a time when I participated in a tent meeting that sticks in my mind. The preacher revealed that I had a vision of a pool of acid. There was a man who swam around, grabbing people by their hair and then letting them go. Someone wanted to know, who is it that you are seeking? The man stated that I was trying to find the teacher who taught me incorrectly. I am suffering here because of that deceitful teacher. The man said that the false teacher had to be here.

It's now past the point of no return. Make sure no one leads you astray. Your soul can find eternal rest if you seek God. Studying the word is my responsibility.

2 Timothy 2:14 Of these things put them in remembrance, charging them before the Lord that they strive not about words to no profit, but to the subverting of the hearers. 15 Study to shew thyself approved unto God, a workman that needeth not to be ashamed, rightly dividing the word of truth.

Seek the truth, impart the truth.

God instructed us to devote ourselves to studying His word. The Holy Spirit will provide you with teachings. It is my job to study the word.

This book should not depart from your mouth.

Joshua 1:8 This book of the law shall not depart out of thy mouth; but thou shalt meditate therein day and night, that thou mayest observe to do according to all that is written therein: for then thou shalt make thy way prosperous, and then thou shalt have success. 9 Have not I commanded thee? Be strong and of good courage; be not afraid, neither be thou dismayed: for the LORD thy God is with thee whithersoever thou goest.

Ever since discovering the truth, I've remained steadfast in my faith and spread the truth. I stand against all opposition. I am not impressed with degrees, titles, miracles, or whatever.

A lake of fire is an actual place; I must love myself to escape it. I remain dedicated to the work of God. Learning the Bible involves more than just listening; it requires action. I haven't found anything impressive yet, except for the truth that is revealed through obedience. I can't explain how great the experiences are; just obey and see what I am talking about. Now I can teach and preach what the Lord is talking about. I cannot fail people or the Lord. He is so real, and His Word is amazing.

The Lord wants us to pray. I start my day by waking up at 3:50 am and praying. At times, I find myself waking up in the middle of the night to pray. It's necessary for us to fast every week. Once a month, we engage in a week-long fasting period. There's a prayer event that goes on throughout the night. People from all over join the phone call and stay on throughout the night. I desire to perform my job according to God's instructions.

1 Timothy 2:1 I exhort therefore, that, first of all, supplications, prayers, intercessions, and giving of thanks, be made for all men; 2 For kings, and for all that are in authority; that we may lead a quiet and peaceable life in all godliness and honesty. 3 For this is good and acceptable in the sight of God our Saviour; 4 Who will have all men to be saved, and to come unto the knowledge of the truth.

I extend my prayers to individuals contacting me through phone, text, or email. Praying and pulling souls from lions, tigers, and alligators is part of my job. In this terrifying jungle, you'll find demons of scorpions, snakes, and misguiders aplenty. Praying for others is essential for intercession and for myself and my family. He is looking down and saying, is there anyone who knows I exist so I can help? Is there anyone who knows

I died and took stripes for them? Is there anyone aware that they can contact me, and I will handle their needs? I am ready and willing to help.

Psalm 46:1 God is our refuge and strength, a very present help in trouble.

Reach out to the Lord for help. He has designed multiple types of angels to fulfill our needs. Our job is to ask for the Angel.

Hebrews 1:13 But to which of the angels said he at any time, Sit on my right hand until I make thine enemies thy footstool? 14 Are they, not all ministering spirits, sent forth to minister for them who shall be heirs of salvation?

People who are hard of hearing are responsible for all the trouble and problems. Begin with prayer, then patiently await a response, or persist in prayer until you witness God's intervention. We need to work. Attending church is not considered labor. Singing in the choir is not working for the kingdom. No one was trained by God for the choir, music, or pulpit operation.

Luke 10:2 Therefore said he unto them, The harvest truly is great, but the labourers are few: pray ye, therefore, the Lord of the harvest, that he would send forth labourers into his harvest.

God will do all you ask Him if you yield the Spirit in the direction where God wants you to go.
He desires to heal your land and various mental, physical, and spiritual illnesses.

However, we have once again become busy and ruined ourselves. Praying to Him grants the almighty complete control over everything.

2 Chronicles 7:14 If my people, which are called by my name, shall humble themselves, and pray, and seek my face, and turn from their wicked ways; then will I hear from heaven, and will forgive their sin, and will heal their land.

LET US PRAY

In Jesus's name, we come before your altar. Please forgive our sins. We ask you to give us your burden. Please give us the desire to work for you. Pour your Spirit upon us. We want to be your laborers to work in your field. We need direction from you. Give us revelation of you and your word. We want to be a teacher of truth. Let your kingdom be established on earth by your true teacher, prophet, and laborer. Make us sincere and diligent for your work in Jesus's name. Amen! God bless you!

APRIL 28

GOD'S WORKS AND PLANS ARE IN ORDER!

God is the author of the order. Explore the formation of God's creation. It happened in an order where there was no confusion or conflicts. We admire the master plan of God as He finished. God's system is so beautiful that it is beyond the understanding of the human mind. It's amazing to see the order and power behind creation. He consistently viewed his actions and expected them as good. God is both good and actively engages in doing good things.

Genesis 1:31a And God saw everything he had made, and, behold; it was very good.

God showed Moses the template of the worship center. Moses did exactly according to God's plan. God is a God of planning. He works with planning. He created and continues creating with the mastermind. Make sure you have His approval before making any plans. Any alternative to God's plan is considered confusion. The plan of God includes the opportunity to be like Abraham and Isaac. Abraham's actions during the plan with Ismael resulted in damage.

Exodus 25:9 And thou shalt rear up the tabernacle according to the fashion thereof which was shewed thee in the mount. 40 And look that thou make them after their pattern, which was shewed thee in the mount.

Exodus 26:30 And thou shalt rear up the tabernacle according to the fashion thereof which was shewed thee in the mount.

God's mastermind orchestrated everything with a profound reason. Praise God!

I was instructed by God to move to Texas from California in 2004. I've been contemplating the idea of purchasing a house and settling down in any part of Texas. I initiated a search and grew frustrated with my failure to obtain God's approval. Upon the arrival of evening, I heard the voice of God saying that I am unaware of the blessings He has in store for me. I had a conversation with the realtor who was both patient and understanding. They agreed. I sold my house after coming back to California. Once I sold my California house, I went back to Texas and began searching for a new home. I searched for a few days but couldn't locate it. On the final day, I located the house and received confirmation from the Lord that it belonged to me. I completed the paperwork and departed for California. The house's city, place, and plan are a concern for the Lord. I've been a resident of Texas for 16 years (since 2005). Don't forget that people's plans can often go against God's plan, just like Eve and Adam, King Saul, Priest Eli, and King Jeroboam. They aim to harm you, your family, and cause desolation in the country.

Divorces, prison incarcerations, mental illnesses, suicide, and various other issues demonstrate a deviation from God's plan. It will fail.

Since God says in Ephesians 2:10 For we are his workmanship, created in Christ Jesus unto good works, which God hath before ordained that we should walk in them.

Many of us had planned, but as we find Jesus or He finds to restore from chaos. Isn't that fantastic? I love to see the alcoholic, possessed, prostitute, wicked, and sinners turn to God and how the Lord fixes, mends, and reconstructs mind, body, and Saul.

Remember the Men with legions; Lord made him whole. Lazarus was brought back to life by the Lord after four days. It is beyond our imagination to comprehend His orderly work and His perfect will to maintain His creation. Is there anything too hard for the Lord? Seeking God's guidance and patiently waiting for Him is a wise decision. He has the power to assume control and restore you to His plan.

In order to protect Jonah, God made a massive fish that kept him alive for three days and nights. It is the work and plan of God that will do all in order.

Have you ever encountered a nation with multiple gods and a lack of structure? Everything is a chaotic mess, disorganized and jumbled. A faithful God is an author of order and mindful of every detail. By turning to Jesus, we experience the incredible ability to reconstruct and transform our personal lives, countries, or communities. You will be amazed by his work. Despite never having witnessed the Garden of Eden, I hold the belief that it must be the most stunning place on earth.

Observing how God orchestrated the liberation of the Hebrews from slavery. He destroyed the land of Egypt and the master plan of routing to the promised land. That is amazing. Taking through the Red sea is not just to let Israel know the power of God but also to destroy the enemy and chariots of enemies. Why do you feel the need to question His work? Or make a plan over His plan?

God's purpose on earth is to grant you a peaceful, temporary abode.

Jeremiah 29:11 For I know the thoughts that I think toward you, saith the LORD, thoughts of peace, and not of evil, to give you an expected end.12 Then shall ye call upon me, and ye shall go and pray unto me, and I will hearken unto you.13 And ye shall seek me, and find [me] when ye shall search for me with all your heart.14 And I will be found of you, saith the LORD: and I will turn away your captivity, and I will gather you from all the nations, and from all the places whither I have driven you, saith the LORD, and I will bring you again into the home whence I caused you to be carried away captive.

Do you think you have a greater understanding than God? Ignoring the plan of God invites immature death, illnesses, curses, and a state of confusion. Religion, denominations, organizations, and non-denominations are examples of deviating from God's plan. The land is experiencing what is known as chaos.

At the appointed time, God delivered the Hebrews from Egypt.

Exodus 3:17 And I have said, I will bring you up out of the affliction of Egypt unto the land of the Canaanites, and the Hittites, and the Amorites, and the Perizzites, and the Hivites, and the Jebusites, unto a land flowing with milk and honey.

Psalm 139:14 I will praise thee; for I am fearfully and wonderfully made: marvelous are thy works; and that my soul knoweth right well.

Psalms 118:23 This is the LORD'S doing; it is marvelous in our eyes.

Psalm 40:5 Many, O Lord my God, are thy wonderful works which thou hast done, and thy thoughts which are to us-ward: they cannot be reckoned up in order unto thee: if I would declare and speak of them, they are more than can be numbered.

Psalms 92:5 O LORD, how great are thy works! And thy thoughts are very deep.

Every mention of God's work in the Bible provides evidence of His greatness. Their disagreement revealed the imperfection of science. We amaze and admire God's knowledge and speak the praises and greatness of God. I rather know nothing and still trust and respect His work. Who knows the mind of God? Not a single person! The season, day, and night are gifts from God to help us structure our lives. We follow his work and learn His deep thoughts behind it. Follow God anyway, whether we understand or not. You won't regret it.

Amen! You will find protection since our limited mind has no clue about the beautiful work of God.

LET US PRAY

In Jesus's name, we come before your altar. Let your work bless our life. We glorify the work of the Lord by doing and obeying His command. We have God, whose plan is to create, bless, and show that He is wonderful. Lord, we are the Work of the Great God. Help us show others the God of Abraham, Isaac, and Israel. God's work and plan give us knowledge of the great God and His work. Help us, oh Lord, in Jesus' Name. Amen! God bless you!

APRIL 29

WE MUST KNOW WHAT IS AVAILABLE.

Power and authority are available in the name of Jesus. You may say, I reign since Jesus paid my price. Yes, the power is taken away from the devil over humans.

Jesus defeated Satan on Calvary. If you know what you hold, then you can claim and defeat the enemy. Use the given power and authority against the devil. Putting the devil in prison by binding him and then destroying his territory to win everywhere. You'll be liberated while the devil faces confinement.

Matthew 18:18 Verily I say unto you, Whatsoever ye shall bind on earth shall be bound in heaven: and whatsoever ye shall loose on earth shall be loosed in heaven.

Paul was given the power to bind.

Acts 9:14 And here he hath authority from the chief priests to bind all that call on thy name.

Seek out the person who can grant you authority. Let me tell you, only Jesus can provide you with authority and empower you as well. Being born in the kingdom of God connects to having authority. I need the power to go into battle with the devil; he has stolen my health, children, spouses, businesses, etc. Satan uses famine or flood to wash away your houses and crops. Go stand in each direction and say, devil, the prince of the air, I bind you and destroy your power. Command the drug dealers, gangs, witches, warlocks, and ouija board called the fun game to get out in the name of Jesus. Bind the work of black, grey, and white magic, palm reader, ruler in high places, and the corrupt system of the nation to be destroyed in Jesus' name. I command all power of darkness to get out and I lose the light. We bind all systems and power over USA and break them in the name of Jesus. I lose the Angels, the Holy Spirit, the Fire of the Holy Spirit, wisdom, knowledge, riches, understanding, protection, and all blessings that belong to me, my family, and my nation in the name of Jesus. Depart from here, Satan, and never return.

Please go around the city, school, market, and downtown, and play shofar on the phone. Either stay in the car or walk around and play the shofar loudly. I tear down all walls of confusion, confinement of drugs, ignorance, and darkness, in Jesus's name. Nowadays, Religious demons are in operation. They act as the spirit of light. The devil doesn't come where I am sending Angels to heal, deliver and set the captive free. I whip Satan and his army; since I have the authority in the name of Jesus. Hallelujah! Winning is possible only when you recognize your rights, authority, and power. What's the issue you're facing? What is the holdout? What is preventing you from moving forward, keeping you stagnant, down, and depressed? Your key has been stolen again.

APRIL 29

Luke 11:52 Woe unto you, lawyers! For ye have taken away the key of knowledge: ye entered not in yourselves, and them that were entering in ye hindered. 46: And he said, Woe unto you also, ye lawyers! For ye lade men with burdens grievous to be borne, and ye yourselves touch not the burdens with one of your fingers.

Before entering any territory, I make sure to fast, pray, bind the enemy, and call upon the power of God and all angels. Remember to always shield everything with the blood of Jesus. I enter with the sword of the Lord, which is the Word of God. I take my shield of faith; never forget this vital weapon.

Despite Jesus giving the key, why is humanity still perishing? The key to the truth is being stolen by the religious demon. If the shadow of the disciple can heal, why isn't it happening now? Break free from the constraints of your religion, organization, denomination, and non-denominational beliefs.

2 Timothy 3:5 Having a form of godliness, but denying the power thereof: from such turn away. 6 For of this sort are they which creep into houses, and lead captive silly women laden with sins, led away with divers lusts, 7 Ever learning, and never able to come to the knowledge of the truth.

Seek the true teachers and prophets to connect with God. Do not believe all but check their fruits.

False prophets and teachers can't change because they never had a connection with God that transformed Paul, Abraham, and Jacob, who later became Israel.

The Lord trains His followers to serve His Kingdom. I'm here to train you and ensure your triumph in the battle. The most powerful weapon is knowledge, the key to success. The key stolen by the enemy devil has caused a decline in the functioning of various religious denominations, non-denominations, and organizations. Where my key is located is never a question for their followers. Why does Satan have the upper hand and continue to prevail over the Church? People do not have the revelation of Jesus; He is Jehovah in the flesh.

The Bible says,

Matthew 16:15 He saith unto them, But whom say ye that I am? 16 And Simon Peter answered and said, Thou art the Christ, the Son of the living God. 17 And Jesus answered and said unto him, Blessed art thou, Simon Barjona: for flesh and blood hath not revealed it unto thee, but my Father which is in heaven. 18 And I say also unto thee, That thou art Peter, and upon this rock I will build my Church; and the gates of hell shall not prevail against it. 19 And I will give unto thee the keys of the kingdom of heaven: and whatsoever thou shalt bind on earth shall be bound in heaven: and whatsoever thou shalt loose on earth shall be loosed in heaven. 20 Then charged he his disciples that they should tell no man that he was Jesus the Christ.

Don't allow the devil and his followers to control and dominate you. Conquer the adversary by challenging falsehoods and pursuing accurate information. You serve one King named Jesus. Religious leaders will dominate you by teaching false doctrine through a few verses. Their motive is to have control over you. The power of setting one free is in the truth.

Allow the truth; love the truth; it will set you free. The condition for it to happen is your obedience to the truth. Lack of knowledge is your enemy.

What is knowledge: It means understanding, schooling, wisdom, information, intelligence, education, grasp, and mastery.

With the help of our Lord, we can discover every key to defeat the devil, known for lying, stealing, killing, and destroying. Don't stop using oil for anointing yourself. I go around anointing schools, markets, and patients in the Hospitals, trees, parks, and houses. I always keep oil in my car and purse. To break the power of Satan, I use oil. It breaks the chain, territory, and yoke. I added anointed oil to my water, food, and clothing. It has a miraculous impact.

Lord said I gave you power over,

Luke 10:19 Behold, I give unto you power to tread on serpents and scorpions, and over all the power of the enemy: and nothing shall by any means hurt you.

Search for the key mentioned in the New Testament, specifically in the Book of Acts. Study the foundation of the Church built by Peter and Paul, the key holder of the kingdom. Those who believed in and followed Jesus possess the key to understanding Jesus' revelation.

The devil can only be brought to tears, bound, destroyed, and silenced if you possess the knowledge of where the power and authority reside. What are the proper ways to utilize one's rights and sovereignty? Your lack of knowledge is causing you to be weak, disabled, dying, and losing the battle. You lack knowledge. The fake false teachers and prophets stole your key. Open the KJV Bible and engage in reading, studying, meditating, claiming, seeking, asking, knocking, and living with it in Jesus's name.

LET US PRAY

Lord, we know you are the God of truth. You meant what you said. Give us a believing heart to believe in you. We need to focus on you for what is available. Let our footsteps be ordered in your ways, truth, and teaching. We will have experience of your power, and so will others by following and obeying you. You gave us true teachers and prophets. We thank you for defeating the enemy and giving us back not only what we lost in the garden of Eden but giving power over the enemy devil and his army. In the name of Jesus, we thank you for loving us so much. Amen! God bless you!

APRIL 30

CHANGE TO ENTER THE PROMISED LAND!

The deceiver, liar, adulterer, murderer, and whoremonger must be corrected before entering the promised land.

Revelation 22:15 For without are dogs, and sorcerers, and whoremongers, and murderers, and idolaters, and whosoever loveth and maketh a lie.

The Bible provides a list of fleshly sins. In order to enter the promised land, repentance and turning to Jesus are necessary.

Mortify all this

1 Corinthians 6:9 Know ye not that the unrighteous shall not inherit the kingdom of God? Be not deceived: neither fornicators, nor idolaters, nor adulterers, nor effeminate, nor abusers of themselves with mankind,10 Nor thieves, nor covetous, nor drunkards, nor revilers, nor extortioners, shall inherit the kingdom of God.

In the New Testament, There is another list of fleshly sins given in the Book of Galatians.

Galatians 5:19 Now the works of the flesh are manifest, which are these; Adultery, fornication, uncleanness, lasciviousness, 20 Idolatry, witchcraft, hatred, variance, emulations, wrath, strife, seditions, heresies, 21 Envyings, murders, drunkenness, revellings, and such like: of the which I tell you before, as I have also told you in time past, that they which do such things shall not inherit the kingdom of God.

The desire in all of us is to enter the kingdom promised by Jesus Christ, the King and Lord of Lords.

In His kingdom, no one practices evil. The evil-doer has a place called hell and a lake of fire. It becomes a physical place if you decide not to repent of sins.

Luke 13:28 There shall be weeping and gnashing of teeth when ye shall see Abraham, and Isaac, and Jacob, and all the prophets, in the kingdom of God, and you [yourselves] thrust out.29 And they shall come from the east, and [from] the west, and from the north, and [from] the south, and shall sit down in the kingdom of God.

You have the chance to be a part of the promised land, where Jesus reigns as the everlasting King.

ELIZABETH DAS

Daniel 2:44 - And in the days of these kings shall the God of Heaven set up a kingdom, which shall never be destroyed: and the kingdom shall not be left to other people, [but] it shall break in pieces and consume all these kingdoms, and it shall stand forever.

Jesus is making preparations for you and me in this place. It's necessary for us to transform and get ready to enter this realm. No one enters the promised land except by meeting the condition first.

John 14:2 In my Father's house are many mansions: if it were not so, I would have told you. I go to prepare a place for you. 3 And if I go and prepare a place for you, I will come again, and receive you unto myself; that where I am, there ye may be also. 4 And whither I go ye know, and the way ye know.

Jacob can't enter the promised land as a supplanter or deceiver. The angel has to fight that evil out by wrestling all night. He stopped Jacob from entering the promised land given to Abraham and his descendants. That night, by the grace of the almighty, it transformed Jacob into Israel. A deceiver to the prince with God! God has to change the name since He is the righteous and Holy God.

God changed Abram's "high father" name to "Abraham," "father of a multitude," and his wife's name from "Sarai," "my princess," to "Sarah," "mother of nations" See the inner personality connected with your physical location and name. As we change, God changes us inside out with our name. You only can enter the promised land if the fleshly nature and name connected with it change.

I talked with many new converts. Taking their names brings battle and the presence of evil spirits. Searching for God, I found out their name has a connection with the gods or goddesses. I advise them to change their name. You are stopping yourself from entering the promised land.

The name of Saul changed to Paul. Paul means "little"; "Saul" means "desired." He abandons the name that prophesied of favor and honor to adopt a name that bears upon its very front a profession of humility. (from Bible hub)

Unless you meet His conditions, you won't be able to enter God's promised land. In the New Testament, lier, alcoholic, adulterer, jealous, wicked, and unrighteous have no place in Heaven. Caution! Rename yourself as sober, loving, joyous, wonderful, faithful, peacemaker, truthful, and more.

The angel of God will stop you at the gate of Heaven. Those who are willing to obey and submit are the ones who truly belong in heaven. Before we can be granted the promise, we need to make a change within ourselves. Meet the living God; He can help you change before entering.

Lord said,

Mark 10:15 Verily I say unto you, whosoever shall not receive the kingdom of God as a little child, he shall not enter therein.

Servants of God must repent and mortify the flesh that defiles. And become good, righteous, and faithful to the Lord.

Matthew 25:21 His lord said unto him, well done, thou good and faithful servant: thou hast been faithful over a few things, I will make thee ruler over many things: enter thou into the joy of thy lord.

APRIL 30

We must repent, wash away our sins in Jesus's name and receive the Spirit of God to be born again, as the Lord said. The surgery of our consciousness and rising in the newness of life is underwater only in Jesus's name. You will see the change. You must experience the change within, or you cannot enter the Promised land of the Kingdom of God.

Colossians 1:13 Who hath delivered us from the power of darkness, and hath translated us into the kingdom of his dear Son:

It's not about converting to a different religion, but rather about your connection with your creator. You have now established a connection with God and headed towards the promised land. Your journey begins towards a place known as the Kingdom of Heaven.

Hebrews 11:5 By faith Enoch was translated that he should not see death; and was not found, because God had translated him: for before his translation he had this testimony, that he pleased God.

Translated means transfer. How did Enoch go to the promised land?

Genesis 5:24 And Enoch walked with God: and he was not; for God took him.

If you want to redeem promises over five thousand, you need to transform your personality that stops, blocks, and hinders. You speak; it is God's will for me to be healthy, wealthy, and prosperous. Yes, you can enter the promised land of health and wealth by doing what is required. Conquer your carnal nature by taking a necessary step.

Jacob confessed to Angel, I am Jacob, meant; I am a supplanter and a deceiver. And as he confessed, God changed His name to Israel, which means May God prevail.

You also acknowledge and disclose your true self. God said in

1 John 1:9 that If we confess our sins, he is faithful and just to forgive us our sins and to cleanse us from all unrighteousness.

LET US PRAY

Lord, we are grateful that you alone can change us. We thank you for the promised land. Help us, Lord, to change every day and turn to be the children of light instead of children of darkness. Sinner to saints, sick to be healed, oppressed, possessed to be free. We were poor, but you made us rich. We were going astray, but we have found our destiny. No one but the Lord has changed us and given us tranquility and peace of mind. Thank you, Lord, for the promised land called the kingdom of Heaven. We long for the place you have prepared for us. Keep us from all evil in Jesus's name. Amen! God bless you!

ABOUT THE AUTHOR

Hello, I am Elizabeth Das Author of the Book Daily Spiritual Diet a devotional for each day and I did it His Way. As I mentioned I am not the author but I obeyed the voice of the Lord to write.

Daily Spiritual Diet is a series of 12 months in English, Hindi, and Gujarati.

My books are published in different languages. The English name is, I did it 'His Way'.

The French name is : Je l'ai fait à "sa manière" The Spanish name is 'Lo hice a " a Su manera "

Gujarati name is 'me te temni rite karyu'.... '□□□ □□ □□□□□ □□□□ □□□□□□'

Hindi name is 'Maine uske tarike se kiya'…'□□□□□ □□□□ □□□□□ □□ □□□□'

Theses both books are available in more than 30 languages. It is also narrated in different languages. Praying to see you saved and most important you find hope.

May the Lord Bless you.

ELIZABETH DAS

Contact: nimmidas@gmail.com, nimmidas1952@gmail.com

YouTube channel:
1. http://youtube.com/@dailyspiritualdietelizabet7777/videos
2. http://youtube.com/@newtestamentkjv9666/videos

web addresses: https://waytoheavenministry.org/

www.ingramcontent.com/pod-product-compliance
Lightning Source LLC
Chambersburg PA
CBHW082314230426
43667CB00034B/2722